PENGUIN BOOKS

HAUNTED ENGLAND

ennifer Westwood's books include *Albion: A Guide to Legendary Britain* 985), *Gothick Cornwall* (1992), *Lost Atlantis* (1997) and *On Pilgrimage* 003). Dr Jacqueline Simpson's books include *Icelandic Folktales and egends* (1971, 2004), *The Folklore of the Welsh Border* (1976, 2004), *ritish Dragons* (1980, 2000) and, with Steve Roud, *A Dictionary of nglish Folklore* (2000).

Books may als
phone and

D0278088

3

Haunted England

The Penguin Book of Ghosts

JENNIFER WESTWOOD *and*
JACQUELINE SIMPSON

Edited by Sophia Kingshill

PENGUIN BOOKS

PENGUIN BOOKS

Published by the Penguin Group
Penguin Books Ltd, 80 Strand, London WC2R ORL, England
Penguin Group (USA) Inc., 375 Hudson Street, New York, New York 10014, USA
Penguin Group (Canada), 90 Eglinton Avenue East, Suite 700, Toronto, Ontario, Canada M4P 2Y3
(a division of Pearson Penguin Canada Inc.)
Penguin Ireland, 25 St Stephen's Green, Dublin 2, Ireland (a division of Penguin Books Ltd)
Penguin Group (Australia), 250 Camberwell Road, Camberwell, Victoria 3124, Australia
(a division of Pearson Australia Group Pty Ltd)
Penguin Books India Pvt Ltd, 11 Community Centre, Panchsheel Park, New Delhi – 110 017, India
Penguin Group (NZ), 67 Apollo Drive, Rosedale, North Shore 0632, New Zealand
(a division of Pearson New Zealand Ltd)
Penguin Books (South Africa) (Pty) Ltd, 24 Sturdee Avenue, Rosebank, Johannesburg 2196, South Africa

Penguin Books Ltd, Registered Offices: 80 Strand, London WC2R ORL, England

www.penguin.com

The Lore of the Land first published 2005
This selection of stories taken from The Lore of the Land published in hardback as
The Penguin Book of Ghosts 2008
Published in paperback as Haunted England 2010
1

Copyright © Jennifer Westwood and Jacqueline Simpson 2005, 2008
All rights reserved

The moral right of the authors has been asserted

Set in 9/10.75 pt Apollo MT
Printed in England by Clays Ltd, St Ives plc

Except in the United States of America, this book is sold subject
to the condition that it shall not, by way of trade or otherwise, be lent,
re-sold, hired out, or otherwise circulated without the publisher's
prior consent in any form of binding or cover other than that in
which it is published and without a similar condition including this
condition being imposed on the subsequent purchaser

ISBN: 978-0-141-03974-9

www.greenpenguin.co.uk

Penguin Books is committed to a sustainable future
for our business, our readers and our planet.
The book in your hands is made from paper
certified by the Forest Stewardship Council.

To Sue Clifford of Common Ground and her co-founder
Angela King, who opened paths for the rest of us.

Contents

Introduction

A clergyman sleeping in an old house awoke in the middle of the night. No candles were lit, but there was a glimmer in the centre of the room which suddenly increased to a bright flame. To his amazement the man saw a beautiful boy clothed in white, who remained staring at him for some minutes, then glided away towards the chimney and disappeared, leaving the room in total darkness. [*See* CORBY CASTLE, Cumberland]

The 'haunted house' (or inn, or wood, or road) is a staple of folklore, and people might have heard one or two such stories relating to places they know, but remain unaware of just how many local tales there are throughout England. This book offers a representative sample, but it must be stressed that there are plenty more. Readers may be surprised to see that a tale they had thought belonged to one place is found elsewhere: this is an international phenomenon, and a number of motifs recur in many different countries.

Folktales and legends are in constant slow movement, like icebergs. It is a modern folklorist's business to pursue the trail as it passes vertically down the ages or horizontally across borders, to see where a tale has come from and where it is going, and thus perhaps to get a glimpse of why people wanted to tell this particular story of their particular place.

Two or three storytellers may have learnt a legend and repeated it orally, in subtly different forms. From here the tale may have passed into written form; so circulated, it may return into oral tradition, sometimes attached to a new place. Other stories may have arrived from abroad and begun their British life in books before becoming part of the supposed indigenous tradition.

Such things are legitimate variation, but there is plenty in print which is not. Writers may embroider or 'make sense of' a story, to fit it into their notion of what a folktale should be, and it can be hard for later readers to tell where the authentic legend ends and a poet's licence begins. We have therefore been careful here to include the oldest sources available, and have generally preferred to quote direct rather than summarize or modernize.

Ghost stories are particularly liable to transmutation. A good story may become attached to more than one historical (or mythical) figure, and certain themes lend themselves irresistibly to ideas of haunting. Any disappointed dead lover may be thought of as unable to forsake the scenes of their passion, any miser as impelled to guard their hidden wealth or direct their chosen heirs to the hoard. Murder victims may seek vengeance, and murderers, once dead, are also likely to return in continued menace or in vain repentance.

In death as in life, the rich and powerful are prominent. An unpopular landlord may remain notorious for long after he has ceased materially to oppress his tenants, taking the reins of one of England's many phantom coaches with its team of fire-breathing or headless horses or even, in one surprising instance, elephants [*see* MARTINHOE, Devon]. The driver of the coach is related in lore to the leader of the Wild Hunt [*see* PETERBOROUGH, Huntingdonshire and Peterborough], an ancient and internationally known legend which tells of a clamorous pursuit across the moors or skies of night. Here folklore begins to cross a line into pagan myth, for these tales can be traced back to the Norse god Odin, and even into early Christian belief that the souls of unbaptized infants eternally range the darkness. The cries of birds may be interpreted as the wailing of these babies, or as the voices of men transformed in death, warning their living comrades of danger. Such legends are particularly linked to callings fraught with risk, such as those of sailors or miners, and kings too may be considered to have undergone metempsychosis, reincarnation in another form: King Arthur is said to have assumed the form of a raven or Cornish chough [*see* MARAZION, Cornwall].

Birds (flying and shrieking) are obvious casting for unearthly roles, but they are not the only creatures with a weird reputation. Dogs, particularly when black and shaggy, are enduring characters of legend, whether demonic like the devastating manifestation at BUNGAY, Suffolk, or, like Shuck [*see* SHERINGHAM, Norfolk], sometimes protective. These are often bogey beasts, supernatural beings in their own right [*see* BRIGG, Lincolnshire], but are sometimes thought of as the ghosts of specific animals. Human souls may shift their shapes and appear in animal form, and inanimate forms such as rolls of linen and trusses of straw may also be assumed by shape-shifters.

Where a body is buried may be of great significance. As late as 1823 suicides were not buried in consecrated ground, making it likely that they would be restless in their unhallowed graves, and even a churchyard burial is no guarantee of quiet lying. If someone asks to be buried in a particular place or even position and the request is ignored, their spirit may be as uncomfortable as someone sleeping in a strange bed.

Skulls are known to be particularly obstinate about their chosen home, and the Victorian cliché of Screaming Skulls was coined for this phenomenon, disturbing to many country houses. Skulls on their own lead one to think of a body without a head – the widely travelled 'headless horseman' or the Silent Woman (so called because to some misogynist writers the only way to keep a woman quiet is to cut off her head) who carries hers beneath her arm. Such haunts are today often explained as caused by actual decapitation, but there are far more historical ghosts than met their end this way [see Sir Thomas Boleyn, BLICKLING HALL, Norfolk] and clearly headlessness is merely a shorthand way of describing a ghost.

Haunts can be family affairs, with regular appearances to many generations. Occasionally the spirits are accepted, like visiting cousins, and places laid for them at table, but more often they are unlucky omens, like the Radiant Boy of KNEBWORTH HOUSE, Hertfordshire. Warnings of approaching death can however be acts of kindness, as in the case of the Duchess of Mazarine who returned to assure her friend that there was indeed an afterlife – as she would soon find out for herself [see ST JAMES'S PALACE, London and Middlesex]. While such ghosts tell the future, others seem doomed to repeat the past. Phantom armies have been seen after certain battles, fighting over the same campaigns for years after the event [see for instance EDGEHILL, Warwickshire].

How to lay a ghost is a problem that has kept many clergymen busy down the centuries. Exorcisms are acts requiring courage, expertise and determination (and often a lot of candles), and up to the last a malevolent spirit can cause injury [see for instance PORLOCK, Somerset].

The living sometimes make use of legend for their own ends. Fraudulent haunts have included the famous case of the COCK LANE poltergeist [London], while cautionary tales are told of those who, pretending to be ghosts, have found that the otherworld has caught them up [*see for instance* NETHERBURY, Dorset]. Often a piece of ghost tradition is explained away in terms of robbers or smugglers (as at BUCKLEBURY, Berkshire), but such rationalization is itself a branch of folklore, albeit of a later and more sceptical age. Very modern ghosts do make appearances, in the form of urban myths such as that of the 'phantom hitchhiker' [*see for instance* BLUE BELL HILL, Kent].

Not all ghosts come with a story attached: there are places where local writers list a whole parade of spectres such as chanting monks, galloping horsemen (with or without their heads), Roman legionaries, Cavaliers, White Ladies, and so forth, with little or no background. While we have mentioned one or two villages with a claim to be 'the most haunted' in their county [*see for instance* PRESTBURY, GLOUCESTERSHIRE], on the whole for something to be included here it has to have some narrative content.

The material is drawn from England alone, since a book attempting to cover the whole of the British Isles would be several times the length of this one. The great majority of legends are 'migratory' – that is, the plot may occur anywhere, provided the setting is appropriate. For ghosts, these settings have few limits: any churchyard, village, street or house may seem eerie, particularly in solitude or late at night, and this gives enduring fascination to such stories, however 'true' they may be considered to be.

Ghost stories are a significant branch of folklore. There are of course also legends of fairies, witches, and demons, and other stories which do not deal with the 'supernatural' but with buried treasure, sunken churches, or features of the landscape: more comprehensive coverage can be found in *The Lore of the Land* (Westwood & Simpson, Penguin 2005), from which most of the material here is taken.

Thanks are due to all those acknowledged in *The Lore of the Land*, especially those who gave us oral traditions never before recorded, the life blood of folklore studies. Our chief thanks for this volume on Ghosts, however, are due to Georgina Laycock at Penguin, supportive in the tradition of the finest editors.

SOPHIA KINGSHILL &
JENNIFER WESTWOOD

Maps

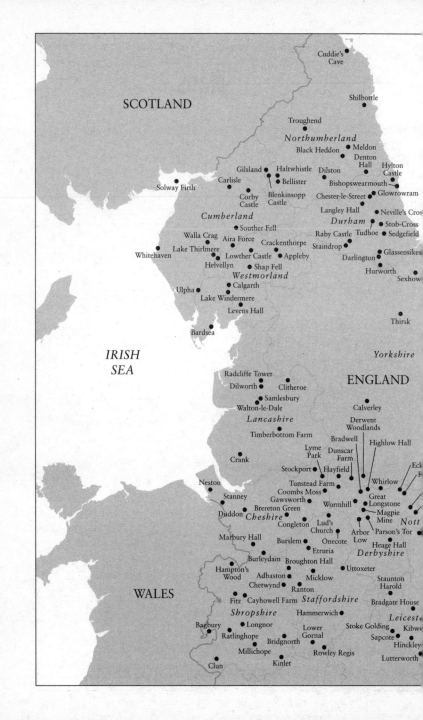

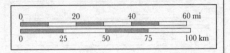

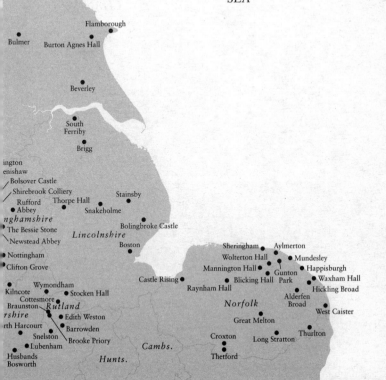

NORTH

SEA

Flamborough

Bulmer   Burton Agnes Hall

Beverley

South
Ferriby

Brigg

ington
enishaw
Bolsover Castle
Shirebrook Colliery
Rufford   Thorpe Hall   Stainsby
Abbey   Snakeholme
nghamshire
The Bessie Stone   Bolingbroke Castle
Newstead Abbey   *Lincolnshire*

Nottingham   Boston
Clifton Grove

Sheringham   Aylmerton
Wolterton Hall   Mundesley
Wymondham   Mannington Hall   Happisburgh
Kilncote   Castle Rising   Gunton   Waxham Hall
Cottesmore   Stocken Hall   Blicking Hall   Park
Braunston   *Rutland*   Raynham Hall   Hickling Broad
rshire   Edith Weston   Alderfen
rth Harcourt   Barrowden   *Norfolk*   Broad   West Caister
Snelston   Brooke Priory   Great Melton
Lubenham   Croxton   Long Stratton   Thurlton
Husbands   *Cambs.*   Thetford
Bosworth   *Hunts.*

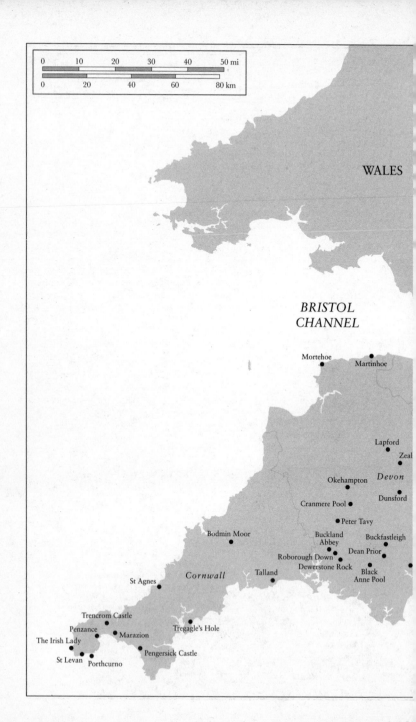

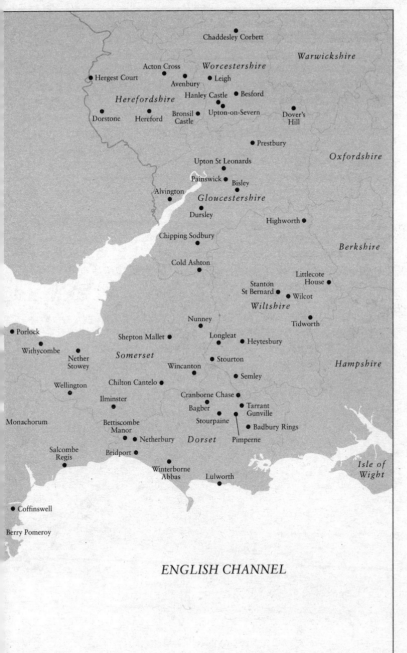

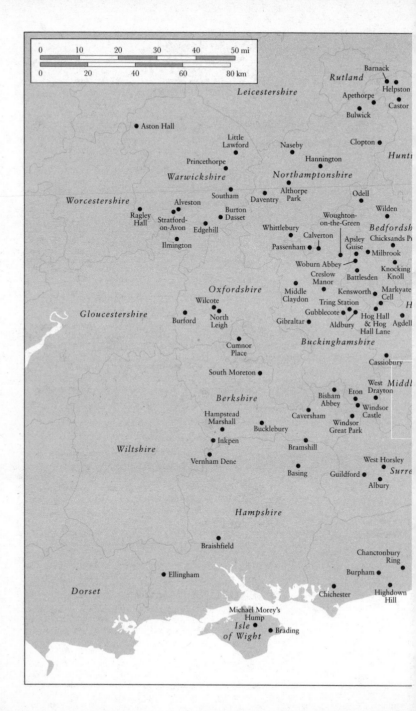

Peterborough

Norfolk

Oulton
Broad

Southery

Bungay ● Barsham
Lowestoft

Littleport to Brandon Creek Road

Bungay
Castle

Upwood
Cambridgeshire

ngdonshire

Blythburgh

Holywell ●

Pakenham

Cambridge - Abbey House /
Corpus Christi College

Debenham

Suffolk

Wandlebury Camp

Boulge

Whittlesford

Clopton ● Dallinghoo

Little Abington

Acton

Burgh

re
iory

Abington

Hintlesham Hall

Seckford Hall

Litlington

Walden Abbey

Hitchin

Earls Colne ●

Wormingford

Knebworth House

Codicote

ertfordshire Sawbridgeworth

The Strood

Tewin ● Ware

Essex

Barrow Hill

Hatfield House

South   Cheshunt   Ambresbury Banks
Mimms
Castle   Loughton

Hockley ●

Rochford

esex   Dagenham
Park

London

Hadleigh
Castle

SEE LONDON &
MIDDLESEX MAP

Blue Bell ●   Rainham
Hill

Epsom

Tadworth

Faversham

Kent

Goodwin
Sands

y

Pluckley ●

Marden

Cuckfield
●

Sussex

Chalvington
●

ENGLISH CHANNEL

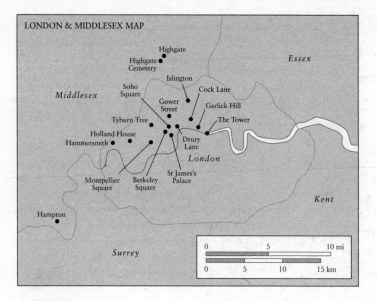

LONDON & MIDDLESEX MAP

Highgate

Highgate
Cemetery

Essex

Islington

Middlesex

Soho
Square

Cock Lane

Gower
Street

Garlick Hill

Tyburn Tree

The Tower

Holland House

Hammersmith

Drury
Lane

London

Montpellier
Square

Berkeley
Square

St James's
Palace

Kent

Hampton

Surrey

| 0 | | 5 | | 10 mi |

| 0 | 5 | 10 | 15 km |

Bedfordshire

Apsley Guise

A house called 'Woodfield' in Weathercock Lane must be one of the few houses in Britain to be the subject of a rates appeal on the grounds of ghosts.

In his *A–Z of British Ghosts* (1971), Peter Underwood reports being invited by the Borough Council to take part in investigations to see if there was any substance to the claim. He says there was a persistent local legend that, 200 years previously, a former house on the site had been lived in by a girl and her father. The girl's secret lover would visit the house whenever her father was away, and one night on his coming back unexpectedly they hid in a large cupboard. Unbeknownst to them, he had spied them through a window, and in fury blocked the cupboard door with a heavy table and other furniture, and left them to die.

Some time later, the highwayman Dick Turpin broke into the house and accidentally discovered the bodies. Waking up the old man and hearing the story, he blackmailed him into allowing him to use the house as a hideout in return for keeping the murders quiet. The lovers' bodies were then buried under the cellar floor.

The owner of Woodfield, Mr B. Key, told Underwood that there was evidence to suggest that Dick Turpin had indeed visited the former house, said by some to have been an inn. In Weathercock Lane, people still heard the sound of a galloping horse, believed to be Turpin's mare, the famous Black Bess. One man told Underwood that he had seen a phantom horseman dismount and hastily enter the grounds, apparently passing through a thick hedge. Underwood established that on that spot, many years before, there had been an entrance. The ghosts of the doomed lovers, especially the girl, were also said to have been seen about the garden and in the house.

Mr Key appealed twice against his rates assessment, arguing that no one would rent the house because it was haunted. In addition to the phantom horseman and the ghostly lovers, he said that a white lady had been seen at the top of an embankment. Although the

Bedfordshire Quarter Sessions Appeal Committee dismissed his argument as 'without point or substance', the affair made a sufficient stir for the BBC to announce the failure of his appeal on the News.

Battlesden

The grounds of Battlesden House, since demolished, are said to be haunted by the restless ghost of a dishonest steward. He is heard rattling milk pails and crying:

> Milk and water sold I ever,
> Weight and measure I gave never,
> And I shan't rest, never, never!

The story belongs to a group of international tales concerning 'The unforgiven dead', ghosts still atoning for crimes committed during their lives. The dishonest steward is one of several ghosts who confess to selling watered milk. A ghost with a similar 'cry' is Old Molly Lee at BURSLEM, Staffordshire.

Chicksands Priory

The house still known as Chicksands Priory was originally a foundation of the comparatively rare Gilbertine Order. Dissolved with other religious houses in the reign of Henry VIII, in 1587 it became the property of the Osborn family and the birthplace of Dorothy Osborn (1627–94), writer of the celebrated *Osborn Letters* to her diplomat husband Sir William Temple.

The remains of the priory – which reminded John Byng, Viscount Torrington, who came on a visit in 1791, of nothing so much as a dairy – were sold to the Government in 1939 and enclosed in an airforce camp. To make up for this lack of romance, they are now said to be haunted by the ghost of the nun Rosata, walled up alive, and still walking here in search of her lover.

The story was connected with a plaque in the remaining cloister on which the inscription reads:

Moribus Ornata Jacet
Hic Bona Berta Rosata

This has been translated as: 'By Virtues guarded and by manners graced, here alas is fair Rosata placed.' A historical consultant who examined it said he knew of no medieval example of the name 'Rosata', and suggested that the epitaph was an eighteenth-century invention, added by one of the Osborn family to give a suitably Gothic touch to Chicksands. Betty Puttick, in *Ghosts of Bedfordshire* (1996), wonders if it was inspired by the name of the founder of the priory, Rose de Beauchamp of Bedford Castle.

As she tells Rosata's story, it is a tale of forbidden romance between a nun and a canon (no doubt suggested by the fact that the Gilbertines were a mixed order and the priory in its heyday was the third-largest house of this order in England, housing 55 canons and 120 nuns). Inevitably, Rosata became pregnant and the discovery of this by the authorities was followed by swift punishment: the canon was beheaded, while she was walled up to her neck and forced to watch him die. Then the wall was sealed up and she was left to perish.

How long this story has been in circulation is uncertain, but Roger Ward in *Legend and Lore* (1983) gives a comparatively early reference. A woman who had worked at the priory for thirty years said that in 1914 or 1915 – 'the time of the battle of Mons' – she was just coming out of the King James's Room, after taking a glass of hot milk to a guest, when a tall woman in white glided past her. 'I heard the rustle of her dress and saw the long white train as she flashed by.' She dropped her tray and fled in terror, telling the other servants she had seen a ghost. This was at about ten o'clock on a winter evening and the light was dim; she had not been drinking. She said, 'I am not sure it was Rosata, but I am sure it was something.'

Also reported are sightings by members of the RAF and USAF, but the descriptions vary greatly and include an old woman, a woman with untidy hair and a lace collar, a middle-aged nun, and a woman in a long, filmy white robe with a hood. In the early 1950s, George Inskip, head gardener at the priory for thirty years, reported seeing a 'dark, greyish shape', coming up the path outside the greenhouse where he was tending the vines. Thinking it was someone coming to see him, he went outside but there was no one there. 'Whatever I saw was wearing a cowl and came straight up the path ... if it was a ghost I don't know, but I'll never forget it.'

Though the paranormal activity at Chicksands has evidently been varied, there is nothing conclusive to link any of the alleged sightings with the legend of Rosata, the walled-up nun.

Kensworth

In her *Folklore of Hertfordshire* (1977), Doris Jones-Baker records the tradition that in Kensworth, south-east of Dunstable, the path running over Bury Hill to the church is haunted by both a witch and a headless milkmaid. No reason is given for either haunt.

In former times, reasons were possibly never required. A witch might well have been assumed to linger after death from sheer malevolence, and formerly there was no need to explain why a ghost had no head. Whereas Peter Haining in his *Dictionary of Ghosts* (1982) says, 'Such phantoms are almost invariably people who were beheaded,' this is not borne out in British tradition, in which *most* headless ghosts did not end their lives by decapitation. Sir Thomas Boleyn of BLICKLING HALL, Norfolk, was not beheaded yet rides round in his phantom coach with his head beneath his arm. There are numerous other examples.

The headlessness of ghosts is a stereotype of popular ghost-lore – at bottom, a shorthand way of talking about apparitions, like ghosts being dressed in white, or, as Daniel Defoe put it in *The History and Reality of Apparitions* (1727), 'dressed up ... in a shroud, as if it just came out of the coffin and the churchyard'. When in the nineteenth century a Norfolk countrywoman described the phantom dog Shuck (*see* SHERINGHAM, Norfolk) as headless but with saucer eyes, this was not peasant illogic but a traditional way of indicating briefly that this was a bogey, just as it was in the seventeenth century when Richard Baxter wrote:

Simon Jones, A Strong and healthful Man of *Kederminster* (no way inclined to ... any Fancies) hath oft told me, that being a Souldier for the King in the War against the Parliament, in a clear Moon-shine Night, as he stood Sentinel in the Colledge Green at

Worcester, something like a headless Bear, appeared to him; and so affrighted him, that he laid down his Arms soon after, and returned home ...

Knocking Knoll

A little to the east of Pegsdon Common Farm, in the parish of Shillington, is Knocking Knoll, sometimes called Money Knoll, the remains of a barrow. Today it looks like a large bowl-barrow, because it has been cut in two by ploughing. It is actually all that is left of a Neolithic long barrow, opened in 1856 though there is no record of the excavator's findings.

According to local tradition, it is so called because it is hollow and an old man can be heard inside it knocking to be let out. In a version current in 1894 given in the *Hertfordshire Illustrated Review*, it is a British chieftain who is buried in the knoll and he is knocking on his treasure chest to make sure it is still there. The Hertfordshire folklorist W. B. Gerish heard from a Mr Aylott that it was a 'warrior in armour' knocking on the chest. Three distinct and loud knocks were to be heard at certain times apparently issuing from the mound. Mr Aylott said 'that he had met with a person who avers that he heard the knockings in question'.

Both versions of the story combine the common idea that there is treasure in every barrow (often there really was until treasure seekers or later archaeologists removed it) with a fanciful explanation of the name (actually from an old Celtic word surviving in Welsh as *cnycyn*, 'bump, hillock'). The name itself, of course, is onomatopoeic – it sounds like knocking.

Millbrook

In 1857, during restoration of Millbrook's hilltop church of St Michael and All Angels, a large Tudor altar-tomb had to be dismantled and for financial reasons was never replaced.

On it had lain the full-length carved figures of William Huett and his wife Mary. They had lived in a house, since demolished, on Millbrook Hill, Mary dying in 1602, her husband twenty years later. Their effigies remained in the church and became known as 'The Warriors' or 'Worriers', although whether this was before or after events following the tomb's removal is unknown.

Before long, however, they indeed appeared to be worried at the way in which their monument had been disturbed. According to village rumour, unexplained cracks and groans were heard emanating from the church, and to put a stop to the talk the rector had the effigies moved to his cellar. However, the groaning went on unabated, and the rectory maid was so frightened that she refused to go down to the cellar to fetch the coal. Now the rector had the statues buried in the churchyard. Even burial in consecrated ground failed to stop the noises, which did not cease until 1888, when work on the church roof revealed timbers devastated by the death-watch beetle. This was thought by many to account for the cracks and groans.

In 1919, the then rector, the Revd H. P. Pollard, decided to dig the effigies up. By that time, however, it was uncertain where they lay. Although members of the Bedfordshire Archaeological Society and Bedford Modern School Archaeological Society joined forces in a dig, they could not find them. However, an old lady in the village, Mrs Bunker, whose husband had been sexton, had in her house a stone head which he had dug up in the churchyard. She showed the archaeological team where he had found it, and this time they uncovered the Huetts, side by side in the shallow grave where they had been placed. William had no head, but Mrs Bunker gave it back so that it could rejoin his body inside the church.

The Huetts now lie peacefully side by side near the altar. William wears armour and a ruff, Mary a gown once carved with flowers, but, like her face, now rubbed almost smooth. Both have been much mutilated, and are missing body-parts. Both their heads appear to have been chopped off at the neck, possibly by the Parliamentarian soldiers credited with so much damage to churches in the time of Oliver Cromwell.

Odell

On the porch of All Saints' church are five marks said to have been left by the claws of the Devil. The local explanation of how they came to be there is that Sir Rowland Alston of Odell sold his soul to the Devil, but when the time came to pay his debt took sanctuary in the church. The Devil (traditionally often conceived of as gigantic) thereupon shook the church in frustrated fury, leaving his claw marks behind. Sir Rowland's ghost allegedly appears on a phantom black horse every hundred years – 2044 is when he is next expected.

The theme of the 'diabolic contract', or selling one's soul to the Devil in exchange for worldly advantage, is usually attached to magicians, and to those like Sir Francis Drake whose speedy rise to fame and fortune was explained in folk tradition in this way (*see* BUCKLAND ABBEY, Devon). Quite how Sir Rowland came to have this theme attached to him appears to have gone unrecorded. There were Alstons at Odell from the early seventeenth century, one of whom incorporated parts of Odell Castle, by John Leland's time 'nothing but straunge ruines', into a new house (since burnt) on the site. They were men of some importance, MPs, Justices of the Peace, and soldiers, to whom there are memorials in the church. The only possible black mark against Sir Rowland himself (at least among Tories) seems to be that he was twice elected as Whig MP for the county (in 1727 and 1734). As with landowners elsewhere, his memory may have been soured by some local grudge.

At all events, Betty Puttick in *Ghosts of Bedfordshire* (1996) calls him 'Wicked Sir Rowland Alston' and says he was the black sheep of his family, 'depraved and wicked in life'. She tells a version of his legend less traditional in form than the first and without the diabolic contract. This says that Sir Rowland haunted the house on the site of Odell Castle so badly that steps were taken to exorcize his restless spirit. He was 'laid' in a pond in the traditional manner and stayed there for a hundred years, but then emerged intending to resume his haunt. However, the Devil was waiting for him and followed him to the church, but Sir Rowland crept in through the keyhole, leaving the Devil outside. As before, the Devil in his frustration shook the church, leaving five scratches on the stone jamb of the porch.

Wilden

In 1872 or 1873, two ladies driving in a pony cart between Wilden and Ravensden saw a horrific apparition. The elder, Mrs Goodhall, noticed a woman coming towards them, walking on the verge. It was daylight and both she and her daughter, who was driving, saw this figure quite plainly, to the extent of noticing that she appeared to glide not walk on the grass. Drawing level with them, she turned her face towards them and they were shocked by what they described as her 'fiendish' expression. Her features were masculine and coarse, and she was clothed top to toe in black garments that trailed on the ground. As she passed by, she turned to look back at them and moments later had vanished.

Mrs and Miss Goodhall were interviewed some time afterwards on behalf of the Society for Psychical Research by Frank Podmore, who was satisfied that what they had seen had been an apparition. At the point where they saw the figure, the road is very wide, with grass margins on either side, and nowhere for a person to have hidden so quickly. Although Mrs Goodhall questioned people in the county, she could discover nothing more about this ghost than that that stretch of road was locally said to be haunted.

Woburn Abbey

Like many stately homes, Woburn Abbey, the seat of the Dukes of Bedford, purports to be haunted. Antony D. Hippisley Coxe, writing in 1973, reports that in a room which has a door at either end, first one opens, then the other, as if allowing an unseen presence to enter and leave. This happened so often that the thirteenth duke stopped using it as a television room.

Hippisley Coxe also says that a summerhouse in the private part of the park was believed by the duke to be haunted by his grandmother, Mary du Caurroy (1865–1937), wife of the eleventh duke. Known as the 'Flying Duchess', she took part in record-breaking flights to India and Africa before being lost off the English coast while flying solo in 1937.

Other writers add to these ghosts a tall man in a top hat who has been seen walking through the antique market, and one from the abbey's medieval past – it was rebuilt in 1746 on the site of a Cistercian monastery founded in 1145. This is a monk in a brown habit who has been seen in several different parts of the house. The Cistercian habit was white, but perhaps he was a lay brother.

Berkshire

Bisham Abbey

This fine Tudor building on the site of a fourteenth-century priory was given by Henry VIII to Anne of Cleves, and then passed to the Hoby family, one of whom (Sir Thomas Hoby) died in 1566, at the relatively young age of thirty-six. His widow, Lady Elizabeth Hoby, married again (her second husband being John, Lord Russell) and lived to be eighty-one; like many aristocratic women of the period, she was learned in Latin, Greek, and theology, and is remembered as a stern, forceful character. Her portrait, by a follower of Holbein, can be seen in the Great Hall of Bisham Abbey (now a national sports centre); her tomb, with marble effigy, is in Bisham church. But according to a legend which arose in the nineteenth century, her tormented spirit has never ceased to roam the abbey and its grounds.

The story goes that Lady Hoby was not only a scholar herself but expected similar intelligence in her sons and daughters. The younger boy (whom most authors name 'William') distressed her by his stupidity; she was particularly enraged by his slovenly handwriting and ink-stained copybooks. One day, when his work was particularly dirty and full of errors, she gave him a severe whipping, as a result of which he died – as Jerome K. Jerome curtly notes in *Three Men in a Boat* (1889):

> The ghost of the Lady Hoby, who beat her little boy to death, still walks there at night, trying to wash its ghostly hands clean in a ghostly basin.

Anne Mitchell's more recent version (1972) is more elaborate: she says Lady Hoby, having whipped the child, locked him in a closet with his books and set off for London, forgetting to tell anyone where he was. The servants assumed the boy had gone to London too, and it was not till many days later that anyone looked for him. He was of course dead.

One writer who did much to publicize the legend was John Meade

Falkner, in his *Handbook for Berkshire* (1902); he cites an alleged confirmation of the story which has also been much repeated:

> It is certainly curious that about 1840, in altering the window shutters, a quantity of children's copy-books of the time of Elizabeth were discovered, packed into the rubble between the joists of the floor, and that one of these was a copy-book which answered exactly to the story, as if the child could not write a single line without a blot.

Falkner does not say that he himself saw these books, whose present whereabouts, if they ever existed, is not known. Moreover, records show there never was a 'William Hoby'. The two sons of Thomas and Elizabeth Hoby, Edward and Thomas Posthumous, both lived to be adults; she did have a son by her second marriage who died as a baby, but his name is given by some authorities as Thomas, by others as Francis – never William – and he was too young for blotted copybooks to be an issue.

Lady Hoby's ghost is generally said to appear in the upper corridors, wandering from one bedroom to another, weeping and washing its bloodstained hands in a spectral basin which glides before it in mid-air. According to Falkner's account, its face and hands are inky black, but its dress is white. He notes that the portrait of Lady Hoby is notable for the extreme whiteness of the face, hands, and coif, contrasting with her black widow's weeds; it has a distinctly spectral air, which may have contributed to the growth of the tale. Anne Mitchell's modern account includes mention of an occasion when Admiral Vansittart, owner of the house in the 1920s, became aware that Lady Hoby was standing in the library behind him – and that where her portrait hung there was only an empty frame.

The church booklet mentions the floating bowl in the 1967 revision but not in the 1990 revision. Both revisions remark of the murdered son: 'Who this child was, whether a Hoby or a Russell, history does not record.'

Bucklebury

In 1977 Cecilia Millson, herself a long-standing resident of Buckle-bury, recorded a local anecdote concerning ghosts that were not what they seemed. At one time, this alleged, the people of the village were afraid to go out at night because of rumours that a ghostly procession would often be seen passing along certain winding lanes. Four figures in white would silently go by, carrying a coffin. But one man, bolder than the others, lay in wait for the ghosts, and when they appeared he jumped out and started beating the nearest one with a stout stick. All four ran away, dropping the coffin – which, on inspection, turned out to be a stolen sheep.

Anecdotes in which supposed ghostly phenomena turn out to be tricks devised by smugglers or poachers are common enough to be themselves a form of folklore-about-folklore.

Caversham

In his diary of 'A Tour to the West, 1781', the Hon. John Byng described a visit on 9 July to some friends at Caversham. He sat with them in the old gallery of their house until supper time, by moonlight, and commented on its atmosphere:

> The gallery gloom may do very well for a few summer evenings and for lovers; but wou'd soon overcome the spirits of a nervous man wishing for cards and candles. As other old galleries are, so this is reported to be haunted, and that at midnight a coach and horses without heads, scour thro' the gallery, terrifying those that are awake, but never awaking the sleepers; as I can well testify: of this coach history the family are ignorant. – Pulleyn, a carpenter, was supposed to have been (in former times) resident in this house, and therein to have kill'd himself; he also alarms the family nightly, by working and making all kinds of hammering noises: one room is call'd Pulleyns room. (In Mr Windhams house in Norfolk, where we pass'd some weeks of last winter, is a similar story of an old woman who spins throughout the night with much noise.)

It is unusual, and rather paradoxical, to hear of a phantom coach manifesting itself indoors, but nocturnal noises are a common feature of hauntings. The house in Norfolk to which Byng alludes is Felbrigg Hall.

Cumnor Place

Amy Robsart's death at Cumnor Place in 1560 was a notorious scandal in an age of scandals. Born in Norfolk, the daughter of Sir John Robsart of Syderstone, she subsequently moved with her family to Stanfield Hall, where she met Robert Dudley, later Earl of Leicester. In 1550, they were married, but when in 1558 Elizabeth I came to the throne, 'Robin' quickly became a royal favourite. His wife, not welcome at Court, was left in a succession of borrowed houses and, when she fell ill, rumours began. On 18 April 1559, the Spanish ambassador wrote to King Philip, 'People . . . say that his wife has a malady in one of her breasts, and the Queen is only waiting for her to die to marry Lord Robert.'

By the end of that year there were accusations that Dudley was hastening Amy's demise. On 15 November, the ambassador wrote, 'I heard from a person . . . accustomed to give veracious news that Lord Robert has sent to poison his wife.' On 16 January 1560, he called the rumour 'an important story and necessary to be known'.

On 6 September, at Windsor for an audience with the queen, the ambassador bumped into Sir William Cecil:

> After . . . many entreaties that I would keep it a secret, he told me that . . . he saw that they were thinking of putting to death Lord Robert's wife, and that now she was publicly reported to be ill, but . . . was quite well, and taking care not to be poisoned. The day after this took place the Queen told me . . . that Lord Robert's wife was dead, or nearly so, and begged me to say nothing about it.

There is a postscript: 'Since this was written the Queen has published the death of my lady Robert, and has said in Italian "se ha rotto il collo"; she must have fallen down a staircase.'

On Sunday, 8 September, Amy had been found dead with a broken neck at the foot of a stone newel staircase in Cumnor Place.

Monastic in origin, this stood secluded among fields and orchards. It was leased by Anthony Forster, formerly Leicester's steward, from Dr Owen, the queen's physician. Owen's wife was one of only two people in the house when Amy died, the other being a widowed dependant of Forster's.

Because of these suspicious circumstances, Amy's death is the *locus classicus* of 'did she fall or was she pushed?' At the time, though the coroner's verdict was death by misadventure, the word on the street was murder.

The scandal was appalling. Elizabeth sent Dudley away from Court, with orders not to reappear before his wife was buried. He did not go to Cumnor, but the day after Amy's death wrote to a relative, Thomas Blount, asking him to go and find out 'whether it happened by evil chance or villany'. He expresses no regret but much concern with what was being said. Blount's response is vague. At no point does he tell Dudley what happened – the manner of death, where and when the body was found, who found it – though he does say that Amy had sent the whole household, except for the two women, to Abingdon Fair.

Curiously impersonal, too, was the disposal of Amy's remains. Though she was given what amounted to a state funeral at Oxford, the chief mourner was Anthony Forster's sister-in-law. Dudley did not attend.

If the pompous funeral was designed to disarm suspicion it failed. On the following 22 January, the Spanish ambassador reported, 'There ... was hardly a person who did not believe that there had been foul play. The preachers in their pulpits spoke of it.' In a minute of Cecil's of April 1566, concerning possible husbands for the queen, in a list of 'Reasons against the E. of L.' appears as no. 4: 'He is infamed by the death of his wiff.'

So what *had* happened to Amy? The choices are accident, suicide, or murder. Even those close to the Court seem never to have learned with certainty what happened. Clearly there was *something* to be hushed up, if only suicide, as then Amy could not be buried with full rites.

Whatever the truth, Dudley's continuing connection with Elizabeth did nothing to allay gossip, and twenty-four years after Amy's death political capital could still be made out of it. In 1584, there appeared an anonymous attack known as *Leicester's*

Commonwealth. It paints Leicester as an English Borgia, a princely villain with poisoners in his train, and a long list of victims beginning with his wife. Among other things, it tells how a 'Professor of ... Physic' at Oxford was asked to prescribe for Amy, but, seeing that she was perfectly well, declined, lest his 'potion' be blamed for her death.

Leicester's Commonwealth was read avidly, and on 26 June 1585 the queen was forced to ban this and other libels on Leicester, 'of which most malicious and wicked imputations Her Majesty in her own clear knowledge doth ... testify his innocence to all the world'. The world remained unconvinced, and the antiquary Elias Ashmole, a hundred years later, was able to add:

> The inhabitants will tell you that she was conveyed from her usual chamber ... to another where the bed's head ... stood close to a privy postern door, when they in the night-time came and stifled her in her bed ... broke her neck, and at length flung her downstairs, believing the world would have thought it a mischance ...

Cumnor Place itself fell into ruin and acquired the name of 'Dudley Castle' from a belief that Lady Dudley's ghost haunted it. According to Alfred Bartlett in his *Historical ... Account of Cumnor Place* (1850):

> The apparition was said to appear chiefly in the form of a beautiful woman, superbly attired, and was mostly to be seen at the foot of a stone staircase, in the north-western angle of the building, where the remains of her Ladyship are said to have been discovered. At length the panic became so general, and the building so dreaded, that the fear-stricken superstitious villagers had recourse to exorcism to expel the spirit; and the tradition yet remaining is, that the ceremony was performed by nine Parsons from Oxford, who laid the ghost in a pond in the adjoining close; and it is said that the water never afterwards froze over the spot. This story exists in the neighbourhood to the present day, and the pond is still pointed out as the receptacle of Madame Dudley's spirit.

However, says Bartlett, not everyone was convinced that the haunt was over. Rather more than a century before he was writing, part of the building had been repaired and used as a dwelling and workplace by a farmer and maltster; later it was patched up and made into tenements for labourers. Their occupancy was not peaceful:

> There is a story now current in the village, that the ghost was never effectually laid, and that it exercised its power to the terror and annoyance of the inmates as long as the place was inhabited; and it is asserted, that at times the candles would become almost extinguished, and the subdued light assume an unnatural hue; while at other times the inmates would be aroused from their slumbers in the dead of night by the most terrific and unearthly noises . . .

In 1810, nearly the whole mansion was taken down to obtain materials for rebuilding Wytham church nearby. In the east wall of the chancel is the window of the chamber above the Long Gallery at Cumnor in which, according to tradition, Lady Dudley spent the night before her death. The site of the house itself was immediately south of the churchyard. Traces of its terraces and gardens are still visible to the west of the site, or were in the 1920s when the *Victoria County History: Berkshire* recorded them.

Hampstead Marshall

Here, the park surrounding the family seat of the Earls of Craven is the setting for a tradition about a death omen. How old this tradition may be is not known, but it was certainly current in 1965. On a dark and stormy night in January of that year, Mr Robert Graham, service manager of a garage in Newbury, was driving back one of the earl's cars on which his garage had been working. The road through the park was full of potholes and wound through dense woodlands, making it even more difficult to see, so he drove slowly and with great care.

After a few minutes he became aware of thudding hooves, causing him to wonder who would choose to be out riding on such a night. Into sight came a horse, ridden at speed, with the rider, dressed in a cloak, bent low down on its neck. The horse veered straight in front of Mr Graham, who braked to avoid a collision. Upon arrival at the house, he was greeted by the chauffeur, Mr Mullins. Mr Graham was quite shaken, and commented that one should keep a look out for people riding horses through the park in such a dangerous way. The chauffeur and his wife were visibly upset by the tale, and asked if the rider had a head. Graham, a very down-to-earth sort of person, was surprised at the question, but had to admit that no, he had not actually seen the rider's head, because he was bent down so low that it must have been almost impossible for him to see where he was going. Mullins then told him that the story went that when the headless horseman was seen in the park, the head of the household was going to die. And William Robert Bradley Craven, sixth Earl of Craven, died shortly afterwards, on 27 January 1965.

Inkpen

There are several prehistoric round barrows on Inkpen Hill, which are supposed to contain buried treasure, including a coffin made either of solid gold or of silver. One particular barrow, on Saddler's Farm, is said to be haunted by a headless ghost; it is also said that nineteenth-century archaeologists who tried to open it up were driven away by violent thunder and lightning – a frequent feature in legends about treasure seekers and others who disturb prehistoric monuments. The barrow was eventually successfully dug in 1907.

South Moreton

This village is the scene for a tale of ghost laying with an unusual twist to it, recorded in 1924 from informants whose memories of it went back into the nineteenth century. The story starts with the suicide in 1804 of a farmer named William Field, who hanged himself in his barn, and then returned as a ghost, to the terror of the neighbourhood. By about 1850 the situation had become intolerable, so eleven clergymen gathered in the barn to conjure him down and lay him in a pond in the farmyard. However, there were two workmen on the farm, brothers named James and John Parker, who had decided to spy on the proceedings and so had hidden themselves under a pile of straw in the barn. When the ghost appeared, it demanded to be given some living creature before it would let itself be laid – either the cockerel on the dunghill or 'the two mice under the straw'. The parsons replied that it could take the cockerel, and at once the bird was seized and torn to pieces. Then they drove the ghost into the pond, and pinned it there with a stake.

An almost identical story is told at Welford, another Berkshire village. The implication seems to be that both the ghost and the parsons were supernaturally aware of the presence of the hidden men; the ghost thought the parsons would be sure to offer him 'mice' rather than a valuable farm bird, but the parsons knew what the ghost meant, and were not tricked.

Windsor Castle

The oldest and most highly developed story connected with the castle is that of Herne the Hunter, which relates to the park, not the building (see below). As regards the castle itself, Hector Bolitho, writing in 1943, reported sightings of two royal ghosts, the first being Elizabeth I:

As recently as a quarter of a century ago [i.e. c.1918], a Guards officer was reading quietly in the Castle library one evening, near the part which survived from Elizabeth's gallery, and he claimed afterwards that he had seen her ghost passing quietly before him. He did not know until afterwards that this was one of the few parts of the Castle which she had built and decorated.

The second story concerns George III, who during the years of his 'madness' spent some time confined to a suite of rooms in the castle and used to enjoy looking from the windows towards the Thames. Whenever sentries patrolling the terrace below looked up and saw him there, they would salute, and the king would raise his hand in acknowledgement.

Long after George III died, the sentry on the terrace looked up at the window one evening and saw a hand parting the curtains. The ghost of George III looked down at the soldier, and a pale hand was raised to the salute. The curtains fell back and the terrified soldier ran to his companion on the East Terrace. Soldiers came to hate their vigil on the North Terrace, for the ghost appeared again and again, until the death of William IV when the Hanoverian regime ended and the ghost apparently retired into tranquillity.

Windsor Great Park

The story of Herne the Hunter, as now known, depends entirely on Shakespeare's *Merry Wives of Windsor* (1597); we cannot tell whether his allusions to local folklore are basically accurate. In Act 4, scene 4, the two heroines decide to make a fool of Falstaff by persuading him to disguise himself as a ghost and meet them at midnight under an oak tree in Windsor Park. Describing this ghost, one says:

> There is an old tale goes, that Herne the hunter,
> Sometime a keeper here in Windsor Forest,
> Doth all the winter time, at still midnight,
> Walk round about an oak, with great ragg'd horns;
> And there he blasts the trees, and takes the cattle,
> And makes milch kine [milking cows] yield blood, and shakes
>   a chain
> In a most hideous and dreadful manner.

A pirated text of 1604 has different lines at this point; interestingly, they say belief in the ghost is exploited by mothers as a 'bogeyman' to control unruly children:

> Oft have you heard since Horne the hunter dyed,
> That women, to affright their little children,
> Says that he walkes in shape of a great stagge.

There is no other early account of this Herne (or Horne), and any attempt to identify him is futile, as it is quite a common medieval surname. In 1792, Samuel Ireland stated that Herne had been a gamekeeper in Elizabeth's reign who hanged himself on the oak, fearing he was about to lose his job for some crime; this fits the traditional belief that suicides are likely to haunt the scene of their death. The rattling chain is also frequent in ghostly apparitions, but other details in Shakespeare's text are less usual. The form he says

Herne takes on, that of a semi-stag, has very few parallels, whereas ghostly dogs, bulls, or calves are common in popular belief. Perhaps he invented it to suit the forest setting, or simply because a disguise involving antlers would be taken as a reference to cuckold's horns, a guaranteed source of laughter on the Elizabethan stage. Another strange feature is the ghost's baneful influence: he causes trees to wither, 'takes' (i.e. bewitches) cattle, and makes cows' milk bloody. Few ghost legends, if any, describe such permanent and far-reaching malevolence.

Shakespeare's influence ensured that Herne became widely known. From the mid eighteenth century, a tree in Windsor Park was pointed out as Falstaff's Oak or Herne's Oak, though sources disagree on which it was. The main claimant, being half dead, was felled in 1796, and its rival was blown down in a storm in 1863; however, other oaks were planted to replace them, the current holder of the title dating from 1906.

Variant stories and speculations began in the nineteenth century. Harrison Ainsworth, in his novel *Windsor Castle* (1843), says Herne was the ghost of a forester whose life was saved by the Devil when he was gored by a stag, on condition that he would wear antlers henceforth, but who ended in despair, suicide, and damnation. Because of the epithet 'the Hunter', Jacob Grimm suggested that Herne had once been imagined as leader of the Wild Hunt – a demonic cavalcade which, in European folklore, sweeps across the midwinter skies, bringing destruction in its path. Its leader may be identified as the ghost of a locally or nationally famous personage, now a lost soul who is doomed to hunt for ever. This notion is attractive, and certainly there are plenty of British traditions telling how some man who loved nothing so much as hunting is doomed to ride eternally at the head of a phantom hunt, accompanied by demonic hounds. However, the Herne legend does not match that of the Wild Hunt, which, by definition, rushes in frenzy from one place to another, usually in mid-air, whereas Shakespeare's Herne simply patrols the area round his tree.

Since the second half of the twentieth century, a tradition has grown up that Herne is seen before national disasters or the deaths of kings; moreover, from about the beginning of that century, a fair number of people have reported personal experiences of hearing his horn or hounds. Further developments have arisen among modern neo-pagans; they claim (incorrectly) that Herne's name is derived from the Celtic antlered god Cernunnos, and see him as a spirit of nature. Shakespeare's text gives no warrant for any of these ideas.

See also PETERBOROUGH, Huntingdonshire and Peterborough.

Buckinghamshire

Calverton

According to the Reader's Digest's *Folklore, Myths and Legends of Britain* (1977), the ghost of 'Lady Grace Bennett' haunts Gib Lane at Calverton, which takes its name from a gibbet that once stood there. She was the owner of the former manor house, now Manor Farm, at the north end of Calverton, next to All Saints church.

The *Victoria County History: Buckinghamshire* (1927), speaking of Manor Farm, says:

> Local tradition places the scene of the murder of Mrs Grace Bennett in the servants' hall, and the spot at which the murderer climbed over the wall and escaped into Gib Lane, an ancient pack-horse track at the back of the house, was said to be shown by a stone in the wall bearing the date 1693.

Mrs Bennett (referred to as 'Madam' in the notice of her burial in the parish register) was the widow of Simon Bennett, who died in 1682, allegedly leaving her a 'prodigious estate'. She is described as 'a miserable, covetous and wretched person', who living by herself in the house, 'and being supposed to have great Store of Money by her, tempted a Butcher of Stony Stratford to get artfully into the House, and as there was no Body to assist her or call for Help, he barbarously murthered her'. This was on 19 September 1694.

The butcher, Adam Barnes, was later hanged and his body suspended in irons from a gibbet until it rotted and fell apart. The site of this gibbet is said to be marked by carvings of two gibbets on a barn built into the high stone wall surrounding the former manor house and its orchard.

Creslow Manor

From the Dissolution of the Monasteries to the reign of King Charles II, the manor of Creslow was Crown property, used as grazing land for cattle for the royal household. Following the Restoration, it was granted to Thomas, Lord Clifford of Chudleigh (1630–73). So much is history.

Parts of Creslow manor house date from the fourteenth century, including the octagonal turret at the west corner, and the crypt beneath it. According to the Revd W. Hastings Kelke, writing in *Records of Buckinghamshire* in 1858, near this was a windowless vault known as 'the dungeon', which in his time contained several skulls and other human bones dug up around the manor house and church. *Murray's Handbook for ... Bucks* (1860) recorded the tradition then current that the bones were those of prisoners kept there.

The *Handbook* adds that, from the cellars, a subterranean passage led to the great pasture. Bones and secret passages both inspire romance, and Murray duly delivers: 'One of the rooms has its ghost, in a silk dress, supposed to be that of Rosamond Clifford.'

This is 'Fair Rosamund', the mistress of King Henry II. She was probably drawn into the traditions of Creslow because she shared surnames with Thomas, Lord Clifford, from a collateral branch of her family. However, in the early nineteenth century, local tradition in Buckinghamshire maintained that as well as a bower at Woodstock, Oxfordshire, Henry had built her another retreat in or near Kingswood, not far from Creslow.

Not everyone explained Creslow's ghost as Rosamund. In the 1860s, Chambers's *Book of Days* identified the haunted room as one above the crypt, formerly reached by a staircase, and having a Gothic door decorated with human heads and grotesque faces. The ghost was seldom seen, but often heard by those who slept in this room or entered it after midnight. She seemed to come out of the crypt or dungeon, and always entered by the Gothic door. Then she would be heard walking about, her long train sweeping the floor. Sometimes her silk dress rustled violently as if she were engaged in a struggle.

Because of the haunt, the room was seldom used and was avoided by servants. However, in about 1850, a gentleman who was forced to stay the night was given the haunted room to sleep in. Next morning at breakfast, he told them he had locked and bolted both doors of his room, and satisfied himself there was no other entrance. He soon fell asleep, but was suddenly woken by a sound like a light footstep, accompanied by the rustling of a silk dress. He sprang out of bed, but there was nothing to be seen. Both doors were still fastened. Returning to bed, he once more fell asleep. Again he was woken by a noise like the rustling of a stiff silk dress. Darting to the spot it came from, he tried to grab the intruder but his arms closed on empty air. The noise passed through the Gothic door, and there was silence.

Eton

A spectre appeared at the Christopher Inn, Eton, in the reign of King Charles II in order to keep a promise.

Major George Sydenham of Dulverton in Somerset had often discussed with his friend Captain William Dyke the existence of God and the immortality of the soul. They promised each other that whoever died first would, if possible, appear between twelve midnight and one o'clock, on the third night after the funeral, in the little summerhouse in the Major's garden.

Sydenham was the first to die, and, shortly after his death, Captain Dyke went to his house with his cousin, Dr Dyke, who had been called to attend a sick child. At half past eleven that night, Captain Dyke called for two candles and went to the summerhouse. Although he waited for two and a half hours, Sydenham did not appear. He reported this to the doctor. 'But I know,' said he, 'that my major would surely have come had he been able.'

Six weeks later, Captain Dyke took his son to Eton to school and put up at the Christopher Inn. His cousin the doctor was again with him. The morning before they left, the captain was later than usual calling on the doctor, and, when he appeared, looked unlike his usual self. His hair stood on end, his eyes were staring, and he was trembling all over. When the doctor asked what was wrong, he answered, 'I have seen my major.' He continued:

This morning after it was light, some one comes to my bed side, and suddenly drawing back the curtains, calls, Captain, captain, (which was the term of familiarity that the major used to call the captain by) to whom I replied, What, my major? To which he returns, I could not come at the time appointed but I am now come to tell you, That there is a GOD and a very just and terrible one, and if you do not turn over a new leaf (the very expression, as by the doctor punctually remembered) you shall find it so.

The ghost then walked about the room, stopping by the table on which lay a sword the major had given him. Drawing the sword and finding it not so clean as it should be: 'Captain, captain, (says he) this sword did not use to be kept after this manner when it was mine.' Shortly afterwards, he vanished.

According to George Sinclair, recording this story in *Satan's Invisible World Discovered* (1789), the captain, who had been 'brisk and jovial', was much altered from that night and those who knew him believed that the words of his dead friend often sounded in his ears during the remainder of his life. He himself died two years later.

This is one of several 'proof of the resurrection' stories, such as that told of Madame de Beauclair at ST JAMES'S PALACE, London.

Gibraltar

A murder that took place near Haddenham in 1828 was connected by the Revd Frederick Lee, in *Glimpses in the Twilight* (1885), with the hamlet of Gibraltar. It was long remembered, and, in *Sketches of the Bucks Countryside* (1934), Horace Harman tells the story as he heard it from Mr Plastow, an old man of ninety, who as a boy had often heard his grandfather and others discussing it.

The victim was a market gardener called 'Noble' Edden (Mr Plastow pronounced it 'Ee-aden') who lived at Thame in Oxford-shire but had land at Creddon. While working there one day, he saw two other men from Thame, Sewell and Tylor, enter a field and kill a sheep. The penalty for sheep-stealing being transportation or hanging, he told no one but could not resist baiting the thieves every time he met them by going 'Baa! Baa! Baa!' To keep him quiet, they decided to murder him on his way home one Saturday night from Aylesbury market.

Edden seems to have had a presentiment of this, as he told a Haddenham man to whom he gave a lift in his cart that something terrible was about to happen. After setting the man down at his turn, Edden drove on alone. The thieves set upon him a little further on, at Anxey. Mr Plastow's grandfather thought he heard the murder as he was coming back from Notley. Approaching Anxey, he heard a terrible row of men shouting and fighting in the bushes. His dog growled and would have gone after them, but he did not want to leave his horse and cart, and drove on.

Meantime, Noble Edden's wife was ironing in the kitchen when suddenly he stood before her. She also saw a man whom she recognized as Tylor hit him on the head with a stone-breaker's hammer. She ran screaming from the house, and roused her neighbours. They went to look for him but found nothing. Not long afterwards, however, a farmhand taking horses to Anxey meadows found his body. His head had been bashed in, but there was nothing to show by whom, so the verdict at the inquest was 'Murder by some person or persons unknown'.

Mrs Edden, however, 'felt in her mind' that Tylor was the murderer, and, as soon as the body was brought to the house, sent for him to touch the corpse. It being widely believed that a murdered body would bleed at the touch of its killer, Tylor refused to come. Time passed, but people in Thame had their suspicions, as Sewell and Tylor had been seen on the night of the murder washing their hands in Close Pond near the church. Then Noble Edden's son was stopped one night when he was driving home by two men who threatened to do to him what they had done to his father. He beat them off with his whip, and knew the voices for those of Sewell and Tylor.

Whether the two men could not hold their tongues, Mr Plastow did not know, but about ten months after the murder Sewell was arrested and jailed. There, he 'split' on Tylor, who was also arrested. When their case came up, the magistrates did not believe Sewell and let Tylor go. He went straight back to Thame, bought ribbons for his jacket and hat, and went and danced outside the houses of the people who had testified against him.

His triumph was short-lived, however. When Sewell came out of prison a few days later, he was immediately arrested again for stealing poultry and sentenced to fourteen years' transportation. He tried to get his sentence reduced by saying he had seen Tylor strike Edden with a stone hammer and kill him. He gained nothing by this, as both men were found guilty and hanged on 8 March

1830 outside Aylesbury Gaol in front of four or five thousand people. Tylor swore to the end that he was innocent, but Mrs Edden knew what she had seen.

According to the Reader's Digest's *Folklore, Myths and Legends of Britain* (1977), Noble Edden's ghost has been seen in a lane branching off the A418 to Haddenham, and anyone who meets it will incur bad luck.

Middle Claydon

In Middle Claydon church is a monument to 'the ever-honoured Sir Edmund Verney, standard-bearer to Charles I. in the memorable battle of Edgehill'.

Sir Edmund Verney (1590–1642) was knighted by King James I in 1611, and under Charles I was appointed Knight-Marshal. He had had a long association with Charles, from before he came to the throne, but was also a Puritan MP frequently opposed to Charles's policies. Nevertheless, when the Civil War broke out, though his family was divided – his older brother and eldest son fighting for Parliament, while his two younger sons fought for the king – Verney stood by Charles, explaining, 'I have eaten his bread and served him near thirty years, and will not do so base a thing as to forsake him.'

Verney was appointed royal standard bearer, but was killed at the battle of EDGEHILL, Warwickshire, on 23 October 1642, two months later. When the Parliamentary troops bade him surrender the standard and live, he answered that his life was his own, but the standard was the king's, and he would not deliver it while he lived. The royal banner was seized and carried off by a Parliamentary ensign, but recaptured in a daring rescue by Captain John Smith, of Lord Grandison's Horse. Opinions differ as to what happened to Sir Edmund's body.

According to a Buckinghamshire proverb, Sir Edmund was 'neither born nor buried', and *Murray's Handbook for ... Bucks* (1860) says 'His body was never found, but there is a tradition that one of his hands was discovered among the remains of the slain on the field of battle, and identified by a ring.' This is accepted as true by some authorities: the National Portrait Gallery's website, for example, says concerning a portrait of Sir Edmund *c.*1640 by Van Dyck (NPG L202), 'His hand was later found still grasping the standard, but his body was never recovered.'

That the body was never found appears certain. Sir Edmund's eldest son, Ralph, sent messengers to the armies of both sides to find out whether or not his father had died. A little later, he wrote in a letter, 'Last night I had a servant from my Lord of Essex Army, that tells me there is noe possibility of finding my Deare father's Body.' The servant had been assured by the army's leaders that 'hee was never taken prisiner, neither were any of them ever possessed of his Body; but that he was slaine by an ordinary Trooper'. Ralph then sent his man to the ministers of parishes where those slain in the battle had been buried, but none could give further information. However, they had kept tallies of the bodies they buried – 'they amount to neare 4,000,' writes Ralph – and one said that men 'of good quality' had been buried with the rest.

As to the severed hand, in *Memoirs of the Verney Family* (1892), Frances Parthenope Verney reports what was evidently the family tradition:

> The standard was taken, and round its staff (says the legend) still clung the hand which had grasped it, faithful in death. On one of the fingers was the ring given to Sir Edmund by the king, and containing his miniature. For two hundred years his disconsolate ghost wandered about the old house at Claydon searching for his hand; the ring still exists and the worm-eaten effigy of Sir Edmund's hand – and if any should dispute the truth of the story, are they not to be seen at Claydon to this very day?

'Claydon' is Claydon House, south of Middle Claydon, Sir Edmund's former home (though not the present building). Antony D. Hippisley Coxe in *Haunted Britain* (1973) suggests that it may be Sir Edmund's ghost that is seen on the Red Stairs. Other twentieth-century authors claim that Sir Edmund appears at the house in times of national crisis, an imitation, perhaps, of the better-known national portent of Drake's Drum (*see* BUCKLAND ABBEY, Devon).

It is now also said that servants claimed to see an apparition of the battle of Edgehill on the lawns of Claydon House at dusk on every anniversary of his death. This no doubt derives from the contemporary report of a re-enactment at Edgehill by phantom armies in the days following the battle. In response to rumours concerning the apparition, King Charles is said in the pamphlet *A Great Wonder in Heaven* (1642) to have dispatched 'Gentlemen of credit' to investigate, who 'heard and saw the fore-mentioned prodigies ... distinctly knowing divers of the apparitions ... by their faces, as that of Sir *Edmund Varney* [*sic*], and others that were there slaine'.

West Drayton

In *Glimpses in the Twilight* (1885), the Revd Frederick Lee reports that at West Drayton, in about 1749, the inhabitants became convinced that the vaults under the church were haunted. Strange noises were said to be heard, and the sexton of the day, 'a person utterly devoid of superstition', was compelled to admit that unaccountable things had occurred. Knockings had been heard from the vaults under the chancel, most often on Fridays, and people from the village used to come to hear them. They were never explained away.

The villagers formed their own theories, some saying that one person had murdered another, then committed suicide, and they had been buried side by side in the same grave (a recipe for trouble). Others said that three people from a nearby mansion had gone together to look through a ventilation grating into the vault and had seen a large raven perching on one of the coffins. This bird was seen more than once by the parish clerk, pecking at the grating and fluttering about inside the vault. On another occasion it was seen in the church itself. The wife and daughter of the parish clerk often saw it. Some bell-ringers, one evening when they came to ring the bells, were told by a youth that a raven was flying about in the chancel. Coming to the church with sticks, stones, and lanterns, the four men and two boys found it fluttering among the rafters and tried to catch it. Having been driven back and forth, and beaten with a stick, so that one of its wings was broken, it fluttered down screaming and they tried to seize it. Although it appeared exhausted and finally in their grasp, all in a moment it vanished.

In 1883, the wife of a former vicar told Dr Lee that she remembered often hearing sounds in the church like the fluttering of a large bird. Dr Lee also heard that, one Saturday afternoon in 1869, two ladies who had gone to the church with flowers each saw a great black bird perched on one of the pews – they thought it must have escaped from the Zoological Gardens or some menagerie.

Some identified this bird with the murderer of the first story. Dr Lee heard through a friend from a Mrs White, whose family lived in the district from 1782 to 1818, that:

> ... the country folks always believed that the Spectral Bird which haunted Drayton Church was the restless and miserable spirit of a murderer who had committed suicide, and who, through family influence, instead of being put into a pit or hole, with a stake through his body at the cross-road by Harmondsworth, as was the sentence by law, had been buried in consecrated ground on the north side of the churchyard.

Fridays (the day the bird usually appeared) were traditionally unlucky, and ravens themselves were not only ominous birds but sometimes also thought to be the vehicles for the transmigration of souls (*see* MARAZION, Cornwall). These seem sufficient reasons why the raven should be thought to hold the spirit of a murderer, who had been buried, contrary to custom up to 1823, in consecrated ground.

Woughton-on-the-Green

According to a tradition recounted by Horace Harman in *Sketches of the Bucks Countryside* (1934), the Old Swan Inn at Woughton became one of the haunts of the eighteenth-century highwayman Dick Turpin when he changed the scene of his activities from the Great North Road to Watling Street. In Harman's time, it was still held locally that it was at the Old Swan that Turpin reversed his horse's shoes in order to escape pursuit.

Turpin was said to travel to and from his exploits by an unfrequented route running over ancient tracks. This route led down a trackway known as Bury Lane into Woughton, past the Old Swan and down what was known as the Roman Road, across a patch of scrub-covered waste known as 'No Man's Land' (an ideal lurking place for robbers), and so to Watling Street. Tradition said that Turpin's ghost was still seen on dark nights riding a phantom horse along Bury Lane. Christina Hole in *Haunted England* (1940) adds to this story that, here as elsewhere, whenever Turpin is seen, he is riding the legendary Black Bess, without whom his ghost would be scarcely recognizable.

The Old Swan was a convenient stopping place for Turpin on what was then an otherwise lonely route, and the landlord may have supplied him with information on travellers' movements. A gloomy and unlighted room in the centre of the building was once known as the Prison Room, and was where prisoners travelling in custody were confined for the night. Tradition, however, said that many a wanted man was hidden there by the landlord until the hue and cry died down.

Turpin and his horse were not the only ghosts at Woughton. Locals in the Old Swan one night warned Harman to watch out when he went home by Bury Lane for 'Old Curley and his dog', who came out of Curley Bush. Harman, however, said he had heard that they never strayed far from the Bush, which he describes as 'on the other side of Woughton', meaning the far side from Bury Lane of the crossroads at which the Old Swan stands, up the road from and on the same side as the church (it is marked on a map Harman gives showing Dick Turpin's route).

He asked if anyone had ever seen Curley and his dog when passing Curley Bush, but the villagers ridiculed the suggestion that the ghosts were anything but imaginary:

> 'Ghooasts be a lot a rot', said one. 'They be caused by narvous people afeard to goo out a nights ... Many old people yeeurs agoo were afeard to goo past Curley Bush on dark nights. They allus expected to see him and their fright done the rest ... I a bin past Curley Bush all hours a the night ... yit I a nivver sin Curley nur his dog nuther.'

Evidently no one told Harman who Curley was and why he and his dog haunted the Bush. Perhaps no one had been interested enough to ask the older generation. It was a different case, says Harman, with those who were dead and gone, for whom Curley was 'a grim reality'.

Cambridgeshire

Abington

On Abington Church Farm is or was a meadow known as Sunken Church Field. Local tradition says that there was once a church or chapel there, which fell into ruins and in the course of time became buried. It was said that at times the church bells could be heard ringing underground, and if you knelt with your ear pressed to the grass on a moonlit night you would hear a ghostly choir singing. 'Few villagers', says Enid Porter recording this story in the 1960s, 'dared to go after dark into Sunken Church Field.' She gives no date for the story, but it may be an old one, as there are similar traditions of sunken churches throughout Britain and on the Continent.

Cambridge, Abbey House

The Augustinian priory of Barnwell was originally founded in 1098 at Castle End, Cambridge, but was moved in 1112 to a new site between the Newmarket road and the river in what was then the village of Barnwell. In 1539, the priory was dissolved and stripped of its contents, roof-tiles, ironwork, and glass, all of which were sold. By this time there was little left of the priory itself, so Alexander Butler, into whose possession it came in 1659, built a new house on part of the site, later known as the Old Abbey or the Abbey House.

Beneath the ground floor of the Abbey House are vaulted cellars, one arch of which is bricked up. Local tradition has it that the arch led to a subterranean passage running from the priory to Jesus College, formerly the Benedictine nunnery of St Radegund.

From the end of the nineteenth century, Abbey House was often lived in by two or three families at a time. From about 1904 to 1910, the greater part was let to a Fellow of Pembroke College. While he and his family lived there, they often saw a woman in long robes like those of a nun pass through a particular room in the house and disappear into the panelled wall.

This was not her first appearance: a Cambridge woman who died in 1960, and who had lived in the north end of Abbey House from 1904 to 1911, said she had heard about the ghost before she went to live there. The ghost was known locally as 'the Grey Lady', and thought to have been one of the nuns of St Radegund's who came regularly via the underground way from her convent to meet her lover, a canon of Barnwell.

The children of the family living in Abbey House from 1904 were often visited by the Grey Lady, who would come to their rooms after they were in bed. They appear not to have been frightened of her, although they did not 'like her very much'. Her visits to the children suggest that she may have had a special concern with them, like the most famous White Ladies of German tradition.

The Grey Lady is reported as having been seen during the Second World War, and, in the 1950s, the house was subject to poltergeist activity, though the Grey Lady herself did not appear. Enid Porter, writing in 1969, said that she had been neither heard nor seen since 1959.

Cambridge, Corpus Christi College

Upper rooms in a corner of the Old Court of Corpus Christi are said to be haunted by a ghost usually supposed to be that of Dr Butts, Master of the college from 1626 to 1632, and Chancellor of the university during the terrible outbreak of plague in 1630. The responsibilities he bore then appear to have preyed on his mind. In a letter to Lord Coventry, High Steward of Cambridge, he writes of the sufferings of the townspeople and adds, 'myself am alone, a destitute and forsaken man, not a Scholler with me in College, not a Scholler seen by me without.' On Easter Sunday 1632, he was due to preach before the university but never appeared. When they looked for him, they found him hanging by his garters in his rooms, and since that time his ghost has haunted the college.

The haunted rooms were above the kitchens, and it was said in the 1880s that no college servant willingly remained in the kitchens at night.

According to an article which appeared in the *Occult Review* of March 1905, in 1904 an undergraduate who had the set of rooms opposite was at work there at about three o'clock one afternoon around Easter-time when he became aware of feeling uneasy. He got up and looked out of the window, and saw a man with long hair leaning out of an upper window in the opposite rooms. Only his head and shoulders could be seen, and he remained perfectly still, fixing the undergraduate with a glare. The student ran upstairs to get a better view, but by this time the figure had gone. He then rushed across the court to investigate but found the door locked. He later discovered that the owner of the rooms had been out all afternoon.

After the apparition had been seen again, the undergraduate asked a friend interested in spiritualism, and four other students, to come to his rooms to hold a seance. They all knelt down and prayed, then commanded the spirit to appear. It duly did so, although only the rooms' occupant and the student interested in spiritualism saw it.

They described it as appearing as a mist which slowly consolidated into the form of a man seemingly shrouded in white and having a gash on his neck. The phantom moved slowly around the room, and the two who could see it advanced on it with a crucifix, but they seemed to be thrust back by some invisible force. Crying, 'It drives me back,' they became altogether unnerved. A few days later, another seance raised the spirit again, but the meeting was inconclusive.

Litlington

There were in Litlington some strips of unenclosed but cultivated land bordering on the north side of Ashwell Street, part of the Icknield Way. In 1821, some workmen digging for gravel came upon a wall of flint and Roman brick. Excavations that took place in the following year uncovered several pottery urns containing ashes of the dead, which showed the site to have been a Roman walled cemetery of the type known as an *ustrinum*, which served for the burial of the ordinary dead without much expense or ceremony. G. L. Gomme, in *Folklore as an Historical Science* (1908), gives a plan of the site, showing a nearby Roman tomb, and, to the north, the foundations of a Roman villa.

According to Gomme, the place had been known since 'time immemorial' as 'Heaven's Walls' and was so-called in 'ancient deeds'. The village children were afraid to go near it after dark, because it was said to be haunted. Gomme gives this as an example of folk memory: more likely, the name reflected earlier finds of funerary urns, and the tradition of the haunting followed, as with more modern churchyards and cemeteries.

Little Abington

According to Enid Porter, writing in 1969, the two Jeremiah's Tea Houses in Little Abington and Lagdon's Grove, a wood near Bourne Bridge, perpetuate the memory of Jeremiah Lagden (with an *e*), an eighteenth-century highwayman. He was the son of Emma Lagden, a servant before her marriage to the Bromley family of Horseheath and later proprietress of the White Hart Inn at Bourne Bridge. She was a Quaker, but an unusual one, as the Cambridgeshire antiquary William Cole, who knew her well, wrote that she 'laid herself out to attract men . . . gallantry was her ruling passion'.

Jeremiah in his youth was post boy at the White Hart – or some said at Horseheath – in which occupation he enriched himself with stolen money. From this he progressed to robbing coaches on the Newmarket to London road. In later life, he lived at the Old House, Little Abington, where a hiding place in the chimney and a well under a living-room floor are said to have been where he hid his stolen loot.

In the garden is a vault known as 'Jeremiah's Grave', although it is his wife who is said to be buried there. Tradition said that Jeremiah himself was eventually captured on the Newmarket road as he lay in waiting for the coach to pass, and was hanged in a field opposite his house. The ghost of the highwayman is said to have been seen here. Certainly the name of Jeremiah was enough to frighten Abington children well into the twentieth century. Presumably he had by then become one of the many traditional bogeys used to make children behave.

Littleport to Brandon Creek Road

Enid Porter wrote in 1969, 'The East Anglian belief in the apparitions of black dogs known as *Shucky Dogs*, or, individually, as *Black
Shuck*, was held until the early part of the twentieth century in the
Fens north of Ely.' An invisible presence would be felt, the rattling
of chains heard and the sounds of heavy breathing. They were
fearsome animals, foretelling death or disaster. While this picture
needs adjusting for the Norfolk Shuck (*see* SHERINGHAM, Norfolk),
not always black, not always a dog, and not always a bad omen, it
seems to be a faithful portrait of Shuck as W. H. Barrett heard of him
in his youth in the 1890s and early 1900s.

He was said to be a big black dog whose master had been
drowned one foggy night when his horse ran down the riverbank
and plunged into the river halfway between Littleport and Brandon
Creek. Shuck was never seen again, but on pitch-black nights way-
farers could hear him padding along the road, whining and howling
for his dead master. Some even declared that they had felt the dog's
hot breath against their legs, while people living in the houses
alongside the road dreaded the dark nights when Shuck's howls
kept them awake as he roamed up and down the riverbank.

In 1906, the haunt abruptly came to an end. A Littleport man
driving home in a motorcar one foggy autumn night crashed into
something on the road and stalled the engine. He landed up off the
road with his front wheel only a few feet from the river at the very
spot where Shuck's master had been drowned nearly a hundred
years before. The animal was never heard of again, and local people
declared that this was the only known case of a phantom dog run
over by a car.

Although this story with a humorous twist at the end explains
Shuck as the ghost of a real dog, he is generally believed to be a
spirit in his own right, that is, an entity that never was corporeal.

The road in the story is the one on the opposite bank of the Great
Ouse to the modern A10.

Southery

'The Legend of the Southery Wolf-Hound', told by W. H. Barrett in *Tales from the Fens* (1963), says that, when Southery was an island, cut off by Southery Fen, monks came from Ely and began building a church. The Southery folk were a wild, rough lot, living in reed-thatched huts, and making their living by catching eels and robbing boats sailing up to Cambridge or Ely. After a number of monks were found with their throats cut, the abbot of Ely sent armed men to search for their murderers in the swamps. This proving a hopeless task, he asked the Baron of Northwold, Norfolk, in whose lands Southery lay, for help. As the baron had lost many men in the Fens already, he sent a pack of wolfhounds to guard the monks.

The hounds arrived, but they refused to eat the fish which was all the monks had, and soon started hunting. At first there were plenty of dead monks and soldiers for them to eat, but they ate their way through those and began hunting the living. The Southery people abandoned the village and went to live in the Fens, and the monks returned to Ely.

Food again becoming short for the wolfhounds, they fell on each other. At last only the fiercest and most cunning of them was left, a bitch as big as a donkey. A Fenman found her dying of hunger in the reeds, and friends helped him carry her home to his hut. His wife had just had a baby, and she soon got the bitch well by feeding her milk to both her and the child. The bitch soon became tame and friendly with the Southery men, who had now returned to the village, but she did not like the monks.

One day she could not be found, and the Fenmen thought the monks had killed her. However, a week or two later she returned, her pads all bloody and torn, as if she had travelled on rough ground beyond the Fens. She was pregnant, which was strange, as there was not a dog left in the neighbourhood. Then one day she carried from a dark corner of the hut a pup neither dog nor wolf but something in between. He grew up to be nearly as big as an ox, and when his mother died he took on the job of catching fresh meat for the Fenmen, often coming home with a stag or a sheep.

When the church was finished, the Bishop of Elmham (in Norfolk) came to open it, riding in with a troop of armed men. One of the soldiers, who had been in Southery when the wolfhounds were there, saw the huge dog and made to kill it. Before he could get within striking distance, the dog was at his throat and began devouring him as he lay kicking on the ground. The other soldiers loosed a rain of arrows at the dog, which crept off into the fen to die.

That happened hundreds of years ago, said old Fenland storytellers in Southery pubs up to about 1900, but, if you go out at midnight on 29 May, the date of the Southery Feast, you will still hear the wolfhound howl as it pads along, and know you will die within a twelvemonth. And if you look at the cornerstones of the charnel house of the ruined church, you will see that they have been gnawed, the marks having been made by the wolf-dog, which comes on that night every year and tries to get to the bones. That is why Southery men take the long way home from the pub, rather than pass those ruins at midnight on the night of the Southery Feast.

Wandlebury Camp, Stapleford

After describing the Gogmagog Hills, near Cambridge, the sixteenth-century topographer William Camden goes on to say:

> On the top of these hilles, I saw a fort intrenched, and the same very large, strengthned [sic] with a threefold rampire ... Gervase of Tilbury seemeth to call it Vandelbiria.

This is Wandlebury Camp, a massive Iron Age hill-fort on the summit of the Gogmagogs. Camden was contemptuous of a local ghost story Gervase of Tilbury (fl. 1211) had to tell about Wandlebury, saying dismissively:

> Touching the Martiall spectre, or sprite that walked heere, which he addeth to the rest, because it is but a meere toyish and fantasti-call devise of the doting vulgar sort, I willing [sic] over-passe it. For it is not my purpose, to tell pleasant tales, and tickle eares.

Gervase himself, writing for the entertainment of the Holy Roman Emperor Otto IV (1197–1212), had no such reservations. He says:

> There is a very ancient tradition, attested by popular report, that if a warrior enters this level space at dead of night, when the moon

is shining, and cries 'Knight to Knight, come forth!' immediately
he will be confronted by a warrior, armed for fight, who, charging
horse to horse, either dismounts his adversary or is dismounted.
But I should add that the warrior must enter the enclosure alone,
although his companions may look on from outside.

This tradition was once put to the test by a knight called Osbert
Fitzhugh, who had been told about it while he was staying at
Cambridge Castle. He and his squire rode up to the Camp, but only
Osbert passed through the ramparts and rode into the inner court.
He cried, 'Knight to Knight, come forth!' as he had been instructed
'and in response a knight or what looked like a knight, came forth
to meet him'. The two knights rushed at each other, and at the
end of their shadowy combat, under the light of the moon, Osbert
unhorsed his adversary and cast him to the ground. He seized hold
of the bridle of the horse to lead it away as spoils – and no doubt
also as proof of the encounter – but at that the knight leapt to his
feet and hurled his spear, deeply piercing Osbert's thigh, then
vanished.

Osbert led the horse out of the Camp and gave him into the care
of his squire. It was a beast of exceptional beauty and strength, tall,
with fierce eyes, and black as midnight, including its gear. Leading
it back to Cambridge Castle, they tethered it in the courtyard and
got everyone out of bed to hear Osbert's adventure. 'At cockcrow,
the horse, prancing, snorting and pawing the earth, suddenly burst
the reins that held it ... fled, vanished, and none could trace it.'
However, another proof that this had been a supernatural encounter
remained. Every year on the night that Osbert had fought with the
phantom, his wound would open and bleed afresh.

Gervase's story of the Black Knight later entered English
literature, being the main source of the 'Host's Tale' in Canto 3 of Sir
Walter Scott's *Marmion* (1808).

Whittlesford

In the neighbourhood of Whittlesford there were three tumuli
or burial mounds known as the Chronicle Hills or (more descrip-
tively) the Conical Hills. When Ebenezer Hollick, the squire of

Whittlesford, levelled the Conical Hills in about 1826, some Roman remains were found, including skeletons.

According to a tradition recorded by W. R. Brown in *Cambridgeshire Cameos* (c.1895):

There is an amusing story told in the village about one of these skeletons. It was one of two which were discovered in a most remarkable position, showing that they were combatants; one was gripping the other so tightly that even in the grave they were not separated[.] This particular skeleton was in a sitting posture; one of the venturesome labourers took a fancy to the skull of this warrior, and accordingly dismembered it from the skeleton and carried it home to his cottage. At night, however, up came the headless skeleton to the labourer's house [.] Knocking at the door, it demanded restitution of the skull. This occurred night after night, so the gossips- say, until the skull was taken back and re-placed.

A more circumstantial version of this tradition was recorded by Enid Porter in 1969 from Mr J. Maynard of Whittlesford, who said that it was still known to old people in the village. According to Mr Maynard, the labourer who stole the skull was a man named Matthews, who took it home and placed it on his bedroom mantelpiece. In the middle of the following night, he was woken by a terrific banging on his door, and, putting his head out of the window, saw a headless skeleton standing in the garden below. In a hoarse, sepulchral voice, the skeleton demanded his skull, and Matthews was so terrified that he at once threw it down to him.

Cheshire

Brereton Green

There is an old legend about the Breretons, formerly owners of Brereton Hall, that they, like many other ancient families, had a death omen peculiar to themselves. In their case, it concerned a lake on their estate; whenever the head of the family was about to die, a black tree trunk would be seen floating in it. There is disagreement among local historians as to whether this lake is Blackmere, which still exists, or Bagmere, which has been drained. The omen is referred to by several writers in the sixteenth and seventeenth centuries; William Camden in his *Britannia* (1586) gives a slightly variant account where it announces the death of the heir, not the head of the family:

> A wonder is that I shall tell you, and yet no other than I haue heard verified upon the credit of many credible persons, and commonlie believed: That before the heire of this house of the *Breretons* dieth, there bee seene in a poole adjoining, bodies of trees swimming for certaine daies together.

Another sinister tradition, recorded by Christina Hole in the 1930s, is that once a year the ghosts of all the Breretons that ever lived gather at Shocklach church; the black phantom coaches in which they arrive block the lane leading to the lonely church.

Burleydam

In the 1950s and '60s, members of Women's Institutes in Cheshire compiled two volumes of 'village memories', which include many interesting items of tradition and belief. Among these is the claim that there is a bottle buried under the doorstep of the entrance to the Combermere Arms Hotel, in which two clergymen once imprisoned a ghost which had been troubling the place. If it is ever broken, the ghost will return, worse than ever. Stories on this theme seem to have been especially popular in the western counties in the early nineteenth century, so it seems likely that this tale may be equally old, though only recorded in the mid twentieth century.

Congleton

In the nineteenth and also the twentieth century, people reported seeing the ghost of a white cat sitting on a post near the remains of Congleton abbey. If human beings approached, it would jump into the air and vanish. It was said to have been a cat belonging to Mrs Winge, a housekeeper at the former abbey. Some accident must have befallen it, for one evening it returned to her cottage only in spirit form, contentedly sitting on the steps but refusing to enter. When she tried to coax it indoors, it slowly disappeared. Every evening the cat would come and sit on the step, but always disappeared before the eyes of friends and neighbours who came to watch it.

This appearing and disappearing cat has been linked with the Cheshire Cat in Lewis Carroll's *Alice in Wonderland*.

Coombs Moss

Fletcher Moss, a local historian writing in the 1890s, was told by one of his informants that when the railway to Buxton was being built, some of the navvies, for a lark, stole an old skull which had been kept for generations in a farmhouse at Coombs Moss. From then on, they had nothing but bad luck: earth slips buried much of the track they had laid, and other stretches were destroyed by subsidence; many of the men fell ill, and all were alarmed by horrible and inexplicable noises. When they told their boss, he ordered them to take the skull back where it belonged, and offered to give its ghost a free pass on his railway line for ever. After that, there was no more trouble, though the scars of the landslips long remained visible.

This particular legend cannot go very far back into the Victorian period, since it involves the construction of a railway line; the general theme of a skull that resents being disturbed is, however, quite widely found (*see* CALGARTH, Westmorland).

Duddon

The pub in this village is named the Headless Woman, and its sign-board does indeed show a woman carrying her severed head under her arm. Pubs displaying this image (now rare) were generally called the Silent Woman or the Quiet Woman, as a joke against chatterboxes – only decapitation could keep them quiet. In this case, however, the explanation offered is a local legend about a servant's loyalty during the Civil War. Jacob Larwood reported in 1866 that the licensee at that time displayed a notice telling the tale:

> A party of Cromwell's soldiers, engaged in hunting down the Royalists in the Chester district, visited Hockenhall Hall, but found that the family being warned of their coming had buried all the silver and other valuables and then fled for safety, leaving only a faithful old housekeeper in charge of the Hall, thinking it unlikely that the soldiers would do her any harm.
>
> The soldiers, being incensed at finding nothing of value, locked up the housekeeper in the top room and proceeded to torture her to tell them where the valuables were hidden. She remained faithful, and was finally murdered by the soldiers cutting off her head. Tradition says that afterwards, on numerous occasions she was seen carrying her head under her arm, walking along the old bridle path between Hockenhall Hall and the spot where it comes out on the Tarporley Road near to the public house.

The story is repeated in more recent books with additional details such as the name of the faithful servant, said to be a cook called Grace Trigg. Some say the soldiers carried her body and the head to a cottage at Duddon to hide them; this building was later on turned into the pub.

Gawsworth

A notable sight in this village is the isolated grave of Samuel 'Maggoty' Johnson, a playwright and music master of the eighteenth century, whose eccentricities won him his nickname (the equivalent, in the slang of the time, to 'batty' or 'nutty'). He was also employed as a jester at the local Old Hall – probably the last professional domestic jester in England. When he died in 1773, he was buried, at his own request, in a little wood rather than in the village church-yard; the lengthy inscription on the tombstone is his own composition. Understandably, there is a local tradition that his ghost can be seen. A twentieth-century sexton reported meeting him one moonlight night riding a white horse, and followed him through the wood towards the grave; he was just in time to hear the bump of the gravestone thudding back into place once Maggoty was inside.

Lyme Park

According to a tradition of the mid nineteenth century, Lyme Park (near Disley) is said to be haunted by a phantom funeral which slowly approaches the house, followed by the ghost of a woman in white; at the same time, bells are heard tolling. This is said to be the re-enactment of the funeral of Sir Piers Leigh, killed at Agincourt and brought home to be buried in his own park, under a mound still called Knight's Lowe. The ghostly woman is not his wife but a local girl who had loved him; when she heard of his death she drowned herself in a stream by a meadow called Lady's Grave.

Marbury Hall, near Comberbach

Up to the 1930s, a skeleton used to be kept in an oak chest in this house. Why this should be so is not known; one explanation might be that some family member had been a medical student, or an art student, who used it in his work. But of course such a dramatic and mysterious object inspired rumours, and by the mid twentieth century a colourful legend had developed, with several variations of detail.

According to this tale, at some unspecified time in the past one member of the Barrymore family (owners of Marbury Hall) travelled to Egypt, where an Egyptian girl fell so passionately in love with him that after he left she made her own way to Cheshire and refused ever to go home again. Some say he then married her; others, that he had meanwhile married his English sweetheart, but installed the Egyptian at Marbury as his mistress. In either case, it is said she grew so fond of the house that she insisted that if she were to die her body must remain there, not be buried in the churchyard. In due course she did die (some say she was murdered on the staircase), but her request was ignored and she received a normal funeral. Soon afterwards, bells began ringing of their own accord, and her ghost was seen riding a white horse. To put a stop to the haunting, the family disinterred her corpse and brought it home, where it was laid in an oak chest. A later generation of owners, it is said, tried to transfer it to the family vault, while others tried to get rid of it entirely by throwing it into Budworth Mere. Each time they were forced to bring it back. It was kept in the chest until the 1930s, but then removed; some say it was reburied in the churchyard at midnight, others that it is bricked up somewhere in the walls of the house.

The park round Marbury Hall is also reputed to be haunted by a more conventional ghost, a lady on a white horse, who can be seen at sunset. She too is supposed to be a Lady Barrymore. The inspiration for this legend was a real mare, the Marbury Dun, so swift that Lord Barrymore wagered the Hall itself that she could gallop from London to Marbury in a single day, between sunrise and sunset. She won his bet for him, but tradition asserts that she dropped dead on arrival, after drinking from a trough in the yard. She was buried in the park, under a stone reading:

> Here lies Marbury Dunne,
> The finest horse that ever run,
> Clothed in a linen sheet
> With silver shoes upon her feet.

The ghost story which grew from this claims that Lord Barrymore had bought this mare as a wedding present to his wife, promising it would be there on the wedding day, and in order to keep his promise insisted on the fatal gallop. Lady Barrymore was so upset that she died soon after of a broken heart, and her last wish was to be buried by the well where the horse died, not in the churchyard. Lord Barrymore refused. Her ghost told him she would never rest, but would ride her lovely mare for ever.

Neston

When she was collecting Cheshire folklore in the 1930s, Christina Hole was told how a Catholic woman had seen the ghost of a priest but had not realized it at the time; her name was Teresa Higginson, and she died in 1905. She was a key-holder for the Catholic church at Neston, and early one morning a priest whom she did not know called at her house and asked to be let into the church so that he could say his daily Mass there. She unlocked the church and attended his Mass – to which, since it was an unscheduled one, nobody else came. Afterwards he went into the vestry to disrobe, but when she followed a little later there was no one in there, though there was no way out except through the church. Perplexed, she told various other parishioners what had happened, and from her description of the stranger the older ones knew that it must have been the ghost of a former parish priest, long since dead.

The implication of the tale probably is that the priest had neglected to say the Masses he had promised to say on someone's behalf, and could not rest till he had fulfilled his promise.

Stanney

The collection of local anecdotes collected from members of Women's Institutes in the 1950s includes a standing joke against the people of Stanney as being timid simpletons. Allegedly, they were so terrified by a duck which used to wander down the lane towards Stoak that nobody dared go that way. Eventually a band of men ambushed it, cut its head off, and buried it at the top of Stoak Lane. But things only grew worse, for now the ghost of the duck haunts the lane, waddling past without a head.

Stockport

In the nineteenth century a ghost known as the Gatley Shouter was said to haunt the Gatley Carrs, a swampy morass near the river in the parishes of Stockport, Northen (now Northenden) and Didsbury, in Cheshire (now Greater Manchester). Fletcher Moss, writing in 1894, told the story 'in the language of the old folks who remember the occurrence', and in 1898 he told another version in many of the same words but with additional details. He says he had been told the whole tale many years before by an old man who was then over eighty: 'I am not sure whether he said he was present at the great hunt or only remembered it.' Both 1894 and 1898 versions may come from this source, the differences in the 1898 text probably being attributable to Moss's adding information gleaned from other informants in the interim.

In both tellings, the Shouter was in life a dishonest tradesman who after death is being punished for giving short measure: in 1894 he is reported as lamenting 'milk short o' measure, butter short o' weight, oh dear, oh dear,' but in 1898: 'The Gatley Shouter sang a verse of an old song, sang it often in Gatley Carrs when the moon was at full:

> "Milk and water sold I ever,
> Weight or measure gave I never."'

Almost exactly the same lament (only two words different) was uttered by Old Molly Lee at BURSLEM, Staffordshire.

Fletcher Moss's two versions with their different details are a salutary reminder that when a nineteenth-century collector says a story is being told 'in the language of the old folks who remember the occurrence', this does not necessarily mean that what follows will be a verbatim transcript of what the storyteller in fact said.

In the earlier account the Shouter is called a boggart, but in 1898 is described as 'an uneasy spirit who came out of the grave in Northen churchyard, and squeaked and gibbered about the Carr Lane to Gatley'. Even in the first telling Fletcher Moss acknowledges that 'Th' mon 'ad bin a Barrow,' and in 1898 he identifies him more precisely:

Aye, sure, th' Gatley Shouter wur Jim Barrow's ghost. 'E cum fro' Cross Acres, t'other side o' Gatley. Them Gatley folk wur allus a gallus [mischievous] lot. Owd Jim wur desprit fond o' brass, an' 'e stuck to aw as 'e could lay ode on. 'E 'd a flayed two fleas for one 'ide, 'e wud, an' when 'e deed Owd Scrat got 'im an' 'e warmt 'im 'e did so, an' Jim mi't a bin 'eard a neets moaning, 'Oh dear, oh dear, wa-a-tered milk, wa-a-tered milk,' till folks got plaguey feart a goin' yon road arter dark. Now there come a new passon to Northen, a scholar fresh from Oxford or Rome or someweers, chok'-fu' o' book-larnin', an' 'e played th' hangment wi' aw th' ghostses i' these parts, an' 'e said 'e'd tackle 'im. So 'e got aw th' parish as could read or pray a bit to cum wi' their Bibles, an' one neet when th' moon wur out Owd Scrat mun a bin firin' up, for th' Shouter wur bein' rarely fettled by th' way as 'e moaned. An' aw th' folk got round 'im, an' they drew toart one another in a ring like, an' kept cumin' closer till at last they 'd gotten 'im in a corner i' th' churchyard by th' yew-tree, an th' passon was on th' grave, an' 'e whips a bit of chalk out o' 'is pocket an' draws a holy ring round 'em aw, an' aw th' folk jooin 'ands and [sic] pray desprit loike, an' th' passon 'ops about an' shouts an' bangs th' book till 'e's aw o' a muck sweat. An' 'e prayed at 'im in Latin too, mind yo', as weel as English, ani' th' poor ghost moans an' chunners an' gets littler an' littler till 'e fair sweals away like a sneel that's sawted. An' at last th' devil wur druv out o' im, an' 'e lets 'im abide as quiet as a mouse. 'E's now under yon big stone near by th' passon's gate. Yo' may see it for yosen. It's theer now."

'You may see it for yosen' – therefore by implication the story was true.

Cornwall

Bodmin Moor

Quite possibly the most terrifying thing ever to happen on Bodmin Moor was the appearance of the death-fetch of William Rufus (r. 1087–1100).

Robert, Earl of Moreton in Normandy, was a special friend of Rufus and another of the same stamp. As soon as he was made Earl of Cornwall by William the Conqueror, he seized the priory of St Petroc at Bodmin and converted its lands to his use.

One day, he was hunting in the woods around Bodmin. During a long chase after a great red stag, he became separated from his huntsmen and found himself alone. Riding clear of the trees on to the moors above, he was astonished to see a large black goat approaching. As it drew near, he saw that it bore on its back 'King Rufus', black, naked, and pierced through the breast. Robert commanded the goat in the name of the Trinity to tell him what it was he bore, and the goat replied, 'I am carrying your king to judgement.'

The goat revealed that he was an evil spirit, sent at the bidding of St Alban, 'who complained to God of him', to wreak vengeance on Rufus for his oppression of the English Church. Having spoken, the spectre vanished. Robert related this apparition to his followers, and shortly afterwards they learned that, at the very hour when he encountered the goat, William Rufus had been slain by the arrow of Walter Tirrell in the New Forest, Hampshire.

This horror story from the Latin chronicler Matthew Paris (c.1200–59) was not the only legend concerning the death of Rufus told by chroniclers (most of them monks) in the Middle Ages, when there was a strong clerical bias against him.

The Irish Lady

Pedn-mên-du, 'the headland of black rock', forms the western boundary of Whitsand Bay. Joseph Blight wrote in 1861:

> [W]estward off the point, is seen towering above the waves a rock of a peculiar and pleasing form; it is known as the Irish Lady. The legend is, that a wreck having happened there, of all the souls that were on board only a lady was seen, clinging to this rock. It was found that the ship belonged to Ireland ... The fishermen of the locality say that the ghost of the drowned lady, with a rose in her mouth, is still often seen sitting on the rock.

Blight also gives the explanation favoured by sceptics, that the rock got its name from its shape, 'not unlike a lady in a long black robe advancing into the sea'.

Robert Hunt gives an altogether more highly coloured version of this tradition: the shipwreck takes place at night, so the Irish Lady is seen only in the morning; the storm rages on and she cannot be helped; days and nights pass while people onshore watch her dying; her dead body is washed into the sea. Neither Blight nor Hunt connects this lady with the one of the same name and way with roses said in the nineteenth century to appear at the fogou of Pendeen Vau, St Just.

The background to the story of the Irish Lady may be largely historical: Sir Humphry Davy (1778–1829), who wrote a poem on the drowning, says that she was shipwrecked at the Land's End about the time of the massacre of the Irish Protestants by the Catholics, in the reign of Charles I.

Marazion

A correspondent of *Notes and Queries* in 1853 drew attention to the apparent survival around Marazion of a very ancient belief. He notes that, in *Don Quixote* (1604–15), Cervantes mentions an English tradition that King Arthur did not die, but by magic art was turned into a raven, and would reign again, 'for which reason it cannot be proved that, from that time to this, any Englishman has killed a raven'.

The contributor, Edgar MacCulloch, goes on to say that, about sixty years before, his father had been about to shoot a raven on Marazion Green when an old man rebuked him, 'telling him that he ought on no account to have shot at a raven, for that King Arthur was still alive in the form of that bird'.

Robert Hunt in 1865 reported asking about this belief and being told 'that bad luck would follow the man who killed a Chough, for Arthur was transformed into one of these birds'. Ravens and choughs are both corvids, as is the bird named in what was probably Cervantes' source, Julian del Castillo, who in 1582 reported that, according to common talk, King Arthur had been enchanted into a crow.

Underlying this legend is belief in metempsychosis, the transmigration of souls, which survived in Western Europe into the early twentieth century and perhaps is not quite dead. Sailors and fishermen in particular held that the souls of drowned comrades might be embodied in storm petrels and gulls, and English miners held a similar belief: the 'Seven Whistlers' are reported as giving warning by their eerie call of impending danger in the mines, and have been explained as the spirits of comrades returning in bird form to alert their fellows. Other traditions, however, place them in the context of the Wild Hunt (see PETERBOROUGH, Huntingdonshire and Peterborough).

Pengersick Castle

Now restored and inhabited, Pengersick or Pengerswick Castle was in the eighteenth and nineteenth centuries a ruin consisting of a single tower standing in a lonely hollow running down to Pengersick Cove. Strange traditions concerning it existed, including one of a lady of Pengersick, who was often seen either as partly or wholly serpent, and in that form long haunted the ruins after her decease. This is an echo of a rambling tale reported by both William Bottrell and Robert Hunt in the second half of the nineteenth century. Hunt says that the first Pengersick, who built the castle, married as his second wife a 'wicked stepmother', who persuaded him to have his son kidnapped and sold as a slave. Subsequently, she poisoned her husband, then shut herself up in her room, having become covered in scales from her poisons, and finally cast herself into the sea.

Meantime, Young Pengersick had escaped abroad, and when he returned brought with him a lady of great beauty whom people said was a 'Saracen'. Only a few servants were allowed within the castle walls, which, or so it was rumoured, were bound by spells. Pengersick would shut himself up in his room for days, and at night and during storms could be heard calling up spirits in some unknown language.

The Saracen lady sat alone in her tower all day looking out of a window over the sea. She seldom spoke, but sang the love songs of her land so sweetly that the fishes raised their heads at dawn to hear her, and mermaids and strange spirits of the waters were drawn to Pengersick Cove.

This mysterious pair long inhabited the castle. Pengersick often rode abroad on a great horse thought to be demonic, and he was feared by all. Years passed until one day a sunburnt stranger was seen in Market Jew (Marazion). People noticed him wandering out at night and sitting on a rock at the entrance to Pengersick valley. At the same time, the lord seemed to stay at home more than usual, and no one heard his spells or his lady's singing.

Then, one stormy night, a burst of flames told the people of Market Jew that Pengersick Castle was ablaze. Its interior was destroyed, and neither enchanter nor lady nor stranger were ever seen again. People later claimed that, as the flames reached their height, they saw two men and a lady amidst them who passed upwards like lightning and vanished.

The legends of Pengersick and its enchanter are probably rooted in the personality of Henry de Pengersick in the fourteenth century. Violently anti-clerical, he was excommunicated by the Church for having laid hands on clergy come to gather tithes. He was perhaps remembered as 'godless' and woven into a story accounting for the castle's ruined state. The castle came after his time, however, its surviving tower being built around 1500. By 1738, when it was visited by the antiquary William Borlase, except for this tower it was ruinous. Not surprisingly, there are rumours of secret passages and of a treasure bricked up within its walls.

Penzance

Perhaps the most notorious haunting in the history of Penzance was that of a house in Chapel Street, near the parish church. The house, as William Bottrell tells us in 1880, was occupied by an elderly lady called Mrs Baines, who, going into the garden one night to make sure that her manservant John was keeping guard in her orchard, found him asleep and shook down some apples in order to pretend that they had been stolen and he was remiss in his duties. But waking, he mistook her for a thief and shot her, and a short time later she died.

Her ghost returned, and was often seen under the tree where she was shot:

> Everybody knew the old lady by her upturned and powdered grey hair under a lace cap of antique pattern; by the long lace ruffles hanging from her elbows; her short silk mantle, gold-headed cane, and other trappings of old-fashioned pomp.

Her walking in the garden might have been put up with, but she started haunting the house, 'tramping about from room to room, slamming the doors, rattling the furniture, and often making a fearful crash amongst glass and crockery'. Finally a parson famed in the neighbourhood as a 'ghost-layer' (Bottrell thought his name was Singleton) was brought in 'and he succeeded . . . in getting her away to the sand-banks on the Western Green . . . where the waves now roll'. Here he single-handedly bound her to spin ropes of sand for a thousand years, unless she could weave one to reach from St Michael's Mount to St Clement's Isle.

In 1890, Margaret Courtney adds to Bottrell's story that the whirring of Mrs Baines's spinning-wheel was often heard long after her ghost stopped appearing, but eventually it was discovered that the sound was made by the wind whistling through loose pieces of leather nailed around a door to stop draughts.

Porthcurno

A belief once prevailed in the western districts of Cornwall that Porthcurno was its principal port until the cove became 'sanded up'. Some said this was the work of Jan Tregeagle of TREGAGLE'S HOLE, but others linked it with the old maritime tradition of ghost ships.

'There is ... a very old belief', wrote William Bottrell in 1873, 'that spectre ships frequently visited Parcurno ... and that they were often seen sailing up and down the valley, over dry land the same as on the sea.' They were regarded as 'tokens' that enemies were about to descend on the coast, their ships equal in number to the number of ghost ships seen. The presage had latterly become attached to a person who had lived more than a hundred years before in a lonely house inland from Porthcurno called Chyg-widden. An old farm labourer of St Levan told Bottrell the story.

Harshly treated by his drunken father and his stepmother, Young Martin went to sea, vowing never to return while they lived. Years passed and he was presumed dead. Old Martin and his wife died, and the house went to relations.

About ten years later, Young Martin returned to Chygwidden, with a companion and several chests. His cousins, a young man and his sister, Eleanor, offered to leave the house, but he said he would only stay a while and they could keep it.

His companion's name was José, and he conversed with 'the Captain', as everyone called Young Martin, in some foreign tongue. The Captain never answered questions concerning his adventures while away, but when drunk he was heard swearing at José, saying that he had risked his life to save him from being hanged at the yardarm. He had plenty of money, which came out of the chests, as did fine clothes and jewels for Eleanor. After about a year, the Captain had a ship built in which he and José would vanish for months. (One is led to suspect they were pirates.)

Time passed, and the Captain, feeling the approach of death, made José swear to take him out to sea to die, and send him to rest on the seabed. However, he died before this was done. He had also laid a curse on anyone burying him in the same ground as his father and stepmother, and, when a coffin was taken to St Levan church-yard and buried near them, it was rumoured that all it contained was earth. When, the next night, José had two chests conveyed to Porthcurno, people suspected that the largest held the Captain. They were put on the ship, and José and his favourite dog climbed on board, and no more was seen of them. Eleanor also vanished.

Presently a tempest arose and, in the week that it raged, Porthcurno was choked with sand. Shortly after that, people began to see a phantom ship driving into Porthcurno against wind and tide. Often she came at dusk, and would sail over the land till she came to Chygwidden. She was generally shrouded in mist, but now and then people glimpsed on her deck the shadowy figures of a dog, two men, and a woman.

After hovering over the farm, this ship with her spectral crew would bear away and vanish near a rock where a hoard of foreign coins was supposedly found. 'Of late the ghostly ship has not been known to have entered Parcurno.'

St Agnes

The landscape around St Agnes is dotted with the shafts of disused tin mines. Polbreen Mine, at the foot of St Agnes Beacon, was haunted by a spirit called Dorcas. In life she had inhabited one of the small cottages adjacent to the mine, but one night, for a reason that has gone unrecorded, she threw herself down one of the shafts. Her dead and broken body was discovered, brought up to the surface, and buried.

Her spirit, however, still remained in the mine. She seemed to take pleasure in tormenting the miners, calling them by name, and luring them from their work. She was usually only a voice. Though a few claimed they had seen her, the miners in general put this down to nerves. 'But', says Robert Hunt, telling this story in 1865, 'it is stated as an incontrovertible fact, that more than one man who has met the spirit in the levels of the mine has had his clothes torn off his back.'

Only on one occasion had Dorcas appeared to act kindly. Two miners, to whom Hunt gives the names Martin and Jack, were working together in the mine when they distinctly heard a voice calling 'Jacky!' Martin said Jacky should go and see who was calling him, but Jacky was afraid, or perhaps thought his senses were deceiving him. Again came the call: 'Jacky! Jacky! Jacky!' this time more vehemently. Jacky threw down his hammer and went to look. He had not gone many yards when a mass of rock fell from the roof of the level onto the spot where he had been working. A projecting rock had deflected it from Martin, who, though they had to dig him out, was unhurt. Jacky declared to his dying day that he owed his life to Dorcas. Hunt adds, 'Although Dorcas's shaft remains a part of Polbreen Mine, I am informed by the present agent that her presence has departed.'

Because of the dangerous nature of their work, tin miners, like coal miners elsewhere, had a deeply rooted belief in presages, and in Cornwall as in other counties there were tales of haunted mines inhabited by warning spirits, sometimes explained, like Dorcas, as ghosts. (*See also* SHILBOTTLE, Northumberland.)

St Levan

In the churchyard at St Levan is the low altar-tomb of Captain Richard Wetherall, of the Scillonian brig *Aurora*, which went down in 1811. It is said that the ship sprang a leak and sank, and he was drowned off Gwennap Head near the Rundle or Runnel Stone. 'This grave is regarded with fear and wonder by many persons,' wrote William Bottrell in 1873. A ghostly bell was said to strike the hour and half-hour in his grave, exactly as on shipboard, and this had gone on since he was buried. The sound could be heard most clearly at midnight, for it was around midnight that he made his crew take to the boat. As she went down, the crew heard him strike 'eight bells', signifying the end of a watch. This was the captain's last farewell as he went down with his ship, and those who hear it ringing from the grave have due notice that their own watch is over.

Talland

In the early eighteenth century, Talland was perhaps best known for its vicar from 1713–47, the Revd Richard Dodge. 'Parson Dodge' was a ghost-layer or exorcist of extraordinary power. Robert Hunt in 1865 told the story of how Parson Dodge was called in by the Revd Abraham Mills of nearby Lanreath, whose parish was haunted by one of England's ubiquitous phantom coaches with headless horses. The two clergymen kept watch one night on the moor where the coach was usually seen, but it did not appear. Arranging to keep vigil another night, each turned homeward.

At the bottom of a deep valley, about a mile (1.6 km) from Blackadon, Parson Dodge's horse became uneasy, as if something was moving across the road in front of her. Defying whip and spur, she kept trying to turn round, and finally Dodge threw the reins over her neck and she started back over the moor. There, to his horror, Dodge saw the phantom coach, with his friend Mr Mills lying on the ground and the demon coachman standing over him. But at the mere sight of Parson Dodge closing in on him, the demon cried, 'Dodge is come! I must be gone!' and sprang back on his coach, whereupon coach, horses and all vanished and did not return.

In the 1970s, local people believed that Dodge was in league with smugglers and that he had spread a story of demonic apparitions in Bridle Lane, leading up from Talland beach to the church, to frighten away onlookers. The smuggler theory is a common corollary of coastal hauntings: in most cases, however, it turns out on investigation to be either smugglers exploiting an existing tradition or else a latter-day rationalization.

Other well-known Cornish ghost-layers were Parson Woods of Ladock, Parson Richards, curate of Camborne, the Revd Jago, vicar of Wendron, and the Revd Polkinghorn of St Ives, who laid the infamous ghost of 'Wild Harris' of Kenegie, setting him to count all the blades of grass at Castle-an-Dinas, Ludgvan.

Tregagle's Hole

Tregagle's Hole is a natural arch in a rocky promontory south of Carne Beacon. Its name commemorates Cornwall's most powerful ghost, Jan or John Tregeagle or Tregagle.

Stories about Tregeagle appear to have coalesced round the memory of a John Tregeagle who lived in the early seventeenth century. He is said to have been the foster-brother and chief steward of John, second Lord Robartes of Lanhydrock. Various episodes in his life brought his name into such ill repute that, by the time of Richard Polwhele's *History of Cornwall* (1803), he was remembered as a very wicked man.

According to traditions current in William Bottrell's time, he was an unscrupulous lawyer who took bribes, forged documents, and bore false witness in pursuit of power and riches. He was also a Cornish Bluebeard, dispatching several wealthy wives, and selling his soul to the Devil. When Tregeagle died in 1655, he was buried in St Breock churchyard. Rumour said he had to bribe the parson to get into consecrated ground, and he has no memorial.

He was summoned from the grave by his name being spoken in court. One man lent another money with Tregeagle as witness, though no documents were signed. After Tregeagle's death, the lender tried to get the money repaid, but the debtor denied having received it. The case went to Bodmin Assizes, and, when the plaintiff said that the loan was witnessed by Tregeagle, the defendant swore, 'If Tregeagle ever saw it, I wish to God that Tregeagle may come and declare it!' The oath was no sooner uttered, than Tregeagle stood before the court and said the debtor had indeed had the money. Then he added ominously, '[T]hou hast ... found it easy to bring me from the grave, but thou wilt not find it so easy to put me away.' Though the debtor repaid the loan, Tregeagle thereafter dogged his footsteps. Conjurors and parsons were brought in, who for a time bound the troublesome ghost to emptying Dozmary Pool on Bodmin with a 'croggan' or limpet shell. Not only did the shell have a hole in it, but Dozmary Pool itself was long believed to be bottomless or to connect with the sea. Richard Carew reports in 1602, 'The country people held many strange conceits of this pool; as ... that a fagot, once thrown thereinto, was taken up at Foy Haven, six miles distant.'

Tregeagle soon completed his task, however, and returned to plague his victim. More exorcists were called in, who bound him and led him to Gwenvor Cove. There they doomed him to make a truss of sand, bind it with ropes of the same, and carry it up what Bottrell in notes given to Hunt describes as 'a certain rock' in Escall's Cliff, but in his own book calls Carn Olva.

Tregeagle laboured fruitlessly at this task, until, one night of hard frost, he poured water from the Vellandreath Brook on the truss so that it froze and he could carry it to the Carn. Then he flew back to the terrified debtor, who summoned more ghost-layers. They bound Tregeagle to sand-spinning at Gwenvor once again, now with the proviso that he must not go near fresh water. 'So

Tregeagle was matched at last,' writes Bottrell, 'for he is still there on the shore of Whitesand Bay vainly trying to make his truss of sand; and he is frequently heard roaring for days before a northerly storm comes to scatter it.'

Robert Hunt's version of the legend says that Tregeagle escaped from Dozmary Pool and raced across the moors until he came to Roche Rock, 'a huge, high, and steep rock, seated in a plain' as Carew calls it, surmounted by the remains of the late medieval St Michael's chapel. From here, an assortment of monks, parsons, unnamed saints, and St Petroc by turns chivvied him to Padstow, to weave ropes of sand, then to Bareppa, to clear the beach by shovelling sand into sacks and carrying them to Porthleven. Crossing the Loe estuary, he one day dropped his sack and thus Loe Bar was created (in point of fact, it formed in the thirteenth century). From there he was finally banished to Land's End, and condemned to sweep the sand from PORTHCURNO Cove round to Nanjizal.

The ghosts of the wicked are often forced to perform everlasting tasks, but Tregeagle is more than the usual ghost. His voice is heard in the roaring of the wind on the moors around the hill-fort of Castle-an-Dinas, St Columb Major. As the Quiller-Couches wrote in 1894, 'The howls of the great spirit Tregeagle ... are among the weirdest sounds of the Cornish hills and moors.'

Trencrom Castle

On the summit of Trencrom Hill, commanding a view over land and sea, is the small Iron Age hill-fort of Trencrom Castle. Like other hill-forts and cliff-castles, it was later said to be the home of giants.

William Bottrell in 1870 told a story of the giant of Trecrobben (Trencrom) and the giant of St Michael's Mount. They were cousins and very friendly. They had only one cobbling-hammer between them, which they would throw back and forth between Trencrom and the Mount as needed. But one afternoon, when the giant of the Mount called, 'Hallo up there, Trecrobben, throw us down the hammer,' just as Trecrobben obliged, the giant of the Mount's wife came out of the cave, and 'down came the hammer, whack, hit her right between the eyes, and settled her.' The lamentation raised over her by the two giants was terrible to hear, and Trecrobben buried his treasure deep among the cairns of his castle, before grieving himself to death.

Many people dug around the cairns on Trencrom, on moonshiny nights, in hopes of finding his crocks of gold, but whenever their spade hit the flat stone covering the mouth of the crock, so it rang hollow, out from among the crevices of the rocks came troops of frightful-looking spriggans, who raised such bad weather that it scared the diggers away.

A variation on this theme is that bad-tempered giants once lived here who hid their treasure in the hill, where it was guarded by spriggans. Robert Hunt relates that, 'not many years since', a man who thought he knew where to dig proceeded one night to the hill armed with pick and spade. When he had been there for a while, the sky rapidly clouded over and hid the moon. The wind rose and whistled around the rocks, but its sound was presently drowned out by great crashes of thunder:

> By the flashes of lightning, the man saw spriggans swarming out from all over the rocks. Although small at first, they rapidly increased in size until they assumed almost giant-stature, looking all the while, he said afterwards, 'as ugly as if they would eat him'.

He was said to have been so frightened that he took to his bed and was unable to work for a long time after. From this it seems that the spriggans were not thought of as fairies, as in some stories, but as the giants' ghosts.

Cumberland

Aira Force

Aira Beck on its journey downhill into Ullswater forms a series of waterfalls, one of which is Aira (earlier Airey) Force. It is the setting for one of the Lake District's best-known stories, told in William Wordsworth's 'The Somnambulist', probably written in 1828, and mentioned in every Victorian guidebook.

The story is connected with Lyulph's Tower, a hunting box in Gowbarrow Park built by Charles, eleventh Duke of Norfolk. A grey, castellated and turreted building, it is picturesque enough in itself, but the story is said to relate to an earlier castle on the site, supposedly built by Ulf the Saxon, first Lord of Greystock, who gave his name to the lake.

Harriet Martineau, in her *Complete Guide to the English Lakes* (1855), says that the tourist visiting the Force 'ought to know of the mournful legend which belongs to this place, and which Wordsworth has preserved'. She tells it, but Mackenzie Walcott a few years later does it better:

In Lyulph's Tower ... lived Emma, the promised bride of Sir Eglamour. The gallant knight had sailed to foreign shores to do some deed worthy of his fair lady; months and months passed away without tidings of him, and every night the distracted girl went down in her sleep to the holly bower on the side of the waterfall, the trysting place where she had often met her lover, and had bidden him farewell. She was thus reposing, when Sir Eglamour, who had suddenly returned, passing through the ravine, saw a white-robed figure in the moonlight come out from the well-known bower, and, sighing, drop leaves into the rushing stream. He recognised his beloved, and rushed forward to save her; his touch awoke her, and in her terror and wonderment on waking she fell into the torrent, which swept her swiftly down. The knight leaped in to rescue her, but when he at length reached and bore out the inanimate form, it was only to receive and reciprocate her assurance of love and fidelity before she breathed her last in his arms. In sorrow and bitterness of heart the knight built a cell upon the spot, and died here mourning.

This romantic story is still said by writers on the Lake District to have 'inspired' Wordsworth. However, far from being a 'legend' that was 'preserved' by Wordsworth, as Miss Martineau and others have evidently thought, if we are to believe the poet himself, he and his friends Sir George Beaumont and Mr Rogers invented it.

In notes dictated to Isabella Fenwick in 1843, Wordsworth says that, while they were visiting this part of the Lake District together, they heard that 'Mr Glover, the Artist', while lodging at Lyulph's Tower, had been disturbed by a loud shriek, which he had learnt came from a young woman in the house given to sleep-walking. She had gone downstairs, and while trying to open the outer door, either because it was difficult or the stone floor was cold on her feet, had uttered the cry which alarmed him. 'It seemed to us all that this might serve as a hint for a poem, and the story here told was constructed, and soon after put into verse by me as it now stands.'

Despite its literary origin, the story of Emma and Sir Eglamore has become widely accepted as local legend. Indeed, possibly because Eglamore in 'The Somnambulist' at first thinks Emma to be a 'wandering ghost', there have been reports of her haunting Aira Force, though Jessica Lofthouse in *North-Country Folklore* (1976) writes, 'I doubt if her frail ghost has been seen in modern times.'

One spectral figure seen here, however, was not a poet's brainchild but the fetch of a living person. Thomas De Quincey, in his *Recollections of the Lake Poets* (1839–40), relates how a Miss Smith, who lived locally, went without a guide to sketch the Force and succeeded in climbing up beside the waterfall for about half an hour. Then she found herself in an 'aerial dungeon', out of which she managed to climb only to find herself trapped on the edge of the chasm. She could see no way out, 'since the rocks stood round her in a semi-circus, all lofty, all perpendicular, all glazed with trickling water, or smooth as polished porphyry'.

Suddenly, however, as she looked around her, she saw about 200 yards (180 m) away a lady dressed in a white muslin robe. The lady beckoned to her to follow, and to her surprise she found an exit which she had not seen before. 'She continued to advance towards the lady, whom now ... she found to be standing on the other side of the *force*, and, also to be her own sister ...' The apparition led Miss Smith safely down to the path, then vanished. Miss Smith continued her descent alone and on arriving home found her sister there, having never left the house.

Carlisle

In a letter written on 12 December 1874 while he was staying at Ripley Castle, Augustus Hare recorded the story of a moment-of-death apparition which he had heard there:

> Another story which Countess Bathyany told from personal knowledge was that of Sir Samuel Romilly.
>
> Lord Grey [Charles, second Earl Grey] and his son-in-law, Sir Charles Wood, were walking on the ramparts of Carlisle ... While they were walking, a man passed them, returned, passed them again, and then disappeared in front of them over the parapet, where there was really no means of exit. 'How very extraordinary! And how exactly like Sir Samuel Romilly!' they both exclaimed. At that moment Sir Samuel Romilly had cut his throat in a distant part of England.

Sir Samuel Romilly (1757–1818), lawyer and law reformer, committed suicide three days after his wife's death.

Corby Castle, near Carlisle

Corby Castle, although a comparatively modern building, incorporates an ancient pele tower, which no doubt set the tone for its tradition of 'the Radiant Boy of Corby'.

Mrs Catherine Crowe, who in *The Night-Side of Nature* (1848) gives several examples of luminous ghosts, says, 'To these instances I will add an account of the ghost seen in C— castle, copied from the handwriting of C— M— H— in a book of manuscript extracts, dated C— castle, December 22, 1824, and furnished to me by a friend of the family.'

The castle had a 'haunted room', part of the old house, adjoining the pele tower. It used to have an old-fashioned bed and dark furniture, but so many complaints were made by those who slept there that these had been replaced with lighter modern versions to relieve the gloom. 'But', adds the writer, evidently the owner of Corby, 'I regret to say I did not succeed in banishing the nocturnal visitor [sic], which still continues to disturb our friends.'

He gives an account of the apparition's having been seen by a clergyman, taken from his own journal, written at the time of the occurrence. On 8 September 1803, among the guests at Corby was the Revd Henry A— of Redburgh, and rector of Greystoke, with his wife. They were supposed to have remained several days, but, on the morning after their arrival, Mr A—, who was extremely agitated, said that they absolutely must leave. All attempts to dissuade them failed, and as soon as breakfast was over they went.

Some time later, Mr A— told the writer what had happened, saying:

> Soon after we went to bed, we fell asleep: it might have been between one and two in the morning when I awoke. I observed that the fire was totally extinguished; but although ... we had no light, I saw a glimmer in the centre of the room, which suddenly increased to a bright flame. I looked out, apprehending that something had caught fire, when, to my amazement, I beheld a beautiful boy, clothed in white, with bright locks, resembling gold, standing by my bedside, in which position he remained some minutes, fixing his eyes upon me with a mild and benevolent expression. He then glided gently away towards the side of the chimney, where it is obvious there is no possible egress, and entirely disappeared. I found myself in total darkness, and all remained quiet until the usual hour of rising. I declare this to be a true account of what I saw at C— castle, upon my word as a clergyman.

Mrs Crowe, who was acquainted with some of the family and friends of Mr A—, still alive at the time of writing, says, 'The circumstance made a lasting impression upon his mind, and he never willingly speaks of it; but when he does, it is always with the greatest seriousness, and he never shrinks from avowing his belief, that what he saw admits of no other interpretation than the one he then put upon it.'

According to T. F. Thiselton Dyer nearly fifty years later, there was a tradition in the family at Corby that the person who saw the Radiant Boy would rise to the summit of power, but then die a violent death. He goes on to give as 'an instance of this strange belief' the appearance of 'this spectre' to the statesman Lord Castlereagh, who later committed suicide. However, he appears to be confusing the Radiant Boy of Corby with the similar apparition seen by Castlereagh, some say at KNEBWORTH HOUSE, Hertfordshire, but, according to Mrs Crowe in *Ghost Stories and Family Legends* (1859), when he was staying in Ireland.

Gilsland

Gilsland, on the Northumberland–Cumberland border, is in modern gazetteers assigned to Northumberland, Gilsland Spa to Cumberland. Nineteenth-century authors do not always make this distinction. William Henderson, for example, in his *Folk-Lore of the Northern Counties* (1866), after talking about the Cauld Lad o' Hilton (*see* HYLTON CASTLE, Co. Durham), writes:

A friend of mine, who was born and brought up in the Borders, tells me of another Cauld Lad, of whom she had heard in her childhood, during a visit to Gilsland, in Cumberland. He perished from cold at the behest of some cruel uncle or stepdame; and ever after his ghost haunted the family, coming shivering to their bedsides before any one was stricken by illness, his teeth audibly chattering; or, if it were to be fatal, laying his icy hand upon the part which would be the seat of the disease, saying,

> 'Cauld, cauld, aye cauld,
> An' ye'se be cauld for evermair!'

This sad (and for the beholder horrifying) apparition plays the part of the Irish banshee, acting as a family death-warning. Few, if any, such warnings, however, were as specific in the information they had to impart.

Helvellyn

Murray's Handbook for ... Cumberland (1866) reports the tradition of a spectral army having been seen marching over Helvellyn on the eve of the battle of Marston Moor, fought on 2 July 1644. The *Handbook* also reports a similar phenomenon having been seen a century later on Blencathra, for which *see* SOUTHER FELL.

Lake Thirlmere

Under the waters of Lake Thirlmere, on its north-west side, lies the village of Armboth along with several farms on the shore of the original lake, Thirlmere having been appropriated in the late nine-teenth century by the Manchester Water Authority and the valley flooded to form a reservoir.

Secluded in woods by the lake stands the old manor house of Armboth Hall, which has been invested with an eerie reputation. The first writer to mention the haunting of Armboth appears to have been Harriet Martineau in her *Complete Guide to the English Lakes* (1855). She writes:

> Lights are seen there at night, the people say; and the bells ring; and just as the bells all set off ringing, a large dog is seen swimming across the lake. The plates and dishes clatter; and the table is spread by unseen hands. That is the preparation for the ghostly wedding feast of a murdered bride, who comes up from her watery bed in the lake to keep her terrible nuptials.

Subsequent authors added to the story. Mackenzie Walcott in 1860 said that the dog who seems to emanate from the lake is a Black Dog. By the time that A. G. Bradley came to write *Highways and Byways in the Lake District* (1901), the 'ghostly wedding feast' was attended by other neighbourhood ghosts: 'Among other gruesome guests at these entertainments the Calgarth skulls are supposed to have put in an appearance, being back in their niche, no doubt before morning.' But by his day, the haunting had come to an end. The house had been acquired by the Mayor and Corporation of Manchester, since when all had been quiet.

This did not prevent the story of Armboth Hall, or House as it is now more often called, being reworked by twentieth-century writers. As it now stands, the story says that, many years ago, the daughter of the house was about to be married. The wedding day was set for 31 October, though the older people in the neighbourhood shook their heads and said that no good could come of a Halloween wedding. The wedding feast was to be held at Armboth House, and family and servants were making ready when a man brought the tragic news that the bride's body had been found in the lake. She had evidently been half-strangled before being thrown into the water to drown. Soon after that, the family abandoned the house, and for years it stood empty.

Neighbours were accordingly astonished one Halloween to see lights shining in its windows. Two men went to investigate and, standing outside, heard sounds of water being drawn from the pump, heavy furniture being moved, and the clatter of crockery. Looking in at a window, they saw that a long table had been set for a feast and chairs arranged for guests. None were to be seen, however. Realizing that it was the anniversary of the bride's murder, the two men were unnerved and went home, concluding that they had witnessed preparations for her wedding feast. Sounds of revelry and eerie music continued coming from the lighted rooms, until all of a sudden the lights went out and there was silence. Later occupants of the house said they would often be disturbed by bangings and thumpings, and the sound of breaking crockery.

Solway Firth

Phantom ships are reputed to haunt the Solway Firth. Elliott O'Donnell, writing in 1954 of 'nasty sea ghosts', says:

> One such story is of a phantom ship that appears in the Solway immediately before a wreck in that water. It is supposed to be the phantom of a vessel containing a bridal party that was maliciously wrecked in the Solway many years ago.

In *The Midnight Hearse* (1965), he adds to this story that the ghosts of the bridal party are visible on the deck before a wreck. There is some similarity here to the story of the phantom ship deliberately wrecked on the GOODWIN SANDS off the coast of Kent.

67

O'Donnell also mentions a tradition reminiscent of 'The Flying Dutchman', saying that at times the spectres of two pirate ships are seen. 'The pirates, on account of their many crimes, are fated to haunt the Solway till Doomsday.'

Another phantom of these waters is described by Gerald Findler in *Legends of the Lake Counties* (1967). He writes, 'I have met several people who have stated that they have seen a ghost ship sailing along the Solway. At Allonby, an old villager said he had seen the ghost ship several times, always about Christmas time.' This spectral vessel is the *Betsy Jane*, a slave ship which sank near Whitehaven on its home voyage laden with ivory and gold. Findler says that, in old copies of the *Whitehaven News*, he found the legend that the *Betsy Jane* was sailing along the coast of the Firth one Christmas Eve, and the church bells were ringing. The godless skipper, however, swore by the powers of light and darkness that the bells could ring till they cracked, but it would be the chink of his gold that rang on Christmas morning. He had made a fortune from the slave trade and was returning a rich man. But now divine vengeance overtook him, and the ship struck the Giltstone Rock. The terrible shrieks and curses of those on the foundered ship went unheard as the bells rang again on Christmas morning, and the waves of the Firth closed over the *Betsy Jane* and all aboard. 'So about Christmas time, the *Betsy Jane* sails again and again along the Solway ... The years roll by, the church bells ... ring out each Christmas morn, and the *Betsy Jane* still sails on and on, never to reach port.'

Souther Fell

In the early eighteenth century, a phantom army was seen on Souther Fell, east of Blencathra. In 1747, the *Gentleman's Magazine* published an account by someone who had spoken to witnesses of a first sighting on Midsummer Eve 1735, and then a second sighting precisely two years later:

> *Wm. Lancaster* ... imagined that several gentlemen were follow-
> ing their horses at a distance, as if they had been hunting, and
> taking them for such, pay'd no regard to it, till about ten minutes
> after; again turning his head towards the place, they appeared to

be mounted, and a vast army following, five in rank ... He then call'd his family, who all agreed in the same opinion; and what was most extraordinary, he frequently observed that some one of the five would quit rank, and seem to stand in a fronting posture, as if he was observing and regulating the order of their march, or taking account of the numbers, and after some time appear'd to return full gallop to the station he had left, which they never fail'd to do as often as they quitted their lines, and the figure that did so, was generally one of the middlemost men in the rank. As it grew later, they seem'd more regardless of discipline, and rather had the appearance of people riding from a market, than an army, tho' they continued crowding on, and marching off, as long as they had light to see them.

The phenomenon was repeated on the Midsummer Eve preceding the Scottish Rebellion of 1745. This time about twenty-six people saw it, and so convinced were some of them that it was real that they climbed the mountain-side next morning looking for hoof-prints. William Lancaster of 'Blake hills' (Blake Hills Farm), on the other hand, said that he never thought it could be a real army because the ground was too difficult and the number of troops too huge. Villagers later thought it was an apparition, a foreshowing of the Rebellion.

Educated writers explained it away as an optical illusion, the editor of the *Lonsdale Magazine* in 1821 stating that it had been a mirage caused by a reflection of the rebels performing their military exercises on the west coast of Scotland. Whatever it may have been, local people gave it a supernatural explanation as a spectral army, such as has also been reported in other places, including EDGEHILL, Warwickshire, and HELVELLYN.

Ulpha

In 1860, Mackenzie Walcott recorded the tradition that, near Ulpha, 'a lady was destroyed by a wolf at the well of Lady's Dub.' Others say that this was the lady of Ulpha Old Hall who, frightened by wolves, fled down the valley and disappeared. According to *Black's Picturesque Guide to the English Lakes* (5th edn, 1851), 'Ulpha' was then locally pronounced 'Oopha'. This suggests that the story is of learned origin, inspired by the written form of the name, assumed to derive from Old Norse *úlfr*, 'wolf'.

Notwithstanding this, in the twenty-first century the lady's ghost is reported as being frequently seen.

Walla Crag

Black's Picturesque Guide relates a supernatural tradition attached to Walla Crag:

> ... within whose ponderous jaws the common people believe that the once errant spirit of Jamie Lowther (the first Earl of Lonsdale) is securely inured ... After his death it was confidently stated that his ghost roamed about these vales, to the terror of all ... until some worthy priest, skilled in the management of refractory apparitions, safely 'laid' him, with the aid of divers exorcisms and approved charms, in the centre of this rock.

According to Mackenzie Walcott (1860), the priest who successfully dealt with Jamie was the vicar of Bampton.

Sir James Lowther, who lived at Lowther Hall (later LOWTHER CASTLE), Westmorland, was remembered in popular tradition as 'the bad lord', an oppressor of his tenants and one who feigned carelessness of his immense wealth. Thomas De Quincey writes of him:

> The coach in which he used to visit Penrith was old and neglected; his horses fine, and untrimmed; and such was the impression diffused about him by his gloomy temper and his habits of oppression, that, according to the declaration of a Penrith contemporary of the old despot, the streets were silent as he traversed them, and an awe sat upon many faces ...

Whitehaven

Given that strange noises made by trickling water, distant tunnelling, and other mining operations were habitually heard by miners working in darkness and often alone, it is scarcely surprising that England has numerous haunted mines. One of these was at Whitehaven. The anonymous author of *The Unseen World* (1847) reports a story told by a miner on his sick bed to his local clergyman about a mine overseer who had been dismissed from his post and replaced by an overseer from Northumberland:

He lived, however, in apparent friendship with him; but, one day, they were both destroyed together by the fire-damp. It was believed in the mine that, preferring revenge to life, the ex-overseer had taken his successor, less acquainted than himself with the localities of the mine, into a place where he knew the fire-damp to exist, and that without a safety-lamp; and had thus contrived his destruction. But ever after that time, in the place where the two men perished, their voices might be heard high in dispute, the Northumbrian burr being distinctly audible, and so also the well-known pronunciation of the treacherous murderer.

William Henderson, retelling this tale in 1866, compares it with one communicated by the Revd Sabine Baring-Gould, who wrote:

I know a man who is haunted by two spectres. He has shaking fits, during which his eyes wander about the room; then he sees the ghosts. He was a miner, and is said to have half-cut through the rope when some men against whom he bore a grudge were going down the pit; the rope broke, and they were dashed to pieces. Their ghosts haunt him night and day, and he can never remain long in one house, or endure to be alone night or day.

Derbyshire

Arbor Low

Arbor or Arbour Low on Middleton Moor, west of Youlgreave, is a double-entrance henge monument dating from c.2000–1600 BC. Standing high above sea level and commanding a wide view, it was probably, like other henge monuments, a ceremonial and political centre. It has been known by this name, meaning 'earthwork hill', since at least 1533, when it is recorded as *Harberlowe*.

Oval in shape, the henge's grass-covered bank and ditch, less imposing than they once were, thanks to erosion, enclose what was perhaps originally an egg-shape rather than a circle of white limestone blocks. Officially numbered at forty-six, these stones are not upright, and perhaps never were. All but one – which leans at a shallow angle – have lain flat on the ground since the monument was first described in 1761. While writers in 1783 and 1824 cite local men as having said that within living memory, or that of their fathers, the stones had stood upright, excavation has failed to reveal any sockets cut into the limestone to hold them.

In the centre of the circle, near three larger stones, was found the skeleton of a man buried in an extended position, and in a round barrow near the south-east entrance of the monument a cremation burial was discovered. Possibly local people knew of these burials, or else assumed the dead were buried here, as in the nineteenth century the site was said to be haunted and avoided after dark. In *Romances of the Peak* (1901), W. M. Turner says that, coming away from Arbor Low after a visit in 1897, he accosted a young herdsman tending some cattle and asked him if he knew how it came there and what its purpose was. The herdsman said he could not tell. He only knew what old people had told him, that it had been there undisturbed for generations. That was all – except there might have been a battle there and people buried about the place.

'How did he come to know that?' 'Well, you see,' he said, 'the folks round about never go that way at night for fear of "boggarts." Several have been seen prowling about, and it is the common talk that people must have been buried there.'

Bolsover Castle

'Of all the houses I have seen,' wrote Louis Jennings in 1880, 'the castle at Bolsover is the most weird and ghostly.' Strung out along a hilltop, its history reaches back to William the Conqueror, who gave the site to William Peveril.

Jennings describes wandering through the ruined parts of the castle, knocking in vain on doors until at length he found the old caretaker. She admitted him to the rooms that were still roofed and furnished – a vaulted hall with portraits, the Star Room with a chair in which the famous Bess of Hardwick (b. 1527) used to sit in her days at Bolsover, bedrooms called 'Hell' and 'Heaven' and 'the Duke's Chamber', dark recesses in the tower with grated windows, one of which, the old woman said, was 'Mary Queen of Scots' dungeon'. The place had a feeling to it which Jennings had not encountered elsewhere. 'It looks like a haunted house,' he said to the woman. 'You would say so if you lived here,' she answered, but for the time said nothing more.

She then took him downstairs to cellars and passages said to be the remains of the Norman castle. Here was the high vaulted chamber used as the kitchen, which was connected by a stone passage with a sort of crypt. Beneath this, she said, was a church, never opened since the days of William Peveril. Their footsteps had a hollow sound, and Jennings thought there must have been empty space below the stone floor, but what it had been used for no one seemed to know. He remarked jokingly that this was where all the ghosts came from, to which the old woman replied seriously:

'It is, sir; and when the family are here the servants sometimes will not come down here except by twos and threes. Oh, many people have seen things here besides me. Something bad has been done here, sir, and when they open the church below they'll find it out.'

She went on to talk of uncanny experiences of her own:

'Just where you stand, by that door, I have several times seen a
lady and gentleman – only for a moment or two, for they come like
a flash. When I have been sitting in the kitchen, not thinking of
any such thing, they stood there – the gentleman with ruffles on,
the lady with a scarf round her waist. I never believed in ghosts,
but I have seen *them*. I am used to it now, and don't mind it.'

What she and her husband, who came to sleep there at night, *did*
mind were the noises, which disturbed them, on occasion seeming
to follow them round the house, carrying on worse when they left a
room but always falling silent when they were in it.

Bradwell

In *Bradwell: Ancient and Modern* (1912), Seth Evans tells the story of
the 'Lumb Boggart' ('Lumb' coming from the Old English word for a
pool). He writes:

It used to be said that about a century and a half ago the body of a
young girl who was supposed to have been murdered was found
buried under the staircase of a house at Hill Head. The ghost of the
girl appeared every night until everybody in the neighbourhood
were terrified and thrown into a cold sweat. Unable to bear it any
longer the people got a well known individual who belonged to
the Baptists . . . to undertake the task of 'laying' the ghost. As this
individual professed to be able to rule the planets, of course no
one doubted his power of getting rid of the ghost.

The time came, and the haunted house was filled with affrighted
spectators when the exorcist appeared among them with his para-
phernalia, and when he prayed until streams of sweat poured from
his face as he knelt within a ring he had chalked on the chamber
floor, the lookers-on kneeling around, and later afterwards
declared that they 'felt the floor move for yards up and down in
quick succession.' Then the magician arose and exclaimed, 'Arise!
arise! I charge and command thee,' when the spirit appeared, and
the man ordered it to depart and assume the body of a fish, and to
locate itself in the Lumb Mouth. He also ordered that every
Christmas eve the ghost should assume the form of a white ousel,
and fly to Lumbly Pool.

(By 'ousel' is presumably meant the ring ouzel, which nests in crevices in cliffs and rocks.) Evans calls this story 'an absurd tale which everybody believed even down to half a century ago'.

Derwent Woodlands

A village of this name once existed, together with its small church, in the area which was submerged when the Ladybower Reservoir was made in the 1940s. In the 1990s, several writers on Derbyshire lore picked up oral versions of an eerie tale about that church. This said that a new vicar, who came to the parish from the south of the county, disapproved of various 'superstitious practices' he found here. In particular, he was shocked when the churchwardens told him it had been the custom since time immemorial for the vicar on the last Sunday in December to preach 'the Sermon for the Dead' in the empty church at midnight. The wraiths of all who were fated to die in the coming year would gather there to listen. The new vicar refused, calling it witchcraft, and saying he would allow no such thing while he was the incumbent. Yet when the last Sunday came, he felt impelled to go, and climbed into the pulpit. All at once, he saw the spectral forms of some of his parishioners in the gallery – among them his own. Sure enough, he was dead within a year.

The plot of this legend is obviously akin to the stories about men who kept watch in a church porch to see wraiths (as at DORSTONE, Herefordshire), though 'the Sermon for the Dead' described here is an intriguing variation. Derbyshire is one of the areas where covert Catholic practices lingered long after the Reformation: a correspondent of the *Gentleman's Magazine* in 1784 described how children at Findern lit bonfires on the common on All Souls' Night, which the adults said were meant 'to light the souls out of Purgatory'. Conceivably, the people of Derwent Woodlands had a custom of praying annually for the dead of the parish, and expected their vicar to co-operate in this.

Dunscar Farm

The skulls still kept in some houses in Derbyshire were probably originally displayed as simple curios or perhaps (judging from the position of some of them in windows, like 'witch-balls') as evil-averting charms. Bones mentioned by S. O. Addy may have had a like purpose, though explained by a ghost story. In *Household Tales* (1895), he writes:

> There is an old farmhouse in the Peak Forest, in Derbyshire, at which, it is said, there once lived two sisters who loved the same man. To put an end to their rivalry one sister murdered the other, but the dying sister said that her bones would never rest in any grave. And so it happens that her bones are kept in a 'cheese-fat' [vat] in the farmhouse which stands in the staircase window. If the bones are removed from the vat trouble comes upon the house, strange noises are heard at night, the cattle die, or are seized with illness.

Though he speaks of a skull rather than bones being kept here, Clarence Daniel, in *Ghosts of Derbyshire* (1973), identifies this unnamed farmhouse as Dunscar Farm, near Castleton. Others says the cheese vat in the staircase window was at TUNSTEAD FARM.

Eckington

From Eckington came a sombre fairytale related by the nineteenth-century collector S. O. Addy. 'The Golden Cup' is a horror story possibly told to children to stop them pestering adults. There was a little girl who owned a golden cup, and one day her mother went out, telling her she could play with her cup that day. So the child asked a maid to fetch it from a cupboard, but the maid said she was too busy. The girl nagged her and eventually the infuriated maid murdered her, burying her body under one of the stone flags in the cellar. When the mother returned, she asked for her child, but the maid claimed that she could not find her:

> Then the mother was deeply grieved, and she sat up all that night, and all the next night. On the third night as she sat alone and wide

awake she heard the voice of her daughter outside the door saying, 'Can I have my golden cup?' The mother opened the door, and when her daughter had repeated the question three times she saw her spirit, but the spirit vanished at once, and she never saw it more.

Great Longstone

Shady Lane, a stretch of road running between Great Longstone and Ashford-in-the-Water, is said to be haunted at twilight by a procession of twelve headless men carrying an empty coffin. Clarence Daniel, in *Ghosts of Derbyshire* (1973), answers the question of why an *empty* coffin with the surmise that the procession is a death omen. He writes, 'My guess is that the coffin is intended for the unfortunate person who meets the strange funeral cortege! No wonder the people living in the district avoid travelling down Shady Lane at dusk or dawn.'

Hayfield

S. O. Addy reports in *Household Tales* (1895) the tradition that, in the sixteenth century, all the dead in the cemetery surrounding the ancient chapel rose from their sleep in golden raiment. Despite the date, he appears to be talking about an event concerning the communal grave of flood victims, recorded as taking place in 1754 in a letter written by the Revd Dr James Clegg, the Nonconformist minister of nearby Chapel-en-le-Frith. He writes:

> ... on the last day of August, several Hundreds of Bodies rose out of the Grave in the open day ... to the great astonishment and Terror of several spectators. They deserted the Coffin, and rising out of the grave, immediately ascended directly towards Heaven, singing in Consert all along as they mounted thro' the Air; they had no winding sheets, about them, yet did not appear quite naked, their Vesture seem'd streak'd with gold, interlaced with sable, skirted with white, yet thought to be exceedingly light by the agility of their motions, and the swiftness of their ascent. They

left a most fragrant and delicious Odour behind them, but were quickly out of sight ...

It is possible that this is an invented story told by a clergyman to demonstrate the truth of the dogma of the Resurrection of the Body. However, it might well be a glamorized version of a true event. As Paul Barber has written in *Vampires, Burial, and Death* (1988), 'The tendency of bodies to return to the surface has generated a great deal of folklore in Europe and elsewhere in the world.' The bloating of drowned bodies, and the shallowness of a mass grave dug in a hurry, would both conspire towards this.

Heage Hall

Heage Hall, later divided into cottages, had the reputation of being haunted. In *Ghosts of Derbyshire* (1973), Clarence Daniel writes that this reputation was actively encouraged to divert attention from criminal activities, as the Hall was said to be one of the hiding places of two notorious highwaymen, Bracey and Bradshaw, and that stories are still told of horses being shod backwards to hinder pursuit.

Of the several ghosts, by far the most interesting is that of Squire George Pole who lived at the Hall in the seventeenth century. For many years, one of the bedrooms contained a large iron-bound chest which had belonged to him. It had many locks and contained his money and the deeds to the Hall, and his sword and pistol always lay ready to hand on its lid. Though Sir George was said to have kept the keys on him day and night, and furthermore had the door to the bedroom barricaded with iron bands, when the chest was opened after he died there was no money in it.

The Hall was already said to be haunted by Pole's wife, to whom he had been so cruel that she died of melancholy. He was later persuaded against his will to build the church at Heage in 1646 in atonement for his misdeeds. This was evidently not enough, as shortly after his death he was seen coursing in the fields with his dogs and riding in his coach across Belper common. It was alleged that he sometimes took the form of a bird 'larger than a crow' (compare the spirit of King Arthur at MARAZION, Cornwall). At other times, he came as a 'shagged foal', one of the traditional bogey beasts (*see* BRIGG, Lincolnshire).

One man nearly died of fright after encountering Pole and his dogs one night when he was returning from a religious meeting. The clergyman of his congregation, 'Pastor Macklin', later conducted a service of exorcism and laid Sir George's restless spirit in Dumble Hole.

Highlow Hall

Highlow Hall is a small manor house of probably the sixteenth century, perched on top of a shoulder leading up to Smelting Hill and by ancient lanes from Hathersage to Abney and Great Hucklow. It was a home of the Eyre family of Hathersage, founded in about 1400 when Robert Eyre of Hope married Joan Padley, a local heiress.

Numerous stories are told of it by modern writers without indicating their source. Some accounts say that Highlow Hall came into the Eyre family when the younger of two sisters of the Archer family then living there married Nicholas Eyre, heir to the manor of Hope. According to legend, the older sister was almost married to him when she found that he was also paying attentions to her younger sister. Jilted, she fled the house and apparently killed herself, as some time later her ghost glided down the great oak staircase to confront Nicholas and put a curse on the house of Eyre. Within the prescribed time, this once great family was no more.

Among other ghosts supposedly seen at Highlow is a man dressed in white who, according to S. O. Addy in 1895, appears at midnight riding a white horse. Other writers mention a workman whose incessant grumbling during the restoration of the Hall in 1360 provoked Nicholas Eyre into murdering him. In another version, he was a mason whom Robert Eyre found playing dice when he should have been working, so immediately killed with his sword. There is also the ghost of one of Robert's friends. They were returning together from a drunken outing in Chesterfield when they quarrelled. In the ensuing fight, Robert killed his friend, as he successfully claimed, in self-defence. The story adds that Robert, too, would have been killed, by a blow to the head, had he not been wearing the same hard hat he wears in what is said to be his image, a man's head in a rolled-brim hat, carved on the north wall of Hathersage church.

One of England's numerous White Ladies also haunted the Hall after it had become a farmhouse. She was often seen crossing the courtyard and entering by the front door, then with a rustle of silken skirts ascending the oak staircase. One farmworker who sometimes saw her by moonlight would politely touch his cap at her approach, and once ventured to speak, but received no reply nor any other sign of having been heard. A carter on his way home to Dronfield saw a woman standing with the palms of her hands resting on the cattle-trough as if gazing at her reflection. This was at about two in the morning, and, remarking on his return that the people at the Hall were astir early, he was told that he must have seen the White Lady. Bumps heard on the staircase from time to time were said to be echoes of the past, a lady in white having been murdered in one of the bedrooms, and her body dragged along the landing and down the stairs to be buried none knew where.

Further fragmentary traditions speak of tables mysteriously set for unseen guests (*compare* WAXHAM HALL, Norfolk), and Clarence Daniel (1973) was told of a lay preacher whom he knew, and who formerly lived at the Hall, conducting a service of exorcism during which the ghosts of a mother and child materialized at the top of the staircase.

Magpie Mine

Magpie Mine, close to Ashford-in-the-Water and now a listed industrial monument, is like a number of other lead mines in the Peak District alleged to be haunted. The mine was worked for 300 years until its closure in 1924, and is said to have been cursed, as it has a record of fires, floods, and rockfalls. According to David Clarke in *Ghosts and Legends of the Peak District* (1991), the curse may have originated in 1833, when three men were suffocated in the lead workings.

R. A. H. O'Neal, in an article on lead mines and mining in *Derbyshire Countryside* (1957), gives an account of a spectre thought to have been seen in the mine in 1946. He writes:

Just after the war a party of speleologists were exploring the mine when one of them reported that he had seen a man with a candle walking along a tunnel from which he disappeared without any trace. A photograph of another member of the party on a raft in a sough [short level for drainage] at the mine showed a second man standing, apparently, on nine feet of water. The Old Man was clearly either trying to protect his ancient rights or to help the twentieth century searchers find the ore, which is reported to be thick and pure in the main vein now 150 feet below the water level.

O'Neal says 'T 'Owd Mon', or the Old Man, was a generic name for the miners of former days, but also describes him as 'a kind of guardian spirit over the mine'. He reputedly also haunted Hanging Flat Mine, near Eyam, where he wandered around the fluorspar workings with a spade over his shoulder and muttering to himself. S. O. Addy says it was the custom of Derbyshire miners on Christmas Eve to leave half a candle burning in the mine for T 'Owd Mon when they finished work for the holiday. If he was inclined to lead miners to good veins of ore, T 'Owd Mon would be one of the more helpful spirits to be found in haunted mines.

Although Magpie Mine is now run as a field centre by the Peak District Mines Historical Society, David Clarke reports that it 'retains an eerie atmosphere'.

Parson's Tor

Towering over the upper reaches of Lathkill Dale, near Over Haddon, is a limestone crag formerly known as Fox Tor. *Murray's Handbook for . . . Derbyshire* (1868), after describing how the River Lathkill issues from a cavern in the limestone opposite Parson's Tor, says briefly, 'This derived its [present] name from a sad accident that befell the parson of Monyash.'

This was the Revd Robert Lomas, incumbent of Monyash, found dead on the tor on 12 October 1776. Already by the time the *Handbook* was written, a ghost story had become attached to this true event. Llewellynn Jewitt, in *The Ballads and Songs of Derbyshire* (1867), reprints a ballad that had first appeared in *The Reliquary* in

1864. Written by the Revd W. R. Bell, a former curate of Bakewell, it was founded 'partly on *facts*, and partly on local *traditions*', and tells the following story.

After a night of disturbing and ominous dreams, the parson of Monyash set out on horseback for Bakewell on a Friday morning, arriving a little after midday. He had hoped to catch the vicar of Bakewell after morning service to have a word with him, but, as chance would have it, the vicar was called away immediately afterwards to attend a dying man. When he got back, he invited the parson of Monyash to dine, and it was six before the latter took his leave. The night grew darker as he rode on his way, the drizzling rain turned to sleet, and by the time he drew near Haddon Grove he was lost in thick mist on the moor. Dismounting, he led his horse, groping his way on. Arriving in the dark and obscurity on the brink of Fox Tor, the horse refused to move. The parson, not hearing the warning roar of the Lathkill above the noise of the gale, continued tugging the reins and, when the horse suddenly backed off and the reins snapped, fell headlong over the edge onto the rocks.

When he did not return, his servants, Hugh and Betty, were anxious – Betty remembering the old superstition concerning Fridays ('A Friday venture's no luck! I've heard say'), but Hugh trusting that his master was staying overnight safely with friends. Next morning, however, the truth of what had become of him was supernaturally revealed to them:

> At dawn of next day, old Betty went forth
>   To milk the cow in the shed; –
> And saw him sitting upon a large stone,
>   All pale, and mute – with bare head.
>
> But a moment she turned her eyes away,
>   A fall she heard and a groan;
> She looked again, but no Parson was there,
>   He'd vanished from off the stone!

The report of the ghost soon spread and a hunt for the parson was made. At length they found his body lying among bloodstained rocks at the foot of the tor and buried his corpse in Monyash churchyard.

Renishaw

Renishaw is the country house of the Sitwells, the Derbyshire family to which Sir Osbert Sitwell, Dame Edith Sitwell, and Sacheverell Sitwell belonged. The original small house, built by Sir George Sitwell *c.*1625, survives at the heart of the present castellated mansion of around 1800.

Like many ancient houses, Renishaw had ghostly associations. Another Sir George Sitwell wrote on 17 September 1909, 'Last Saturday two ghosts were seen at Renishaw.' Happening to look up while speaking to a friend sitting near her, Sir George's wife, Lady Ida, saw out in the passage a grey-haired woman in a white cap who appeared to be a servant. The upper part of her dress was blue, the skirt dark, and her arms were stretched out before her with clasped hands. 'This figure moved with a very slow, furtive, gliding motion,' wrote Sir George, 'as if wishing to escape notice, straight towards the head of the old staircase, which I removed twenty years ago. On reaching it, she disappeared.'

Lady Ida called out 'Who's that?' and then the name of her housekeeper. No one answered, and she asked those nearest the door to run out and see who it was. Two people hurried out but saw no one. Others joined them, but though they searched the hall and passages upstairs they found no one answering the woman's description. Then, as they were returning to the drawing room, Miss R—, a little way behind the others, exclaimed, 'I do believe that's the ghost!' No one else saw it, but she said afterwards that in full light, within twenty feet (6 m) of her, where the door of 'the old ghost room' used to stand until Sir George put in the new staircase, she saw a lady with dark hair and dress, seemingly lost in thought. She cast no shadow, but moving 'with a curious gliding motion' into the darkness, she disappeared within a yard (0.9 m) of the walled-up doorway, formerly leading into the hall.

Sir George rounds off his account by saying, 'There is no doubt that these figures were actually seen as described.' He had his own explanation of them, however. 'They were not ghosts but phantasms, reversed impressions of something seen in the past, and now projected from an overtired and excited brain ... Ghosts are sometimes met with, but they are not ghosts.'

Lady Ida seems not so certain, adding in a note: 'I saw the figure with such distinctness that I had no doubt at all that I was looking at a real person, while, at the same time ... I was conscious of an uneasy, creeping feeling.' She says that the figure was that of a woman of between fifty and sixty years of age with grey hair done up in a bun under an old-fashioned cap. 'I have never seen a ghost before, nor had I been thinking about ghosts.'

As to 'the ghost room', this had its own history. Sir George, born in 1860, celebrated his legal coming of age in 1885, and the large house party on that occasion included Dr Tait, the Archbishop of Canterbury. One of the archbishop's daughters was sleeping in a room at the head of the staircase, and in the middle of the night went to the bedroom of Sir George's sister and told her she had been woken by the sensation of being given three cold kisses. Miss Sitwell made up a bed for Miss Tait on a sofa, saying she was unwilling to exchange rooms and sleep in Miss Tait's room herself, as she thought she had experienced the same phenomenon.

Later, Sir George met his agent, Mr Turnbull, and, thinking to amuse him, told him what Miss Tait thought had occurred. Mr Turnbull, turning pale, responded, 'Well, Sir George, you may make a joke about it, but when you lent us the house for our honeymoon, Miss Crane ... , a schoolfellow of my wife's, came to stay with us, and she had the same room and exactly the same experience.'

Subsequently, it was decided to enlarge the staircase by incorporating both the room in which Miss Tait had slept and the one below it. When work had begun, the Clerk of the Works reported that the men had found something odd. Between the joists of the ghost room's floor was an old coffin, held together with nails, not screws, and apparently dating from the seventeenth century. It was fastened to the joists by iron cramps, but because space was tight had no lid, this purpose being served by the floorboards of the room above. There was no sign of bones, but marks on it suggested it had once contained a body.

These stories about Renishaw were recorded by Viscount Halifax in his *Ghost Book* (1936). Miss Tait's story was believed by Lord Halifax's son to have been given to his father by Miss Tait herself, who was a friend of his. The account of 'The Renishaw Coffin' was given him by Sir George Sitwell, together with Lady Ida's note.

Shirebrook Colliery

Reported in the Sheffield evening newspaper the *Star*, in November 1958, was a spectral incident at Shirebrook colliery. John McGroary, an Irishman working there, saw a ghost and passed out from the shock. 'All I will say now is that I saw a vision and a light,' said Mr McGroary later. 'The vision went past me. It looked like Wilfred Hales.' Another miner, Keith Plant, also reported seeing the apparition and recognizing it as Wilfred Hales, who had collapsed and died in January 1955 aged only thirty.

There was so much talk of this event among the 2,000 men working at the colliery that the management complained that output was severely reduced. It would not be surprising if work had been disrupted: according to traditional miners' beliefs, apparitions in mines generally presaged a disaster, and the ghosts of dead miners frequently returned to deliver warnings to their workmates.

Tunstead Farm, near Chapel-en-le-Frith

For several hundred years this farm was home to a broken skull nicknamed Dickie or Dick. The first published account dates from 1807, in *A Tour Through the High Peak of Derbyshire* by John Hutchinson, who stated that it had 'remained on the premises for near two centuries past, during all the revolutions of owners and tenants in that time'. Hutchinson was told by the tenant of the farm that Dickie 'is looked upon more as a guardian spirit, than a terror to the family: – never disturbing them but in case of an approaching death of a relation or neighbour'. But if anyone spoke disrespectfully about the skull, or tried to remove it from the farm, it showed its displeasure:

> [T]wice within the memory of man the skull has been taken from the premises, once on building the present house on the site of the old one, and another time when it was buried in Chapel church yard; – but there was no peace! – No rest! – It must be replaced!

However, it could be moved about inside the house. G. Le Blanc Smith in 1905 said the family insisted its place was on a downstairs windowsill looking out over the farmland. It was still there in 1938, but has not been seen for many years now; it is said locally that the wife of one of the owners buried it in the garden because so many visitors came to see it.

Stories about Dickie's powers flourished in the nineteenth century. For instance, it was said that in 1863 he forced railway engineers to divert their planned route away from Tunstead Farm by causing the foundations of their bridge to sink in a swamp; the new route passed over what is still called Dickie's Bridge. The best recent investigation was carried out in the 1990s by Andy Roberts and David Clarke, who found many vivid anecdotes still circulating, though these were mostly about events long past. One informant, Margaret Bellhouse, told them in 1993 that Dickie could be very helpful but that:

> People wouldn't dare walk across Dicky's land after dark, and there was a strange black dog which used to follow people down from the main road and then vanish into the hill. The tradition was that this was Dicky's spirit seeing them off his land.

As to the skull's identity, Hutchinson is silent. Most nineteenth-century accounts say that a certain Ned Dickson in the sixteenth century, the rightful owner of the farm, went abroad and on his return was murdered by his cousin to gain the property. Ned haunted the place till his grave was reopened and his skull brought into the house; alternatively, it reappeared of its own accord, and could never be got rid of. Others thought 'Dickie' was a woman and identified her as the murdered sister in a story told by S. O. Addy (1895) of 'an old farmhouse in the Peak Forest', said to be DUNSCAR FARM.

Wormhill

According to tradition, the neighbourhood of Wormhill was once a forest and crowded with trees. It was then the haunt of wild animals. The antiquary and historian William Camden, writing of Derbyshire in the *Britannia* of 1610, observes:

> ... there is no more danger now from wolves which in times past were hurtfull and noisome to this Country; and for the chasing

away and taking of which some there were that held lands here at *Wormhil*, who thereupon were surnamed *Wolvehunt*, as appeareth plainely in the Records of the Kingdome . . .

It may have been this feudal tenure by wolf-hunt that inspired the tradition reported in 1991 by David Clarke that the last wolf in England was killed here in the sixteenth century. This in turn may be connected with reports of a phantom animal on the B6049 linking Miller's Dale with the A6 north-east of Buxton. Motorists have allegedly been chased at night by a strange wolf-like beast running and leaping at immense speed after their cars.

Devon

Berry Pomeroy

The ghosts of Berry Pomeroy Castle have particularly grim tales to account for them, which have been printed in several popular books over the past hundred years, the most detailed survey being by Deryck Seymour in 1982. On the battlements of one tower there walks a Lady Margaret Pomeroy, said to have been imprisoned for nineteen years by her elder sister, Lady Eleanor, because they both loved the same man. Deryck Seymour notes that current oral versions are becoming more dramatic, with the hapless victim being starved to death or walled up alive. The name 'St Margaret's Tower' is recorded in John Prince's *Worthies of Devon* in 1702, but throughout the nineteenth and twentieth centuries it has been *Lady* Margaret's Tower. However, the family tree shows no sisters with the right names. Several compilers of ghost-lore books say the tower is haunted by Lady Margaret; others say it is Lady Eleanor, the wicked sister, who walks. One, Elliott O'Donnell, relates in his *Screaming Skulls and Other Ghost Stories* (1964) that in 1913 the International Club for Psychical Research were told (at third hand) about a young army officer who saw a beautiful girl beckoning to him from the top of the ruined tower; thinking she needed help, he tried to climb up, but the masonry gave way and he was almost killed in the fall.

One of the ruined rooms is haunted by another, unnamed, Pomeroy girl; she is allegedly a victim of incest who had a child by her own father, and strangled it. In the late eighteenth century, Dr (later Sir) Walter Farquhar wrote an account of how he once was visiting the sick wife of the steward of the castle when he encountered a richly dressed lady who hurried past, wringing her hands in anguish and despair. This, he later learned, was the ghost, whose appearance always portended death; sure enough, his patient died.

Black Anne Pool

Commemorated in an anonymous Victorian poem entitled 'A Legend' is the story of Tom Treneman, a fifteenth-century squire of Sowford House, Ivybridge, who reappeared in his kitchen after his funeral, frightening his scullion to death. Twelve parsons were summoned, got a halter round the ghost's neck, and led him to Black Anne Pool in the River Erme, which rises on Dartmoor and flows through Ivybridge on its way to Bigbury Bay. There Treneman was given the endless task of making a beam of sand. When the river is in spate, the grinding of boulders is said to be Tom roaring for more rope.

The poem is cited by Elias Tozer in 1873, and by various more recent writers: Tozer recalled how as a boy he had thought he saw Treneman working by the river, wearing a red cap.

Buckfastleigh

At Brooke Manor in this parish, in the seventeenth century, lived Richard Capel or Cabell (d. 1677). The Devon folklorist Theo Brown wrote in 1982:

> We know practically nothing about him, except that he rebuilt part of his house (the date 1656 is carved over the door) and enjoyed a horrible reputation as a persecutor of village maidens. Having captured one he would keep her under lock and key across the valley at Hawson ... So he had an unenviable reputation as a violent and powerful squire, and when he came to die in 1677 his end was unpleasant. One version says that as he lay dying whisht hounds [demonic dogs] gathered round the house, howling horribly. Another says that he was out and a pack of whisht hounds chased him across the moor till he dropped dead.

He was buried very deep outside the south porch of the church (now partly demolished) on a hill outside the village. An altar-tomb was erected over him, on top of which is a little square chamber with a massive iron grille on the side facing the church porch, and on the opposite side a small oak door with a large keyhole. 'To this day', wrote Theo Brown, 'the children of the village climb the hill, walk thirteen times round [the tomb], and then dare each other to insert a small finger in the keyhole and feel Capel gnaw the tip.' Children still performed this ritual in the 1990s, calling this 'the vampire's tomb'; there is a popular tendency nowadays to class all corporeal revenants as vampires. In 1992, one observer noticed that 'a little cross of twigs carefully tied together' had been laid on the tomb, presumably as protection.

As a supernatural punishment for hunting maidens, Capel is pursued by the spectral hounds once a year, every year, down the drives of his two mansions: on Midsummer Eve at Hawson and on 5 July (Midsummer Eve by the Old Calendar) at Brooke.

Theo Brown believed Capel was the prototype for Conan Doyle's wicked Sir Hugo Baskerville in *The Hound of the Baskervilles*, who in Chapter 2 sets out with his pack of hounds to hunt down a fleeing girl he intends to rape, but is himself followed by 'a great black beast, shaped like a hound, yet larger than any hound that ever mortal eye has rested upon', which rips out his throat. Thereafter the Baskervilles are plagued by 'sudden, bloody and mysterious' deaths, often preceded by apparitions of the Hound. According to Conan Doyle's dedication of his novel, this highly melodramatic tale was suggested by a friend's account of a West Country legend. The friend was Fletcher Robinson, who lived at Ipplepen, a mere six miles (9.6 km) from Buckfastleigh.

Buckland Abbey

Sir Francis Drake, whose home this was, is the hero of many legends recorded by two Victorian folklorists active in the area, Mrs Anna Eliza Bray in the 1830s and Robert Hunt in the 1860s. Already in his lifetime the Spaniards had feared him as a magician who could command the winds by the Devil's aid and had a magic mirror enabling him to spy on their fleets. Devonshire people gleefully adopted this notion; they told how Drake created fire-ships by magic, to defeat the Armada; how he led a stream of fresh water from Dartmoor down into Plymouth by simply riding ahead of it, uttering a spell of summoning; how he turned Buckland Abbey from a ruin into a mansion in just three nights, with the Devil's help; and how his magic mirror (or a spirit) warned him, while he was in the Antipodes, of his wife's impending remarriage.

After Drake died off Panama in 1595, various mementos were brought home to Buckland Abbey, including a drum painted with his coat of arms, traditionally believed to have come from the ship on which he sailed round the world in 1577–80; this became, much later, the focus for what is now the most famous Drake legend. The first hint of this comes from the folklorist Robert Hunt who, writing before 1865, says that 'old Betty Donithorne, formerly the housekeeper at Buckland Abbey', told him that 'if the old warrior hears the drum which hangs in the hall of the abbey, and which accompanied him round the world, he rises and holds a revel.'

This homely and cheerful belief was transformed into something of national significance by Sir Henry Newbolt's vivid patriotic poem 'Drake's Drum', written in 1895 for the tercentenary of the hero's death. It was immediately popular, and was set as a rousing song. It was Newbolt who launched the idea that Drake on his deathbed sent the drum home, saying it should be beaten to call his spirit back to defend England in any hour of danger:

> If the Dons sight Devon, I'll quit the port of Heaven,
> And drum them up the Channel, as we drummed them long ago.

The patriotic message of the drum for a nation at war was further developed by another poet, Alfred Noyes, who wrote in an article on submarine warfare in *The Times* on 28 August 1916:

> There is a tale in Devonshire that Sir Francis Drake has not merely listened for his drum, during the last 300 years, but has also heard and answered it on more than one naval occasion. It was heard, as men of the Brixham trawlers can testify, about a hundred years ago, when a little man, under the pseudonym of Nelson (for all Devonshire knows that Nelson was a reincarnation of Sir Francis) went sailing by to Trafalgar ...
>
> It was only a little before the great naval action in the North Sea [the battle of Jutland, 1916] – perhaps the greatest British victory since Trafalgar – that word came from the Brixham trawlers again. They had 'heard Drake's drum beat' and were assured that the ghost of Sir Francis Drake was inhabiting the body of Sir John Jellicoe.

Whether this is authentic tradition is doubtful; nothing like it had been previously reported by local historians or folklorists. But it certainly developed into a powerful new legend, both locally and nationally, and was exploited again in the Second World War. It has been reinforced by reports of people actually hearing the drum at moments of crisis in both wars.

Coffinswell

It is presumably through a pun on the name of this village that there arose the tale that some unknown lady was buried, for reasons unknown but presumably sinful, beside the village's holy well rather than in the consecrated ground of the churchyard. Once a year, at precisely midnight on New Year's Eve, she is permitted to rise and move towards the churchyard for the distance of one cockstride. It will take her till Judgement Day to get there, but when she does she will find salvation. The story was recorded by the folklorist Sabine Baring-Gould towards the end of the nineteenth century; the motif of the ghost's painfully slow journey is found in several other West Country legends.

Cranmere Pool

Cranmere Pool lies about five miles (8 km) south of Okehampton, in the northernmost of the two great blanket bogs of Dartmoor. It is not a real 'pool' today, though it must once have been one, for the name Cranmere means 'Crow's Mere'. It consists, rather, of peaty puddles draining into West Okement Head, a few yards to the north. Stories from the nineteenth century, however, talk of the banishment of ghosts under water in this lonely and desolate spot – indeed, a contributor to *Notes and Queries* in 1851 called it 'a great penal settlement for refractory spirits':

> Many of the former inhabitants of this parish [St Mary Tavy] are still there, expiating their ghostly pranks. An old farmer was so troublesome to his survivors as to require seven clergymen to secure him. By their means, however, he was transformed into a

colt, and a servant boy was directed to take him to Cranmere Pool. On arriving at the brink of the pool he was to take off the halter, and return instantly without looking round. Curiosity proving too powerful, he turned his head to see what was going on, when he beheld the colt plunge into the lake in the form of a ball of fire. Before doing so, however, he gave the lad a parting salute in the form of a kick which knocked out one of his eyes.

Most notoriously, the pool contains the ghost of Benjamin Gayer ('Benjie Geare'), who was three times mayor of Okehampton and died in 1701. One of his duties had been to administer the funds of a charity which ransomed English sailors held prisoner by Barbary pirates, and at some time during the eighteenth century a legend grew up to the effect that one year he secretly appropriated some of its money for himself, so his spirit could not rest.

There are several versions of how he was laid. Some time before 1869, a journalist was told by a local:

Old Mayor — was in the abbit of hanting his dwelling yander a gude while arter he was daid, but the passens [parsons] took en in hand, and laid en at Cranmere Pool, where he's got to mak a sartain nimber of bindles of sand, and to bind em with raups of the same, afor he can com bak to trouble his howze agen.

According to a version in *Murray's Handbook for . . . Devon* (1879), 'a spirit (Bingie by name) is confined in it [the pool] by a conjuror, and condemned to the hopeless task of draining it with an oat-sieve; but one day Bingie found a sheepskin on the moor, which he spread across the bottom of his oat-sieve, baled out the water, and drowned Okehampton town.'

An account in the *Western Antiquary* in 1883 is the first to name the troublesome mayor. Twenty-three parsons gathered and uttered prayers of exorcism in Latin, Greek, Hebrew, and English, but in vain; at length one, more learned than the others, tried the effect of Arabic. 'Now thou art come, I must be gone!' cried Benjie. They were then able to transform him into a black colt, and put an unused bit and bridle on him; a young man was told to ride him out to the edge of Cranmere Pool, never allowing him to turn his head, and there pull off the harness at once and let him go. The young man was given the Sacrament to fortify him for the task. The colt did all it could to throw the rider off, but failed, and when it reached the pool it dived in and was never seen again. (This young man, unlike the lad in the earlier version, obeyed orders exactly and got away scot free.)

Some twentieth-century informants told Theo Brown that as additional punishment, Benjie was ordered to go on baling out the pool, this time using a thimble with a hole in it; it is because of his toil that there is so little water there now. Others believed the ghostly black colt could still be seen near the pool, and that one could raise a thunderstorm by walking three times round the pool (or even round a table) chanting:

> Benjie Geare! Benjie Geare!
> If thou art here, do thou appear!

Dean Prior

In traditional tales of exorcism, the troublesome ghost is usually a member of the local gentry, but at Dean Prior (also called Dean-combe) it is a mere weaver. It is not clear when he lived – only that the story about him already existed in 1850, when a certain 'R.J.K.' sent an account to *Notes and Queries* of his banishment to the Hound's Pool at the foot of a cascade in a narrow valley in this parish:

There once lived in the hamlet of Dean Combe a weaver of great fame and skill. After long prosperity he died, and was buried. But the next day he appeared sitting at the loom in his chamber, working diligently as when he was alive. His sons applied to the parson, who went accordingly to the foot of the stairs, and heard the noise of the weaver's shuttle in the room above. 'Knowles!' he said, 'Come down, this is no place for thee.' 'I will,' said the weaver, 'as soon as I have worked out my quill' (the 'quill' is the shuttle full of wool). 'Nay,' said the vicar, 'thou has been long enough at thy work; come down at once!' – So when the spirit came down, the vicar took a handful of earth from the church-yard, and threw it in its face. And in a moment it became a black hound. 'Follow me,' said the vicar; and it followed him to the gate of the wood. And when they came there, it seemed as if all the

94

trees in the wood were 'coming together', so great was the wind. Then the vicar took a nutshell with a hole in it, and led the hound to the pool below the waterfall. 'Take this shell,' he said; 'and when thou shalt have dipped out the pool with it, thou mayst rest – not before.' And at midday, or at midnight, the hound may still be seen at his work.

Theo Brown wrote in 1979, 'I have myself seen the site where the weaver's house once stood. The Hound's Pool is in a dark impenetrable thicket, but the locals still say that when the stream is in spate you can hear an odd grinding noise; this, of course, is the hound scraping the bottom with his nutshell!'

Dewerstone Rock

This great mass of rock looming above the river Plym, on the southwest edge of Dartmoor, is linked with the Devil. According to a contributor to *Notes and Queries* in 1850, 'During a deep snow, the traces of a naked human foot and of a cloven hoof were found ascending to the highest point,' though the writer unfortunately does not make clear whether he is referring to something recently seen, or to mere tradition. He adds, 'The valley below is haunted by a headless black dog.'

But there was more than one spectral dog in the valley, according to *Murray's Handbook for ... Devon* in 1879; this, after mentioning the footprints, continues:

... and on stormy nights the peasant has heard the 'whishhounds' sweeping through the rocky valley with cry of dogs, and 'hoofs thick-beating on the hollow hill'. Their unearthly 'master' has been sometimes visible – a tall, swart figure with a hunting-pole.

The 'whish-hounds' or Wisht Hounds are the Dartmoor version of the Wild Hunt (see PETERBOROUGH, Huntingdonshire and Peterborough), the 'tall, swart figure' probably the Devil. Slaugh Bridge was said to be one of his favourite haunts; from there he would lure travellers to the Dewerstone and then drive them over the edge, so that they fell to their deaths.

Some other mid nineteenth-century accounts call the demon huntsman of Dartmoor 'Dewer'; hence, they say, the name of the rock (though the reverse is far likelier to be true). He hunts the souls of babies who die unbaptized. A man riding home one night across Hamel Down, north of Widecombe, was startled by the sound of a hunting horn and the belling of a pack of coal-black hounds with fiery eyes which swept past him, followed by the huntsman. The man recklessly called out, 'What sport, Mister? Give us some of your game!' Laughing, the huntsman threw him a bag, telling him to keep it. When he reached home he unwrapped the bundle and found inside it the dead body of his own child.

Dunsford

According to a tale recorded in 1936, there was once a certain Squire Fulford who haunted Fulford House 'because they didn't bury he proper, where he'd wished'. A parson advised them: 'You must take up old Squire and bury he *in the sand* down by the river, and you must *bind he down* wi' straw beens [binds].' And so they did, 'but every night he takes *one cockstride* nearer Fulford House. And I suppose one night he'll get back there again,' said the local narrator. 'Anyone can see him at 12 o'clock at night, for I expect it goes on just the same.'

This tale ingeniously combines the motif of a corpse or a skull which refuses to lie in a churchyard and insists on some peculiar resting place, with that of a banishment from which the dead man returns at the rate of one cockstride a year. Theo Brown doubted that the squire's body was reburied in the sand; she thought that 'judging by other stories, it was more likely his clothes and personal belongings, which, if left in the house, were supposed to attract the spirit home.' She was probably referring to the story of Mr Lyde's ghost at SALCOMBE REGIS.

Lapford

The parish of Lapford has good cause to remember its 'hunting parson', John Arundel Radford (1799–1861). The West Country folklorist Theo Brown wrote in 1979 that 'it is remembered clearly that he allowed his hounds to terrorize the village children', while others say that he ran up huge debts – forcing one tradesman to eat his bill between two slices of bread – and fathered innumerable bastards. One girl he seduced drowned herself, and her ghost is said to appear occasionally. The picture painted of him, under the name of Rambone, by R. D. Blackmore in *The Maid of Sker* (1872) is too kind, says Theo Brown – 'there is no doubt that he was a horrible man.'

Rumour went so far as to claim that he had murdered his curate, either by cutting his throat or by hanging him with his own hands. Mrs Barbara Carbonell, in notes compiled between about 1923 and 1931 from information given her by a deaconess who had worked in Lapford for a number of years, adds that the hanging was from a beam in the rectory.

> He was brought to trial, but was acquitted by a jury largely empanelled from his own parish. After the acquittal the Judge asked why the jury, in the face of all the evidence against him, had acquitted the Rector. The jury replied, 'us haven't hanged a parson and us wasn't going to now.'

Theo Brown records that Radford wished to be buried inside the chancel of his church, but this seems to have been more than the much-tried parishioners could bear, for they laid him outside the north wall of the chancel. Until fairly recently, the north side of a churchyard was customarily reserved for those whose salvation was uncertain or improbable: unbaptized babies, strangers of unknown antecedents and doubtful characters, and, later, suicides. The practice probably stemmed from the apocryphal tradition that Hell lay in the north. Burying the hated Parson Jack on the north side of his own church was perhaps the best revenge the villagers could think of. Mrs Carbonell, however, tells it somewhat differently; she says the villagers made 'determined efforts' to carry out his wishes, because he had threatened to haunt the village for ever if he was not laid in the chancel, but 'so much opposition was shown by the authorities' that he had to be buried outside, beside the vestry door.

But, whether because his wishes were not fulfilled or in punishment for his misdeeds, Radford lies uneasy in his grave. The cross over it reputedly refused to remain straight and had to be cemented into place, with the result that, as Belinda Whitworth observes in *Gothick Devon* (1993), 'It is now the only cross in the graveyard *not* slewed.' He was said to emerge from a small hole in the grave every night and try to return to the Old Rectory at the traditional speed of a cockstride a year. Numbers of people claim to have seen the ghost.

Radford is not the only cleric haunting this churchyard: the ghost of Thomas à Becket, familiarly known as 'Old Tom', is today said to ride round the church wearing a hat at midnight on 7 July, his feast day. Mrs Carbonell heard a slightly different tale: that on St John's Eve (Midsummer Night) he gallops through the village on a white horse, on his way to Nymet. The reason the tradition is attached to this church is that it was restored by one of Becket's murderers, William de Tracy, as penance for the crime; it is dedicated to Becket, and the Lapford 'revel' or village feast was customarily held on the first Sunday after his day.

Martinhoe

Round Martinhoe roams the ghost of Sir Robert Chichester, doomed never to rest on account of his crimes, including a cruel attempt to rob one of his own tenants. Sir Robert had let his manor at Crosscomb to a farmer who as rent day drew near had prepared enough money to pay. The night before it was due, the house was attacked by a party of mounted robbers, but it happened that the farmer had given shelter for the night to a passing soldier, who came to the assistance of his host with his bow and arrows; he shot a tall man who was riding a white horse at the head of the gang. This turned out to be Sir Robert himself, who was trying to make sure of both getting the rent and regaining the manor.

Since he had died in the midst of his crimes, his spirit could not rest:

> He nightly traversed the country in the shape of a black dog, sometimes on foot and sometimes in a flaming carriage drawn by four elephants which he drove at full speed up and down a perpendicular cliff near Crosscombe still known by the name of Sir Robert's Path.

At midnight he always returned to his house, his bedroom, and even his bed, which was kept permanently made up for him. A servant who had the bad luck to see him arrive would have been burnt to death in the surrounding flames, had he not been holding a loaf made with leaven, a powerful protective charm.

The country people eventually asked the help of Parson Bringwood of Bratton Fleming, a famous 'conjuror' or exorcist. He got all the neighbouring priests together and conjured Sir Robert's ghost into a circle, then with their help bound him to the task of making a bundle of sand, tying it with a rope of sand, and carrying it on his back up the steep cliff from Woodsbay to Crosscomb. Every time the rope broke, the ghost roared so loud that he was heard for miles (like Jan Tregeagle not far off in TREGAGLE'S HOLE, Cornwall). It is said that he failed to perform his task in the allotted time and so was carried off to Hell.

W. R. Halliday, whose family owned the manuscript containing this tale, discussed it in *Folk-Lore* 65 (1954); he judged that it had been written down late in the eighteenth or early in the nineteenth century. He could not find any record of a Parson Bringwood at Bratton Fleming, but a much later parson, William Gimmingham (1820–37), was popularly believed to have magical powers.

According to another version (printed by the Revd George Tugwell in 1863), Sir Robert is doomed, like Sir William de Tracy at MORTEHOE, to wander along the shore of north-west Devon making ropes of sand; these he has to use as traces for his carriage, which he must then drive up the crag and through a narrow fissure known as 'Sir Robert's Road'. He is sometimes followed by 'a pack of eager hounds whose fiery tails gleam like will-o-wisps in the covering darkness'.

Mortehoe

Though medieval chronicles report that William de Tracy, one of Thomas à Becket's murderers, died abroad, there was a strong local tradition that he fled back to Devon after the crime, and died and was buried there.

Initially, he is said to have hidden in Crookhorn or Crewkhorne Cave, west of Ilfracombe, which is dry at low water but filled at high tide, except for three months of the year. According to Ilfracombe boatmen in the nineteenth century, it was within those three months that 'Sir William Tracy' hid there for a fortnight and was fed by his daughter.

He is also connected with the beautiful headland of Morte Point ('Death Point', so called because its rocks and razor-sharp slate stacks have claimed so many lives), where he is said to have retired to a manor belonging to the Tracys. An old farmhouse close to the seashore, known as Woolacombe Tracy, allegedly marks the spot where he lived in banishment.

In expiation of his crime he is said to have founded several churches: Nymet Tracy near Yeoford Junction; Bovey Tracy; a chapel which formerly stood on Barnstaple Bridge; and the parish church of Morte (now Mortehoe), just north of Woolacombe. In the south transept of the latter stands an altar tomb which, as Dean Stanley wrote in 1857, 'was long supposed, and is still believed by inhabitants of the village, to contain the remains of the murderer'.

The tomb was identified as de Tracy's because of a partly defaced inscription on its black marble lid, reconstructed as: '*Syr William de Tracey git ici, Deu del alme eyt mercy*' ('Here lies Sir William de Tracey, Lord have mercy on his soul'). In fact the tomb is that of another Sir William de Tracey, a rector of Morte who died in 1322. His effigy on the lid is clad in clerical robes, a problem explained away by supposing that on retiring to Devon de Tracy became a priest. Likewise figures on the north side of the tomb representing Sts Margaret and Catherine (to whom the chantry containing the tomb was dedicated) were said to be de Tracy's wife and daughter, buried with him.

Tristram Risdon, writing *c.*1630, said that people who stole the lead in which the dead body of de Tracy was wrapped never prospered afterwards. Perhaps this was because they had violated the tomb of a priest, perhaps because they were haunted by the ghost of a murderer. For de Tracy is one of the restless dead. Along the south edge of Morte Bay is Woolacombe Sand or Sands, a two-mile (3.2-km) long beach to which (so the locals told Dean Stanley) he was banished 'to make bundles of sand and binds [wisps] of the same'. According to later traditions, his penance is everlasting, for whenever the rope is nearly woven, along comes a Black Dog with a ball of fire in his mouth and breaks it. People living in cottages along the shore were said sometimes to hear his shrieks and wails – the more cynical explain these as the foghorn of Flat Holm.

This uneasy spirit also haunted the northern landing place of the ferry from Braunton Burrows to Appledore. According to a tradition recorded in 1919, a long-drawn cry of 'Boat ahoy!' would at times come ringing out of the dark across the waters:

> No one answers that call now after dusk, for once, many years ago, the ferryman, who is well remembered among the Appledore people, went over, and no man was there, but a black dog jumped into the boat. The ferryman, not much liking this, put back again as fast as he could, but when Appledore was nearly reached the dog swamped the boat, made his way to shore, and was lost in the shadows of Northam Burrows.

Black dogs were commonly regarded as ominous apparitions (*see also* SHERINGHAM, Norfolk).

Okehampton

'Okehampton Park is the scene of the nightly penance of Lady Howard,' says *Murray's Handbook* (1879). Elsewhere Murray tells us that the former mansion of Fitzford at Tavistock belonged in 1644 to Sir Richard Granville, who possessed it in the right of his wife Lady Howard, daughter and heiress of Sir John Fitz. A curious legend was told of her in the town.

Granville was her fourth husband, and local tradition asserts that she murdered the first three. As penance, she has to set out from home every night in a coach constructed of human bones, with a skull at each corner of the roof, which is driven by a headless coachman. Alongside it runs a ghostly black dog, which may or may not be headless; if it does have a head, there is one glaring eye in the middle of its forehead. In some versions, this dog is Lady Howard herself, transformed. The coach drives round the moor to the mound of Okehampton Castle, where the dog tears off one blade of grass, after which they all return to Fitzford House. This must continue till the mound is stripped bare – which it never can be, as the grass grows faster than the dog can pluck it. The coach and/or the dog reportedly appear at various places along the route.

The story was well known, and still is. It is told by Mrs Anna Eliza Bray (1790–1883) in her historical novel *Fitz of Fitzford*, and by Mrs Whitcombe in 1874. Lady Howard was a childhood bugbear of the Revd Sabine Baring-Gould:

> I frequently heard of the coach going from Okehampton to Tavistock when I was a boy ... I remember the deadly fear I felt lest I should be on the road at night, and my nurse was wont to comfort me by saying there was no fear of the 'Lady's Coach' except after midnight.

Peter Tavy

A stone on a low mound, at the crossing of a footpath and a bridleway on the parish boundary, is said to mark the site of 'Stephen's Grave'. The first printed account of the associated legend, in *Notes and Queries* in 1851, says 'Stephen' committed suicide and so received the degrading form of burial usually accorded to a suicide until 1823, being laid by a crossroads with a stake through his body. However, this did not prevent him from 'coming again' as a very troublesome ghost, until the curate laid his spirit one Sunday afternoon, a ritual which was followed by a violent storm.

More recent accounts have elaborated details of the tragedy, saying that Stephen was a young man who murdered his unfaithful sweetheart just before their wedding, and then killed himself. There are different versions; one says he poisoned an apple, got the girl to eat half, and watched her die. After that he went home and fed his pigs, and then ate the rest of the apple himself.

Roborough Down

Besides packs of demon dogs, Devon traditions also mention individual Black Dogs – or perhaps *a* Black Dog appearing in many places. One of the most circumstantial reports of this spectral beast, written by Sarah Hewitt in 1900, concerns a man who met him while crossing Roborough Down, Dartmoor, on a frosty, moonlit December night.

[H]e fancied he heard the pit-pat of feet gaining upon him. Thinking it was a pedestrian bound for Plymouth, he turned to accost his fellow traveller, but there was no one visible, nor were any footfalls then audible. Immediately on resuming his walk, pit-pat, pit-pat, fell the echoes of the feet once more. And suddenly there appeared close to his right side an enormous dog, neither mastiff nor bloodhound, but what seemed to him to be a Newfoundland of enormous size. Dogs were always fond of him, and he of them, so he took no heed of this (to him) lovely canine specimen. Presently he spoke to him: 'Well, doggie, what a beauty you are; how far are you going?', at the same time lifting his hand to pat him. Great was the man's astonishment ... for his hand passed right through the seeming body of the animal. 'Hulloh! What's this?' said the bewildered traveller. As he spoke the great glassy eyes gazed at him; then the beast yawned, and from its throat issued a stream of sulphurous breath. Well, thought the man, I am in for it now! ... With heart beating madly ... he hurried down the hill, the dog never for a moment leaving him, or slackening his speed. They soon reached a crossway, not far from the fortifications. When suddenly the man was startled by a loud report, followed by a blinding flash as of lightning, which struck him senseless to the ground. At daybreak, he was found by the driver of the mail-cart, lying in a ditch at the roadside ... unconscious.

Sarah Hewitt adds that tradition says a man was murdered long ago at this spot, and that the ghost of his dog will roam this road and kill every man it meets, until it kills the murderer himself. Similar folk explanations of Black Dogs as ghosts of real dogs are given in other counties (*see also* SHERINGHAM, Norfolk).

Salcombe Regis

In the 1920s, the local historian J. Y. Anderson-Morshead compiled archives on the history of this parish, including an account of the ghost of Mr Lyde of Sid House given many years previously by John Bastin, a villager of Salcombe Regis born in 1818, who remembered hearing it in his childhood:

[Mr Lyde was from] an old Salcombe family and at first appeared in the Orchard, then every year he drew a cockstride nearer and sat on the road gate. Six ministers were called to lay him but they could not and next year he got into the cellar and next sat down to dinner with them. Then they rode wildish up to Paccombe for Mr George Cornish who came with a small Bible but laid him at once. The reason that the others could not was that it takes an Oxford scholar to lay a bad ghost. It was fine to hear Mr Cornish tell him he was in Hell and lay him. Next day to make sure they drove a donkey cart up to Pepperell's field with his things and laid him with gravel for fifty years in a pit. Some are only bound with sand, but they generally work free, and have then to be bound with bricks ... The fifty years are up now.

The Lydes were an old family in Sidmouth. The most likely original for this ghost was Thomas Lyde, who died in 1824 and is buried in the family vault at Sidmouth parish church; his dates match those of the Revd Mr George Cornish, who seems to have lived at Paccombe only from about 1821 to 1828, after which he moved to Cornwall. John Bastin would surely have been too young to attend Mr Cornish's exorcism (if it really occurred); presumably he was repeating gossip he had heard as a boy.

Despite the successful laying, Mr Lyde's ghost was seen in 1870 and 1920, and Theo Brown in 1979 reported being told that he was still around. As to the reason for his haunt, it was probably guilt; he is rumoured to have murdered his uncle, and there is a tradition of a treasure buried under an elm tree (to die leaving one's wealth hidden was regarded as a grave injustice to one's heirs, and those who did so were unlikely to rest easy).

Punishment for blasphemy is hinted at in another version of the story, given in J. Y. Anderson-Morshead's printed work in 1930, which says: 'He, when ill, heard a robin singing and died swearing.' This requires explaining. It was a widespread belief in Britain in the nineteenth and twentieth centuries that robins served as death omens when they tapped at the window of a sick person's room, or, as a writer put it in the *Sussex County Magazine* in 1932, 'When they sings a mournful "weep, weep", that's when 'tis unlucky, that means death.' The belief is still found; one of the present writers has letters from informants in the 1990s recording the tapping or singing as a personal experience before deaths in the family. It was the knowledge that the robin was prognosticating his death that made Mr Lyde die swearing.

Zeal Monachorum

A farm in this parish was the setting for a series of events made famous in a pamphlet of 1641 entitled *A True Relation of an Apparition in the likenesse of a Bird with a white brest, that appeared hovering over the Death-Beds of some of the children of Mr James Oxenham, of Sale Monachorum Devon, Gent*. This describes the death in 1635 of Mr Oxenham's eldest son, a pious young man, 'to whom, two dayes before he yeelded up his soule to God, there appeared the likenesse of a bird with a white breast, hovering over him'. A few days later the same thing happened to the young wife of Mr Oxenham's second son, then to her baby, then to another related child; other members of the family who were sick but recovered had no such visitation. In each case several witnesses reported seeing the bird; they were later questioned by the Bishop of Exeter, who found 'all their sayings to be true and just'. The pamphleteer says it was then remembered that the bird had appeared earlier, in 1618, at the death of Mr Oxenham's mother. Another writer of that period described seeing a memorial tablet recording the same four deaths and mentioning the bird, in a London stone-cutter's shop. But it was never delivered to the church it was intended for, and nobody has seen it since.

The story has been much repeated, though the Victorian folklorist Sabine Baring-Gould thought it was probably an invention. Further episodes have been added in popular books in the twentieth century, some alleging earlier sightings in Elizabethan times, others bringing the story up to date by claiming that the bird has been seen shortly before deaths in the family in the nineteenth and twentieth centuries. One melodramatic variant says its first apparition was to a certain Margaret Oxenham (date unspecified) shortly before she was murdered on her wedding morning by a jilted lover.

Dorset

Badbury Rings

In 1883, Edwin Guest argued that this large Iron Age hill-fort about two miles (3.2 km) west of Shapwick was the 'Mount Badon' where, according to early chronicles, King Arthur won his great victory over the Saxons. The same claim has been made for several other places whose names begin with *Bad*, including Badbury in Wiltshire and Badbury Hill in Oxfordshire; there is no supporting evidence either here or elsewhere. But Guest's theory became known to members of the Dorset Field Club in 1889, and spread out into the wider community, where it soon inspired further legends.

One concerns a colony of ravens which nested in pine trees on the hill, and whose presence was supposed to ensure prosperity for the family of the lord of the manor. In 1908, the archaeologist A. Hadrian Allcroft linked them to the Badbury/Badon hypothesis:

> The Arthurian tradition lingers obstinately on the spot, and in view of the ancient superstition that the dead hero's soul passed into a raven until in the fullness of time it shall be embodied in human shape and 'Arthur shall come again', it is curious to read that the solitary clump of trees which now crowns the hill was the haunt of the last pair of ravens to linger in Wessex.

He is referring to the belief about ravens and Arthur found in Cervantes' *Don Quixote* (1604–15), and at MARAZION, Cornwall. The idea of a 'last pair' is romantic, but must have been erroneous, for the following year the local ornithologist R. Bosworth Smith, while equally enthusiastic for Arthurian links, spoke of the ravens in the present tense:

> Don Quixote himself tells us that King Arthur did not die, but was changed by witchcraft into a raven. . . . What place would be more appropriate for King Arthur to haunt, during his inter-vital state, than the scene of his greatest victory, Badbury Rings? Long may he haunt it! The raven has continued to build, with few inter-

missions, every year since 1856, either at Badbury Rings or in the adjoining park of Kingston Lacy.

These ideas became part of local knowledge and underwent further elaboration. In the *Dorset Magazine* in 1968, for the first time a ghostly cavalcade of Arthur and his knights is mentioned; moreover, the ravens have become not merely the last in Wessex but the last in England:

'They do say if you'm up to the Rings come midnight, you'll see un.' . . . Badbury Rings has many associations with King Arthur. Legend maintains he is still here, that at midnight he and his knights ride round the pre-Roman hill-fort in a ghostly cavalcade . . . People hereabouts will tell you that, of course, Arthur must have been at Badbury Rings for some period of his life. After all, was this not the last place in England where wild ravens lived? Trying to unravel this, one may recall that in Celtic mythology there is not only Arthur but also a goddess called Badb Catha, the Raven of Battle. Is it possible that Badbury Rings bears her name?

Then, in the 1970s, Stanley J. Coleman offered a lively evocation of Arthur as a raven ghost:

Legend has it that the victorious Arthur reappears on the anniversary of the battle every year since those stirring days, in the shape of a raven. He flies around croaking his satisfaction as he surveys the scene of his triumph, then off he flies, to reappear the following year.

Bagber

The Dorset dialect poet William Barnes (1801–86) spent his youth in this village, and in later life told his grandchildren how he used to believe that a house he often passed on the lane leading from there to Sturminster Newton was haunted, and how on one occasion 'all at once he saw the ghost in the form of a fleece of wool, which rolled along mysteriously by itself till it got under the legs of his horse; and the horse went lame from that hour and for ever after.'

Vague shapes encountered in dark lanes were sometimes

interpreted as ghosts, as here and at UPTON ST LEONARDS, Gloucestershire, and sometimes as other types of supernatural being such as boggarts.

Bettiscombe Manor

For several generations the owners of this manor house near Bridport (who, until recently, were the Pinney family) have declared that its luck depends on a certain skull, the true age and history of which is unknown. The house itself was built around 1694, replacing an Elizabethan one. The skull was first described in 1847 by Mrs Anna Maria Pinney; it rested on a beam in an attic, near a main chimney, and she was told it brought good luck 'and while this skull is kept, no ghost will ever invade Bettiscombe'. Later, a niche was made for it in the attic; by the 1980s, it was being kept in a cardboard shoebox in the study, but still fairly close to a chimney. This may well reflect old customs, for when objects credited with magical powers of protection are hidden in buildings, they are often in the brickwork of a chimney, or in the roof-space, to guard these vulnerable points from supernatural attack.

J. S. Udal, a Dorset antiquarian, wrote to *Notes and Queries* about the skull in 1872, saying it had remained in place because of a belief 'that if it be brought out of the house, the house itself would rock to its foundation, whilst the person by whom such an act of desecration was committed would certainly die within the year.' In a further letter he added that he had been told it was the skull of 'a faithful black servant of an early possessor of the property, a Pinney, who, having resided abroad some years, brought home this memento of a faithful follower'. Udal's informant was an eighty-year-old woman who had often stayed at the manor in her youth and had 'learnt and treasured up the legend'.

Later sources identify this Pinney as Azariah Pinney, transported to Nevis in the West Indies for supporting Monmouth's rebellion in 1685; he bought a plantation, and returned home a rich man early in the eighteenth century. Unlike Udal's informant, these sources say Pinney brought the black man to England alive, as his servant. Here he soon fell ill, and asked that his body be taken back to Nevis after death. His request was ignored, and he was buried in the local churchyard; at once, the house was plagued with bad luck and ghostly noises. The body was exhumed and decapitated, and the skull placed in the attic with instructions that it must never be removed; oddly, this put an end to the trouble.

In the 1880s, Udal re-examined the skull, concluding that it looked like a woman's, not a man's (as was confirmed by scientists in 1963); indeed, some informants told him it was the remains of a woman imprisoned or murdered in the attic. He also recorded a story that one of the owners had thrown the skull into a pond, but a few days later went stealthily to fish it out again and put it back in its place, for, though he was embarrassed to admit it, he had been 'disturbed by all kinds of noises'.

Meanwhile, other outsiders had been taking an interest. In the 1880s, Udal noted that 'the legend has gained both in volume and romance. It has now, I understand – and this without any justi-fication from local sources – gained the reputation of being a "Screaming Skull".' This term has since become firmly established; one farm worker in the 1960s claimed that he used to hear it 'screaming like a trapped rat in the attic'. Further variations devel-oped in the twentieth century. Some now say the servant was beaten to death by his master, or imprisoned in a barred recess by the fireplace; some believe that the skull sweats blood before national calamities.

Possibly, it could be prehistoric – a curio from some local archae-ological dig. Whatever its true origin, it still features prominently in local tradition, journalism, and TV documentaries.

Bridport

Writing in 1922, J. S. Udal records that it was thought in the 1880s that Bagley House near Bridport had long been haunted by a noisy but usually invisible ghost which caused rappings, rustlings, foot-steps, and the noise of doors opening and closing, and of crockery being violently moved about. A male figure in old-fashioned clothes was occasionally to be seen. Supposedly this was due to events more than a century earlier, when a certain Squire Light drowned himself after a day out hunting; his groom, having a premonition of tragedy, rode after him to the pond but was too late to save him. As the groom was returning to Bagley House, the Squire's ghost appeared before him and knocked him off his horse, after which he became so desperately ill that his entire skin peeled off. A group of clergy then laid the ghost in a chimney of the house for a set period of years, but it returned once the time was up, and caused perpetual disturbances – which, the neighbours fervently believed, would continue until the house was demolished.

Cranborne Chase

According to a strong local tradition recorded early in the nineteenth century, there was a violent encounter between deer poachers and forest keepers in Cranborne Chase in 1780, known as the battle of Chettle Common. The worst fighting took place at a gate leading to a path through the woods and on towards Bussey Stool Farm, in the parish of Tarrant Gunville; this is still called Bloody Shard Gate ('shard' being a dialect word for a gap in an enclosure), and the wood is Bloodway Coppice. Here the keepers ambushed the poachers. The latter were led by a trumpet-major, whose hand was cut off by the keepers; it is supposed to have been buried in the churchyard at PIMPERNE. But the man survived the wound and died years later in London, where he was buried; since his hand was not reunited with his body in death, it was said to be haunting Bloody Shard Gate and the lane leading to Pimperne. In the 1970s, people still reported seeing it, and they regarded the whole area as eerie.

Lulworth

The ancient hill-forts and groups of barrows strung out along the crests of the Purbeck Hills are the setting for repeated sightings of phantom armies, according to tales which apparently originated in the seventeenth century and were revived strongly in the twentieth. Several accounts, including the earliest one, mention Flowers Barrow, a promontory fort just south of Lulworth Castle.

The first time the phantoms were sighted, in December 1678, they were initially assumed to be real living soldiers, and caused great alarm. A local squire, Captain John Lawrence of Creech, together with his brother and four workmen who had been out digging clay, thought they could see 'a vast number of armed men, several thousands, marching from Flowers Barrow, over Grange Hill' (a distance of at least five miles (8 km)), and could hear 'a great noise and clashing of arms'. They roused the inhabitants of nearby hamlets and cottages; in all about a hundred people declared they could see a host of foot soldiers and horsemen. Messengers were sent to nearby Wareham, where the militia was called out and the bridge barricaded; Lawrence himself rode to London to warn the Privy Council of a possible Popish uprising. But as no attack came, and no material trace of the passage of the Grange Hill army was ever found, it was concluded that it could only have been a vision.

In modern local belief, as recorded in the 1930s, the phantoms are firmly identified as ancient ghosts – usually Romans, but occasionally prehistoric warriors. According to Marianne Dacombe's informants in Lulworth in 1935, 'on certain nights a phantom Roman army marches along Bindon Hill to their camp on King's Hill; the thud of the tramping of horses and men is plainly heard, and their indistinct forms seen as the fog drifts. On those nights no rabbits run and no dog can be induced to go near.' The following year, another writer spoke of 'an army of skin-clad folk' coming down from Flowers Barrow, and there are further references in books from the 1970s, some of which claim that the phenomenon is an omen of coming war, or that it occurs chiefly in wartime.

Netherbury

The folklorist J. S. Udal, who collected much Dorset material in the late nineteenth century, published the following anecdote in 1922. There was once a sexton at Netherbury whose cottage backed onto the churchyard, and who was annoyed that a certain half-witted village girl used to sit in the church porch night after night singing psalms, which kept him awake. So one moonlit night he wrapped himself in a sheet and crept about among the graves, meaning to scare her away for good and all.

But the girl cheerfully greeted the supposed ghost: 'Here's a soul a-coming! Whose soul be you? Be you my granfer's or granmer's, or so-and-so's?' – naming someone recently buried. Then she went on: 'H'm! Souls be about tonight! There's a black 'un too, and he's trying to come up to the white 'un, and he's coming on so fast that if the white 'un don't take care the black 'un'll catch him.' Terrified, the sexton fled, while the half-wit clapped and shouted: 'Run, white soul; black soul'll catch 'ee!' He never stopped till he was back home, where he lay gravely ill from the shock, so ill that all the skin peeled off him from head to toe. And from then on nobody tried to stop the girl singing her psalms in the porch at night.

Similar tales are found in other parts of Britain, for example at Garstang, Lancashire, and TUDHOE, Co. Durham; beneath their humour, they carry a serious warning against frivolity in relation to the supernatural, which is liable to bring rapid retribution.

Pimperne

According to tales collected orally around 1970, something invisible, but which drags rattling chains, can be heard running wildly from Letton Hill to Pimperne; those that have tried to grab hold of it report feeling soft fur, so it is generally thought to be a ghostly dog.

Pimperne graveyard is haunted by the spectral form of a hand which lies buried there. Some say it is the hand of a soldier, cut off during a bloody clash between deer poachers and keepers in 1780 at CRANBORNE CHASE; others, that it was cut off during a battle between Roundheads and Cavaliers. Either way, its owner or his companions retrieved it and buried it in holy ground, yet it cannot rest.

Stourpaine

Here, as at PIMPERNE, the ghost of a dog dragging a rattling chain is said to run invisibly through the village square, heading for the hills. According to an informant in about 1969:

> The dog had apparently been well treated in its early life, but when its owner moved across the hill it was given to another. The other owner, who lived around the square, treated the dog badly

and tied it with a chain. The dog tried many times to escape from its imprisonment, and one day it did. It ran through the square with its chain dragging behind it. Just as it rounded the corner a horse-drawn wagon came round the corner, trampling the dog before it had time to get away. The dog died, and there is supposed to be the ghost of this dog. It cannot be seen, but all that can be heard is the rattling of its chain as it runs to its old master.

Although this account makes no mention of the ghostly dog's colour, the rattling chain links it to traditional descriptions of Black Dogs, which are sometimes rationalized as ghosts of dead dogs.

Tarrant Gunville

This village can boast of a vivid ghost legend recorded in the 1880s, the modern versions of which have developed hints of vampirism. The ghost is that of a certain William Doggett who in the eighteenth century was the steward of Eastbury House, the seat of Lord Melcombe. According to the traditions recorded by John H. Ingram in 1884, Doggett had long been defrauding his employer, and when this was found out he shot himself in one of the rooms of the mansion, leaving an indelible bloodstain on its marble floor. This, as local historian Edward Griffiths has pointed out, is chronologically impossible, for Eastbury House was demolished between 1775 and 1782, and its supposedly defrauded owner, Lord Melcombe, had died in 1762, whereas the date of death of Doggett himself was 1786. But tradition insisted that his ghost continued to haunt the area, headless, driving round the park in a phantom coach – which some said was drawn by headless horses and driven by a headless coachman. When this arrived at the mansion, Doggett would dismount and re-enter the house, where he would shoot himself once again, in the same room as before.

Taken alone, these rather commonplace details would not explain why Doggett's ghost appears in several modern books on the supernatural. But Ingram's informant, a Miss M. F. Billington who collected local folklore, had also heard something more striking from her own informant. About forty years previously, in 1843–5, the old parish church had been thoroughly repaired and restored, and in the course of the work some old vaults were demolished. Miss Billington said:

> The old man who told me much of this story, said it fell to his share to pull Doggett's vault to pieces. They found the self-murdered man's body in a fair state of preservation, and the course of the bullet from the jaw through the head was distinctly visible. The old man described him as 'a short, ginger-haired man'. His legs had been tied together with a broad yellow ribbon, which was as fresh and brightly coloured as when it was buried. My informant added that he had abstracted a piece of the ribbon, and a lock of the hair, which he had kept as curiosities for many years and much regretted that he had not got them still to show me.

This account, it should be noted, is not presented as supernatural; it is not uncommon for bodies in vaults to be 'in a fair state of preservation', and the old man who saw the corpse expresses no surprise at the presence of the ribbon, only at its freshness. Tying feet or legs together was a normal procedure in laying out a corpse. Some later writers, however, found these details reminiscent of vampire beliefs from south-east Europe, which became known in England through literary channels in the nineteenth century. Charles Harper, for instance, in 1907, declared that 'the credulous country folk averred that he was a vampire'; A. D. Hippisley Coxe repeated this claim in 1973 and also speculated that the ribbon was an attempt to prevent Doggett from walking after death. There is no necessity for such a dramatic interpretation.

Another line of development in recent decades is signalled by a version collected orally by Kingsley Palmer in the 1970s from an informant who, after speaking of the phantom coach, ended with 'quite some time ago blue ribbons were found on one of the tombs in the churchyard. They were thought to be the driver's garters.' This seems to be influenced by versions of the modern urban legend of the Vanishing Hitchhiker, where some item of clothing left draped over a tombstone is subsequently discovered and serves as proof of the ghost's reality.

Winterborne Abbas

Here, as at LULWORTH, there is a story of a seventeenth-century sighting of a phantom army initially assumed to be real and subsequently interpreted as some form of ominous vision linked to present events – not, as would probably be the case nowadays, as ghosts from the past. The account comes from a tract entitled *Eniantos Teratios, Mirabilis Annus*, published in 1662:

> Upon the 29th June, a reverend and godly Minister, one of the King's chaplains, as he was travelling with his man between Winterbourne and Dorchester, saw a great troop of horses upon the top of a hill with colours flying, some of them alighted and walked down the hill; his man also saw the same, and did both really believe that they were a troop of horse, in as much that they put on and rode hard, that they might get in to Dorchester before the horsemen, to provide themselves of convenient quarters. But they still expecting when the troop should come, and none coming, upon enquiry found that there were really no horsemen thereabouts that day.

Durham, Palatinate County of

Bishopswearmouth

In the eighteenth century, Building or Beyldon Hill had an eerie reputation. In 1767, during a lawsuit against a man called John Thornhill, a woman deposed 'that her father went to the hill one night ... and saw a "waugh"'. More phonetically spelled 'waff', this was the wraith of a living person, which would appear shortly before his or her death.

John Wesley (1703–91), the founder of Methodism, left in his journal an account of another appearance on Building Hill. He was told of it by a young woman named Elizabeth Hobson, born in Sunderland in 1744. From conversations with her in May 1768, he learned that, from her childhood, she had seen the waffs of neighbours shortly before they died, and in April the previous year had seen that of her brother John who had died in Jamaica. By his death she became entitled to a house left them by her grandfather, John Hobson, 'an exceeding wicked man'. Though she had employed an attorney to recover it from her aunts, they resolutely clung on, so that in December she had given it up. Three or four nights afterwards, her grandfather appeared to her and said if she gave the house up, he would never rest, and she must get an attorney from Durham who would recover it for her. 'His voice was loud, and so hollow and deep that every word went through me. His lips did not move at all (nor did his eyes), but the sound seemed to rise out of the floor.'

Despite this, she did nothing, and one midnight in January he came again, and kept up regular appearances for about three weeks. 'All this time he seemed angry, and sometimes his look was quite horrid and furious.' Sometimes he would pull off the bedclothes, and eventually, worn out by his visits and 'having taken much cold', she went to Durham and hired another attorney. Still nothing happened and the ghost continued appearing. Elizabeth's conversations with Wesley ended with her saying that, one Friday, she saw the waff of an aunt against whom her grandfather had warned her, and on the Saturday heard she was dead.

This seemed to resolve the matter, for now a friend of Wesley's takes up the story. Having already told Wesley that Elizabeth had got the house, he wrote to him in July to say that, on the very same night that she got possession, her grandfather appeared again and said she must meet him on Beyldon Hill the next Thursday just before midnight. 'You will see many appearances, who will call you to come to them; but do not stir, neither give them any answer,' he warned. She asked if friends might come with her. He answered, 'They may; but they must not be present when I come.'

Wesley's friend was one of a group of twelve who met at a house about a quarter of a mile (400 m) from the hill and spent some time in prayer. Then six of them, including himself, went on with Elizabeth to the hill, leaving the rest to pray for them.

> We came thither a little before twelve, and then stood at a small distance from her. It being a fine night we kept her in sight, and spent the time in prayer. She stood there till a few minutes after one. When we saw her move, we went to meet her. She said, 'Thank God, it is all over and done.'

She had followed her grandfather's instructions regarding the apparitions, and when he himself appeared he remarked, 'You are come well fortified.' He explained to her why he could take his leave on the hill, and not in the house, without 'taking something from her'. But, he said, if she told this to anyone, he would trouble her as long as she lived. 'He then bid her farewell, waved his hand, and disappeared.'

Presumably Elizabeth kept his secret, as Wesley does not explain either.

'Vulgar tradition has it,' says William Brockie, writing in 1886, 'that Mr Wesley went out himself to Beyldon Hill, and laid the Ghost', but Wesley makes it plain that he was not present. Whereas some writers refer to what happened as an exorcism, it is also clear that, while Elizabeth was protected by the prayers of the twelve ('You are come well fortified'), the ghost was not dismissed.

In the nineteenth century, people believed the ghost still 'walked'. Brockie reports that 'an intelligent middle-aged lady tells me that she remembers quite well how, when she was a young girl, the people used to go out to the hill at midnight to see the ghost'.

Chester-le-Street

John Webster, in his *Displaying of Supposed Witchcraft* (1677), gives an account of a murder here that was revealed by a ghost. He says that, about the year 1632, near Chester-le-Street, there lived a man called Walker, a well-to-do yeoman who was a widower and had a young relative to keep house. One night she was fetched away by Mark Sharp, a Lancashire-born collier, and not heard of again. As neighbours already suspected that she was pregnant, not much talk was occasioned by this.

Then, the following winter, a local miller called James Graham or Grime was alone late one night at his mill grinding corn. At about midnight or one o'clock, he came down the stairs and, though the mill doors were shut, there stood a woman in the middle of the floor, with her hair hanging down, five large wounds on her head, and all bloody:

> He being much affrighted ... at last asked her who she was, and what she wanted; to which she said, I am the Spirit of such a Woman, who lived with *Walker*, and being got with child by him, he promised me to send me to a private place, where I should be well lookt to until I was brought in bed, and well again; and then I should come again, and keep his house. And accordingly (said the apparition) I was one night late sent away with one *Mark Sharp*, who upon a Moor (naming a place that the Miller knew) slew me with a pick ... and gave me these five wounds, and after threw my body into a coal-pit hard by, and hid the pick under a bank, and his shoos and stockings being bloody he endeavoured to wash, but seeing the blood would not wash forth he hid them there. And the apparition further told the Miller that he must be the Man to reveal it, or else that she must still appear and haunt him.

Despite this warning, the miller said nothing of what he had seen and tried to avoid being in the mill alone at night thereafter.

The apparition was repeated, however, until he revealed the

matter, when the body was found in the coal-pit as described, and also the pick, shoes, and stockings, 'yet bloody'. On this evidence alone – for they never confessed to the murder – Walker and Sharp were executed. Some claimed that the apparition also appeared to the judge or the foreman of the jury, 'but of that I know no certainty'.

The account of the murder appeared also in a letter written by Dr Henry More, printed in Joseph Glanvill's *Saducismus Triumphatus* (1681). More adds details learned from his 'discreet and faithful intelligencer', a Mr Shepherdson, and from the testimony of William Lumley of Great Lumley, present at the trial. Lumley testified that the young woman, whose name was Anne Walker, was sent to her aunt in Great Lumley, where she told her that the father of her child would look after her 'and bid her not trouble her self'. After a time, Sharp came to Lumley, 'being a sworn Brother of the said *Walker's*', and together they called her out of the house. It was fourteen days afterwards (not the lengthy interval reported by Webster) that she appeared to Graime (not Graham or Grime), 'a fuller' (not a miller), with the same consequences as before.

Darlington

W. Hylton Dyer Longstaffe, in his history of the parish of Darlington (1854), speaks of 'the unearthly tread of *Lady Jarratt* who still inhabits the old Manor House'. This house, on the south of the churchyard, had long been a residence of the Bishops of Durham, having originally been built by Bishop Pudsey. By Longstaffe's day, however, the site was occupied by the Union Workhouse.

Current in his time were oral traditions of Lady Jarratt's having been murdered by soldiery, and leaving on a wall 'a ghastly impression of thumb and fingers in blood for ever'. As with other 'indelible bloodstains', no amount of scouring or whitewash could remove it. Though the arrangements for the workhouse had destroyed the handprint itself, Lady Jarratt's fate was still remembered. The ghost had only one arm, for the other had been cut off and carried away by the ruthless soldiers, for the sake of a valuable ring she wore.

Within doors, says Longstaffe, 'she invariably makes a rustle-me-tustle with her stiff silk dress', and like the Silkies of the north of England, her behaviour was compounded equally of mischief and benevolence:

> Her grand sanctum is a supposed subterranean passage leading from the mansion to the church, which has been ... sometimes discovered but never dared to be explored, yet she is fond of perambulating in the midnight chill and the golden sunrise. She sits on the boundary wall and terrifies children on their road to toil on the opposite side of the stream at the factory which she mortally hates, making a house near it perfectly untenantable.

She was given to jingling pans and rattling an old pump handle even when locked, and to pulling the bedclothes off sleeping servant girls, sometimes even tumbling them out of bed and onto the floor. This mischief was generally perpetrated before births and deaths in the workhouse community. 'On these occasions she relents, and *makes coffee for* the sick.'

When she manifested herself in the town, it was as one of 'the very numerous community of white rabbits scampering about the market place' (in other words, she was not simply the revenant of a murdered woman but, like traditional bogeys, also a shape-shifter). An old pair of spectacles were claimed by the master of the workhouse ('rather fond of a joke by the way') to be Lady Jarratt's, and Longstaffe, who had seen them, says they were indeed rather extraordinary, 'being large goggle glasses set in a *leather* frame, which has no legs, but is fixed by squeezing the nose'.

William Brockie, in *Legends and Superstitions of ... Durham* (1886), adds that Lady Jarratt was said to have been the wife of Charles Gerrard, Esq., and the daughter of Dr John Cosin, Bishop of Durham, who restored the house in 1668. He also says that the 'soldiery' were Parliamentary troops during the Civil War. Of Lady Jarratt's sitting on the boundary wall of the churchyard, Brockie says, 'why she chose that place would be difficult to explain'. However, her behaviour is that of a typical boundary ghost, which hovers outside the churchyard because it cannot cross into consecrated ground.

Glassensikes, Darlington

According to W. Hylton Dyer Longstaffe, writing in 1854, the name 'Glassensikes' referred to 'certain closes' watered by a small stream of this name flowing into the Skerne. Glassensikes was haunted by numerous ghosts who may have been different manifestations of the same bogey: headless men who vanished in flame, headless ladies, white cats, white rabbits, white dogs, black dogs, 'shapes that walk at dead of night, and clank their chains'.

'The Glassensikes witnesses are not all thoughtless, and superstitious men,' he writes:

> An old gentleman of Darlington was, at the witching hour of midnight, returning from Oxeneyfield. It was a bright moonlight night, and ... he thought that if nothing was to be seen in the day, nothing could well haunt Glassensikes by night ... Accordingly, when he came to the place where the road to Harewood Hill now turns off, he ... was greatly surprised to see a large animal's head popped through the stile at the commencement of the footpath, leading by the present Woodside to Blackwell. Next came a body. Lastly, came a tail. Now my hero, having at first no idea that the unwelcome visitant was a ghost, was afraid that it would fly at him, for it bounced into the middle of the road and stared intently at him ... [I]t was much larger than usual, and unlike any dog he had ever seen ... in the neighbourhood; moreover it was as black as a hound of hell.

The 'dog' stood immoveable in his path, so rather than approach nearer, he turned his back and walked on. To this account, Longstaffe adds, 'Of late years, this harmless sprite has seemingly become disgusted with the increased traffic past its wonted dwelling, and has become a very well-behaved domestic creature.'

Glowrowram

In a green lane called Petty Lane at Glowrowram, near Chester-le-Street, used to be seen the ghost of a woman. When approached, the figure would fall down and spread out like a sheet or a great pack of wool. When anyone went forward to pick it up, it would suddenly disappear. It startled both men and horses, and a Glowrowram farmer's horse took fright as he was coming home late one night, and arrived at the stable door all in a tremble, though the farmer himself saw nothing.

The Glowrowram ghost often used to appear when the girls went out at night to milk the cows, and frighten them so dreadfully that they spilled the milk, though there was never a drop on the ground to be seen the next morning. The carters driving up the lane with coals would also have their carts upset. Although the ghost's behaviour is that of a typical bogey, with its inheritance of shape-shifting and mischief from medieval demons, that the apparition was indeed the revenant of a woman seemed confirmed when, while digging up the ground to improve the road, they came on a woman's skeleton. The ghost never walked after that.

Hurworth

W. Hylton Dyer Longstaffe, writing in 1854, says that a spirit known by the name of Hob Hedeless (Headless) haunted the road between Hurworth and Neasham. His haunt was restricted because, like evil spirits, witches, and ghosts, he could not cross running water, in his case the Kent, a little stream flowing into the Tees at Neasham. Eventually, he was exorcized and 'laid' for ninety-nine years and a day under a big stone by the wayside. Local tradition said that if anyone sat on this stone, he or she would be stuck there for ever. This was not a sufficient deterrent, however: when the road was altered, the workmen 'fearlessly' removed the stone.

According to William Brockie, in *Legends and Superstitions of . . . Durham* (1886), before being laid under the stone, Hob Hedeless was last seen by a man called Robert Bone but usually known as Bobby Byens. He attributes a somewhat different fate to the stone, saying that, when Anthony Moss of West Middleton built his garden house near that spot, the stone was smashed up by the mason's labourer and part of it used as a foundation stone. Neither author mentions repercussions from this breaking of the implicit ban on moving the stone.

Hylton Castle

'Every castle, tower, or manor-house, has its visionary inhabitants', says Robert Surtees in 1820, and goes on to tell of perhaps the most famous in the County Palatinate of Durham, the Cauld [Cold] Lad who once inhabited Hylton Castle, a fifteenth-century tower house in the north-west part of Sunderland:

> *'The cauld lad of Hilton'* ... was seldom seen, but was heard nightly by the servants *who slept in the great hall*. If the kitchen had been left in perfect order, they heard him amusing himself by breaking the plates and dishes, hurling the pewter in all directions, and throwing every thing into confusion. If, on the contrary, the apartment had been left in disarray (a practice which the servants found it most prudent to adopt), the indefatigable goblin arranged every thing with the greatest precision. This poor *esprit folet*, whose pranks were at all times perfectly harmless, was at length banished ... by the usual expedient of presenting him with a suit of cloaths ... At twelve o'clock the sprite glided gently in ... and surveyed the garments provided ... tried them on, and seemed delighted with his appearance, frisking about for some time ... till, on hearing the first cock, he twitched his mantle tight about him, and disappeared with the usual valediction: Here's a cloke, and here's a hood, The cauld lad o' Hilton will do no more good.

Surtees classes the Cauld Lad as a brownie, hence the 'usual' in his description – these domestic spirits often inhabited tower houses in the north of England and Scotland. However, he adds that the boy had become identified as the ghost of a servant killed by 'one of the old chiefs of Hilton' and thrown into a pond 'where the skeleton of a boy was (in confirmation of the tale) discovered in the last Baron's time'.

Surtees thought the story might be founded on fact, as a coroner's inquest recorded the death of Roger Skelton accidentally killed on 3 July 1609, with the point of a scythe held by Robert Hilton of Hilton. Surtees notes that a free pardon for the manslaughter appears on the Durham episcopal rolls, dated 6 September 1609, but it seems that what the coroner judged accident, local rumour turned into murder, and provided the traditional vengeful ghost.

Surtees observes that the Cauld Lad's apparent glee on being released from his haunt by the gift of clothes was untypical, as brownies are often sad to leave 'their' homes. But the Cauld Lad is by no means a typical brownie. His very name links him to the Cauld Lad of GILSLAND, Cumberland, who was a ghost, and he shares the character of Silky of BLACK HEDDON, Northumberland, half-bogle, half-revenant.

Local storytellers themselves may have seen the Cauld Lad's reaction as a departure from brownie traditions and sought to redress this. M. A. Richardson, in 1843, gave a corollary of the Cauld Lad's story mentioned by neither Surtees nor Sir Cuthbert Sharp in his *Bishoprick Garland* (1834), which explains the spirit's jubilation. He says, when the inhabitants of Hylton Castle decided to get rid of the Cauld Lad, he got an 'inkling' of their intentions, and would often be heard exclaiming sadly at dead of night:

> 'Wae's me. Wae's me,
> The Acorn is not yet
> Fallen from the Tree
> That's to grow the wood
> That's to make the cradle
> That's to rock the bairn
> That's to grow to a Man
> That's to lay me!'

Richardson judged that the Cauld Lad was comforting himself with the (mistaken) thought that the man was not yet born who could 'lay' him, but the rhyme links him with ghosts who accost people in *hope* of being released.

According to Richardson, the Cauld Lad was not banished entirely, but, long after, his voice would be heard at midnight dolefully singing:

> 'Here's a cloak, and here's a hood,
> The cauld lad o' Hilton will do no more good.'

'Certain it is', he writes, 'that there was a room in the castle long distinguished by the name of the "cauld lad's room", where "unearthly wailings" could be heard.'

William Howitt, when he visited Hylton Castle, heard a different version of the legend. In *Visits to Remarkable Places* (1842), he writes that a woman there told him that the boy had been kept in confinement in a cupboard and had consequently acquired the epithet 'the Cold Lad'. She also said that he had no head. Others speculated that his name meant not 'cold' but 'cowed', having close-cropped hair.

Langley Hall

The ruins of Langley Hall, built in the reign of Henry VIII and sited picturesquely on a hillside east of Durham, inspired a legend of a phantom coach. William Henderson in *Folk-Lore of the Northern Counties* (1866) records, 'Night after night ... when it is sufficiently dark, the Headless Coach whirls along the rough approach to Langley Hall, near Durham, drawn by black and fiery steeds.'

He adds that the death of one John Borrow, of Durham, was said to have been presaged by the vision of a coach drawn by six black pigs and driven by a black driver, and compares belief in Northumberland, where the 'death-hearse', drawn by headless horses and driven by a headless driver, whirling silently towards the churchyard, was a sure omen of the imminent death of some important person in the parish.

Neville's Cross, Durham

Neville's Cross, the mutilated remains of which are now a listed ancient monument, gave its name to a battle fought here on 17 October 1346 between the army of King David of Scotland and that of Queen Philippa, wife of Edward III, who was absent at the French wars. King David had burnt Lanercost abbey, pillaged Hexham priory, and then encamped only two miles (3 km) from Durham. The Bishops of Durham and Lincoln, and the Archbishop of York, together with Lords Neville and Percy, mustered an army of 16,000 men to defend St Cuthbert's shrine (as well as their lands), and together defeated the Scots.

The echoes of the battle of Neville's Cross were heard for centuries afterwards. William Brockie, writing in 1886, records that a lady teaching Sunday School in Durham, and dilating on the horrors of war, heard one of her pupils observe that there had once been a great battle at Durham. 'And where was it fought?' she asked. 'At Neville's Cross,' replied the boy. 'I go there very often of an evening to see the place; and if you walk nine times round the Cross, and then lay your head to the turf, you'll hear the noise of the battle and the clash of the armour.'

Raby Castle

In a letter to Sir Cuthbert Sharp, the county historian Robert Surtees told him that Christopher, first Lord Barnard, was persuaded by his wife into such an irrational jealousy and hatred of his eldest son that he determined to pull down Raby Castle (which the younger man would otherwise have inherited). He had got as far as stripping the lead off the roof when his son stopped him by an injunction in Chancery. As for the unnatural mother:

> This old jade after her death used to drive about in the air, in a black coach and six; sometimes she takes the ground and drives slowly up the town to Alice's well, and still more frequently walks the battlements of Raby, with a pair of brass knitting needles, and is called Old Hell Cat.

Why she carries brass knitting needles, and why she hated her son so, is unexplained. Loose ends are a hallmark of authentic popular traditions, unprocessed by rationalizing writers – these things would have been understood by local people at the time.

Sedgefield

The Revd John Garnage, rector of Sedgefield, died in the second week of December 1747, about a week before the tithes payable to the incumbent fell due. It is said that his widow, who, observed William Brockie in 1886, was a woman 'with all her wits about her', prudently laid his body up in salt and kept it hidden until after the twentieth of the month, on which day the tithe-farmers came to pay their rents. Thus she received all the payments of the living that year, which would otherwise have gone to the Bishop of Durham, and only after the money was safe did she announce her husband's death. Her deception did not please the ghost of the departed, however. 'The Pickled Parson', as he was popularly known, proceeded to haunt the parsonage and create nightly disturbances in the neighbourhood. This continued for the better part of half a century, until finally, on New Year's morning, 1792, a fire broke out in the rectory and most of the building was destroyed. From that day on, 'the Pickled Parson' was never seen again.

Staindrop

In the *Newcastle Magazine* of June 1872 appeared an account of a haunting experienced by Mrs Brook, a dressmaker then living at Oakland, not far from Darlington. She had on one occasion to go and work at a public-house in Staindrop, where she was sitting sewing in the parlour when the landlady asked her to go up to the 'long room' and bring down some onions she would find there. As Mrs Brook came downstairs with the onions, she was terrified to hear invisible footsteps following her from the room – the sound of a person wearing clogs treading heavily on each stair.

Once downstairs, she nearly fainted, but the landlady, hearing her story, only uttered a scornful 'howts!' However, later that morning, at another house in Staindrop, on being asked why she looked so white and ill, she gave an account of her fright and was told that she had heard 'Old Cloggy'. It appeared that someone formerly living at the public-house had had a son of unsound mind who hanged himself in the long room, and his unhappy ghost had haunted the house ever since. He was frequently heard, and also, after dusk, seen. When Mrs Brook, on returning to the inn, told the landlady what she had heard, the other laughingly admitted that it was true but said that she had not wanted to frighten Mrs Brook. For her own part, she had heard 'Old Cloggy' so often that she cared nothing for it.

Stob-Cross

Robert Surtees in his *History ... of Durham* (1816–40) writes of
Stob-Cross, near Cornforth:

> And here Stobcross 'brings on a village tale.' A few fields to the
> South stands a ruined dove-cote, shaded by a few straggling ashes,
> and haunted by a brood of wood-pigeons. Here a poor girl
> put herself down for love, in the homely phrase of the country, on
> the very spot of her appointments with her traitor lover; and her
> spirit still hovers round the cote, the scene of her earthly loves
> and sorrows, in the form of a milk-white dove, distinguished from
> its companions by three distinct crimson spots on the breast. The
> poor maid was laid in the churchyard ... The traitor ... drowned
> himself some years after in the Floatbeck, and being buried where
> four roads meet with a stake or stob driven through his body, left
> the name of the transaction to Stobb cross.

An old farmer told Surtees he had seen this dove twenty times
and added that she was (unusually among bird omens) always a
harbinger of good weather and a fruitful harvest.

For other traditions of the transmigration of souls into birds,
see MARAZION, Cornwall, and TROUGHEND, Northumberland.

Tudhoe

Towards the close of the eighteenth century, says M. A. Richardson, writing in 1842, the occupier of Tudhoe mill, a quiet, steady,
sober man, had been to Durham on business and was returning
home, but by the time he reached Sunderland bridge it was nearly
dusk. He felt like company on the road, and the wish was father to
the thought, for he suddenly saw a man in a broad-brimmed hat
about twenty paces ahead whom, though the road was straight, he
had not noticed before. He made haste to catch up with him, but,
strangely, the faster he walked the faster the person moved ahead of
him. They kept at about the same distance the whole way until they
arrived at 'Nicky-nack bridge', and the miller was about to turn off
to the gate on the right hand. He took his eye off the man ahead for
a moment and, when he looked again, there was no one on the

bridge, nor yet in the lane beyond. When later someone suggested that the man might have passed behind a tree, he replied that, as he had never harmed anyone and so had no need to fear ill things, he had looked everywhere that a man might be hidden from view, but he had vanished like the morning mist.

Many years beforehand, a company of reapers had assembled at a farmer's house in Tudhoe to enjoy a 'Mell supper' (harvest feast). Though a good supply of ale and spirits had been laid in by the farmer, it unexpectedly ran out and so the men clubbed together and sent a poor mental defective to buy more at the nearest public-house, at Sunderland bridge. When he had been gone three hours, one of them swore 'a deep oath' to frighten him by dressing in a sheet and meeting him at 'Nicky-nack field'.

Thus disguised as a ghost, he set off but never returned. Just as dawn was breaking, the simpleton rushed in, pale and trembling. When they asked if he had seen anything, he said, 'Yes, I saw a white ghost which came and frightened me much, but I saw a black one behind it, so I cried, "black ghost catch white ghost".' At that, the white ghost looked round and, seeing the black one, screamed and tried to run away, 'but *blackey* was too swift for him, and after much struggling, he flew away with *whitey* altogether!' When day dawned, the harvesters went out to look for their comrade, but all they found in the 'Nicky-nack field' were a few fragments of sheet. The man himself was never seen again.

A similar story was told of Meg of MELDON, Northumberland. At Tudhoe, the harvester made his first mistake when he swore 'a deep oath', always an attractant to the Devil and evil spirits. His second was to set out to torment an 'innocent'.

Richardson does not say if 'Nicky-nack bridge' and 'field' were so-called before or only after these events. 'Nicky' suggests Old Nick, the Devil, but 'nick(e)y' also meant a simpleton.

Essex

Ambresbury Banks

Epping Forest is a remnant of the primeval forest that once stretched from the Thames to the Wash and from the Lea to the Essex coast. In this forest were two Iron Age earthworks, Loughton Camp and Ambresbury Banks, in the parishes of Epping Upland and Waltham Holy Cross.

Ambresbury Banks, thrown up some time between 300 BC and AD 10, is a rectangular plateau fort defended by a single rampart in places still seven feet (2 m) high, and a ditch twenty-two feet (6.7 m) wide and ten (3 m) deep. Traces remain also of a counterscarp bank. It is impressive still, and must have been more so in the past. Local guides in the nineteenth century glamorized it further by calling it the Roman Camp, and the Loughton earthwork Boadicea's Camp, and accordingly Essex tradition claims that the last battle of Queen Boadicea was fought here, and that her ghost wanders around the fort.

The Roman historian Tacitus says that, after destroying the Roman *colonia* at Camulodunum (Colchester), Boudica, as she is more properly called, turned on Londinium (London). The British governor, Suetonius, hurriedly returned from campaigning in Wales, necessarily without most of his army, so ordered an evacuation. Boudica set fire to the town and any remaining inhabitants were massacred. Meantime, Suetonius had gone north to meet up with his main forces – the Fourteenth Legion, part of the Twentieth, and auxiliaries from the nearest forts – and Boudica stopped to torch another hated *colonia*, Verulamium (St Albans), before following on.

Suetonius had sent word to the Second Augusta, stationed in Exeter, to join him, but its acting commander would not budge (disgraced, he afterwards fell on his sword, some said compelled by his own troops). Though Suetonius consequently had only 10,000 men to pit against Boudica's great host, he decided not to wait for more reinforcements, but make a stand while he could still choose his battleground. Tacitus records:

He chose a position in a narrow defile, protected to the rear by woods: he was sure there were no enemy forces except to his front, where the open plain was without cover, so that there was no fear of a surprise attack.

The Iceni and their allies were less circumspect. Knowing they outnumbered the Romans roughly ten to one, they had brought their wives and children to witness their latest victory, stationing them on wagons round the battlefield, cutting off their own retreat.

'Don't worry about these yelling savages,' said Suetonius, in a speech perhaps passed on to Tacitus by his father-in-law Agricola, who had been the staff officer at Suetonius' side. Having disposed his small forces, the legionaries in the centre with the lighter-armed auxiliaries on either side and the cavalry on the wings, he awaited the attack.

Boudica began the battle, her troops advancing in loose array, some historians say uphill, always disadvantageous. The Romans broke her charge with a hail of javelins (their normal procedure, as might have been anticipated) and then launched the counter-attack. The Britons were driven back and trapped against the wagons. Though not normally wasteful of valuable animals, the legionaries slaughtered the draught oxen, so the wagons could not be moved. Having created a killing ground, they conducted a general massacre. Tacitus put the final toll at 80,000 Britons, 400 Romans.

Tacitus gives no idea of the whereabouts of Boudica's last battle, but archaeologists now suggest that it was near Mancetter in Warwickshire. This is a few miles north-west of High Cross, near Hinckley, Leicestershire, where Watling Street, up which Suetonius himself had come from London, and down which his infantry had come from North Wales, meets the Fosse Way along which the Second Legion was expected. The local terrain fits Tacitus' description, and the area has also produced evidence of a battle.

In the past, in the absence of archaeological evidence, Essex imaginations got to work. According to the Revd Sabine Baring-Gould in his gloomy novel *Mehalah* (1880), this last, decisive battle took place on Tiptree Heath, while a contributor to William Andrews' *Bygone Essex* (1892) declares as fact that it was fought at Ambresbury Banks – this in defiance of both Londoners (who set it around Battlebridge Road near King's Cross Station) and of the people of Middlesex (who said it took place on Stanmore common).

Tacitus says that, after the fatal battle, Boudica ended her own life by poison. There is no record of what happened to her body, hence a proliferation of 'Boadicea's Graves', including sites in Wales, Norfolk and London. Wherever and however the real queen perished, Essex legend said that, having seen that her men were losing, she committed suicide with her daughters by eating poisonous berries near Epping Upland.

Barrow Hill, Mersea Island

Although most modern accounts attribute the haunting of THE STROOD to a Roman centurion, some say it goes back to the time of the Danes, and that the victims of a tragic love-triangle are buried in Barrow Hill, a mound twenty feet (6 m) high in West Mersea, listed as an ancient monument under the name Mersea Mount.

The story is told by the Revd Sabine Baring-Gould, rector of East Mersea in the 1880s. In his novel *Mehalah* (1880), he speaks of a 'great barrow with ... Scotch pines on top', which he calls 'Grim's Hoe'. His villain (Rebow) asks his heroine (Mehalah) if she knows the tale of Grim's Hoe, and then tells her that in olden times, when the Danes wintered on Mersea, and in summer cruised along the coast, burning and plundering, their two leaders were twin brothers, born in the same hour, who loved one another. One spring they sailed up the creek to St Osyth's nunnery, where they killed Osyth but carried off her beautiful sister. When they got back to Mersea, each wanted her for his own, and their love turned to jealousy. Drawing their long swords, they hacked one another and by nightfall both were dead. Then the Danes drew their ship up to the top of the hill just above the Strood, and put the woman in the hold with a dead brother on either side, sword in hand, raised a howe above them 'and buried them all, the living and the dead together':

> When the new moon appears, the flesh grows on their bones, and
> the blood staunches, and the wounds close, and breath comes back
> behind their ribs ... and if you listen at full moon on the hoe you

can hear the brothers fighting below in the heart of the barrow. You hear them curse and cry out, and you hear the clash of their swords. But when the moon wanes the sounds grow fainter, their armour falls to bits, their flesh drops away, the blood oozes out of all the hacked veins, and at last all is still.

When there is no moon, you can hear the woman weeping until the new moon reappears, and then she falls silent as the brothers revive to renew the fight. 'This will go on month after month, year after year, till one conquers the other ... but that will never be, for the brothers are of the same age, and equally strong, and equally resolute.'

Archie White, who tells a version of this in *Tideways and Byways in Essex and Suffolk* (1948), locates it at Barrow Hill and evidently accepted it as local legend – as by the 1940s it may have become. However, Baring-Gould later admitted to inventing it, probably by using themes drawn from his reading in Norse literature. The combat between rivals for a woman is told in the *Saga of Hervör and Heithrek*, surviving from the fourteenth century. Hjalmar and Angantýr, one of the twelve berserker sons of Arngrim, are rivals for the hand of Ingibjörg, the king of Sweden's daughter. She chooses Hjalmar, and Angantýr challenges him to a fight on the island of Samsø. Meantime he returns to his patron, Earl Bjartmar, and marries his daughter. Later, Angantýr and Hjalmar meet and fight, and Hjalmar kills Angantýr, but not before himself receiving his death wound from Angantýr's sword Týrfing. On Samsø, mounds are raised over Angantýr and his eleven brothers, all killed in this conflict, but Hjalmar's body is returned to Sweden. On seeing it, Ingibjörg falls dead and is buried with him in the same howe. This tale was popular and had a long life: by the time it reached ballad form, the rivals were brothers, as in the Danish ballad of 'Angelfyr and Helmer the Warrior', known from the sixteenth century, and the Faroese ballad of 'Hjalmar and Angantyr', recorded in 1846.

The notion of continuing life in the mound appears in the same saga. Hervör, Angantýr's daughter, goes to the howes of the sons of Arngrim on Samsö, though they are shunned by all after sunset as fires play over them and phantoms stand outside. Nevertheless, she approaches and wakes Angantýr, and asks him to give her Týrfing,

'Hjalmar's bane'. He does so, saying no good will come of it, which proves true.

For the 'everlasting battle', Baring-Gould could have turned to one of the most popular tales in Germanic literature, the 'battle of the Hjathnings', referred to in the Old English poem *Widsīth* in the seventh century and still being told in the eighteenth in the Shetland ballad of *Hildina* (1774). The core of the tale is that Hethin loves Hild, the daughter of Högni, and they elope in his ship. Högni catches up with them on an island; the two men and their armies fight, and no man is left standing. Unable to part with either lover or father, Hild magically wakes the dead and they rise and renew the battle next morning. And, says the Icelandic historian Snorri Sturluson (1179–1241), who sets the story on Hoy in the Orkneys, it is told in songs that the Hjathningar will go on fighting till Doomsday.

Dagenham Park

At Dagenham Park, near Romford, it was said in the early nineteenth century that the ghost of James Radcliffe, Earl of Derwentwater, walked the gallery adjoining the chapel.

According to one tradition, after his execution at the Tower of London for rebellion in 1716, Lord Derwentwater's body was buried in London at St Giles-in-the-Fields, but another says that he was taken to the Catholic chapel at Dagenham Park, before being carried back to DILSTON, his home in Northumberland.

Lady Derwentwater had rented the house at Dagenham Park during her husband's imprisonment. It was not far from Thorndon, the residence of Lord Petre, who married the earl's daughter Anna Maria in 1732 after her father's death. William Howitt, who reports the haunting in the second series of his *Visits to Remarkable Places* (1842), also gives details evidently handed down among the Petres. He says that some years previously, in the almshouses at Ingatestone, founded by Lord Petre's family, there had been an old woman who said she had frequently heard from her mother that she had assisted in sewing on Lord Derwentwater's head. (Whether this is true or a tradition is a moot point: it conflicts with later evidence that the head was placed in the coffin *beside* the corpse.)

Still at Thorndon in Howitt's time were pathetic relics of the earl and more macabre ones of the execution itself. He writes:

> At Thorndon there is an oaken chest, with an inscription in brass engraved by Lady Derwentwater's orders, containing Lord Derwentwater's dress which he wore on the scaffold – coat, waistcoat, and breeches of black velvet; stockings that rolled over the knee; a wig of very fair hair, that fell down on each side of the breast; a part of his shirt, the neck having been cut away; the black serge that covered the scaffold; and also a piece which covered the block, stiff with blood, and with the marks of the cut of the axe in it.

Lord Derwentwater's execution shocked local people in the places he lived, with whom he was popular, and this inspired traditions concerning him. It was only to be expected that in Essex, where both memories and physical memorabilia survived, people should tell ghost stories connected with his regrettable end.

Earls Colne

Richard Baxter, in his *Certainty of the Worlds of Spirits* (1691), gives an account of a phantom bell at Colne priory, the foundation of which as a cell of Abingdon abbey in Berkshire was confirmed by royal charter in 1111. By Baxter's time, following the Dissolution of the Monasteries, it had passed into private hands. The tale of the bell was one of four 'Stories' sent to Baxter accompanying a letter from Mr Thomas Woodcocke dated 17 July 1691:

> Mr *Harlakenden* ... lived at *Coln-Priory* in *Essex*, (where I often was, his only Son being my Pupil,) ... Off from the House was a Tomb-House, with a Chamber over it; his Butler, *Robert Crow*, and *William*, his Coach-man, used to lie in that Room. At Two of the Clock in the Morning there was always the sound of a great Bell tolling: They affirming it so, Mr *Harlakenden* slept in the Evening, so as to be awaked at One of the Clock, and lay betwixt his two Servants to satisfie himself. At Two of the Clock comes the usual Sound of a great Bell tolling, which put him into a Fright and Sweat, so as he jogg'd his Servants; who awaking, said, *Hark*,

Tom *is at his Sport* ... Upon a particular Occasion, Mr *Thomas Shepheard*, (who after went to New England,) with some other Ministers, and good People, spent a Night in Prayer, and had some respect to the place, serving God, to cast out the Devil: And from that time, never was any such noise heard in the Chamber.

'This', says the narrator, 'I had from Mr *Harlakenden*'s own Mouth, and his Servants, Ear-witnesses, when I was upon the place.'

Hadleigh Castle

The remains of Hadleigh Castle, built in about 1231, once had an eerie reputation. In his *History of Rochford Hundred* (1867), Philip Benton says that, among other 'superstitious' tales of the village concerning them, one was told him by an old lady who spoke of a tradition that a 'woman in white' formerly haunted the ruins. According to this, a milkmaid living at the castle farm met her in the castle precincts in the early dawn, and was told to meet her there again at midnight, when she would disclose 'mysteries' connected with the place. This the girl could not summon the courage to do. She was surprised next morning to encounter the same lady, who bitterly upbraided her for not obeying her command, and gave her a cuff on the ear which almost dislocated her neck. She never got over this blow, and from then on was always known by the nickname 'wry-neck Sall'.

The Hadleigh 'woman in white' is one of the more intriguing English White Ladies as, like German 'key maidens' and similar apparitions in Wales, she haunted castle ruins, appeared at dawn, and had a secret to impart – possibly here as elsewhere concerning hidden treasure.

Hockley

Great Hawkwell Wood at Hockley was once notorious for its 'shrieking boy'.

In the wood was an oak tree known as 'the double tree' as it divided into two trunks, joining again above the ground. Philip Benton, in *The History of Rochford Hundred* (1867), says:

> The neighbourhood of this tree was believed at one time by the
> weak and credulous to be haunted, as being at, or near the spot,
> where a woman is said to have killed her child, and during
> the night noises were heard resembling 'Oh mother, mother, don't
> kill me.'

People used to come for miles to listen to the 'shrieking boy', whose
voice would retreat when followed. Various hoaxers, including
a ventriloquist, played on people's fears, evidently for money, and
eventually the haunting was looked into, and a nearby pond was
dragged.

Finally, a horned owl was identified as the source of the
'shrieking boy's' cries and it was shot. Benton quotes Gilbert White
in his *Natural History of Selborne* (1789) on the subject of owls as
saying, 'I have known a whole village up in arms from the snore
and hisses of the white owl, imagining the churchyard to be full of
goblins and spectres.'

We do not have to accept the owl story as true: disclaimers
attributing what had appeared a supernatural event to natural
causes are sometimes built into their narrations by storytellers not
wanting to appear credulous.

Loughton

According to local legend, ever since his death in 1739, the ghost of
the highwayman Dick Turpin, born at Hempstead, visits Loughton
three times every year. He gallops down Trap's Hill on his famous
mare Black Bess and, at a certain point in his journey, an old woman
jumps up behind him. The two then career madly over the
countryside, bringing misfortune to anyone who meets them.

This second ghost is said to be that of an old woman of Loughton
whom Turpin tortured by holding her over the fire to make her
reveal where she had hidden her money. Edward Hardingham, in
Lays and Legends of the Forest of Essex (1907), says that, as Turpin
approaches the farmhouse where the widow lived, he quickens his
pace. The old lady waits for him by the lime tree at the farm gate
ready to spring up onto his horse.

As Peter Haining remarks in his *Dictionary of Ghosts* (1982), 'This

story is the only recorded example of one ghost being tormented by
another!'

Rochford

Rochford Hall was once owned by Sir Thomas Boleyn, also of
BLICKLING HALL, Norfolk. According to a persistent tradition, it
was the birthplace in 1507 of his daughter Anne. Charlotte Mason,
writing in 1928, says, 'There is a very large room ... called Anne
Boleyn's Nursery, which she is still supposed to visit at night.'
Though some argue that, even if not born at Rochford, she may
have spent some of her early years there, it was not in the present
building which appears to date to the end of the reign of Henry
VIII. However, it is natural that, given her fame and horrific death,
she should be connected in local legend with any place associated
with the Boleyns. She is perhaps England's most ubiquitous ghost,
traditionally said to haunt not only Rochford and Blickling, but also
Hever Castle in Kent and THE TOWER of London.

The Strood, Mersea Island

According to Peter Haining, the Revd Sabine Baring-Gould, writing
in 1904, was the first to record a local belief that the figure of a
Roman centurion was seen patrolling the Strood (pronounced
'strode'), the causeway linking the island to mainland Essex. This
centurion would be seen at certain times of the year, especially on
the night of the autumn equinox, around 23 September. Some
people claimed that other figures would be seen approaching this
lone man and the clashing of arms would be heard. One version of
the story suggested to Baring-Gould that these other men were not
attacking the centurion but helping him repel invaders.

Baring-Gould, though he several times walked across the Strood
in the hope of seeing or hearing the phantom, never did.
Nevertheless, he wrote:

I believe the sounds the people of Mersea heard were the ring of
the swords and the clang of the armour of Roman soldiery who

fought and died here centuries ago. Whether there be one soldier or more I do not profess to know.

In 1926, testimony of an encounter with the ghost was given by Mrs Jane Pullen, landlady of the fifteenth-century Peldon Rose on the edge of the salt marshes on the Colchester to Mersea road. James Wentworth Day, in *Ghosts and Witches* (1954), says he was told the story by Mrs Pullen herself, who had then been eighty-one years old and remembered Baring-Gould.

Mrs Pullen believed in ghosts, as she herself encountered the centurion on the road from Barrow Hill down to the Strood one warm summer's evening on her way home from seeing friends. Wentworth Day records Mrs Pullen as saying that she heard the steady tramp of a soldier marching alongside her all the way to the Strood: 'I could see no one, yet the feet were close beside me, as near as I could have touched him. I bopped [crouched] down to look along the road in the moonlight, yet no one was there.' She kept on walking until she met a man she knew, who was 'all a-tremble'. He said he could hear a man, but was unable to see anyone. Mrs Pullen, with great presence of mind, said, 'keep all along of me ... 'Tis only one of those old Romans come out of the barrows.'

Peter Haining adds to this story that, in 1962, a man digging in the mound suddenly felt the ground beneath him collapse and fell into a hollowed-out chamber. As it appeared to be a burial mound, he reported it to the local authorities. Later excavation brought out some Roman artefacts and an urn containing human ashes, seeming to confirm that a Roman of some rank had been laid there.

Local people drew the obvious conclusion that the cremation was that of the ghostly centurion, and there was a feeling that he might never appear again. However, this proved unfounded, as one winter night, when two naval officers were driving across the Strood to Mersea, caught in the headlights was what seemed to be a human figure, wearing a helmet, and having vertical and horizontal white lines across it. They screeched to a halt, fearing they had hit someone, but when they got out of the car no one was there. When they spoke of this later that night, they were told about the centurion – of whom they had never heard – and concluded that the white lines they had seen were the metal plates on his kilt. The phantom has been seen since then, not least in September 1989 when the 'sighting' turned out to be an elaborate hoax. Not everyone agreed that the haunt was Roman, however. Archie White, in *Tideways and Byways in Essex and Suffolk* (1948), attributes it to a tragedy of the Viking Age connected with BARROW HILL.

Walden Abbey, Saffron Walden

Sir Geoffrey de Mandeville, Earl of Essex, who had a castle on Bury Hill, was the arch-villain of the reigns of Stephen and Matilda (Maud). His notoriety has inspired legends in many of the places with which he was connected, including SOUTH MIMMS CASTLE, Hertfordshire.

'The Wicked Sir Geoffrey' seems to have believed that, despite a career of treachery and godlessness such as to warrant excommunication, he could secure a place in Heaven by benefiting the Church: he founded a priory at Walden in, say the chroniclers, 1136, although they call him Earl of Essex and he was only given this title in 1140, four years before his death. He endowed the new priory, later abbey, with no fewer than nineteen churches, together with the hermitage of Hadley.

Such was his reputation, however, that even these pious endowments became the stuff of legend. At the Dissolution of the Monasteries, Walden abbey and its manors were surrendered on 22 March 1538 to the king, who immediately (27 March) granted the whole property to Sir Thomas Audley in fee.

As often with ecclesiastical properties taken from the Church and distributed among secular owners, it came with a terrible curse. According to a tradition current in the late nineteenth or early twentieth century, Sir Geoffrey laid this curse on anyone who seized lands he gave Walden to buy Masses for the repose of his soul. Until they are returned, he walks his former domains from South Mimms to East Barnet every six years near Christmas, dressed in armour and a red cloak, and accompanied by a spectral dog.

Wormingford

According to Winifred Beaumont in *The Wormingford Story* (1958), local tradition says that during the Danish incursions an English nun, who was a chieftain's daughter, was cruelly slain by the invaders. In response, the local men threw them, alive or dead, into the Mere, a deep pool in the Lower Pastures draining into the River Stour. Since that time, the nun's white spirit supposedly walks the Mere whenever an invader threatens the valley. Winifred Beaumont writes, 'This story is as frail as a man's breath on a frosty morning. No-one has seen her or knows anyone who has, but the tradition persists.' She gives no clue, however, as to how long this story has been current in Wormingford.

Gloucestershire

Alvington

A chapbook printed in 1703 and entitled *A Gloucestershire Tragedy* gives a lurid account of a scandal and crime which had supposedly just occurred at Alvington; its title page sums up the affair:

> Being a True, but very Dreadful Relation of one Mary Williams of Alvington near Glocester; who, leading a wicked and lewd Life, was got with child by a Farmer's Son, who often had use of her Body. With the manner how her Mother's Ghost appear'd to them while they were in the very Act; and he thereupon forsaking her, she was afterwards brought to Bed of Two Sons; but he refusing to Marry her, she Drowned one of them in a Pond, and in a most Wretched and Barbarous manner Cut the other in Pieces, Bak'd it in a Pye, and sent it to him fill'd with Blood, on the Day he was Married to another. With an account of her Apprehension, Tryal, Conviction; and Confession at the Place of Execution.

The hack writers who produced cheap pamphlets for the popular market always declared that their astounding or horrifying contents were absolutely true, but it would be rash to believe them unless they are supported by court records or other factual documents. It is not clear whether there really was a Mary Williams of Alvington who committed infanticide in 1703; it is plausible that she might have drowned one of the twins in a pond, but baking the other in a pie and feeding it to the father as revenge is a motif from myth or melodrama, found, for example, in the ancient Greek story of Atreus and Thyestes, and in Shakespeare's early tragedy *Titus Andronicus*.

Bisley

Near Bisley there is a large round barrow known as Money Tump which had the reputation of being haunted. J. B. Partridge reported in 1912 a tale of some men coming home from a fair who, seeing people ahead of them whom they assumed to be friends of theirs, hurried to catch up with them as they drew near Money Tump – only to find that these figures had no heads. The local historian Edith Brill, writing in 1985, tells how she asked an old man the way to Money Tump, and he said, 'he wished he could borrow a bulldozer and search for the money that lay hidden inside it and then he would be rich for the rest of his life.' Yet she goes on to offer her readers a comment which enshrines an equally traditional view:

> I hesitated to tell him that the legend says it got its name during one of the forays of the Saxons when a wealthy chief fleeing for his life dropped his money as he fled.

Chipping Sodbury

According to a story recounted to the folklorist Roy Palmer, a cat haunts the junction of Broad Street and High Street, but it is not precisely a ghost, for it has never died – indeed, it is immortal. Once, long ago, it was the pet of an alchemist who was trying to concoct a potion which would give him everlasting life. He succeeded, but, alas, left the saucer containing it where the cat could get at it . . . He never managed to repeat the experiment.

Cold Ashton

One winter afternoon in the 1930s, the painter Olive Snell set out for Cold Ashton to visit a friend living there. She had been advised to set out early, as it would be hard to find the way in the dark, but the walk took longer than she expected, darkness came on, and she did lose her way. Eventually her road led past a large house with wrought-iron gates and ornamental stone pineapples on the gateposts, and she decided to ask her way there. The door was answered by a very helpful servant, who gave her clear directions; in thanks, she tipped him half a crown. But when she told her friend about this, the friend was puzzled, for the only house answering to the description had been empty for some time. Next day, Olive Snell and her friend set off by car to look for the house; they found it, but it was all locked up and empty, and there was a half-crown lying on the front door step.

Dover's Hill

Ghost stories which involve the tragic doom of star-crossed lovers are likely to date from no earlier than the nineteenth century, and probably circulated among people with a literary background, not among the older rural population. A ghost story of this type is mentioned in Roy Palmer's *Folklore of Gloucestershire* (1994); he says it was told to account for the white-cloaked figure which can be seen at 'White Lady's Gate' on Dover's Hill on the first night after a full moon. Her name in life was Beatrice, and her brothers fought for Cromwell in the Civil War; after the war ended they prospered, but a Royalist neighbour, Sir Roger, found himself reduced to poverty and became a highwayman. One day, he held up a coach in which Beatrice was travelling; they recognized one another and fell in love. They used to meet secretly by the gate on the hill, where Beatrice would signal to him by waving her white cloak. But her brothers spied on her and Roger; they imitated the signal and so drew him to the trysting-place, where they killed him. Beatrice went mad with grief, and has haunted the place ever since.

Though this romantic melodrama cannot be taken seriously as folklore, the name 'White Lady's Gate' merits attention. There are spectral White Ladies in many places in Britain, generally without any explanatory anecdote attached, and gates, like crossroads, are sites where supernatural creatures were expected to manifest themselves.

Dursley

Phantom buildings are not so common in British folklore as ghostly riders or coaches, but they are occasionally mentioned. One such tale, which was told to the folklore collector Ruth Tongue in 1970, concerns a traveller caught in a heavy snowstorm on the wolds near Dursley, who was delighted to see the lights of an inn ahead of him.

A little old groom came out to attend to his horse, and he himself was shown to a warm, comfortable bedroom by 'a servant in green livery', and well fed. He woke before dawn, wanting to press on as soon as possible to Stroud, and, as he could find nobody about, he left two guineas on the table and rode off.

The friends waiting in Stroud had been anxious about him, so he told them he had stopped off at 'that splendid inn above Dursley'. 'There's no inn at Dursley,' said his friends. To settle the argument he led them back to the spot, but all they could find were the tracks of the traveller's own horse, and two guineas lying in the snow. 'I'm told they come out on stormy nights,' said his friend's wife, 'and they never take payment. They never stay after cockcrow. It's lucky you went early or you'd have waked in the snow.'

There are details in this story implying that it is fairies, not ghosts, who help the traveller; the servant's green livery is one such, and another is the final remark about waking in the snow, for this is often said to be the real fate of those who are deluded into thinking they are guests in fairy dwellings. However, there are similarities with the tale at COLD ASHTON, which does seem to involve ghosts.

Painswick

A remarkable number of ghostly traditions have been collected in and around this town in the mid twentieth century. A typescript in the Gloucestershire Record Office, compiled in 1962 by Kenneth Cooke, lists thirty-four in the parish itself, and twenty-five in nearby lanes and woods. Standard motifs are well represented: there are Civil War soldiers, grey and white ladies, a ghost searching for its own buried treasure in a cellar, ghostly highwaymen, phantom coaches, black dogs, headless women. A 'goblin-like figure' dances round a milestone on the road to Gloucester.

Prestbury

This claims to be the most haunted village in Gloucestershire (though PAINSWICK might well say the same), with many phenom-

ena centred round Prestbury House (now a hotel) and a nearby
street called the Burgage. These traditions are listed by Roy Palmer
in his *Folklore of Gloucestershire* (1994), from a variety of printed
and oral sources of the twentieth century. The chief ghost is a
barely visible horseman, whose mount can be heard galloping
wildly down the Burgage, then halting abruptly. Currently, the
usual explanation is that during the Civil War Prestbury House was
occupied by Roundheads, but Gloucester itself was Royalist, and
there was a Royalist army encamped on Cleeve Hill. Knowing this
army would try to send word to Gloucester by night, the Roundheads laid a trap by stretching a rope across the Burgage at just
the height where it would sweep a rider off his horse. This duly
happened; the king's man was injured in the fall and executed by
his captors, and now his ghost rides through the village. Another
version tells the same tale, but in the setting of an earlier war; the
messenger is said to have been trying to reach Edward II's camp at
Tewkesbury in May 1471. This is linked to the discovery in 1901 of
a skeleton with an arrow in its ribs, found during road repairs at the
north edge of the village.

Other Civil War soldiers haunt an old cottage, and ghosts of
eighteenth-century revellers haunt the grounds of the hotel; a 'Black
Abbot' has been frequently seen in the church, the churchyard, and
in many parts of the village; there is a Phantom Strangler at Cleeve
Corner, where a young bride is said to have been asphyxiated by a
burglar who was after her jewels; a girl's ghost plays the spinet in
one cottage, and a woman is heard singing in another. Roy Palmer
comments, 'There are still more ghosts in Prestbury, including
headless horsemen, phantom shepherds and sheep, an old lady in
antique dress, and a misty form, identified as a former Mrs Preece,
which drifts across the fields.' And when Walnut Cottage was being
renovated, the ghost of a former owner appeared, saying, 'Here's
Old Moses. You see I likes to look in sometimes.'

Upton St Leonards

One of the traditional motives for a ghost to appear is to reveal
the fact that it had been murdered. This is well illustrated by an
anecdote recorded by Roy Palmer about a carpenter at Upton

St Leonards who was found lying dead in his garden. People were surprised at this, for the man had been healthy and there was no obvious cause of death; it was rumoured that his wife had murdered him, but, if so, how had she done it? After this, the churchyard began to be haunted by a dark, shapeless spectre which even appeared to the parson 'as big as a woolpack', but this did not help to explain the mystery.

Time passed, and some twenty years later the sexton was digging a grave when the parson came to tell him that the dead carpenter's ghost had appeared to him in a dream that night, saying something would happen next day to cast light on his death. As he dug the new grave, the sexton began uncovering bones from an older one, including a skull, which he recognized as the carpenter's. This, when examined carefully, was seen to have a long brass pin driven into the back of it. The carpenter's widow confessed to the murder, and died soon after.

Hampshire and the Isle of Wight

Basing

The ruins of Basing House are all that remains of a sixteenth-century mansion, built on the motte of a former Norman castle. During the Civil War it was the home of Charles Paulet, Marquis of Winchester, who defended it for three years against Cromwell's troops, but was forced to surrender in 1645; the Roundheads then blew it up. When members of Hampshire's Women's Institutes in the 1930s pooled their information on local history and traditions to make their book *It Happened in Hampshire*, they included several stories about Basing House. It was said that Cromwell's ghost walks in this neighbourhood, going from the big barn at Lyckpit to Plover's Dell. 'No doubt,' said one informant, 'his spirit felt uneasy at the sight of the ruins he had made.' Another tradition was that before abandoning their home the Paulets melted down their gold plate into the form of a Golden Calf, which still lies hidden somewhere in the ruins. A ghost in Cavalier costume could sometimes be seen at nearby Hook, walking on the common; he may have been a casualty of this battle.

Brading (Isle of Wight)

The name of Centurion's Copse, a wood on a hillside east of Brading, is a corruption of 'St Urian's Copse', Urian being an eighth-century Breton saint to whom a small medieval chapel and well which once stood there had been dedicated. There was also a medieval mansion, destroyed some time in the sixteenth century. Inspired by the traces of these fallen buildings, there grew up the legend of a whole lost 'city' called Wolverton, which allegedly lies beneath the wood. It is said that an evil merchant (possibly the Devil in disguise) tricked the inhabitants into murdering an innocent pilgrim who had come to pray at St Urian's chapel, telling them he was trying to poison the chapel's holy well. The pilgrim's blood dripped into the well, desecrating it; in consequence, the great cliff of Culver's Ness collapsed into the sea, and Wolverton was burned to the ground. Thereafter, the cowled, grey-clad figure of the murdered man haunted Centurion's Copse.

Braishfield

Traditionally, ghosts are often associated with hidden treasure. Sometimes it is said that they have forgotten where it lies and are searching desperately; sometimes, that they feel guilty over depriving the living of money and want to show someone where it is. The Braishfield ghost, however, is credited with unpleasant motives. In 1937, a member of the Braishfield Women's Institute wrote that many years previously a wealthy woman hid her money somewhere near a lonely cottage, and had told nobody, for fear it might be stolen. Soon afterwards she fell ill and was taken to hospital, where she died without revealing her secret. Since then her ghost has been seen or heard many times wandering round outside the cottage, or even knocking at its door, but those who were living there in the 1930s declared that they were quite used to the noises and took little notice. Sometimes dogs were aware of her presence even though she could not be seen, and would snarl and growl. The general opinion at that time was that the ghost wanted to prevent anybody from finding the hidden wealth.

Bramshill

The ghost of a young woman dressed in pale grey or white was said to haunt one of the bedrooms of Bramshill House. The Cope family, who for many generations owned this fine seventeenth-century mansion, believed that it was the true setting for the tragic tale of the 'Mistletoe Bride'.

The story was made the subject of a ballad by the songwriter Thomas Haynes Bayly (1797–1839), set to music by H.R. Bishop, and entitled 'The Mistletoe Bough' from its refrain, 'Oh! the Mistletoe Bough, Oh! the Mistletoe Bough.'

Its setting is the Christmas season, when 'the castle hall' is hung with mistletoe and holly. The company is 'blithe and gay', but the baron's beautiful daughter, 'young Lovel's bride', grows tired of dancing and starts to play hide-and-seek. Her friends and her lover search high and low for her, but in vain: she cannot be found. The years roll by, until:

> At length an oak chest that had long lain hid,
> Was found in the castle. They raised the lid,
> And a skeleton form lay mouldering there,
> In the bridal wreath of the lady fair.

This song, also published in Bayly's *Songs, Ballads and Other Poems* (1844), was hugely popular at English village concerts in the Victorian and Edwardian eras. In the USA, too, it spread by word of mouth, sometimes being altered in the process – for example, by the lost bride becoming a lost princess, or, as in an oral version collected in Kansas in 1959, the tune scarcely changed but unfamiliar words replaced. Because of the popularity of the song, several English 'halls' claimed to be the one in the story.

There appears to be no European version of the legend, suggesting that it arose in England. Though conceivably based on a historical incident, surviving versions are undoubtedly the same story, with only minor variations. It was probably current by the eighteenth century, as it forms the plot of 'Ginevra' in Samuel Rogers' blank verse poem *Italy* (1822–8).

His version is set in Modena, in an old palace of the Orsini. There, in an empty room, stands 'An oaken chest, half-eaten by the worm', on the wall above it a portrait of a beautiful girl named Ginevra. The last of her race, at fifteen she married an only son, 'Her playmate from birth, and her first love', Francesco Doria.

Ginevra enjoyed the irrepressible high spirits of youth and was given to 'pranks'. The day of the wedding arrived:

> Great was the joy; but at the Bridal feast,
> When all sat down, the bride was wanting there.
> Nor was she to be found!

Heart-broken, Francesco threw his life away fighting the Turk; Ginevra's father, old Orsini, died; and the house went to strangers.

> Full fifty years were past, and all forgot,
> When on an idle day, a day of search
> Mid the old lumber in the Gallery,
> That mouldering chest was noticed ...

They try to move it:

> but on the way
> It burst, it fell; and lo, a skeleton,
> With here and there a pearl, an emerald-stone,
> A golden clasp, clasping a shred of gold.
> All else had perished—save a nuptial ring,
> And a small seal, her mother's legacy,
> Engraven with a name, the name of both,
> 'GINEVRA.'

Rogers observes: 'This story is, I believe, founded on fact; although the time and place are uncertain. Many old houses in England lay claim to it.' They do: the Copes at Bramshill maintain that the chest in which the bride had hidden was kept in the house until about 1815, and other places to which the legend has been attached include Marwell Old Hall and Malsanger, also in Hampshire, Brockdish Hall near Harleston in Norfolk, and Bawdrip and Shapwick in Somerset, where it is related to a stone in a nearby church commemorating a local heiress who died on 14 June 1681, 'Taken away by a sudden and untimely fate at the very time of the marriage celebrations'.

The story is also linked to Minster Lovell in Oxfordshire, probably attracted by the double coincidence of the family name and the finding of a skeleton by workmen building a new chimney in 1809. The skeleton was that of a man, but the very word 'skeleton' seems to have been enough to hang the story on.

Ellingham

In 1685, the elderly and aristocratic Dame Alice Lisle offered shelter in her home at Moyles Court to two men who had taken part in the Duke of Monmouth's rebellion and were now trying to flee the country after their defeat at Sedgemoor. This was discovered; not only were the men captured and killed, but Dame Alice herself was condemned to death as a traitor by the notorious Judge Jeffreys. He sentenced her to be beheaded; the execution took place in Winchester on 2 September, outside the Eclipse Inn, where Dame Alice spent her last night.

This much is history. Dame Alice's fate is also recalled in local lore. Her ghost, it is said, is sometimes to be seen in the inn – a tall, quiet figure in a long grey dress, standing in the upstairs corridor. It used also to be said that she walked in the courtyard of her old home at Moyles Court, and drove through the lanes between Ellingham and Dibden, as she often did in her lifetime, since her favourite son lived at Dibden. She rode in a black coach drawn by headless horses, and carried her own head in her lap. One of the informants for a Women's Institute survey of Hampshire villages in the 1930s recalled encountering it in childhood, but said the haunting seemed to have ceased by then:

> One dark night when Mother and I was coming up Ellingham Lane, we heard wagon wheels a-rattlin' behind us. 'Run, child,' says Mother, 'run to the side-long by Ellingham cross, lane's too narrer for it ter pass.' So us ran, all of a trimble, to the side-long, and Mother said, 'I allow t'will be Dame Lisle a-coming to Moyles from Ellingham Churchyard.' So 'twas – wagon passed us all a-rattling, drawed by four horses with never no heads and no driver, but inside wagon Dame Lisle was a-setting. Horses knowed their way and rattled 'cross high road and up backway to Moyles. She must have got there, for they do say she were heard along the passages o' the house; and her high heels went tap-tap-tap and her silk dress went swish, swish, swish, agen the bare floorboards. But they don't hear en nowadays. I allow it's got sort o' tired, wore out by time along.

Michael Morey's Hump, Arreton (Isle of Wight)

This is a Bronze Age round barrow, but its name comes from its being used as a place of execution in 1736. Michael Morey (or Moorey) was a woodsman who murdered his own grandson for the sake of some money the boy had inherited, and then tried to disguise the death as an accident by carrying the corpse back to his cottage and setting fire to it. He was hanged on the Hump, and his decaying corpse was gibbeted there for many years; some say that when the remains were at last taken down they were buried in the barrow. His ghost is said to ride round it three times at midnight, calling out 'Michael Morey's Hump' in wailing tones. A nearby pub, the Hare and Hounds, still (2003) displays a beam said to be from this gibbet, and a skull said to be Michael Morey's.

Vernham Dene

According to a tragic legend, so many people of this village became infected in the Great Plague of 1665 that the rector of the parish persuaded them to encamp on the isolated top of Haydown Hill, just across the Wiltshire border, so as not to spread the disease further. He promised that he would bring them regular supplies of food. In truth, however, he was so terrified of catching the plague himself that once he had isolated his sick parishioners in this way, he never went near them again, and they eventually starved to death. But he was punished for his selfishness: in spite of all his care he became infected, no one knew how, and died. It is said that his remorseful ghost has often been seen on the old Roman road called Chute Causeway, climbing the hill towards the spot where his victims died.

There are no records to show that the village did suffer this calamity in 1665, but the *Victoria County History: Hampshire* notes that there is a gap of twenty-six years in the parish registers of births, marriages, and deaths, from 1628 to 1654, presumably indicating that one volume of the registers was mislaid. It may well be that someone, observing this gap, leapt to the dramatic conclusion that the whole population of the village had been wiped out; in the course of time this supposed disaster could easily have become identified with the slightly later and far more famous Great Plague. The tale seems to have been designed as a bitter counterpart to the well-known (and historically true) account of the heroic vicar and people of Eyam, Derbyshire, who went voluntarily into isolation to prevent the disease spreading to neighbouring communities.

Herefordshire

Acton Cross

This village, like many others, had a traditional tale about a ghost and how it was laid; in 1921 Andrew Haggard, a writer who collected examples of local words and phrases, reproduced a conversation in which he heard a man telling his friend George that he remembered just how and where it happened when he was a boy. The ghost was a Mrs Hodges, the local blacksmith's first wife, and the parson had 'read her small', put her in a matchbox, and thrown the matchbox into a pond in the village. His friend seemed doubtful, so he explained further:

'Well, I were about ten and afore I starts work at Mr Cooke's father's in Acton it was, that Mrs Hodges dies and leaves two children, and the blacksmith he marries again, and very quick he did too – warn't that so, George? – and her was bad to the children of the first wife. And the first wife's sperrit took to haanting her children, not tarrifying them as you might say, but just standing at their beds. And the children they warn't frightened neither, 'cos you see her had her clothes on [i.e. she was dressed, not in her shroud]. But her come that strong that all the place was talking on it. And they tells parson and he lays un and says – parson says he don't never want no such job again – fair made him sweat, it did. Copeland, yes, Copeland were parson then. And he got eleven other parsons so there was twelve on 'em, each with a lit candle, and they starts to read her small. Least they raised un first 'cos with sperrits you got to raise un afore you falls un. And her come that big and the lights went out and at last there was only one candle left, and fortunate that candle kept burning else she'd 'a bested them. And they got reading her smaller and smaller and got her real small and pushed un in a matchbox and throwed un in Amstell Pond as I was telling you, and her aren't troubled no one since, ent that so, George?'

'Ah.'

This tale is somewhat unusual in that the ghost's motives for the haunting are so benign; she returns in order to comfort her children, who are being ill-treated by their step-mother. Nevertheless, she is causing such disturbance that the harsh decision to exorcize her in the customary fashion has to be taken.

Andrew Haggard points out that the parson mentioned, the Revd William Copeland, was rector from 1828 to 1854 and died in 1865, so the storyteller, Ted L., who was no more than sixty-five in 1921, could not possibly have witnessed the event as a boy of ten. However, he might well have *heard* the story at that age, from people whose reliability he would never think to question, and later claimed it as his own. Haggard also notes that by the time he printed the tale, in 1972, the pond had been filled in for some years.

Avenbury

In the late nineteenth and early twentieth centuries, Avenbury church (now disused) was reputed haunted; organ music could be heard at a time when there was nobody inside the building. A local man told Andrew Haggard he himself had heard it, to his great alarm, and explained the reason for the haunting. There had once been two brothers living at Brookhouse:

> The one, he were a good chap and 'a used to play the organ in the church reg'lar. Everybody liked un. T'other he were a sclem [good-for-nothing], never did no work, and was allus [always] a-pothering his brother for money and such. Nobody couldn't suffer un. How it come to happen I don't rightly know, but one evening they comes to blows on the water bridge over the prill [brook] just off the Bromyard road, and the one he kills his brother for dead. And that weren't the end of it, not by no manner of means, for arter that the organ used to play nights, and no lights nor nobody there. A could hear un on the road and all quiet — there's scores heered un one time or another.

The informant went on to explain that this haunting 'come on so powerful' that the vicar decided to conduct an exorcism on the bridge at the same hour as the murder had taken place; as usual in such tales, it was an exhausting task and two out of three candles went out, while 'the passon he prays that hard till the sweat fair runs off his nose.' The third candle flared up brightly, and the job was done. 'That didn't stop the music altogether,' said the informant, 'but the pain had gone out of it and them as lived about there didn't take a lot of notice, but strangers as knowed about it wouldn't go near or nighst the place arter dark, and them as didn't know, well they got tarrified.'

Bronsil Castle

Richard Gough, an eighteenth-century antiquary who published in 1789 a translation of William Camden's *Britannia* with additional material, describes a curious heirloom associated with the medieval Bronsil Castle, the ruins of which are near Eastnor. This was a cedar box containing a few human vertebrae, and labelled 'Lord Beauchamp's Bones'. It was said to date from late in the reign of Elizabeth I; at first it was kept in the castle itself, but later in the owners' new residence at New Court, Lugwardine. It was still in existence in the 1760s, but was lost or destroyed at some later period.

Gough gives a story linked to these bones, involving both a ghost and a treasure. It is said that in Elizabeth I's time the castle was so noisily haunted that the then owner, Gabriel Reede, went to a learned man in Oxford for help, and was told that the only way to stop the disturbances was to get hold of 'a bone of the first Lord Beauchamp' and keep it always in the castle; Lord Beauchamp had died in Italy, and could get no peace unless he – or at least part of him – was returned to his ancestral home. So the box with his backbone in it was sent from Italy, and all was peaceful once more. The motivation is the same as in the more common legends about skulls which insist on remaining in houses they had owned, or lived in, when alive.

The legend developed further details in the course of the nineteenth century. Folklorist Mrs Leather was told that the treasure is a large chest of gold and silver which Lord Beauchamp is said to have buried somewhere in the castle grounds; some say, before setting out for the Crusades. It is guarded by a demonic raven. In one version, the precondition for finding the chest is that the seeker must be the rightful owner, and must also possess the bones of Lord Beauchamp; if so, one has to wonder why Mr Reede did not find it, for he certainly had the bones – perhaps local tradition did not think him a rightful owner of the castle? In another version, the Crusader had ordered that if he was killed in the Holy Land his body must be brought home for burial, otherwise the treasure would never be found; the body was indeed brought home, but only in the form of boiled bones (as was often done for those who died in foreign lands), and this was not good enough to fulfil his demand. And now even the bones are lost; but the treasure must still be there, for sometimes the raven is heard croaking at midnight.

Dorstone

In the nineteenth century and earlier, there was a fairly widespread belief that on one night of the year anyone bold enough to keep vigil in the church porch would see the spectral forms of all those in the parish fated to die in the coming twelvemonth entering the church. The date most often mentioned was St Mark's Eve (24/5 April), but in Herefordshire it was Halloween. To try to peer into the future in this way was regarded as both wicked and dangerous. In 1892, the Welsh folklorist Sir John Rhys was given the following account by a Mrs Powell of Dorstone:

> On Allhallows Eve at midnight, those who are bold enough to look through the church windows will see the building lighted with an unearthly light, and the pulpit occupied by his Satanic Majesty clothed in a monk's habit. Dreadful anathemas are the burden of his preaching, and the names of those who in the coming year are to render up their souls may be heard by those who have the courage to listen. A notorious evil-liver . . . once by chance passed the church at the awful moment: looking in, he saw the lights and heard the voice, and his own name in the horrid list; and, according to some versions of the story, he went home to die of fright. Others say that he repented and died in good repute, and so cheated the evil one of his prey.

The folklorist Ella Leather also heard this story from the same informant in virtually identical terms; the only substantial difference is that the date is given as 'the Eve of All Souls', not Halloween. This is the night between 1 and 2 November; in the Catholic calendar All Souls' Day (2 November) is set aside for prayers for the dead.

Hereford

According to the Bible, to defraud others of part of their land by secretly shifting boundary markers is a particularly serious sin; 'cursed be he that moveth his neighbour's landmark' it says (Deuteronomy 27:17), and the curse is one of those solemnly repeated in the Commination Service which used to be held in Anglican churches on Ash Wednesday. In folklore, the sinner may become a ghost, forced to walk until the effects of his deceit are undone. A correspondent using the pseudonym 'Nonagenarian' recorded a tradition about this in the *Hereford Times* in 1876; the White Cross mentioned is a medieval monument on the road from Hereford to Hay, about a mile (1.6 km) outside the city's former limits:

> There was old Taylor's ghost, that used to walk about at the White Cross. He couldn't rest, because he had moved a landmark. He used to ride upon a little pony, and sometimes he would be seen sitting on a stile. I have never seen old Taylor myself, but have heard many say they had seen him. At last his ghost was laid ... One stormy night a fellow whose name I have forgotten walked into the bar of the Nag's Head, and said he had seen old Taylor, and had promised to meet him in the Morning Pits that night at twelve. Of course nobody believed him, and as the night wore on the others jeered at him, and said 'I wouldn't go out on such a night as this.' He said he would not; but as the hour drew near he was obliged to go.
>
> Something forced him to run, so that he reached the Morning Pits as the clock struck twelve. There the old man was waiting. 'Follow me,' said he; the other followed him into some strange place, which they seemed to reach in a very short time. In the place were two immense stones. 'Take up these stones,' said Taylor. 'I can't,' said Denis (he was nicknamed Denis the Liar). 'You can,' said Taylor, 'try.' He tried, and tilted them easily. 'Now

come with me,' said Taylor, 'and place them where I shall show you.' He carried them, and put them down with ease. 'Now,' said the other, 'I caution you never to tell anybody what you see here this night.' He promised. 'And now,' said he, 'lie down on your face, and as you value your life, don't attempt to look either way, until you hear music, and then get away as fast as you can.' He lay for a long time without hearing what he earnestly desired, but at last the welcome sound was heard ... He was a very different man after that, though he died soon after from the effects of his fright.

Tales giving this specific explanation for a haunting are common in some Continental countries, for instance in Denmark, but are rare in England. More usually, English ghosts (as at SEXHOW, Yorkshire) feel guilty at having hidden money away, and order a living man to take it to the rightful heir.

Hergest Court

In the nineteenth century, many tales were told of the eerie happenings in and around Hergest Court, a fifteenth-century manor house a little over a mile (1.6 km) to the south-west of Kington, because one of its past owners, Black Vaughan, was too wicked to rest in his grave. He is usually identified as a Sir Thomas Vaughan killed in battle in 1469, whose effigy is in Kington church, together with that of his wife Ellen; but some think he was another Sir Thomas, beheaded in 1483 as a traitor to Richard III. Always malevolent, Black Vaughan would manifest himself as a bull or as a fly; he would haunt the lanes, overturning wagons and terrifying women as they rode home from market at dusk by leaping onto the crupper of their horses; he would lurk by a certain oak, where his footprints showed as two bare patches burnt into the grass. Those who thought he had been beheaded would say that the disembodied head was sometimes to be seen hovering above the moat. There was also a sinister black dog that prowled through the house and grounds, clanking its chains, which would appear as an omen before any deaths in the Vaughan family; in life it had been Black Vaughan's favourite hound, though now it was a demon.

Vaughan's fearsome spirit was eventually laid, though it took the combined force of twelve parsons, a woman, and a newborn baby to do it. Armed with a silver snuff-box, and each carrying a candle, they summoned him and tried to master him by their prayers and 'read him down' into the box, but he only grew more and more menacing. One version of the tale was told to the Revd Francis Kilvert in the 1860s by a mole-catcher in Radnorshire; another was recorded by Mrs Leather from a local storyteller in about 1910:

> Well, they read, but it was no use; they were all afraid, and all their candles went out but one. The parson as held that candle had a stout heart, and he feared no man nor sperrit. He called out, 'Vaughan, why art thou so fierce?' 'I was fierce when I was a man, but fiercer now, for I am a devil!' was the answer. But nothing could dismay the stout-hearted parson, though, to tell the truth, he was nearly blind, and not a pertickler sober man. He read, and read, and read, and when Vaughan felt himself going down, and down, and down, till the snuff-box was nearly shut, he asked, 'Vaughan, where wilt thou be laid?' The spirit answered, 'Anywhere, anywhere, but not in the Red Sea!' So they shut the box, and took him and buried him for a thousand years in the bottom of Hergest Pool, in the wood, with a big stone on top of him. But the time is nearly up!

A tradition so vigorous and multi-faceted is likely to have grown over several generations, though there is no way of knowing whether it actually goes back, in any form, to the fifteenth century. The folklorist and local historian Roy Palmer, collecting material in this area in the 1990s, found that even in the twentieth century some people thought Vaughan still manifested himself, in spite of the exorcism:

> In the 1930s his ghost was regularly seen by the pool at Hergest Court, and horses were known to refuse to pass the spot. Half a century later [1980s] a visitor to the district ... was terrified to see in Kington Church the ghostly figure of a bull outlined against the blue curtain covering the north door. The daughter of the present owner of Hergest Court told me that her father ... decided some years ago to have the pool filled in but abruptly changed his mind and dismissed the contractors when, as JCBs prepared to begin work, the water started to bubble ominously.

Hertfordshire

Agdell

Memories were still vivid in the 1930s of 'the Agdell ghost'. Edwin Grey, in *Cottage Life in a Hertfordshire Village* (1935), remembered listening to working men talking about it. One said that 'ole Charlie Angell' reported being 'frit putty tidy' (frightened pretty badly) by seeing it two or three times walking down Hatching Green drive. Another said:

> I mind th' time when ole Jimmy Luck an' ole Charlie Angell was lookin' arter th' 'osses at th' 'ole lady's place (meaning Rothamsted Lodge). They've told me as 'ow, when they went ter feed 'em in th' early mornin', they found 'em sometimes all of a muck sweat an' a trimble; they reckoned th' ghost 'ad bin about there in th' night.

The supernatural being usually credited with giving horses the sweats at night was the night-riding hag called the Nightmare (the 'mare' coming from Old English *mara*, a demon). However, human witches were also said to do this, and, although Grey did not know it at the time, 'the Agdell ghost' was supposed to be a witch. He learned her name later in conversation with an old lady who had lived all her life in the neighbourhood of Hatching Green.

> 'I often think,' said she, 'of the time when I was a young girl, and of how we girls were afraid to go down Agdell path to the village on a dark night, for fear we might meet the ghost of old Ann Weatherhead ...'

The old lady explained that in her young days this ghost was said to be that of an old witch or hag who lived years before somewhere in Agdell. Grey wondered if the tradition was connected with the place-name, which some wrote 'Hagdell'.

Aldbury

The children of Aldbury once lived in fear of the bogeyman Simon Harcourt. A barrister of the Inner Temple and lord of Pendley Manor (1694–1724), he was used, like other bogeys, as a threat when they were naughty: 'Simon Harcourt will get you – rattling his chains.' The chains are traditional appurtenances of a penitential ghost, but why Simon Harcourt should be condemned to haunt the village is unexplained. He may have been numbered among the 'wicked gentry', although the Hertfordshire historian John Cussans records that in Harcourt's will dated 29 July 1721 he gave £150 to buy land, the rental from which was to buy bread to be distributed every Sunday among the poor regular attendants of the church.

Cassiobury

The great mansion of Cassiobury, demolished in 1927, was the home of the Earls of Essex for over 250 years and was said to be haunted by the ghost of Arthur, Lord Capel, created Earl of Essex in 1661. Because of his involvement in the Rye House Plot (1683), he was sent to the Tower of London, where he was found with his throat cut, having probably committed suicide. W. B. Gerish noted in his *Folk-Lore of Hertfordshire* (1911) that the haunt reputedly took place each year on 13 July, the anniversary of his death.

Lord Capel was not the only ghost in the neighbourhood. Adjoining Cassiobury on the north is the Grove, in the nineteenth century locally said to have been built by Arthur-Mohun St Leger, third Lord Doneraile. The historian John Cussans reports as 'a fiction devoutly believed in by all the labourers on the estate' the tradition that, on stormy nights, Lord Doneraile, on a phantom horse, accompanied by phantom hounds, pursues a ghostly fox around the park, whatever the season. He was condemned to do this for ever as a punishment for having converted the ancient chapel into a kitchen. This is a version of the old tradition of the Wild Hunt (*see* PETERBOROUGH, Huntingdonshire and Peterborough), often attached to local magnates and squires for having committed sacrilege or blasphemy.

The story, as Cussans remarks, is a curious combination of fact and fiction. Lord Doneraile indeed bought the estate in 1743, but, except for the third storey, the house as it appears today was probably the work of the first Earl of Clarendon c.1760. When the fourth Earl was altering the basement, he discovered in the kitchen walls evidence of its having formerly been a chapel. This no doubt prompted the legend – here, as elsewhere, interference with former ecclesiastical property calling down the direst retribution.

Cheshunt

David Hughson (Dr David Pugh) writes in his *Walks through London . . . with the Surrounding Suburbs* (1817):

> Passing on to *Cheshunt:* here is a plain brick edifice, in which Cardinal Wolsey is said to have resided. It has been nearly rebuilt since his time; but is still surrounded by a deep moat. In the upper part of this house, called Cheshunt-House, is a room, the door of which is stained with blood; the tradition is – an unfortunate lady became a victim to the Cardinal's jealousy, and that he dispatched her with his own hand. If so, it is unaccountable that the murderer should have suffered those marks of his violence to have remained.

It was not 'unaccountable' in terms of folklore, however, it being 'common knowledge' that blood shed by violence could never be removed, hence the many tales of supposedly indelible bloodstains.

Mrs Crowe in *The Night-Side of Nature* (1848) tells the story of another haunted house which has all the makings of a murder mystery. About six years before the time of writing, a Mr C— heard of an old house not far from London which was being let very cheaply. He moved his family in, joining them as his business allowed.

They had been in the house some time when Mrs C—, entering what was called the oak bedroom, saw a young woman with long dark hair, wearing a silk petticoat and short white robe, looking out of the window as if expecting someone. Mrs C— covered her eyes, 'thinking she had seen something she ought not to have seen', and when she looked again the woman had vanished.

Soon afterwards, a young nursery maid came to her in a fright having seen an ugly old woman looking in through a window. Then the family began to be disturbed by noises in the night, and both Mrs C— and one of the servants heard footsteps following them upstairs.

One night this same servant, sleeping in Mrs C—'s room, became very agitated, murmuring 'Wake me! Wake me!' When Mrs C— did so, the servant said she had dreamed she saw a young woman with long hair and an old-fashioned dress in the oak room, with an ugly old woman. The old one said, 'What have you done with the child, Emily? What have you done with the child?' To which the young woman replied, 'Oh, I did not kill it. He ... grew up and joined the — regiment, and went to India.' Then she told the sleeping servant that her name was Miss Black, and the old woman was the family nurse. Here the old woman interrupted by laying her hand on the dreaming girl's shoulder and saying something, she could not remember what, because the touch was so painful that she had begged to be waked.

Mrs C— now inquired in the village and was told that, seventy or eighty years before, a Miss Black had lived there with her aunt. Subsequently she saw Miss Black in the oak room again, wringing her hands, and staring mournfully into a corner, though when they took up the floorboards they found nothing.

Three years later, they were about to move when one morning Mrs C— awoke to see at the foot of her bed a dark-complexioned man wearing a fustian jacket and a red comforter. He suddenly disappeared, and this was the last apparition seen. But it was not the end of the story. Needing some coal, Mr C— said he would order it on his way to London. When next day Mrs C— told him it had arrived, he confessed he had forgotten to do so. On making an inquiry to the supplier, Mrs C— was told that it had been ordered by a man in a fustian jacket and red comforter.

Mrs Crowe heard this story from the actor Charles Kean and his wife. William Howitt, who had also heard it from the Keans, adds that the house was in Cheshunt, that Mr C— was Kean's brother-in-law, Chapman, the publisher, and that the Chapmans later heard that several families had left because of similar disturbances. The Chapmans sold their lease to a clergyman who kept a school, but he had to give it up for the same reason. Finally, after standing empty for years, it was partly pulled down and rebuilt, and that seemed to put a stop to all ghostly activity, as Howitt reported in 1863 that it was inhabited again and free from haunting.

Codicote

Sissavernes, earlier Sissavens, Farm at Codicote probably gets its name from a historical lord of the manor, William de Sisvierne, mentioned in 1166. In the nineteenth century, the original old manor house on the site (demolished and rebuilt 1870–80) not only was said to possess a mysterious, dark, underground passage leading to the church but was, according to local legend, haunted by Sissavernes, now transformed into 'the wicked farmer of Codicote'. He loved his land so passionately that he vowed he would never leave it, and so, when he died, his body was buried on the hilltop, 'whence his unquiet shade is said to haunt his earthly dwelling-place'.

According to another version of this story, his bier became so heavy that the horses could not drag it as far as the churchyard, so it was buried where they stopped. Sissavernes' ghost, like traditional bogeys, was used to subdue naughty children. He was commemorated in verses written by the Welwyn parish clerk William Nobbs, about 1820:

> To Sissafernes, where many a tale was told
> Of fam'd old Sis, renowned in days of old,
> Who play'd such pranks they say in days of yore
> No other ghost had power to play before . . .
> Grandames of him did tell most wondrous tales
> To frighten children from the lonely vales . . .

Gubblecote

In 1751, John Butterfield, publican of the Black Horse at Gubble-cote, managed to rouse a mob against an old woman named Ruth Osborne, of Long Marston, and her husband, John. Butterfield claimed that, some years before, when he was a dairyman, he and his cattle had been bewitched by her. Despite the fact that the death penalty for witchcraft had been abolished in 1735, on 18 April the town crier of Hemel Hempstead, William Dell, announced in the marketplace: 'This is to give notice, that on Monday next a man and woman are to be publicly ducked at Tring for their wicked crimes.' The same information was 'cried' at Winslow and Leighton Buzzard.

Accounts of what happened next are conflicting, but from the deposition of John Osborne himself, the Coroner's inquisition and the evidence of witnesses, we hear that the first he knew of it was when neighbours warned him that he and his wife were to be ducked. They were advised to leave their house, and took refuge in the Tring workhouse. On the Monday morning, as a precaution, they were locked in the church, but, in the interests of public safety, were given up when a mob attacked the workhouse.

The crowd bore the old couple off to Wilstone Green. According to the *Gentleman's Magazine*, reporting the affair in April, May, and August of 1751:

> The poor wretches were stript stark naked by the mob, their thumbs tied to their toes, then dragged two miles, and thrown into a muddy stream; after much ducking and ill usage, the old woman was thrown quite naked on the bank, almost choaked with mud, and expired in a few minutes, being kick'd and beat with sticks, even after she was dead; and the man lies dangerously ill of his bruises; to add to the barbarity, they put the dead witch (as they called her) in bed with her husband, and tied them together.

The pond they were 'swum' in for witchcraft was known as Wilstone 'Were' or 'Wear'.

At the Coroner's inquest, although thirty or so people were found guilty of murder, only one was hanged. This was Thomas Colley, a chimney-sweep. Ruth Osborne, who was over seventy, had survived most of her long ordeal, but Colley, when they dragged her across the pond for the last time, pushed her face down with his stick. The sheet she was wrapped in came untied, and she managed to get her head above water and grasp the stick, but he tore it out of her hand and again shoved her under. On being finally taken out of the water, she was dead. Cause of death was pronounced by the surgeon who examined her to be partly exposure, partly suffocation by mud and water. Her husband John died not long after.

When it came out that Colley had not been content with drowning the old woman but had gone round the bystanders collecting money by way of reward, he was sentenced at Hertford Assizes to be hanged and hung in chains at the scene of his crime. Some locals complained about the verdict, 'grumbling and muttering that it was a hard case to hang a man for destroying an old wicked woman that had done so much mischief by her witchcraft'. Nevertheless, Colley was executed, not by Wilstone Were, because people living nearby protested, but at Gubblecote Cross, and his body hung from the gibbet in chains.

There it remained for years, doubtless fuelling local talk of a ghost. The Revd Frederick Lee, in *More Glimpses of the World Unseen* (1878), writes:

> It is remarkable that the spot where this man was hung ... is still reputed to be haunted. I recently learnt from John Reeves, parish clerk of Long Marston, that he and others, notably Edward Oakley and Mary Nunes of Gubblecote, have seen a spectral animal near a field called Gibraltar, and that the conviction of the reality of the apparition is firmly held by many.

Later sources specify that Colley's ghost appeared as a great black dog. One who saw it was the village schoolmaster, whose account was printed in 1911:

> I was returning home late at night in a gig with a person who was driving. When we came near the spot, where a portion of the gibbet had lately stood, he saw on the roadside bank a flame of fire as large as a man's hat. 'What's that!' I exclaimed. 'Hush,' said my companion, and suddenly ... made a dead stop. I then saw an immense black dog just in front of our horse ... He was as big as a Newfoundland, but very gaunt, shaggy, with long ears and tail, eyes like balls of fire, and large, long teeth, for he ... seemed to grin at us. In a few minutes the dog disappeared, seeming to vanish ... or to sink into the earth, and we drove over the spot where he had lain.

Bogey beasts elsewhere are sometimes likewise explained as ghosts (*see also* BRIGG, Lincolnshire).

Hatfield House

Hatfield House, home of the Cecils, used to be haunted by a family ghost, James, sixth Earl of Salisbury. It was his mother's fault, as the Victorian raconteur Augustus Hare was told while staying at Hatfield. He recorded in his journal on 14 December 1872 that, in Lady Salisbury's own room, the house-guests were shown among other portraits 'a curious picture of a lady'.

> 'She looks clever but bad,' said I.
>
> 'She *was* desperately wicked,' said Lady Salisbury, 'and therefore it is quite unnecessary to say that she was very religious. She endowed almshouses – 'Lady Anne's Almshouses,' – they still exist, and she sent her son to Westminster with especial orders that he should be severely flogged, when he was seventeen, and so soured his temper for life and sent him to the bad entirely ... The son lived afterwards at Quixwold, and led the most abominably wicked life there, and died a death as horrible as his life ... His is the phantom coach which arrives and drives up the staircase and then disappears. Lord Salisbury heard it the other night when he was in his dressing-room, and dressed again, thinking it was visitors, and went down, but it was no one.'

Twenty years later, on 29 July 1902, Hare recorded in his journal remarks made by Eustace Cecil, great-grandson of the sixth Earl. Eustace Cecil spoke of the ghost, saying that his great-grandfather had run away from Westminster when he was eighteen. He added to Lady Salisbury's account that, as well as the phantom coach, the sixth Earl himself was 'often seen in the room which is now used as a smoking-room'.

Hitchin

A number of ghosts have appeared at Hitchin, including the Ancient Greek poet Homer, who, according to the poet George Chapman (c.1559–1634), appeared to him on Hitchin Hill and commanded him to translate the *Iliad* and the *Odyssey*. The most attractive phantoms, however, are those of two Hertfordshire clergymen, Mark Hildesley (1698–1772), vicar of Hitchin, and Edward Young (1683–1765), rector of Welwyn and author of the elegiac poem *Night Thoughts*, written after the death of his wife.

These clergymen used to play bowls together of a summer evening behind the Sun Inn, where there was a bowling green running down to the River Hiz. Still on summer nights, according to Reginald Hine, writing in the 1930s, 'those who inhabit the nearer rooms can hear the chink and kiss of the "woods," and Young's deep voice as he disputes the score.'

Hog Hall and Hog Hall Lane

'Old Keeper Mayling', who died a very old man, sixty years before Vicars Bell published *Little Gaddesden* (1949), was a lively raconteur who used to tell, among other stories, tales of his own experiences 'back of Hog Hall and them parts'.

One concerned a phantom funeral apparently coming along Hog Hall Lane, like Hog Hall itself in the parish of Little Gaddesden but close to Dagnall:

> There was six men in black coming up from Dagnall way, and they had summat in black on their shoulders, and there was others follering 'em two and two and all as black as Newgate's knocker. So I gets down by the hedge to watch. But on they comes, so near I could ha' touched 'em, and never a sound. Couldn't even hear their feet fall, and it was a corpse as they carried, like they was going to bury it. They went right on till they come to the Barn, and all went in. I waited a bit, but I couldn't hear nothing so I went and took a peek inside. And what do you think I see? Nothing. Not a sign of anything. They was all vanished.

'Black as Newgate's knocker' was a proverbial saying referring to the door knocker on the old Newgate Prison, London.

Knebworth House

The present mansion of Knebworth House replaced an older house begun in the last decade of the fifteenth century, its mainly Elizabethan fabric dated over a doorway to 1563. It was this old house that the novelist Edward Bulwer-Lytton (1803–73) knew in boyhood and of which he later wrote:

> I remember especially a long narrow gallery ... which terminated in rooms that were called, 'haunted'. They were of great antiquity, covered with gloomy tapestry ... In another room ... was a curious trap-door that gave access to a chamber beneath ... which had neither doors nor windows ... How could I help writing romances when I had walked ... through that long gallery, ... mused in those tapestry chambers, and peeped ... into the shadowy abysses of Hell-hole.

All but one wing of the old house had been demolished in 1811 or 1812, including the 'haunted' rooms. But before this they had inspired not only Bulwer-Lytton, who later inherited Knebworth, but a house-guest called Miss James, who stayed there one Christmas in about 1800. Members of the house-party had asked the gatekeeper and villagers about 'the ghost', but no one knew anything more than that there was one. Each of the house-party undertook to write a history for it. Miss James's story was entitled 'Jenny Spinner; or, the Ghost of Knebworth House', and concerned an apparition whose spinning-wheel was often heard. Miss James apparently did not invent her: a Knebworth inventory of 1797 mentions 'Spinning Jenny's Room'. This may have been 'the Haunted Chamber' referred to earlier, in a deed of 1707, in the Knebworth archives.

Certainly traditions of other spinning ghosts are known, including Mrs Baines of PENZANCE, Cornwall, and a Spinning Jenny, attached, according to Mrs Crowe in *The Night-Side of Nature* (1848), to 'a Scotch family of distinction'. She was heard spinning in their house, and accompanied them to their town house on visits to London. She was supposed to be the ghost of a former housemaid. Both Jennies perhaps got their name from James Hargreaves' famous invention (1764).

The most extraordinary apparition connected with Knebworth is that of 'the Radiant Boy'. He appeared to the English statesman Viscount Castlereagh (1769–1822), according to most reports when staying at Knebworth. Sir Walter Scott, who frequently told the story, said that he heard Lord Castlereagh speak of the Radiant Boy 'at one of his wife's supper parties in Paris in 1815'. Seven years later, Scott wrote in a letter to Lady Abercorn:

I remember his once telling seriously and with great minuteness the particulars of an apparition which he thought he had seen. It was a naked child, which he saw slip out of the grate of a bedroom while he looked at the decaying fire. It increased at every step it advanced towards him, and again diminished in size till it went into the fireplace and disappeared. I could not tell what to make of so wild a story told by a man whose habits were equally remote from quizzing or inventing a mere tale of wonder.

With hindsight, he could see that Castlereagh was probably 'subject to aberrations of mind which often create ... phantoms'. For what had followed, on 12 August 1822, was that Lord Castlereagh committed suicide by severing the carotid artery with a penknife, earning himself the cruel posthumous epithet of 'Cut-throat Castlereagh'. Accordingly, on 1 November 1826, Scott wrote in his journal, 'He is gone ... I shall always tremble when any friend of mine becomes visionary.'

Since Lord Castlereagh's suicide, the Radiant Boy or Burning Babe has frequently been said to be a Lytton hereditary 'death omen', although it is unclear if it was so thought of by Castlereagh himself. Certainly it was enough to terrify anyone witless: Scott's son-in-law Lockhart, who had often heard him tell the story, says that, as it grew in size, the naked child 'assumed the appearance of a ghastly giant, pale as death, with a bleeding wound on the brow, and eyes glaring with rage and despair'.

After receiving Scott's account, Lady Abercorn wrote to him, 'I never heard of his [Castlereagh's] having named it to any one else.' If that is true, one might suspect that Castlereagh was not 'fey' but simply entertaining Scott with the kind of story he liked. However, Scott is said by contemporary writers to have heard the story at the house of the Duke of Wellington, at his own request, implying that it was already in circulation.

Unless Lord Castlereagh's story spawned imitators, which is possible, the Radiant Boy seems not to have been a single individual, but a particular kind of ghost – there was another at CORBY CASTLE, Cumberland.

Markyate Cell

Here from the twelfth century up to the Reformation stood the priory of St Trinity-in-the-Wood, founded in about 1145. At the Dissolution of the Monasteries, it was confiscated by the Crown and eventually sold to George Ferrers of St Albans, according to the *Gentleman's Magazine* (1846) by Henry VIII in 1536, according to others by Edward VI in 1549. It remained in the Ferrers family until it descended to Katherine Ferrers, who married Thomas Fanshawe, afterwards Viscount Fanshawe.

Known as Markyate Cell, the house was burned down three times, the last time in 1840. Popular tradition blamed this final destruction on the malignant ghost of a highwaywoman, 'Wicked Lady Ferrers'. The Hertfordshire historian John Cussans writes:

> It is said, that in the disguise of male attire, and mounted on a coal-black horse with white fore-feet, she robbed travellers on the high way, but at length was fatally wounded, at No Mans Land, when so engaged. She was found lying dead outside a door leading, by a secret staircase, to a chamber where she changed her dress.

Cussans says that this doorway was built up, and when, after the 1840 fire, the then owner, 'the late Mr Adey', was demolishing much of the old building and wished to reopen it, none of the local labourers could be induced to do the work, and he had to get men from London. Opening the doorway, they discovered a narrow stone staircase leading up to a stout oak door. They broke this down, but found afterwards that it opened by a hidden spring. There was nothing in the room beyond, apart from bats.

During the final fire, many of the labourers who were trying to put it out swore that they saw Lady Ferrers swinging herself on a branch of a large sycamore tree growing near the house. So convinced were they of the reality of the apparition that they took it on themselves to saw off the branch. They were greatly surprised when Mr Adey did not reward them for their zeal. 'Such', says Cussans, 'is the story of "Wicked Lady Ferrers," which in this present year of 1878 is religiously believed in by the majority of the inhabitants of Markyate Street.'

The Victorian raconteur Augustus Hare, in 1894, added to this account that the Wicked Lady was once a familiar sight about the house. He writes:

> She constantly haunts the place. Mr Ady [*sic*] ... meets her on the stairs, and wishes her good-night. Once, seeing her with her arms stretched out in the doorway, he called out to his wife who was outside, 'Now we've caught her!' and they rushed upon her from both sides, but caught – nothing!

Others assert that she revisits the scene of her crimes, and rides the roads nightly from Markyate Cell almost to Dunstable.

The Wicked Lady's identity is uncertain: although the story may have no historical foundation, later writers have claimed that the last of the Ferrers left a young widow, Katherine, who became the Wicked Lady, or that the historical Katherine Ferrers probably did take to highway robbery as an amusement after the failure of her marriage.

Whatever the truth behind the legend, it became famous world-wide from Leslie Arliss's 1945 film starring Margaret Lockwood as 'the Wicked Lady'. The story is still commemorated locally by the sign of the Wicked Lady freehouse at Nomansland, the large tract of common west of the road between Sandridge and Wheathampstead where she was supposed to have been shot.

Sawbridgeworth

Hyde Hall in this parish was said to be haunted by the ghost of Sir John Jocelyn, the third Baronet. Tradition said that, during his life, he quarrelled with the vicar of Sawbridgeworth because he refused to let him be buried with his favourite hunter in consecrated ground. Consequently, he left the following instructions:

> I will my body to be buried in the circle of yews in the grand avenue to Hyde Hall, attended only by my servants, or such relations or others as shall happen to be at Hyde Hall at the time of my decease, or such neighbours as please to come the day after my decease, at the setting of the sun ...

It has been generally supposed that his wishes were carried out when he died, on 1 November 1741, and his horse slaughtered and buried with him. 'It is said ... that at certain seasons of the year, Sir John ... his charger breathing fire, rides at full speed down the avenue – and then vanishes.'

Some suggest that this phantom horse had its origins in Sir John's instructions that his best ox should be given to the poor of Sawbridgeworth, which is presumed to have been slaughtered to provide them with funeral 'baked meats'.

Sir John's eccentric burial arose, some said, because he was an ardent Dissenter who held Nonconformist services at the hall. A Puritan was similarly said to have been buried with his horse at Houghton Hall, Houghton-le-Spring, Durham.

South Mimms Castle

The extraordinary career of the historical Geoffrey de Mandeville inspired many strange traditions concerning him both in the Middle Ages and long after. There are conflicting tales of how he met his end, whether shot in the head by an arrow and then hung from a tree in London, or down a well here at the overgrown motte-and-bailey of South Mimms Castle, in Mymmshall Wood, north-west of Potters Bar.

Hertfordshire tradition says that Sir Geoffrey, being hunted down for one of his crimes, hid from his pursuers in a hollow tree. He could not escape divine retribution, however, and this tree immediately sank into the castle well, where he perished. His ghost is said to walk his former domains from South Mimms to East Barnet every six years at Christmas, dressed in full armour, with a red cloak, and accompanied by a phantom dog (*see* WALDEN ABBEY, Essex).

South Mimms Castle itself was probably built by Geoffrey, around 1140–2. By the time the sixteenth-century topographer William Camden was writing his *Britannia*, it was already in ruins. Tradition, however, says that, in its heyday, it had gates so huge that they could be heard closing as far away as Winchmore Hill.

W.B. Gerish does not mention the legend in *The Folk-Lore of Hertfordshire*, his useful checklist of traditions current in 1911, and indeed South Mimms Castle was only rediscovered in 1918. The story may therefore have been adapted from the pre-existing one concerning Camlet Moated Site, Enfield, on the north side of what is now Trent Park, where Geoffrey's treasure is said to be hidden in an ancient well. That being said, both versions are now established.

Tewin

Originally in the churchyard of St Peter's, now inside the church, is the massive marble base supporting a huge pyramid flanked by urns which marked the last resting place of General Joseph Sabine, governor of Gibraltar, who died at Gibraltar on 24 October 1739, aged seventy-eight. He was a professional soldier, who bought the estate of Tewin in 1715. It was his first wife, Hester Whitfield, whom a well-known story concerns.

According to a letter of 30 November 1759 printed in the *Gentleman's Magazine* in 1783, General Sabine was once dangerously ill of his wounds after a battle abroad, and, as he was beginning to recover, lay awake one night in his bed. By the light of a candle burning in his room, he suddenly saw the bed-curtains at the foot of the bed drawn back and his wife, 'a lady whom he greatly loved', and who was then in England, standing there. As suddenly as she had appeared, she vanished. Much struck, he wrote this experience down in his notebook. Not long afterwards, news came that she had died, at the exact time, as far as he could recollect, that she had appeared.

The writer of the letter heard this story from Dr Yarborough, rector of Tewin, who had known General Sabine well for many years. When the general told Dr Yarborough of the apparition, he added that the prevailing disbelief in ghosts of his contemporaries was one that he could 'confidently oppose on the strongest grounds'. The rector accepted his story, believing him to be 'a person of great honour and veracity, and much good sense'.

Tring Station

According to a tradition recorded around the turn of the nine-teenth century, on the site of Tring Station, just inside the parish of Aldbury, stood the castle of Sir Guy de Gravade, a legendary sorcerer in the reign of King Edward III.

Like Faust, Sir Guy sold his soul to the Devil in return for the secrets of alchemy and necromancy, and made himself rich by his magic arts. Disaster befell him, however, when one night his servant, John Bond, secretly tried to use one of his master's spells. Discovering what he was up to, Sir Guy (in the words of a burlesque poem by T. Dyke Nunn):

> ... gave vent to a fresh invocation,
> Which shook the whole [house] from roof to foundation,
> And roused for some miles the entire population,
> The bolder of whom made an investigation,
> And found on arriving at the situation
> That nothing at all remained on the scene
> Where Sir Guy, house, and John just lately had been.

One day in every year, on the anniversary of the fatal day, the phantoms of Sir Guy and John Bond were said to reappear on or near the scene.

This is a dramatic local variation of the international tale 'The sorcerer's apprentice', which reached its apogee, with the apprentice played by Mickey Mouse, in Walt Disney's *Fantasia* (1940). This cartoon version is set to the symphonic poem by Dukas, first performed in 1897, which illustrates Goethe's story (itself based on Lucian, second century AD) of someone who finds he can start a spell working but not stop it.

Ware

Now in the Victoria and Albert Museum, but once housed in the Saracen's Head at Ware, was the Great Bed of Ware, made of oak and just over ten feet long and ten feet wide (3 m by 3 m). According to popular tradition, the Great Bed was made by Jonas Fosbrooke, a journeyman carpenter of Ware, who presented it to King Edward IV in 1463. Although the date 1463 is painted on the headboard, seemingly verifying this tale, the bed is actually thought to have been made as a publicity stunt for the White Hart at Ware around 1590. It was famous enough by the time that Shakespeare wrote *Twelfth*

Night (first performed 1601) for him to include an allusion to it (Act 3, scene 2). Later, the Great Bed was housed at several different inns – the George, the Crown, and finally the Saracen's Head, where it remained until 1870. It was then sold to the proprietor of the Rye House Hotel at Hoddesdon and acquired by the Victoria and Albert Museum in 1931.

Meantime, the Great Bed went on being mentioned by travellers, historians, poets, and playwrights into the nineteenth century, the stories told about it becoming increasingly fanciful. Its size was enormously exaggerated – a writer in 1706 said it could lodge a troop of soldiers if supplemented with a trundle bed; another in 1732 said it would hold twenty couples; while one in 1736 spoke of the twenty-six butchers and their wives who had slept in it on the night that King William III was crowned.

The bed was famous not only for its size but because it was supposed to be haunted. Those who tried to sleep in it were kept awake by 'the pinching, nipping, and scratching that went on all night long'. It was said that Harrison Saxby, Master of the Horse to King Henry VIII, fell in love with the daughter of a rich miller living at Chalk Island near Ware and swore that he would do anything to make her his wife. King Henry, who happened to be passing through Ware on his way to Hertford Castle, heard this and ordered the girl and her many suitors to appear before him. He promised her in marriage to the man who would spend the night in the Great Bed (this before the real bed was made). Only Saxby took up the challenge and withstood the tormenting of the ghost though next morning he was covered in bruises. Naturally, he won his bride. As to who did the haunting, it was said by many to be the ghost of old Fosbrooke, angry at the common use his great bed was being put to.

Huntingdonshire and Peterborough

Authors' note. Historically, a number of towns and villages in these two counties have been debatable ground. Barnack, for example, was included by the authors of *Place-Names of Northamptonshire* (1933) under that county, as being in the double Hundred of Nassaborough, which coincided with the Soke of Peterborough. It later came under the administrative district of Cambridgeshire. Now it is back in Peterborough. Castor, too, is something of a moveable feast – in the past two centuries, it has been variously assigned to Northamptonshire, the Soke of Peterborough, Cambridgeshire, Huntingdonshire, and now, like Barnack, again to Peterborough. Here we have followed the example of Simon Jenkins in *England's Thousand Best Churches* (1999), where he writes, 'Fenland boundaries may have mattered as little to modern bureaucrats as to Saxon warlords but, to most local people, Huntingdonshire and Peterborough still form a natural entity.'

Barnack

The rector of Barnack church in the early nineteenth century was the father of the novelist and historian Charles Kingsley, author of *The Water Babies* (1863), and Charles lived as a child in Barnack rectory. His wife, who edited his papers, tells us that the rectory, a fine old fourteenth-century house, contained a celebrated ghost chamber known as 'Button Cap's'. Charles, a nervous and highly sensitive boy, was once moved into this room during an attack of brain fever. For years afterwards, his imagination was haunted by the memory of the weird sights and sounds he experienced. She continues:

> 'Of Button Cap,' he writes in 1864, 'he lived in the great north room at Barnack. I knew him well. He used to walk across the room in flopping slippers, and turn over the leaves of books to

find the missing deed, whereof he had defrauded the orphan and the widow. He was an old Rector of Barnack. Everybody heard him who chose. Nobody ever saw him; but in spite of that, he wore a flowered dressing-gown, and a cap with a button on it. I never heard of any skeleton being found; and Button Cap's history had nothing to do with murder, only with avarice and cheating. Sometimes he turned cross and played Poltergeist, as the Germans say, rolling the barrels in the cellar about with surprising noise, which was undignified. So he was always ashamed of himself, and put them all back in their places before morning.'

One marvels a little at parents who would put a feverish child in a famously haunted room. 'But', says his wife, 'as he often told his own children ... he had seen too many ghosts at Barnack to have much respect for them.' And Kingsley himself, as an adult, rational-ized harmless old Button Cap out of existence:

'I suppose he is gone now. Ghosts hate mortally a certificated National Schoolmaster, and (being a vain and peevish generation) as soon as people give up believing in them, go away in a huff – or perhaps some one had been laying phosphoric paste about, and he ate thereof and ran down to the pond, and drank till he burst. He was rats!'

Castor

The large and richly decorated church at Castor, consecrated in 1124, has the distinction of being the only church in Britain dedicated to St Kyneburgha (also Kyneburga, Kyneberga, Kyneburg, Cyniburg or Cyneburg). Indeed, Castor's modern name is short for its Old English one: (to) *Kyneburga cæstre*, (be) *Cyneburge cæstre*, *cæstre* coming from Latin *castrum* and, like the place-names Caister and Chester, denoting a Roman fort or town. One early medieval author says it was previously called *Dormundescastre* and only later named *Kineburga castrum*, presumably once the cult of St Cyneburg got well under way.

St Cyneburg was one of Anglo-Saxon England's many royal saints. She is said to have been a daughter of Penda, King of Mercia (d. 654), who married Alcfrith, the son of Oswiu of Northumbria.

Later, she became a Benedictine nun and, in about 650, founded a convent here with her sister St Cyneswith (Kyneswitha, Kyneswith, Cyneswide), to whose shrine the medieval reredos at the east end of the north aisle probably belonged. Another relative who came with them was St Tibba.

St Cyneburg died in c.680, and was buried here, but the great relic-collector Abbot Ælfsige of Peterborough (d. 1042) translated the remains of all three women to Peterborough Abbey, where they were venerated. Subsequently they were moved to Thorney, but returned to Peterborough in the reign of Henry I (1100–35). St Cyneburg's feast day is 6 March.

Though the people of Castor lost their saint, they cherished her memory. The *castrum* referred to in Castor's name is the Roman settlement on the left bank of the river, facing the Roman fort and town of Durobrivae ('The Castles') at Chesterton and Water Newton on the right. Ermine Street passed through the station, and the whole of the ground occupied by Castor was once covered with Roman buildings. Later generations connected a ridge or track running through these remains with the saint.

The Revd John Morton, writing in 1712, says it was locally known as 'my Lady *Conyburrow's* Way', and that it appeared to have been paved, and to have been a continuation of a road beginning on the other side of the river, at or near Water Newton, and running northwards through 'Castor Field':

> It is not to be traced so high as the Town; but by the pointing it seems to have lead thither: and according to a Tradition that they have there, it went directly to the ancient Four-square Well in that Churchyard at *Castor*.

He describes Lady Conyburrow's Way as in his time being 'only a narrow Tract ... of Ground three or four Foot [approx. 1 m] broad, distinguishable from the rest of the Field, thro' which it passes, by its being barrener than the Ground, on both sides of it'. As to the local explanation of why the track was barren ground, he continues:

> Those who desire to know how this Way in particular came by its Name, may take this Traditionary Account of it from an old Story that is told at *Castor*, *viz.* That *Kinneburga's* Honour being

attempted she fled from the Ruffian thro' those Fields: and that the Path she took was thus miraculously mark'd out, as a Trophy of her Purity and Innocence, to be seen in future Ages, and to be distinguished by the Name of *Kinneburga's* Way.

This legend is shown among the piers and capitals of the Norman crossing, with the variation that, as she was being chased, the contents of her basket spilled out and turned into bushes, which trapped the men in their branches.

Murray's Handbook for ... Rutland in the nineteenth century, instead of the 'barren ground' theme − the path trodden by the saint being miraculously imprinted on the land − gives a different origin legend for 'Lady Coneyborough's Way', saying that 'the road unrolled itself before her as she fled' (compare 'leading the tide' at MORPETH, Northumberland).

Already by the mid eighteenth century, the name 'Lady Conyburrow' − presumably the approximation of a difficult name to words that were familiar, 'coney' (rabbit) and 'burrow' − had evolved even further from 'Cyneburg', and a supernatural twist had been given to the story. William Stukeley noted in his diary:

> 10 Sept., 1737 I went to Castor ... They have still a memorial at Castor of S. Kyniburga, whom the vulgar call Lady Ketilborough, and of her coming in a coach and six, and riding over the field along the Roman road, some few nights before Michaelmas.

Stukeley refers later to the abbess and her nuns as having been murdered by the Danes. He interprets the tradition of Lady Ketilborough and her phantom coach as the 'remains' or fading memory of her festival celebrated here, until the abbot of Peterborough removed her relics, on 15 September, the anniversary of her death.

Helpston

Woodcroft Manor, near Helpston, in the Soke of Peterborough, was where Dr Michael Hudson, one of King Charles I's chaplains, met an untimely end. He had assembled a band of yeomen to protect the surrounding area from plundering Roundheads in Cromwell's army.

At first he was successful, but at length he met with an overwhelming force and fell back on Woodcroft Manor, and was besieged there. The Roundheads broke through, slaughtering his small force until he found himself the only survivor. Though he offered to surrender, the Roundheads refused and six of them forced him over the parapet of the roof. As he clung to the parapet, a soldier cut off his fingers and he fell into the moat. He managed to struggle to the bank, but there was dispatched by the pikes of his enemies. The manor was said by Christina Hole, writing in the 1940s, to be still haunted by the sound of clashing steel and cries of 'Mercy!' and 'Quarter!'

Holywell

Just beyond Holywell, on the edge of the River Ouse, stands the Ferry Boat Inn, according to Peter Underwood, writing in 1971, 'haunted, for perhaps nine hundred years, by the ghost of Juliet'. She was said to be a young girl who deeply loved a rough local woodcutter named Tom Zoul. He preferred the company of his workmates, and she finally hanged herself for unrequited love from a willow tree on the banks of the river. As a suicide, she could not be laid in consecrated ground, so was buried on the riverbank, her grave marked by a plain slab of grey stone. The Ferry Boat Inn was later built on the site of Juliet's 'gravestone', still to be seen in the floor of the bar.

Local tradition says that Juliet died on 17 March, and Underwood reports that for many years people have gathered at the inn on that day to watch for Juliet's ghost, said to rise from the flagstone and drift out of the inn towards the riverbank where she died.

In 1955, the Cambridge Psychical Research Society sent a team of investigators, but their instruments showed no abnormality. The landlord told Underwood in 1965 of a dog that would not go near the 'gravestone' (a not uncommon phenomenon in old churchyards), adding, 'of course the local women don't come near the inn on March 17th.'

A rather different version of the story was given to Joan Forman in the 1970s or earlier by a local man who said he remembered his grandparents speaking of it and even then the story was old.

According to this version, a lady in white walks into the pub and points to a certain flagstone on the floor of the bar. She was assumed locally to be pointing at the stone because it concealed treasure. Joan Forman says that it was 'a psychical research society' (possibly the Cambridge team of 1955) who claimed to have identified the protagonists in the story as Juliet Tewsley and Thomas Zowl (for Underwood's Tom Zoul).

Guy Lyon Playfair in *The Haunted Pub Guide* (1985) adds that, in the past, the inn obtained a special licence to stay open until midnight (the witching hour) on 17 March in the hope that Juliet would appear, but that the last person to have claimed a sighting of her died in the 1960s.

Peterborough

The earliest recorded manifestation in England of the Wild Hunt took place at Peterborough, in connection with the arrival of a new abbot, Henry of Poitou, who 'did nothing good there and left nothing good there'. These are the words of the monk who kept up the chronicle of events now known as the *Anglo-Saxon Chronicle* at Peterborough Abbey. Under the year 1127 he wrote:

> Let it not be thought remarkable, when we tell the truth, because it was fully known over all the country, that as soon as he came there ... then soon afterwards many people saw and heard many hunters hunting. The hunters were black and big and loathsome, and their hounds all black and wide-eyed and loathsome, and they rode on black horses and black goats. This was seen in the very deer-park in the town of Peterborough, and in all the woods that there were between this town and Stamford, and the monks heard the horns blow that they were blowing at night. Trustworthy people noticed them at night, and said that it seemed to them there might well be about twenty or thirty hornblowers. This was seen and heard from the time he came there all Lent up to Easter.

Similar packs of spectral hounds are known all over England. They go under various names: in Devon, the Yeth (Heath) or Wisht Hounds; in Cornwall, Dando and his Dogs. The 'wide-eyed' Peterborough hounds also sound very much like the Norfolk Shuck (*see* SHERINGHAM, Norfolk). Often such packs are not seen, but heard passing overhead at night during bad weather, like, in the North, the Gabble Ratchets or Gabriel Hounds (*see* HAMMERWICH, Staffordshire).

The apparition of huntsmen riding black horses and accompanied by black hounds was said to have been witnessed in many places in Western Europe, and was mostly encountered in forests and woods, its coming heralded by thunder and the noise of wind in the trees. In 1803, John Leyden characterized it as '*invisible* hunting':

> . . . heard at midnight, or at noon,
> Beginning faint, but rising still more loud
> And nearer, voice [*sic*] of hunters, and of hounds,
> And horns hoarse-winded, blowing far and keen . . .

The name Wild Hunt is now often applied by folklorists to other noisy, invisible, aerial phenomena, such as the Gabriel Hounds and the Seven Whistlers (*see* MARAZION, Cornwall), which may or may not have been originally connected: possibly, in the course of time, different themes have become merged.

A spectral procession, not always a hunting party, and usually seen on the ground, was several times reported in the Middle Ages. Walter Map, writing *c.*1190, speaks of 'nocturnal companies' known as *familia Herlethingus*, 'the household of Herlethingus', and led by King Herla, an ancient British king. Last seen in the marches of Wales in 1154 about noonday, when the countryside was raised against them, they rose into the air and vanished. 'Herlethingus' is one of several names associated with this procession from the eleventh century: *familia Herlechini, maisniee Helequin, Hurlewaynis kynne*, all meaning the household of some being possibly related to Harlequin, who first appeared on the Paris stage towards the end of the sixteenth century.

When a Norman parish priest named Walkelin encountered them one moonlit night in 1092, says Ordericus Vitalis (1075–1143), they appeared as a great crowd, their heads burdened with sheep and bundles of clothes like robbers, accompanied by an army 'in which no colour was visible, but only blackness and fiery flames', all mounted on great war-horses and fully armed. Walkelin said to himself, 'Doubtless these are Herlechin's people.' He had often heard of them, but never seen them.

Walkelin saw in the procession neighbours who had lately died, and among the *familia Herlethingus* 'many persons were seen alive who were known to have died'. This is no doubt why the Hunt is associated with midnight and midwinter – Walkelin saw it in early January – the times when the dead in European tradition are most active.

The presence of the dead in these processions link them to an early 'Fairy Rade', or riding of fairies. In *Sir Orfeo*, a medieval version of the classical story of Orpheus and Eurydice, Orfeo, after the loss of his wife, retires to a wilderness, where:

> He might se him bisides
> (Oft in hot vnder-tides)
> The king o fairy with his rout
> Com to hunt him al about
> With dim cri and bloweing,
> & houndes also with hi*m* berking . . .

Among them on that hot afternoon (vnder-tides) is Heurodis, his dead wife.

Other long-dead kings than Herla were also said to lead the Hunt. One of these was King Arthur. In France, the name *la Chasse Artu*, 'Arthur's Hunt', goes back to the early thirteenth century; in the nineteenth, his hunting horns sounded above the wind on moors around Castle-an-Dinas, Cornwall. In Germany and France, it was often Charlemagne (742–814). Other historical figures included Edric Wilde, lord of the manor of Lydbury North, Shropshire, in the eleventh century.

In north-west Europe, the Hunt was called by names such as *Woedende Jager* and *Odinsjagt*, its leader Woden (Odin), the Germanic god of war, who received slain warriors in Valhalla. As the gatherer-in of pagan (therefore unredeemed) souls, he became a target for the Church and in the Middle Ages was equated with the Devil, consequently also said to lead the Hunt. Thomas Heywood, in his *Hierarchie of the Blessed Angells* (1635), records a curious tradition that the Devil's minions, necromancers, could likewise turn themselves into aerial huntsmen.

The Hunt was exploited before and after the Reformation to frighten congregations. It pursues and punishes the wicked: Walkelin saw a man tortured by demons and women riding on saddles stuck with red-hot nails. In nineteenth-century Devon, tradition said that on the stormy night in 1677 when Sir Richard Capel of BUCKFASTLEIGH died, the Wild Hunt raged around the house waiting for his soul.

Blasphemy and Sabbath-breaking are common sins. In Denmark, King Valdemar rides out every night between Burre and Gurre Castles, Zealand, having said Our Lord might keep his Heaven so long as he was able to hunt. Dando, a parson of St Germans, Cornwall, was so passionately fond of hunting that he rode to hounds even on Sundays. One Sunday they were joined by a stranger on a fiery horse. Afterwards, as this stranger took a share of the game, Dando cried, 'You shan't have it! I'll go to hell for it rather than you shall get it.' 'So you shall,' replied the other and bore Dando off on his horse, the hounds behind them. Plunging into the Lynher, they went down amid fire and steam, but, says Robert Hunt in 1865, Dando and his Dogs can still be heard pelting past in full cry early on Sunday mornings.

Upwood

Upwood House was once lived in by the Hussey family. Charles Tebbutt in *Huntingdonshire Folklore* (1984) reports that, in 1757, the occupants were Thomas Hussey and his daughter Maria Ann. She wanted to marry Captain Richard Bickerton, but he had no money, so her father refused his consent.

Then one night, when Thomas Hussey had had to go to London, Maria woke from sleep to see her father pulling aside the curtains of her bed and smiling down at her. Her maid, who was sleeping in the room with her, also saw him. The next day, a horseman brought the news from London that her father had died and that his last words were: 'Tell my daughter that I withdraw my opposition to her marriage.'

Maria duly married Captain Bickerton, who died in 1792. His career had prospered: he was created a baronet in 1778, and was Member of Parliament for Rochester and Port Admiral of Plymouth.

Kent

Blue Bell Hill

A common feature in twentieth-century folklore is the phantom hitchhiker, victim of a tragic road accident, and so is the ghost which horrifies a driver by apparently throwing itself under his wheels. Both can be found in the series of stories linked to Blue Bell Hill, a steep stretch of road between Maidstone and Chatham, which has been much discussed in the local and national press, on TV, and on the Internet.

The first printed reference is an article in *The (Maidstone) Gazette* of 10 September 1968, based on research by Tom Harber, a local man interested in the paranormal; the apparition of an unknown girl is said to have repeatedly hitched a lift by the Lower Bell pub at the foot of the hill to go into the centre of Maidstone, where she vanished from the still-moving car. At this stage, Harber told the reporter he had failed to find any first-hand witnesses, though he had gathered about thirty second-hand accounts. Several years later, however, he assured the researcher Michael Goss that he had interviewed twelve people who claimed they themselves had given the ghost a lift, though he did not reveal their identities. This always occurred around 11 p.m., and during the ride the girl would talk excitedly about her forthcoming wedding, due next day. One informant said this had happened to him in 1966; the girl mentioned her home address in Maidstone, and when he went there to check up, alarmed at her disappearance, he learned that she had been killed in a road accident exactly one year before. In some cases, however, the girl stopped a car going the other way, towards Chatham, and spoke of having just been in an accident. None of these witnesses came forward publicly, though the press still showed sporadic interest in the affair.

At midnight on 13 July 1974, a Mr Maurice Goodenough came into Rochester police station to report a most alarming incident. While driving up Blue Bell Hill, his car seemed to strike a little girl of about ten who appeared suddenly in the middle of the road; he halted, carried her to the verge, covered her with a rug, and drove off to fetch help. The police accompanied him back to the scene, but the child had vanished (though the rug was still there); there were no traces of blood either on the road or on the car. Later, a police spokesman told journalists the incident was the latest in a series of strange events on Blue Bell Hill, and described some reported encounters with the hitchhiking ghost. Despite the differences in the physical appearance and behaviour between the child ghost and the hitchhiking ghost, local tradition usually regards them as identical; it is now generally said that the girl of Blue Bell Hill may *either* hitch a lift *or* deliberately step into the road and let herself be run over.

These apparitions are supposedly the consequence of a crash on 19 November 1965, when three out of four young women travelling in the same car were killed as it skidded on Blue Bell Hill; one was due to be married next day, while another was to be bridesmaid. Rather surprisingly, it is the bridesmaid, not the bride, who is usually said to be the ghost.

The story is now well established in Kent lore, being periodically reinforced by further sightings; in the course of November 1992, for instance, the local paper *Kent Today* reported several incidents where motorists had recently thought they had run over a young woman who appeared out of nowhere. A teenage driver described the experience:

> She ran in front of the car. She stopped and looked at me. There was no expression on her face. Then I hit her, and it was as if the ground moved apart and she went under the car. I thought I had killed her, because it was not as if she was see-through or anything. She was solid – as real as you are.

Just as in 1974, when the horrified drivers alerted the police, there was no corpse to be seen, and no material trace of any impact.

Faversham

According to traditions collected late in the twentieth century, an old inn called the Shipwright's Arms, in a lonely spot among the marshes, is haunted by the ghost of an old sailor, wearing a reefer jacket and peaked cap, and smelling strongly of rum and tobacco. The story, as recently summarized by Richard Jones, is that his ship ran aground and sank in the Swale one night in the nineteenth century; he managed to get ashore and stumbled across the mudflats to the inn, where he beat upon the door. But the owner, frightened to open his door so late, shouted at him to go away. Next morning the sailor was found dead on the doorstep. His ghost is said to appear at the foot of people's beds, glaring at them – or even, according to the son of a former landlord, trying to get into one's bed.

Goodwin Sands

This treacherous and ever-shifting sandbank some five miles (8 km) off the coast at Deal has caused many shipwrecks over the years, and features in many guides to ghost lore as the setting for periodic appearances of Britain's most notorious phantom ship, the *Lady Lovibund* (or *Luvibund*), supposedly to be seen once every fifty years on 13 February.

The tragic tale alleges that this was a three-masted schooner sailing for Portugal under its captain Simon Reed (or Simon Peel), who brought his newly wedded bride Annette on board, together with some friends. Unknown to him, John Rivers, who was the first mate (or the helmsman), was crazed with jealousy, for he too was in love with Annette. As the schooner neared the Sands, the wedding party were celebrating below deck, unaware that Rivers had deliberately changed course so as to run the ship aground; it sank, and all on board were drowned. In some versions, Rivers kills Reed with a blow to the head before steering to disaster. It is alleged that fifty years later, on the exact anniversary, the spectral *Lady Lovibund* was seen re-enacting its doom, and that this happens every fifty years.

The earliest version of this story so far traced was printed in the *Daily Chronicle* in February 1924; it claimed that the disaster occurred on 13 February 1724. However, a book about the Goodwin Sands by George Goldsmith-Carter, published in 1953, gives the year as 1748, and claims that the spectral ship had been sighted on 13 February in 1798, 1848, 1898, and 1948. Consequently, journalists and others were on the lookout for a further sighting in 1998, but were disappointed – nothing whatever was seen.

After the 1998 fiasco, one of the present authors appealed for documentary evidence for the existence of a *Lady Lovibund*, for the year of its wrecking, and for contemporary reports of the alleged phantom sightings. So far, none has appeared. It seems virtually certain that the story was concocted by the *Daily Chronicle* in 1924, exploiting the emotive possibilities of '13 February' as both an unlucky date and the eve of St Valentine's Day, and setting the tragedy precisely 200 years previously. What caused Goldsmith-Carter to alter the year to 1748 is not known.

Marden

In 1901, the Kentish writer Sir Charles Igglesden noted a tragic and picturesque tale of haunting on the Hawkhurst road at Marden. It seems that one Christmas Eve towards the end of the eighteenth century, a notorious highwayman named Gilbert stopped a coach in which an elderly man and his daughter were riding, and ordered them out onto the road at this spot. The girl had just got out when the horses bolted, carrying off the father and the coachman, and leaving the girl and the highwayman alone together.

As soon as the men could bring the horses under control, they returned as fast as they could to rescue the girl, but there was no sign of her; instead, they found Gilbert bleeding to death from a wound in his side. He just managed to explain that the girl had recognized him because he had murdered her brother in a previous ambush; she had produced a dagger and stabbed him. She had then run off. She was found next day hiding behind a tree some miles away, raving mad.

The highwayman was thought to be buried by the roadside at the scene of the crime. In the nineteenth century, local people shunned the spot, saying that every Christmas Eve a silent ghostly re-enactment of the deadly struggle could be seen, but by 1900 the story was almost forgotten.

Pluckley

It is a curious trait in twentieth-century attitudes that tales of haunting can be either a cause of fear or, very frequently, a matter of pride for the people in the area concerned. It is rarely possible to ascertain the age of such stories, yet they circulate vigorously in the press, in guidebooks, and of course orally. And where there is one, there are likely to be more, for publicity generates imitation.

Writing in 1983, Alan Bignell lists a numerous and richly varied company of ghosts reputedly seen in and around Pluckley in past generations, giving it the reputation of 'the most haunted village in England' – even though he adds that 'it becomes more and more difficult to find anyone who will admit to having seen or heard of any of them.' Several are linked to the Dering family, landowners in this area for many generations, but this need not mean that the tales themselves are old. There is a Red Lady, wearing a fifteenth-century red gown, who wanders round the family chapel in St Nicholas' church and also in the churchyard. She is said to be searching for the grave of her dead baby, and a more recent writer (Richard Jones, in 2001) offers the plausible theory that the baby died at birth, which would mean that it was never baptized, and so had to be laid in an unmarked grave, not in the family vault. Returning to Bignell's list, we note that the site of the Dering home (burnt down in 1950) is haunted by a White Lady holding a single red rose; she also sometimes appears in the churchyard. She too is said to be the wife of a former Dering, who died young, to the despair of her husband; hoping to preserve her beauty, he had her buried in the family vault in four airtight coffins, three of lead and one of oak, placed one inside the other, with a red rose on her breast. Mysterious lights, hammering sounds, and wailing voices have also been reported as coming from the Dering chapel.

In the 1970s, a group of psychic researchers were allowed to spend a night in the vault; next morning they told the vicar that their vigil had been boringly uneventful. 'We were quite glad that your dog came to join us from time to time.' 'Actually,' said the vicar, 'I don't have a dog.'

The Black Horse Inn has occasionally suffered, it is said, from mild poltergeist pranks; the road outside it is reputed haunted – by a schoolmaster who hanged himself, say some. Outside a house called Rose Court, one can hear a dog (or dogs) barking and a woman's voice calling; in the grounds of another house, Greystones, the ghost of a monk has been seen. Some tellers choose to link these two traditions, telling how a Tudor monk at Greystones fell in love with a woman at Rose Court, who had a pet lapdog; she was already the mistress of one of the Derings, so, being unable to follow her true love, she poisoned herself, and the monk soon died of a broken heart.

There is also a phantom soldier, a ghostly miller, an old tramp, an old gypsy woman who accidentally burnt herself to death when her pipe set light to the haystack where she was sleeping, and a young farmer at Elvery Farm (now a hotel) who is said to have killed himself in the 1850s because his wife had died and his farming was a failure. And there is a highwayman who haunts the crossroads aptly named Fright Corner. When alive, he used to hide inside a hollow oak there, to ambush passing travellers, till one day someone who had heard of his trick drew his sword *before* reaching the tree and drove it right through its thin shell. The highwayman perished, skewered inside his tree.

Rainham

The headless revenant who carries his head under his arm is a cliché of literary ghost stories, but is less common than one might expect in folk traditions, and generally remains unexplained; at Rainham in the late twentieth century, however, Alan Bignell found a tale which accounts logically for this feature. In Tudor times a house in Rainham known as Bloor Place (which no longer exists) was the home of a certain Christopher Bloor, a notorious seducer of local women. One night as he was driving home along Bloor Lane, his coach was attacked by a crowd of local men whose wives and daughters he had disgraced, who overpowered the coachman and footman, and then dragged Bloor out of the vehicle and cut off his head. They stuck the head on a pole outside Rainham church and sent the coach with the headless corpse in it back to Bloor Place. Ever since then, it is said, a phantom coach can occasionally be seen at midnight driving down the lane from the church to Bloor Place.

The horses, the coachman, and the footman are all headless; so is Christopher Bloor, sitting inside the coach, but he has retrieved his head from the churchyard, and is holding it under his arm.

Lancashire

Bardsea

In most parts of northern England, 'dobbie', 'dobby', or 'dobie' is a name for a helpful household elf or goblin. In James Bowker's *Goblin Tales of Lancashire* (1883), however, there is an account of a sinister spectre known as the White Dobbie, which was said to appear on stormy nights on the coastal road from Bardsea to Rampside. It looked like a gaunt, weary pilgrim, with sorrowful face and feverish eyes, and would hurry along the road without ever speaking to anyone; ahead of it ran 'a ghastly-looking, scraggy white hare with bloodshot eyes'. The sight of this hare would terrify any dog, and cause it to flee, howling.

One night, after this haunting had continued for many years, the bell-ringer and sexton of Bardsea church was in the ringing-chamber of the belfry, tolling the passing bell to announce a death that had just occurred. Suddenly, though the church door was shut, she saw the white hare leaping about in the belfry, and heard the White Dobbie whisper, 'Who for this time?' The spectre stood beside her as she rang, while the hare leapt into the dobbie's pocket but went on staring at her from there. Eventually two men entered the church, causing the unearthly beings to vanish, but from then on the dobbie and the hare regularly appeared in the belfry whenever the passing bell was rung after dark, as well as con-tinuing to haunt the coast road. The local theory, as reported by Bowker, was that both were ghosts, the dobbie being doomed to wander for the sin of murder, while his victim had become the hare; in other parts of the country, however, dobbies and dobies were differently explained.

Clitheroe

Bungerley bridge, spanning the River Ribble near Clitheroe, replaces an old ford with stepping stones, the setting for a legend.

In their *Lancashire Folk-Lore*, compiled in the 1860s, John Harland and T. T. Wilkinson mention it twice. The first time, they say the place is haunted by a 'malevolent sprite' who assumes many forms:

> He is not known by any particular designation, nor are there any traditions to account for his first appearance; but at least *one* life every *seven* years is required to appease the anger of the spirit of the Ribble at this place.

In their second passage, the malevolent spirit has changed sex and acquired a name, 'Peg (or Peggy) of the Well' (i.e. a well in the grounds of Waddow Hall, beside the river). She was held responsible not only for drownings but for any other fatal accidents in the vicinity. A focus for the legend was a battered headless statue which stood (and still stands) beside Peggy's Well. They write of it:

> There is a mutilated stone figure by the well, which has been the subject of many strange tales and apprehensions. It was placed there when turned out of the house at Waddow, to allay the terrors of the domestics, who durst not continue under the same roof with this mis-shapen figure. It was then broken, either by accident or from design, and the head, some time ago, as is understood, was in one of the attic chambers at Waddow. Who Peggy of the Well was, tradition does not inform us.

Some years later, another Victorian collector, William Henderson, was told that Peg was the ghost of a servant girl at Waddow Hall. One wintry night she was sent out to draw water from the well, or (in other versions) from the river itself; she slipped on the ice and broke her neck (or fell in the river and drowned). She had initially refused to go, saying she was afraid of falling, but her mistress just said, 'Get along with you! And may you break your neck indeed!' From then on, every accident, sickness or other misfortune at Waddow Hall, and indeed throughout the district, was blamed on Peggy's ghost. This is now the standard version of the story.

As for the statue itself, Harland and Wilkinson were told that it was originally a Catholic image of some saint, brought to Waddow Hall after the Reformation but regarded by later owners with 'distrust and aversion' and so banished to the well. They were also given an amusing account of how it lost its head. At one time the Hall belonged to a Mrs Starkie, who had a great admiration for

Puritan preachers – a detail which would point to the seventeenth century. She had sent for a preacher to exorcize her ten-year-old son who was thought to be either possessed by a demon or tormented by Peggy. The night was stormy, and the preacher had not arrived. She sent servants to look for him, fearing he might have fallen in the river, as indeed he had:

> In a few minutes two trusty men-servants returned, panting under the huge weight of the dripping parson. He told his tale. 'Tis Peg', she suddenly exclaimed, 'at her old tricks! This way, all!' She hurried from the apartment, rushed into the garden, where Peggy stood quiet enough near a spring, and with one blow of an axe, which she had seized in her passage, severed Peggy's head from her body.

By the end of the nineteenth century, further elaborations were being reported. The Yorkshire folklorist Thomas Parkinson, writing in 1889, said it was believed that 'Peg O' Nell' claimed a life on 'Peg's Night' every seven years (he does not say what date this is), and that people would deliberately drown an animal to placate her, otherwise some human being would surely die in the river before morning. He tells of a young man who arrived at dusk and insisted on crossing the ford, even though the locals warned him that this was the fateful night, and that no animal had yet been drowned; a sudden rush of water swept his horse downstream, and both horse and rider perished.

Crank

Writing in 1982, Terence Whitaker published the account of the ghost of a large, white, lop-eared rabbit which used to haunt the area around Crank and Rainford in the days before the latter became a railway junction. It was said to jump out at people walking the roads at night, and hop along beside them; to see it was bad luck, for it meant trouble or even death. Most ghost animals have no tale to explain their presence, but in this case Whitaker was told a quite elaborate one.

According to this, in Stuart times an old woman who lived in the village of Crank was regarded with awe because of her knowledge of herbs and also, it was alleged, of the black arts. She had a grand-daughter called Jennie, and Jennie had a pet white rabbit. There was also a man called Pullen who had come to the old woman for a remedy for some wasting disease he suffered from, but, when it proved useless, Pullen had become convinced that she was in fact a witch who was harming, not helping, him. Together with a ruffian named Dick Piers, he broke into the old woman's cottage one night and stabbed her in the arm as she slept, thinking that drawing blood would break her magic power. They had blacked their faces as disguise. Jennie, hearing her grandmother's screams, went to help her, with her rabbit in her arms, but then panicked and ran from the house and across the hill, pursued by Pullen and Piers. They lost track of Jennie, but near the crest of the hill the rabbit ran out in front of them from a hedge, and they kicked it to death. Next day, Jennie was found 'cold and stiff, her feet torn and her head cut where she had fallen'. The grandmother recovered, but left the village.

Then the rabbit's ghost began to manifest itself. It showed itself first to Piers, troubling his conscience so much that he wrote a confession and then killed himself by jumping into a quarry. Then Pullen saw it too, one night when he was passing the old woman's abandoned cottage; terrified, he fled towards his home, but it kept up with him and drove him out into the open fields where he was found next day, suffering from exhaustion and exposure. He died a few days later.

Some of Whitaker's informants insisted that, railway or no railway, the white rabbit was still occasionally seen on dark nights, and always meant misfortune. The story as he heard it is rather modern in sentiment and suffers from a central implausibility – would a girl going to her grandmother's help in the middle of the night bring her pet rabbit? Yet one can guess at traces of an underlying older and authentically folkloric plot, since Jennie's death follows so quickly after that of the rabbit: maybe the rabbit originally *was* Jennie, just as so many witches in local legends take the form of hares, and are pursued and wounded in that form.

See also THETFORD, Norfolk.

Dilworth

In the village of Dilworth, on the slope of Longridge Fell, a steep-sided lane leads to what is known either as Written Stone Farm or Rafe Radcliffe's Farm. There, in the bank at the entrance to the farmyard, lies a massive stone, nine feet (3 m) long, two feet wide, and a foot thick, inscribed:

> Rauffe: Radcliffe: laid: this:
> stone: to lye: for: ever A.D. 1655:

The real reason for its presence has long been forgotten, but a flourishing legend has grown up around it. Local writers of the nineteenth and twentieth centuries all agree that it was set there to pin down an especially troublesome boggart, which was a ghost rather than a household spirit. The account by John Harland and T. T. Wilkinson in 1873 states:

> Tradition declares this spot to have been the scene of a cruel and barbarous murder, and it is stated that this stone was put down in order to appease the restless spirit of the deceased, which played its nightly gambols long after the body had been 'hearsed in earth'. A story is told of one of the former occupants of Written Stone Farm, who, thinking that the stone would make a capital 'buttery stone', removed it into the house and applied it to that use. The result was, that the indignant or liberated spirit would never suffer his family to rest. Whatever pots, pans, kettles or articles of crockery were placed on the stone, were tilted over, their contents spilled, and the vessels themselves kept up a clatter-ing dance the livelong night, at the beck of the unseen spirit.

The stone was of course replaced. Twentieth-century writers such as Jessica Lofthouse, Terence Whitaker and Ken Howarth add details that show that the story has developed further traditional motifs. It is said, for instance, that removing the stone was extremely difficult. No one horse could shift it, nor two, nor even four; a team of six had to be harnessed to haul it out of the ground and drag it from the gate to the dairy – yet on the return journey the stone was easily drawn by a single horse. Once it was replaced, a holly hedge was planted along the lane for greater security, to bind the boggart so long as there are green leaves on the tree.

Radcliffe Tower

The medieval Radcliffe Tower, now in ruins, was once the seat of the powerful Radcliffe family and the scene of a particularly gruesome murder – if, that is, one can trust the pen of John Roby, whose *Lancashire Traditions* of 1829 consists of leisurely and highly coloured retellings of local stories, in which a core of traditional material lies almost hidden by the author's sentimentality. In the present instance, the core is an old ballad entitled 'The Lady Isabella's Tragedy', from which he quotes, but there is nothing to show why he localized it at Radcliffe Tower and changed the heroine's name to Ellen. However, the popularity of his book ensured that this is the version remembered nowadays.

Fair Ellen, said Roby, was the daughter of Richard Radcliffe, much loved by her father but hated by her jealous stepmother. The latter conspired with the master cook at the Tower to murder Ellen, sending the girl herself to him with the message that it was time to kill and cook a 'fair and milk-white doe', the loveliest in the park. The cook seized Ellen and slaughtered her, despite the protestations of the kitchen scullion, baking her flesh in a pie and threatening to murder the boy, too, if he revealed the crime. That evening Ellen's father returned from hunting, and, when he asked where his daughter was, the stepmother said she had gone into a convent. In the words of the ballad:

> O then bespake the scullion-boye,
> > With a loud voice so hye:
> If now you will your daughter see,
> > My lord, cut up that pye,
>
> Wherein her fleshe is minced small,
> > And parched with the fire;
> All caused by her step-mother,
> > Who did her death desire.

The wicked stepmother was condemned to be burnt, and the cook to stand in boiling lead, while the simple scullion-boy was made heir to the lord's land.

There is no historical justification for attaching this tale to the Radcliffe family, for though it is true that at one point the direct line became extinct and the estates were settled on a more remote relative, Lord Fitzwalter Radcliffe, the latter was certainly no scullion boy. Nevertheless, Roby's tale has often been repeated; a bloodstain on the floor of one of the rooms of the Tower was said to mark the murder, and a Black Dog which haunts the ruins is sometimes said to be Ellen's ghost. Even nowadays the tale is remembered; in the 1990s, the 'dinner lady' of Radcliffe High School told the local author Ken Howarth:

> Fair Ellen was baked in a pie at the Old Tower and they say there are secret passages under Radcliffe. They say that one of the passages goes right across Radcliffe and under the senior school and when we serve up meat pie for school dinners they say Fair Ellen comes, 'cos everything goes wrong that day ... When we have meat-pie switches go off, cookers get switched off, boilers, different things like that, a pan fell from underneath a shelf for no reason at all.

Samlesbury

In this village, midway between Preston and Blackburn, stands a fine though much-restored timber-framed mansion, the High Hall, parts of which date from the fifteenth century. The ghost which is said to haunt it is one of the many British White Ladies having a historical context. In the reign of Elizabeth I (1558–1603), this mansion was the seat of Sir John Southworth, the sheriff of Lancashire, who died in 1591. Although a loyal servant of the Crown, he was in his personal convictions equally loyal to the Roman Catholic faith, and suffered heavy fines and even imprisonment as a recusant.

According to a tradition recorded by the folklorists John Harland and T. T. Wilkinson, one of his daughters, named Dorothy, fell in love with a knight whose parents were Protestants; when the young couple applied to Sir John for permission to marry, he declared that 'No daughter of his should ever be united to the son of a family which had deserted its ancestral faith', and he forbade the youth his presence for ever.

The lovers continued to meet in secret, however, on the wooded banks of the Ribble, and finally decided to elope. They fixed on a day and place to meet, but were unfortunately overheard by one of Dorothy's brothers. On the evening that the knight came with two friends to fetch his beloved, her brother and his servants ambushed and killed the men, and dragged Dorothy back into the Hall. She was sent to a convent in France, where she went mad with grief; the three murdered men were secretly buried in the precincts of the chapel at the Hall.

Harland and Wilkinson in their *Lancashire Legends* (1882) say that, some years before they were gathering their material in the 1860s, three human skeletons had been found near the walls of Samlesbury Hall, which popular opinion connected with the tradition:

> The legend also states that on certain clear, still evenings a lady in white can be seen passing along the gallery and the corridors, and then from the Hall into the grounds: that she there meets a hand-some knight who receives her on his bended knees, and he then accompanies her along the walks. On arriving at a certain spot, most probably the lover's grave, both the phantoms stand still, and, as they seem to utter soft wailings of despair, they embrace each other, and then their forms rise slowly from the earth and melt away into the clear blue of the surrounding sky.

If three skeletons really were discovered, it presumably explains why tradition says the young knight had two companions, who, from a narrative point of view, are superfluous to the tale.

Timberbottom Farm (Turton Towers)

A pair of damaged skulls used to be displayed in a glass case in the fifteenth-century manor house of Turton Towers (now a museum), but they are currently kept locked away in a storeroom. They are often referred to in guidebooks as the Timberbottom Skulls, from the name of a nearby farm where they were kept for many years on the mantelpiece of the main room. From there they were transferred to Bradshaw Hall when Timberbottom Farm was demolished in 1939, and thence to Turton Towers in 1949. They used to be kept – and perhaps still are – upon a large family Bible, a method said to have been adopted by the farm tenants on the advice of Colonel

Hardcastle, a late nineteenth-century owner of Bradshaw Hall, to prevent ghostly disturbances.

The early history of these relics is unknown, the various stories about them showing considerable disagreement. Harland and Wilkinson offer no theory as to origin, but describe their supposed behaviour, on the basis of tales told them in the 1860s:

> They are said to have been buried many times in the graveyard at Bradshaw Chapel, but they have always had to be exhumed and brought back to the farmhouse. They have even been thrown into the adjacent river, but to no purpose for they had to be fished up and restored to their old quarters before the ghosts of their owners could once more rest in peace.

According to one account gathered by Jessica Lofthouse in 1976, the river was where they originally came from; they were said to have been found in the water in 1751, and to be the remains of two robbers beheaded by servants when they got into the farm in 1680. A different explanation given to her was that a daughter of the upper-class Bradshaw family fell in love with a farm labourer at Timberbottom; her brother, outraged by this disgrace, killed the man, and the girl died of grief soon afterwards; violent ghostly disturbances persisted until the skulls of both lovers were recovered from their graves and reunited, never to be separated again. Or again it may be said, as John Harris was told in the 1960s, that they are those of a farmer and his wife; he killed her, then committed suicide.

Despite the inconsistency of the explanatory narratives and the lack of early evidence, the fame of the skulls is still considerable.

Walton-le-Dale

According to a story collected by the folklorist James Bowker in the 1880s, there was once a young vicar in this village whose reclusive habits and scholarly tastes caused his parishioners to suspect him of dabbling in the Black Arts. He struck up a friendship with 'Owd Abrum', the village herb-doctor and astrologer. One day he told Abrum that he was curious to know which of his parishioners would die in the coming year, and had read that the way to find out was to keep watch in the church porch at midnight on Christmas Eve, when their wraiths would appear. Abrum said he would come too, so, arming themselves with protective leaves of vervain, bay, holly, and mountain ash, the two men began their vigil. Before long, they saw 'a procession wending its way towards the porch; it consisted of a stream of figures wrapped up in grave-clothes, gleaming white in the dim light'. And one, which paused long enough to be clearly seen, had the vicar's own form. He fainted at the sight. He left the parish soon afterwards, and died within a year of a fever caught while ministering to the sick. The herb-doctor refused ever to repeat the experiment.

One might be tempted to wonder whether this legend was connected with the fact that it was at Walton-le-Dale that Edward Kelley, the medium who worked with the famous sixteenth-century astrologer and magician Dr John Dee, is alleged to have experimented with necromancy (at some time prior to meeting Dee in 1582) in order to ascertain when a certain person would die. According to John Weever, writing in 1631, Kelley and an associate called Paul Waring first raised a demon in a park in order to learn 'the manner and time of the death of a Noble young Gentleman, then in Wardship', and then went to the churchyard to dig up the newly buried corpse of a pauper, 'whom by their incantations, they made him (or rather some evil Spirit through his Organs) to speak, who delivered strange Predictions concerning the said Gentleman'. A slightly later version, in Meric Casaubon's *True and Faithful Relation of what Passed ... between John Dee and Some Spirits* (1659), sets the event in 1560, asserts that Dee had been present too, and says the corpse raised was that of a wealthy man whom they wished to question about money he had hidden in his lifetime.

The anecdote was certainly notorious. However, folklore collections in the nineteenth and twentieth century contain so many references from different parts of Britain to watching in church porches in order to see wraiths that there is no real need to make the connection. Various dates are mentioned, the most common being St Mark's Eve (the night of 24/25 April).

Leicestershire

Bradgate House (Hall)

On the south-east border of Charnwood Forest, near Newtown Lindford, is Bradgate Park, and the ruins of the brick mansion built c.1490–1505 by Thomas Grey, Marquis of Dorset.

It is chiefly remembered as the birthplace of Lady Jane Grey, the 'Nine Days' Queen', executed on 12 February 1554 in the Tower of London. William Kelly, in his *Royal Progresses* (1884), calls Bradgate 'an ever-enduring place of pilgrimage' and notes visits by various members of the royal family to all those spots which tradition particularly connected with her, among them the terraces where she and Lord Guildford Dudley were said to have spent much of their time before their marriage.

In the park itself, the party accompanying the Prince of Wales (later Edward VII), there in January 1882 for the shooting, were shown some fine old oaks whose tops 'were said to have been severed when Lady Jane Grey was beheaded in the Tower, because, said the foresters, a "sweet oak of the forest had fallen."' A contributor to *Folk-Lore*, when driving round Charnwood in the spring of 1893, was likewise told by a driver hired from Loughborough that the old oaks 'lost their tops' when Lady Jane Grey was beheaded.

Although Lady Jane Grey famously haunts the White Tower (*see* THE TOWER, London) on the anniversary of her execution, she is said also to appear in Bradgate Park, riding in a phantom coach, every New Year's Eve. According to others, she appears on Christmas Eve, and the coach and its passenger drive either to Newtown Linford church or to the old ruined mansion in the park before vanishing. As with so many phantom coaches, the four horses are sometimes said to be headless and Lady Jane herself to carry her head on her knees.

Hinckley

Appearing in the *Leicester Chronicle*, 20 June 1874, was notice of 'The Bloody Tomb' at Hinckley. Children and strangers used to be taken in the month of April to see the 'bloody tears' on the inscription on this tomb, that of Richard Smith, who died on 12 April 1727. It looked as if every letter had 'gouts of blood, which were not there before', and which in time disappeared. People were told that this young man had been killed by a recruiting sergeant in Duck-puddle for some light-hearted joke and that the stone cried yearly for vengeance.

The legend may have been inspired by his rhyming epitaph, which begins:

> A fatal Halberd his mortal Body slew
> The murdering Hand God's Vengeance will pursue.

As with the 'bloody tears' wept by holy images to this day, sceptics explained the 'gouts' as being caused by the washing down of friable bits of red sandstone in the wall.

The 'motts' (moats) at Hinckley were originally fish-stews belonging to the priory, which was by the Old Hall, later part of the vicarage grounds. Thomas Harrold, in a paper entitled 'Old Hinckley' (1888), writes:

In a conversation with our much-respected and venerable ex-sexton, old Tom Paul (eighty-six years old) ... I ... obtained ... a very interesting piece of folk-lore ... which, as a lad, I had often heard talked of, but never could understand before. It was enacted at 'the Old Hall' ... He said he had often heard his mother (who lived to a great age) relate, how a child had been flogged to death there, and she remembered hearing its cries, having resided near to, or adjoining the churchyard at the time, and this poor child's spirit haunted the place afterwards, and in order to 'lay the spirit,' I understood a certain number of ministers had to be got together in the room where the affair took place, a short religious ceremony was gone through, and they proceeded to 'lay the spirit,' by exorcising and enticing it into a bottle, securely corked, which was afterwards thrown into the 'motts,' and I perfectly well remember hearing lads say that at night these spirits could be heard buzzing or humming on the surface.

Husbands Bosworth

The Hall at Husbands Bosworth is haunted by a ghost thought to be the restless shade of a Protestant lady suffering eternal remorse for refusing to allow a Catholic priest to come into the house to administer the last rites to a dying servant. It is said that the Catholic chapel built in the grounds of the Hall in 1873 was an effort to expiate her guilt. However, the lady still walks or her footsteps are heard.

Although the main block of the hall was built in 1792, the back of the house has brickwork from the sixteenth or seventeenth century. This gives credibility to the tradition of a stain on the floor that is said to be still damp after 300 years. It is explained as either Communion wine spilt by a priest in his haste to escape from Cromwell's men, or else his own blood.

What modern authors, including Roy Palmer in 1985, do not say is whether the reference here is to the commissioners of Thomas Cromwell (c.1485–1540), the so-called *malleus monachorum* ('Hammer of the Monks') at the Reformation, or to the soldiers of Oliver Cromwell (1599–1658), remembered in folk tradition for the destruction of churches and other buildings. The same ambiguity hangs over many local traditions of Oliver Cromwell as the great destroyer.

Kibworth Harcourt

An account of 1875 speaks of a house at Kibworth known for 'upwards of half a century' to be haunted. It is said that one man killed another there, and afterwards ghostly figures were seen fighting, or the noise of fighting or of pacing footsteps was heard. The householder appears to have taken these goings-on calmly, referring to the manifestation simply as 'the bogey'.

A miller at Kibworth Mill who died as the result of a bet was thought thereafter to walk. At a celebration at the Coach and Horse, he drank gin for a wager, and to make sure he lost his cronies slipped him double measures. He managed to drink them all off and won his bet, but then fell to the floor unconscious. Later, he was pronounced dead, and placed in his coffin. Though noises were allegedly heard coming from the coffin, no one seems to have said anything at the time and he was duly buried. But afterwards, there was a horrified suspicion that he had been buried alive, because his ghost was seen.

Kilncote

A contributor to the *Gentleman's Magazine* in 1790 sent the editor a brief account of 'the *very best ghost* which ever made its appearance in England'. He writes:

> It appeared for several years but very seldom, only in the church porch at Kilncote, in Leicestershire, and was discovered by a lady now living, and *then* the rector's wife.
>
> N.B. It was not a ghost that could appear *ad libitum*; sometimes it did not appear for four years. The lady determined to approach it; and the nearer she advanced, the more confident she was that the substance or shade of a human figure was before her.

This is a convincing account of an alleged supernatural encounter, not because it was the rector's wife that saw the ghost, but because no attempt is made to give it a life history to justify its presence.

Lubenham

One of the family from whom Papillon Hall at Lubenham got its name was David Papillon (d. 1762), locally known as 'Pamp', 'Old Pamp', or 'Lord Pamp'.

He was greatly feared in the neighbourhood as people believed that he had the 'evil eye' and, like many witches and rural wizards, could 'set' or 'fix' people who offended him. One story says that he so disapproved of the way some men were ploughing that he 'set' them so that they could move neither hand nor foot until he released them at the end of the day.

In 1985, Roy Palmer reported that some Lubenham people remembered stories of Old Pamp and a mysterious mistress, probably Spanish, that he kept at the Hall before his marriage. She was not allowed to go outside but took her exercise on the flat leads of the roof. Palmer gives the date of her death as 1715, but also says that there was no record of her death or place of burial. However, the skeleton of a woman was allegedly found walled-up in the Hall during alterations made there in 1903.

It is said that, when dying, the Spanish mistress pronounced a curse on any owner who permitted her shoes to be taken out of the Hall. Consequently, whenever the Hall was sold, the shoes (in fact a pair of silver and brocaded slippers and a pair of pattens) were handed over with the title deeds to the new owner, except in 1866, when they were removed to Leicester. The new occupants were woken at night by the crashing of furniture and the noise of shutters slamming until the shoes were returned.

Six years later, the house was sold again and this time the new owner lent them for a year-long exhibition in Paris. Life thereupon became so intolerable that he and his family had to move out until the shoes were returned. The next occupant, who took over in 1884, had a fireproof cupboard with a padlocked metal grille constructed so as to keep the shoes safe from interference.

However, Captain Frank Belville, who assumed ownership of the Hall in 1903, had the shoes taken to his solicitor's office during alterations. Accidents immediately started happening to the building workers, and one was killed by a falling brick. The men downed tools, but only when Belville himself was in an accident with his pony trap and sustained a broken skull were the shoes brought back. Still he had not learned. In 1908 or 1909 he lent the shoes to Leicester Museum for an exhibition: while they were away, he fractured his skull (again) while out hunting. Then, during a tremendous storm, amid thunder and lightning, the Hall was set on fire, three horses were killed, and some people say that two men also died. Belville got the shoes back, locked them behind their grille, and threw the key in the pond.

Even now they were not safe. During the Second World War, the Hall was used for billeting American airmen. On two occasions, men who had taken the shoes away were killed in action, although somehow the shoes were returned except for one patten. In 1950, just before the Hall was about to be demolished, the remaining shoes passed into the care of Mrs Barbara Papillon and no more has been heard of the curse.

This chapter of accidents has some gaps and also coincidences that strain credulity (two exhibitions, and the same skull broken twice), and is evidently an accumulation of local rumours about the curse rather than a connected narrative.

Lutterworth

In the forepart of the seventeenth century, Lutterworth was the scene of a disturbance by a 'rapping spirit' or poltergeist. Richard Baxter, in his *Certainty of the Worlds of Spirits* (1691), recalls the sensation it made:

> In *February*, 1646. falling into great Debility by Bleeding ... I removed to Mr *Noel's* House at *Kirkby Malory* in *Leicester-shire*, where I lay weak three weeks in *March*, in which time the Neighbours went to see a House in *Lutterworth*, reported to be haunted: Multitudes flockt to see it, and affirmed, that at a certain hour of the day, stones were thrown at those that were present, which hit them, but hurt them not: And that what ever time any one would whistle, it was answered by a whistle in the Room: And no search could discover any Fraud: What became of it after, I heard not; but it continued believed commonly by the hearers, those three weeks that I staid in that County.

Sapcote

A respectably antique ghost is one reported by John Nichols in his *History ... of Leicestershire* (1795–1811). He writes:

> About midway between Sapcote and Stoney Stanton, over a rivulet, is a stone arch called *Scholar's Bridge* about which super-natural appearances are said to have been seen; and, though such appearances are generally exploded, the Scholar's Bridge Ghost has been for ages, and still continues, a nightly terror to many of the inhabitants of both these villages.

Possibly the bridge got its name from some scholar who met his end here. Possibly not. In earlier sources, apparitions are often unaccounted for by a narrative explaining their history (how they came to be ghosts), because people accepted the presence of supernatural entities in the landscape. To some extent they *expected* certain spots to have ghosts: bridges in particular, like other transitional places, such as crossroads, have from antiquity been notoriously haunted.

Moreover, not all 'ghosts' were revenants (the returning dead) requiring identification; they could be supernatural beings of some other kind. Nichols gives a hint of what it might have been supposed to be in the following circumstantial and therefore uncommonly valuable account of an alleged 'sighting':

A friend, who is no wise given to be superstitious, relates the following circumstance, which happened to himself at this bridge ... 'I was,' says he, 'walking between Stoney Stanton and Sapcote one very fine night, in the autumn of 1806, between the hours of eleven and twelve, my mind anxiously engaged upon a problem in mathematicks. In the middle of the meadow adjoining Scholar's Bridge, and at the distance of about 80 or 90 yards from the Bridge, I heard suddenly a groaning sort of noise; which I could not at that time account for ... The ... foolish old women's tales I had so frequently heard about the ghost of Scholar's Bridge rushed instantaneously into my mind, and I was in some measure prepared for the extraordinary circumstance that followed. The night was fine, but rather dark; so that I could distinguish objects at the distance of a few feet only; and had got across the meadow, as far as the stile, which stands close to the Bridge, before I saw any object whatever. This stile stands upon ground raised somewhat above the level of the meadow, and a stone-step is placed for the ease of passengers in getting over. Just as I had set my left foot upon the stone, and in the act of throwing my right leg over the stile, an animal, apparently larger than a fox, and which I suppose to be a shagged dog, brushed by my right shoulder with a surprizing velocity. The darkness of the night prevented me from seeing the animal before its spring over the stile, and I never saw it but only its descent to the ground after touching my shoulder, and I verily believe it was either a fox or a dog; but, meeting with it in the middle of the night, upon the wing as it were (for I never saw it on the ground), in the very place where so many people had been frightened, I was very much startled at first; and the animal ... seemed to be ... as much frightened as myself.'

This is a first-class report, taking into account both physical and psychological conditions, of an experience supposed at the time to be supernatural. Though afterwards rationalized ('I verily believe it was either a fox or a dog'), what Nichols' friend may have supposed at the time was that it was not a real 'shagged' (shaggy) dog, but a spirit in that form.

Tall tales are called 'shaggy dog stories' for the good reason that the shape-shifter often manifesting itself as a dog (black or white) was traditionally rough-coated, and sometimes locally bears names that reflect this, as in the case of the Norfolk Shuck (*see* SHERINGHAM, Norfolk).

Staunton Harold

Staunton Harold Hall was the home of Laurence Shirley (1720–60), fourth Earl Ferrers, the last English peer to suffer a felon's death. Although normally perfectly capable of managing his business affairs, he was given to manic outbursts of rage, exacerbated by drink. He once ordered a manservant to shoot his brother, and the servants themselves he would beat, horse-whip, kick, and on one near-fatal occasion stab.

He was such a monster to his wife, whom he married in 1752, that Parliament passed an Act granting her a separation and maintenance out of his estates. These were vested in trustees, who appointed as receiver of rents John Johnson, who had served the Ferrers family nearly all his life. This was at the earl's suggestion, evidently because he thought an old retainer would help him cheat his wife, but (according to T. B. Howell's *State Trials*), finding Johnson to be incorruptible, 'his ... mind ... altered towards him'. He gave Johnson notice to quit a farm promised him before his appointment. When Johnson produced a legal lease, granted by the trustees, his resentment grew. However, the matter was dropped, and seemingly amicable relations resumed.

Consequently, when the earl asked Johnson to come and see him on 18 January 1760, Johnson went. But Earl Ferrers had packed his household off for the day apart from a few women servants. On arrival, Johnson was shown into the parlour:

> After Mr Johnson had been there the best part of an hour, one of the maids ... heard my lord ... say, ... Down upon your knees; your time has come; you must die; and presently after heard a pistol go off ...

Johnson did not die immediately but was led upstairs to bed. Someone went to inform Johnson's children and summon the surgeon. After a couple of hours, Dr Thomas Kirkland, from Ashby-de-la-Zouche, arrived. The earl told him that he had shot Johnson 'coolly' and 'desired he might not be seized till it was known ... whether Mr Johnson would die or not'. At the same time, he threatened 'that if any person attempted to seize him, he would shoot him'.

Later, after he had been drinking, he began to rail at the dying man and made to pull him out of his bed. He would not hear of Johnson being carried to his own home, as he wished to keep his eye on the 'villain'. At last he himself went to bed, and Kirkland spirited Johnson out of the house to his home, where he died next morning.

Attempting to run away, Ferrers was intercepted by two colliers and arrested. On Wednesday, 16 April 1760, he went on trial before the House of Peers in Westminster Hall. He pleaded 'not guilty' and conducted his own defence, during which witnesses were called to give evidence of the insanity in his family. However, on the third day, the peers unanimously found him guilty of murdering Johnson 'feloniously, wilfully, and of his malice aforethought'. Condemned to death, he petitioned, as a peer, to be beheaded in the Tower of London, but the king refused. He was to be hanged at Tyburn like an ordinary felon.

Earl Ferrers carried off his execution with style. According to the sheriffs' report, 'dressed in a suit of light clothes, embroidered with silver' (some say his wedding suit), he drove from the Tower to Tyburn in his own landau, drawn by his own six horses. A crowd of 'many hundred thousand spectators' turned out, so that the short journey took two and three-quarter hours, during which 'he appeared to be perfectly easy'.

Earl Ferrers mounted the scaffold calmly. There was one concession to his rank: he would not swing off the hangman's cart but be executed from what Horace Walpole termed 'a new contrivance for sinking the stage under him' – the first modern-style scaffold used in Britain. However, it 'did not play well' and he took minutes to die. His body was taken for dissection and 'anatomizing' at the Surgeons' Hall, then privately interred at St Pancras.

The flamboyance of his life and death, inspiring tittle-tattle and rumour, has turned Earl Ferrers' history into fantasy. It is frequently said that he was hanged with a silken rope, but it was common hemp. Though Roy Palmer was told as a boy that the room where the murder took place had been locked ever since, it must have been opened when the house was remodelled as a Palladian mansion from 1763 on.

The surgeon, Thomas Kirkland, supposedly had a prevision of the earl's funeral four months before the event. On 18 January 1760, he was out riding when, at about four in the afternoon, he stopped to allow his horse to drink from a stream. Falling into a trance, he saw a magnificent funeral pass, including a coach drawn by six horses and bearing the Ferrers arms. On reaching home, he was summoned to Staunton Harold, where he learned that Johnson had been shot at 4 p.m. In reality, it was nearly a quarter of a century before Earl Ferrers' remains were exhumed and taken home to Staunton.

Stoke Golding

Not far from Stoke Golding is the site of the battle of Bosworth Field (22 August 1485). Like other battlegrounds, it is said to be haunted: in 1985, Roy Palmer reported that phantoms of a headless soldier and a spectral horseman had been seen here, but he gives no dates for these alleged sightings.

Wymondham

Platts Stile on the footpath from Wymondham to Edmondthorpe was said to be haunted. Within living memory, said Roy Palmer in

1985, children were told not to pass that way after dark for fear of experiencing the feeling of being hit by a heavy money-bag. When they asked why, they were told that two men had quarrelled over money there and come to blows, and one was killed. The dead man's ghost haunted the spot and gave passers-by the sensation of being struck. One man going that way despite the warnings was sent staggering by a heavy blow on the back of his neck. When he reached his friend's house at Edmondthorpe, he found a big red mark there. 'Oh,' said his friend, 'that would be the ghost of Platts Stile.'

Lincolnshire

Bolingbroke Castle

Earthworks and ruins at Old Bolingbroke, west of Spilsby, are all that remain of thirteenth-century Bolingbroke Castle, believed in the seventeenth century to be haunted by an animal ghost.

Gervase Holles, in notes on Lincolnshire made in 1634–42, wrote:

> One thinge is not to be passed by, affirmed as a certaine truth by many of ye inhabitants of ye towne upon their owne knowledge, which is, that ye castle is haunted by a certaine spirit in ye likenesse of a Hare; which att the meeting of ye auditors doth usually runne betweene their legs, & sometymes overthrows them, & so passes away.

Sometimes they chased it down into the castle yard and saw it go in through a grating into a cellar below. Though they followed it there with a light, and though there was no other way out except by the door or window, yet they could never find it. On different occasions it was seen running through gratings into other cellars, of which there were many, and they sent for hounds and put them down after it, 'but after a while they have come crying out'.

Although Holles does not say so, people may have thought that the hare was a witch's familiar, rather than the ghost of a once-living hare or one of the county's many bogey beasts (*see* BRIGG). He does not mention its colour: in Lincolnshire in the nineteenth century, phantom hares and rabbits were thought, if white, to be dead people's spirits and it was unlucky to see them. At the turn of the nineteenth century, a white rabbit with luminous eyes regularly appeared near Caistor, but its reason for doing so was unknown.

Boston

According to old writers, such was the medieval prosperity of Boston that when, during the proclamation of a tournament at fair time, a band of marauders dressed as monks fired the town and plundered the merchants' stalls, the molten gold and silver ran down the streets in a stream. This was towards the end of the reign of King Edward I (1272–1307). In 1371, the town became a staple for wool, and Hanse merchants established a guild here, the Hanseatic League having a steelyard, warehouses, and a dock here for the weighing and export of wool.

Local tradition later said that, in order to secure a firm foundation, the great tower of St Botolph's church was built on woolpacks. This is the 'high steeple' of the rhyme, the world-famous Boston Stump, 262 feet 9 inches (80.07 m) high, and 40 feet 3 inches (12.27 m) square, which can be seen forty miles (64 km) out at sea and served as a beacon over Lynn Deeps. As the tower stands within a few feet of a tidal river, something to consolidate the peaty fenland soil was probably needed, although the fairly widespread tradition of churches and bridges 'Built upon woolpacks' probably has more to do with the wool trade than medieval technology.

Boston Stump was connected with an extraordinary event in the mid nineteenth century:

> On Sunday, Sept. 29th, 1860, a strange portent occurred. A cormorant took up its position on the steeple of Boston Church, much to the alarm of the superstitious among the townspeople. There it remained with the exception of two hours' absence till early the following morning, when it was shot by the caretaker of the church. The fears of the credulous were singularly confirmed when the news arrived of the loss of the 'Lady Elgin' at sea, with three hundred passengers, among whom were Mr Ingram, member for Boston, with his son, on the very morning when the bird was first seen.

A cormorant is unusual as a death omen. Although in Lincolnshire the omen in the form of a bird suddenly appearing or tapping at a windowpane might be of unknown species, it was most often said to be a pigeon or white dove, like the celebrated Oxenham Omen (*see* ZEAL MONACHORUM, Devon). However, the episode of the cormorant was curiously echoed more than a century later by the experience of Bob Lane of Boston, apparently previously unaware of the earlier event:

... just before my father-in-law's death in November 1980 a very strange thing happened ... my wife and I were in bed, I was really sound asleep, and suddenly heard a horrible screech a bit like a heron in the night – it so alarmed me that I woke up with a start ... my wife was awake – she asked if I had heard this noise ... Well, that weekend we went to visit my in-laws ... about a mile away as the crow flies ... mother-in-law had heard the shriek, but father-in-law was convinced that what he heard was the old woman next door's budgie ... not long after he died of cancer.

Brigg

A well-known phantom in the neighbourhood of Brigg was an apparition called the Lackey Causey Calf (causey = causeway). Sometimes described as headless, it was reported by Mabel Peacock in an unpublished collection of Lincolnshire folklore (1909–20) as emerging from a 'tunnel' over a stream between Brigg and Wrawby. After crossing the road, it would vanish.

It might have been a ghost in animal form, as a human skull and bones were said to have been found near the place where it walked. Mabel Peacock writes, 'There is reason to think that no small number of boggarts are murdered people, or suicides "coming again" in the aspect of cattle, dogs or rabbits.' According to one account, the Calf appeared after dark with the intention of tricking people into the water, a trait which could connect it with the Tatterfoal or shag-foal, of whom the Northamptonshire poet John Clare writes (1821):

Old Ball – You mean – the shagg'd foal. It's a common tradition in village that the devil often appears in the form of a shagg'd foal: and a man in our parish firmly believes that he saw him in that character.

A shag-foal is a foal whose baby fuzz is giving way to its adult horsehair, hence the tatters.

Bogey beasts such as these might have been perceived in the Middle Ages as petty demons; in Shakespeare's time people could have thought of them as hobgoblins, like Puck or Robin Good-fellow, which sometimes manifested themselves as animals. By the eighteenth and nineteenth centuries such shape-shifting beings were frequently interpreted as revenant spirits, usually of wicked people.

The boundaries between various forms of the supernatural seem never to have been very stable, and the classification of different apparitions as ghost, goblin or demon is largely the work of later interpreters. Bogey beasts can also appear in human shape, or even as inanimate objects: at GLASSENSIKES, Co. Durham, the bogey shifted between human form and white cats, rabbits, and white or black dogs, but also once manifested as 'a great *gulph of fire*', while W. Hylton Dyer Longstaffe, in his *History ... of Darlington* (1854), relates of Norton, Yorkshire: 'Two gentlemen (one a very dear friend of mine ... now deceased) saw near a water an exquisitely beautiful white heifer turn into *a roll of Irish linen.*'

Snakeholme

In her collection of Lincolnshire folklore in the archives of the Folklore Society, Mabel Peacock gives a tradition from Snakeholme current probably in the later nineteenth century. She writes:

> A.G., a Lincolnshire girl, was told some years ago that a spectral huntsman with his hounds, is to be heard by night at Snakeholme, a hamlet in the parish of Bardney: 'There are people who say they have listened to them in the wood, and along the railway side; and they say that they come because a pack of hounds was once run into by a train.'

The explanation that the spectral hounds are the revenants of once-living dogs is perhaps a late one: in the Middle Ages no such explanation was needed for phantom hunts, which were thought to be demonic spirits existing in their own right as omens. The earliest recorded such phantom hunt appeared not far off at PETERBOROUGH, Huntingdonshire and Peterborough.

South Ferriby

At South Ferriby, on the Humber, in the nineteenth century, 'there used to be something at a house'. This something came every night until the old man and his daughter who lived there hardly dared to stay there alone. The father's bed had rods and curtains, and at night-time the curtains would draw themselves backwards and forwards, and twist round the old man's neck, trying to strangle him.

One night when the daughter's young man called to see her, and they were talking by the fireside, a frightful racket started in the room above their heads. The young man, who had heard of the ghost, asked what was the matter. The girl tried to pass the event off, but almost at once a dish began jerking about, and the old man told her that the ghost had ordered him to meet it alone on the hill behind the church that very night.

When evening came, he was too afraid to go, but instead sat up late, shivering by the fire. When he finally went to bed, something grabbed him on the stairs and nearly strangled him.

This was enough warning: the next night he went to the hill, and on his return seemed much shaken. When asked what he had seen, all he would say then, or ever afterwards, was, 'Ask me no questions – the thing will never trouble us no more.' And it never did.

Stainsby

According to a report from 1900, a ghost used to be seen here and there in the neighbourhood of Stainsby House. It also appeared in the 'ash plantin' afore you go down to the brig ower the brook'. Many people saw it, especially near the bridge. Among them was a wagoner living at Bag-Enderby, the next village to the east. He said, 'It was a misty kind o' a thing. You couldn't see head or tail, or hand or foot, but you knew it was there, and it flitted unaccountable.'

Thorpe Hall

Thorpe Hall, on the edge of the Louth Borough boundary, is one of several places in England that has become associated with the story of 'The Spanish Lady's Love', which tells of a beautiful Spanish lady who falls in love with an Englishman. When he finally confesses that he is already married, the Spanish lady gallantly sends gifts to his wife, and herself enters a nunnery. A popular ballad on the subject by Thomas Deloney, printed in 1603 and probably based on an already existing tradition, excited interest in the identity of the unnamed Englishman, and the tale became attached to several different men who took part in the capture of Cadiz in 1596, including Sir John Bolle of Thorpe Hall, one of the Earl of Essex's captains in the campaign.

It was said that, when Sir John departed Cadiz, the Spanish Lady sent as presents to his wife a great many jewels and other valuables, among which was her own portrait 'done on green' (wearing green), a beautiful tapestry bed embroidered in gold by her own hands, and several casks full of plate, money, and other treasures. Some of these things were said in 1810 to be still in the possession of the family, although the portrait had by some accident been disposed of about half a century before.

Meantime, the portrait had led to her being known as 'the Green Lady' in the neighbourhood, 'where to this day there is a traditionary superstition among the vulgar, that Thorpe Hall was haunted by the green lady, who used nightly to take her seat in a particular tree near the mansion'. It was also believed that, during the life of Sir John's son, Sir Charles Bolle, a knife and fork were always laid for her at table, if she chose to make an appearance.

Another tree-sitting ghost, the Wicked Lady of MARKYATE CELL, undoubtedly haunted her former home in Hertfordshire as an atonement for her crimes, but it is hard to see why the blameless and great-hearted Spanish Lady should be condemned to haunt Thorpe Hall or anywhere else. Probably the portrait generated the ghost story. Whatever the reason for her haunt, she is said to have been frequently heard, though not apparently seen, between 1860 and 1880.

London and Middlesex

Berkeley Square

In Victorian times, a grisly legend circulated about No. 50, Berkeley Square. It apparently arose in the 1850s, when the house was occupied by an eccentric recluse, Mr Myers, who let it fall into decay and lived in one room only; he was said to have gone mad when jilted on the eve of his wedding. By 1879, according to the magazine *Mayfair*, the dreary house was standing empty, 'with windows caked and blackened by dust', and was strongly rumoured to be haunted – though why, and by whom, or by what, was never clear. The magazine repeated some of the tales, while urging the owner to clean up his property. The evil, it seems, was centred in one of the top-floor rooms. A maid was given it as her bedroom, with disastrous results:

> An hour or two after the household was at rest, it was awakened by fearful screams from the new servant's room, and she was found standing in the middle of the floor, as rigid as a corpse, with hideously glaring eyes – she had suddenly become a hopeless and raving mad woman, who never found a lucid interval wherein to tell what had made her so.

The room was then left unused, but some while later a sceptical guest insisted on spending the night there; he arranged with his hosts that if all was well he would ring the service bell once, but that if he rang twice, someone should come at once. After a while, the bell rang frantically; his friends rushed upstairs, and found him dead. Indeed, said the *Mayfair* journalist, it was rumoured that many people had met the same fate. Moreover, the owner only came to the house once every six months, when he would enter a locked upstairs room – possibly to practise black magic.

The rumours had also been discussed in an exchange of letters in *Notes and Queries* earlier in the 1870s, some supporting the alleged tragedies (though always at second or third hand), and others debunking them; maids who had worked in the house in Mr Myers' time, and a butler who had served the previous owner in the 1850s, all denied any ghostly happenings.

Fictional writers picked up versions of the legend, wittingly or unwittingly. Rhoda Broughton, a novelist, agreed that one of her short stories ('The Truth, the Whole Truth', 1873) closely resembled the supposed events in Berkeley Square, but said she had actually been inspired by something that she had been told happened in a country house, not in London at all. In her version, the maid and the rash young visitor both cry out, 'Oh my God, I've seen it!' before falling dead.

Virtually every popular writer on the paranormal in Britain offers his own version. Several stress an episode which had not formed part of the earliest accounts, that of two sailors who had broken into the deserted house to sleep there, but encountered something so terrible that one jumped from an upstairs window to escape, and died, impaled on the railings below. In some versions his companion goes mad; in others he escapes and tells the tale. R. Thurston Hopkins describes the 'horrible intruder':

> It stood for a moment in a dark corner, and the sailors could not see what manner of face the thing possessed – animal or human. But soon it began to move towards them ... it crept, panted, shuffled across the room, making scratchy sounds on the bare boards which might have been the scraping of horny claws.

J. A. Brooks, on the other hand, speaks of a 'horrible shapeless object [which] slid into the room'.

The supposed cause for the haunting is variously given. Antony Hippisley Coxe lists three: that one owner kept his mad brother locked away in that room; that a girl threw herself out of the window to escape a sexual assault by her uncle; and that a Scottish maid was tortured there. It was said that when the house was eventually let again, towards the end of the nineteenth century, the new tenants were charged only a peppercorn rent for the first three years, but would have to pay a huge forfeit if they lost their nerve and quitted.

Cock Lane

The scandalous affair of the Cock Lane poltergeist in 1760–2 aroused much interest, and was eventually proved to be a fake. At the centre of events were two men, William Parsons, a landlord, and his lodger William Kent. The latter was a widower, but he had with him as his mistress his late wife's sister Fanny. Kent had lent money to Parsons, who was so unwilling to repay it that they quarrelled, and Kent sued Parsons. At about this time Kent went off on business, and in his absence Fanny became very alarmed at scratching noises in her bedroom, which she believed were made by her sister's ghost, and were a warning that she herself would soon die too. In view of what happened later, it is significant that during Kent's absence Fanny was sharing her room with Liz Parsons, the landlord's eleven-year-old daughter. When Kent returned, he and Fanny changed their lodgings to Bartlett Court, where Fanny caught smallpox and died.

The manifestations then began in earnest in Cock Lane. Scratching and rapping were constantly heard in Liz's room, and the 'spirit' announced, through the child, that she was Fanny's ghost, and that William Kent had poisoned her. Crowds flocked to the house, for which Parsons charged them an entrance fee, and crammed themselves into a small, dark, and airless room where the ghost might, or might not, be willing to answer questions by rapping once for 'yes' and twice for 'no'. The prevailing mood, according to contemporary reports, was somewhat frivolous, and all the taverns of the area were making a fortune by supplying food and drink to the visitors.

However, a local clergyman, seeing how serious was the accusation made against Kent, called upon various gentlemen 'eminent for their rank and character' to investigate; one of them was Dr Johnson. They visited the crypt where Fanny was buried, and found that, contrary to what Parsons had promised, the ghost did not communicate with them by rapping on the coffin lid. When Liz was caught with a wooden clapper hidden in her clothing, the fraud was exposed. Parsons was found guilty of conspiracy, pilloried, and imprisoned for two years.

There are many references to the affair in contemporary newspapers, and in the letters of sophisticated Londoners such as Horace

Walpole and William Hogarth. An indignant pamphlet attributed to the writer Oliver Goldsmith gives a detailed account, protesting that a man of good character, such as Kent, should never have had his reputation destroyed by an accusation of murder made upon such flimsy evidence.

Drury Lane

The Theatre Royal is the haunt of what is probably Britain's most famous 'theatre ghost', the Man in Grey, who can be seen sitting in a particular seat in the upper circle (always at a matinée); he then rises and walks calmly along the gangway behind the seats until he melts into the wall at a certain spot, and disappears. He wears old-fashioned clothing: powdered hair (or a wig), a grey riding-cloak, boots, and a three-cornered hat. Legend claims that he was a wealthy young man of the early eighteenth century who was having an affair with one of the actresses, whom he used to meet in the upper circle after the performances ended – until the day that a rival stabbed him there, as he waited for her. The murderer then hid the body in the recess of a nearby passage, which he walled up. This tale was prompted by the discovery of a skeleton with a dagger in its ribs, found bricked up in the thickness of a wall abutting on the upper circle when the theatre was undergoing alterations in 1848.

The Man in Grey is regarded by theatre folk as a good omen, whose apparition guarantees that the play then in rehearsal or production will be successful. There are numerous accounts of actors and theatre staff who have seen him.

Garlick Hill

In this district (which gets its name from the fact that garlic was formerly sold there) stands the beautiful church of St James Garlick Hythe. A legend has grown up over the last 150 years or so, to the effect that it is occasionally haunted by a grey, withered figure, with its hands crossed over its chest, to be glimpsed standing rigidly in some obscure corner, apparently staring towards the altar. This is 'Jimmy Garlick', the ghost linked to a naturally mummified corpse which was discovered in 1855 when the vaults were being cleared out. The dead man's real identity is unknown, since the church records were lost when the building was gutted in the Great Fire of London, and this has given rise to much modern speculation, unsupported by evidence. He has been variously asserted to be Belin (a legendary king of the Britons), a Roman general, Henry Fitzailwyn (a medieval Lord Mayor, who died in 1212), Dick Whittington, or a youth called Seagrave Chamberlain who died of fever in 1765 and is commemorated by a plaque in the north aisle.

The body was so well preserved that for almost a hundred years it was displayed in a glass case bearing the traditional verse:

> Stop Stranger Stop As You Pass By.
> As You Are Now So Once Was I.
> As I Am Now So Shall You Be.
> So Pray Prepare To Follow Me.

The choirboys used to take it out on Sundays and prop it up in a pew. Some have supposed that this glass case was the actual coffin, but this can hardly be so; more likely, it was constructed to display the mummy after its discovery. During the air raids of 1942 a bomb shattered the case, and the mummy is now kept out of view, in a chamber of the tower. The church is also haunted by a phantom cat, which some regard as confirmation of the Dick Whittington connection.

Gower Street

In the main corridor of University College stands a handsome glass-fronted case containing the mummified body of one of its founders, the philosopher Jeremy Bentham (1748–1832), who objected to Christian burial. He held that a corpse should be used for scientific instruction and then preserved as a permanent memorial, so in accordance with his instructions his body was publicly dissected – to the accompaniment of a violent thunderstorm, a circumstance which traditionalists might consider an appropriate symbol of the wrath of God. It was then mummified and put on display. The head, however, is a wax replica, since the real one responded less well than the body to the treatment; it used to be in a closed box in the same case, but is now kept elsewhere in the college – allegedly because students were once caught playing football with it. Bentham's body is dressed as he was in life, and holds his favourite walking stick; it is said that sometimes he leaves his case and can be seen walking along the corridors towards the library – or, if not seen, the tapping of his stick is heard. The story has been passed down among college students throughout the twentieth century, and surely goes back far into the nineteenth.

Hammersmith

For about two months during the winter of 1803, the inhabitants of Hammersmith were much alarmed by reports of a malevolent ghost 'stalking up and down the neighbourhood'. The affair led to a violent death, and hence was reported in the press and eventually resulted in a criminal trial. The trouble had reportedly begun after a woman who was pregnant fainted with terror when a very tall white figure arose from among the tombstones, pursued her, and grasped her in its arms; she was carried home in a state of shock, and died a few days later. Others described the phantom as wearing a calf-skin, or draped in white robes and having horns and glass eyes; on one occasion it had ambushed a wagon, causing the horses to bolt, to the great danger of the passengers. It was rumoured to be the ghost of a man who had slit his throat a year before.

There were some people, however, who rejected supernatural explanations; believing that some practical joker was at work, they lay in wait for him on several nights, but there were too many paths and alleys for him to be caught. One of these vigilantes, an excise officer called Francis Smith, went out armed on 3 January 1804 to keep watch in Black Lion Lane, where he saw a white figure coming towards him; as it did not answer his challenge, he shot it. Unfortunately, it was quite human – it was a bricklayer named Thomas Millwood, who was no hoaxer but was simply wearing the white jacket, trousers and shoes which were the normal working dress of his trade. His mother-in-law later testified that it was not the first time he had been mistaken for the 'ghost', and that she had advised him to wear a dark greatcoat, for his own safety.

At Smith's trial on 13 January 1804, the jury at first gave a verdict of manslaughter, but the judge pointed out that however much one must detest the callous trickster who was terrorizing the neighbourhood, this did not justify anyone in shooting a suspect; Smith must either be found guilty of murder, or acquitted entirely. He was therefore condemned to be hanged and dissected. However, the sentence was soon commuted to a year's imprisonment.

Meanwhile, the real hoaxer had been caught, thanks to information given by a neighbour shocked by Millwood's death. It turned out to be an old shoemaker called James Graham, who had been going about by night wrapped in a blanket 'in order to be revenged on the impertinence of his apprentices, who had terrified his children by telling them stories of ghosts'.

There was a sequel twenty years later, as J. A. Brooks describes in his *Ghosts of London*. In 1824, local papers reported the appearance of a new Hammersmith Ghost, also dubbed the Hammersmith Monster, who, not content with scaring women in unlighted lanes, would jump on them and scratch their faces 'as if with hooks'; he turned out to be a young farmer and hay-salesman from Harrow. He was 'sent by the magistrates to the House of Correction to undergo a little wholesome discipline for his pranks'.

Nor was this the end; in 1832, another spectral figure was attacking women in lanes around Hammersmith and Acton. According to one report, he was 'attired in a large white dress, with long nails or claws, by which he was enabled to scale walls or hedges for the purpose of making himself scarce'. Others said he was dressed in armour, and had wagered that he would strip the clothes from a certain number of women within a specified time, and needed only one more victim to win his bet.

These episodes show the interplay between popular tales of the supernatural and the deliberate pranks of copycat hoaxers. However, there are some who still claim that there is a true ghost which appears in the churchyard of St Paul's, Hammersmith, once every fifty years at midnight when the moon is full. This was publicized in the *West London Observer* in July 1955, causing such a crowd to gather that police cordoned off the churchyard. Nothing was seen at midnight (apart from 'Teddy Boys in white shirts'), but the few people who, mindful of Summer Time, continued their vigil till 1 a.m. were rewarded with the sight of a figure draped in brilliant white gliding among the tombs.

Hampton

In Hampton church is the imposing funeral monument of Mrs Sybil
Penn, who died on 6 November 1562 of smallpox. She is shown
lying full-length beneath a marble canopy supported on pillars. Her
rhyming epitaph declares:

> Pen is here brought to home, the place of long abode,
> Whose vertu guided hath her shippe, into the quyet rode . . .

and includes the information 'To courte she called was, to foster up
a Kinge'.

Mrs Penn was the wife of David Penn, one of the Penns of Penn,
Buckinghamshire, lords of the manor in the sixteenth century.
In October 1538, a year after Lady Jane Seymour's death, Mrs Penn
became nurse and foster-mother to her son, the sickly Prince
Edward. From various marks of favour bestowed on her by Henry
VIII, Edward when he came to the throne, and Elizabeth I, she
seems to have been highly regarded.

In 1829, when the old church at Hampton was pulled down, Mrs
Penn's monument was moved into the present church.

> The story goes that, immediately after the disturbance of her
> tomb, strange noises as of a woman working at a spinning-wheel,
> and muttering the while, were heard through the wall of one of
> the rooms . . . in the south-west wing of Hampton Court Palace.
> On search being made, an ancient and till then unknown chamber
> was discovered, in which an antique spinning-wheel and a few
> other articles were found . . .

Reporting this in his *History of the Parish of Penn* (1935), Gilbert
Jenkins adds that, about fifty years previously, the phenomena
had recurred. Several mysterious happenings had been recorded,
and one person claimed to have encountered, in the haunted room,
Mrs Penn's tall, gaunt form, dressed in a long, grey robe with a
hood over her head, her lanky hands stretched out before her. The
description of Mrs Penn corresponds closely to her appearance on
the tomb and this was regarded as a coincidence so startling as to
shake the doubt even of sceptics. (There is, of course, an obvious
explanation – someone had seen the tomb.)

Jenkins suggests that Mrs Penn may have been unable to rest

because her husband, in his will dated 5 January 1564, directed that her body be removed from the place where she then lay buried and be re-interred beside his body. While ghosts were thought sometimes to return because of the flouting of their own or a loved one's wishes, what is perhaps more likely to have generated the haunting tradition is the widespread superstition that disturbing or destroying ecclesiastical property, including church monuments, brings dire consequences.

According to Peter Haining, writing in 1982, 'the restless shade of the old nurse has continued to be seen and heard in the palace, and makes a visit to the south-west wing of Hampton Court a must for every ghost-hunter.' This does not square with the fact that the royal nurseries were at Ashridge, near Berkhamsted, Hertfordshire.

The story of Mrs Penn may have been part of a fashion for spinning ghosts, like those heard in a house in PENZANCE, Cornwall, and in KNEBWORTH HOUSE, Hertfordshire, set at Hampton Court partly because it was a known royal palace but also because it was suggested by both 'Hampden', Mrs Penn's maiden name, and that of the place where she was buried.

Highgate

Spectral animals and birds are common in British folklore, but it is fairly unusual for them to be interpreted as the ghosts of specific individual creatures that died in known circumstances. Among these, the one haunting Pond Square in Highgate is unique, for it is the ghost of the world's first frozen chicken.

On a snowy day in March 1626 (as John Aubrey records), Lord Francis Bacon, politician, philosopher, and one of England's first experimental scientists, was riding in his carriage through Highgate and pondering on the preservative effect of snow and ice. How effective might this be with meat? He told his coachman to buy a chicken from the farm they were passing (Highgate was a rural area then), kill it, pluck it, and clean out its innards. Then Lord Bacon himself began stuffing the bird with handfuls of snow and stashing it away in a bag filled with more snow. While doing so, however, fits of vomiting and shivering which he had already felt on the coach journey from Gray's Inn to Highgate grew worse, and he took refuge in a friend's house in Highgate, where he died a few days later.

It is not known in what icy hell the chicken's spirit spent the next 300 years or so, but (according to Peter Underwood and other modern writers) during the air raids of the Second World War several aircraftmen, firefighters, and residents of Pond Square reported seeing a fairly large bird, unable to fly because almost all its feathers had been plucked, running round in circles and pathetically flapping the stumps of its wings. It was reported again in the 1960s and '70s, apparently dropping out of the sky with a pathetic squawk. Whenever it is seen, it is shivering.

Highgate Cemetery

It is natural that this large, dramatic Victorian cemetery should be the subject of ghostly rumours. What is more startling is that its most notorious spectre has been classed as a vampire, since physical revenants have scarcely figured in British folklore since medieval times, and blood-sucking ones are unknown. The Highgate Vampire owes his title to the literary and cinematic *Dracula* tradition, in which Dracula's London base is represented as being in the Hampstead/Highgate area. When the apparition was first discussed in the local press in 1970, it was merely called a ghost.

The publicity was initiated by a local group interested in paranormal phenomena; they began roaming the cemetery in the late '60s, and on 21 December 1969 one member, David Farrant, spent the night there and glimpsed a very tall figure with inhuman, hypnotic eyes. He wrote to the *Hampstead and Highgate Express* on 6 February 1970, asking if anyone else had seen anything similar. On the 13th, several people replied that there was a tradition of a 'tall man in a hat' seen either in the cemetery or in Swains Lane, which runs alongside it; there was also a ghostly bicyclist said to chase women down Swains Lane, a woman in white, a face glaring through the bars of a gate, a figure wading into a pond, bells ringing in the disused cemetery chapel, and voices calling. Some related personal experiences:

'My fiancée and I spotted a most unusual form about a year ago. It just seemed to glide across the park. I am glad someone else has spotted it' ... 'To my knowledge the ghost always takes the form of a pale figure and has been appearing for several years' ... 'Suddenly from the corner of my eye I saw something move ... which seemed to be walking towards us from the gates, and sent us running up Swains Lane as fast as we could' ... 'My advice is to avoid Swains Lane during dark evenings, if at all possible.'

Hardly two informants gave the same story – quite a common situation when famous local 'eerie places' are discussed – but this natural diversity was about to be subsumed into a single melo-dramatic image.

Besides Farrant, another local man, Sean Manchester, was keen to identify and eliminate the supernatural entity in the cemetery. He told the *Hampstead and Highgate Express* on 27 February that he had seen corpses of foxes drained of blood, and deduced that what the paper called a 'King Vampire from Wallachia' had been brought to England in a coffin in the eighteenth century and interred on the site which later became Highgate Cemetery, and that modern Satanists had roused him; unfortunately, said Manchester, the tradi-tional staking, beheading, and burning were now illegal. The paper gave this the headline 'Does a Wampyr [*sic*] walk in Highgate?' The influence of the *Dracula* story is blatant, but Farrant took the same line, and the label stuck.

The ensuing publicity, enhanced by an escalating rivalry between Farrant and Manchester, culminated in an ITV interview with both of them on Friday 13 March. Within two hours, a mob of would-be vampire hunters from all over London, and beyond, swarmed into the cemetery and were with difficulty expelled by police. Over the next few years, Farrant and Manchester both independently explored the cemetery with their supporters, claiming to find traces of black magic; both conducted rituals of exorcism; each poured scorn on the other's expertise. The affair received further press publicity when rumours arose that the rivals would hold a 'magical duel' on Parliament Hill on Friday 13 April 1973, which never came off; and when Farrant, who had persistently entered Highgate Cemetery at night to conduct ceremonies, was jailed in 1974 for damage to memorials – damage which he insisted had been caused by Satanists. The feud between Farrant and Manchester has remained vigorous to this day; both continue to investigate and combat various supernatural phenomena, and both have written and spoken repeatedly about the Highgate events, each stressing his own central role.

The Highgate Cemetery vampire has featured in several books of popular ghost lore, and inspired various Halloween pranks; it looks set to become a permanent part of London's folklore.

Holland House, Kensington

To see one's own 'fetch' or 'wraith' (or 'astral body', in the language of paranormal studies) has always been regarded as a death omen. John Aubrey, in his *Miscellanies* of 1696, has an anecdote illustrating this belief:

> The beautiful Lady Diana Rich, Daughter to the Earl of Holland, as she was walking in her Father's Garden at Kensington, to take the fresh Air before Dinner, about Eleven a Clock, being then very well, met with her own Apparition, Habit and every thing, as in a Looking-glass. About a Month after, she died of the Small-pox. And 'tis said, that her Sister the Lady Isabella (Thinne), saw the like of herself also before she died. This account I had from a Person of Honour. A third Sister, Mary, was married to the Earl of Breadalbane, as we are informed, and it is recorded that she also, not long after her Marriage, had some such warning of her approaching Dissolution.

However, the theme is rare in English folklore; it occurs chiefly in tales about people who rashly keep watch in a church porch to see the wraiths of those fated to die in the coming year, and are horrified to see their own form among them.

Islington

A booklet of 1842 entitled *The Islington Ghost* describes the strange happenings which were said to have followed the burial in 1517 of a wealthy landowner, Richard Cloudesley, who had been a generous benefactor of the parish church, Holy Trinity. He had left instructions that he be buried in its churchyard, but later rumours suggested that this had not been done, and that he had been laid in a nearby field (which, presumably, was unconsecrated ground), though no reason is given. It was apparently in consequence of this that at some later but unspecified date there was a minor local earthquake:

> It is said that in a certain field, near unto the parish church of Islington, there did take place a wondrous commotion, the earth swelling and turning up on every side towards the midst of the said field, and by tradition of this, it is observed that one Richard Cloudesley lay buried in or near that place, and that his body being restless, on the score of some sin by him peradventure committed, did shew, or seem to signify, that religious observance should there take place, to quiet his departed spirit; whereupon certain exorcisers (if we may so term them) did at dead of night, nothing loth, using divers exercises at torchlight, set to rest the unruly spirit of the said Cloudesley, and the earth did return to its pristine shape, nevermore commotion proceeding therefrom to this day, and this I know of a very certainty.

This curious tale draws on the old belief that the earth itself may sometimes refuse to hold the corpse of a sinner. Whether or not there is any truth in the idea that Cloudesley's body was at one time in the field, it is now indisputably inside the church, having been reinterred there in 1813, as an inscription attests.

Montpelier Square, Kensington

'A wonderful modern ghost-story', wrote Charles Harper, 'obtained much publicity at the close of December 1913 ... The principals were said to be people of the highest social position.' It is presumably out of respect for this social status that Harper carefully avoids mentioning any names, or indicating what form the 'publicity' took. There seems to have been considerable interest in psychic experiences among the upper classes from the late nineteenth century onwards, exemplified, for instance, by many anecdotes in Augustus Hare's *Story of My Life* (1900).

The story given by Harper is as follows. The vicar of a Kensington church was about to leave the church after choir practice one evening when an agitated lady, who was unknown to him, begged him to come at once to an address nearby where a man was dying. 'He is extremely concerned about the state of his soul,' she pleaded, 'and anxious to see you before he dies.' The lady had a taxi waiting; the vicar got in at once, and the two of them drove to the house, where the vicar rang the bell, and told the butler he had come in answer to his sick master's urgent summons. The butler, amazed, answered that his master was in the best of health. 'But this lady said – ' said the vicar, and then, turning, saw that both the lady and the taxi had vanished.

At this point the master of the house appeared, and when the situation had been explained he commented that it was very strange, for though in no way ill he had indeed been troubled lately about something that was on his conscience, and had been thinking of calling some clergyman to talk about it. He and the vicar talked together for an hour or so, and the gentleman said he would come to church next morning to continue the discussion.

He never came, so the vicar went back to the house, where he was told that the gentleman had died the previous evening, just ten minutes after they parted. Going into the bedroom to pray beside the corpse, the vicar was startled to see a portrait which he recognized at once, that of the lady who had summoned him. 'Who is that?' he asked. 'That, sir,' said the butler, 'is my master's wife. She died fifteen years ago.'

Soho Square

A Victorian cheap magazine entitled *Mother Shipton's Miscellany* once carried a story about strange events at a house in Soho Square in 1704. Its owner lived in part of it, and the rest was let out as furnished lodgings, the current lodgers being a seemingly wealthy man and his two servants. One day this man told the landlord that his brother had died, and asked whether the coffin could be kept in the house overnight before being taken to the family vault next day. The landlord agreed, and it was laid in the dining room.

Late that night a servant girl, the only person still up, was horrified to see a tall figure, deathly pale and wrapped in a shroud, enter the kitchen. She fled upstairs to rouse her master and mistress, only to find that the spectre followed her into their bedroom, where it seated itself by the door, glaring and grimacing. Simultaneously, the house was filled with clatter and crashing; the girl fainted, and the landlord and his wife cowered under the bedclothes. After a long while, the noises stopped. The ghost had gone. But so had a great deal of silverware and other valuables; the 'ghost' was in fact a notorious robber, whose accomplices had smuggled him into the house in the coffin, and who acted the part of a spectre so that they could plunder it undisturbed.

Such tales about robbers' tricks were common, but it is usually said that a servant girl's cleverness and courage thwarts them.

St James's Palace

One of the standard traditional motives ascribed to a ghost's apparition is that it has come to warn a living acquaintance to prepare for death. A very detailed account of such a case was given by T. M. Jarvis, a writer concerned to uphold the reality of ghosts, in a book in 1823. The alleged events are not precisely dated, but presumably occurred early in the eighteenth century. After the deposition of James II in 1688, his mistress Madame de Beauclair was given an apartment in St James's Palace; the Duchess of Mazarine, formerly the mistress of Charles II, also had an apartment there, and the two ladies became close friends. They both felt a great curiosity about life after death, and solemnly promised one another that whoever died first would come back to tell her friend about it. The duchess was the first to die, and on the last day of her life she renewed her promise. But, to the intense disappointment of Madame de Beauclair, her spirit did not appear.

Years passed, and Madame de Beauclair grew old; having had no sign from the duchess, she had completely ceased to believe in the afterlife. Then one evening a younger acquaintance of hers received an urgent message to come at once to see her, otherwise they would never meet again in this world. The younger lady was unwilling, as she was suffering from a heavy cold, but after a second message and a gift of jewellery, she agreed. She found Madame de Beauclair in apparent good health, but convinced that she would die that very day and enter that eternal life which she had so much doubted, for the Duchess of Mazarine had at last appeared to her:

> I perceived not how she entered but, turning my eyes towards yonder corner of the room, I saw her stand in the same form and habit she was accustomed to appear in when living: fain would I have spoken, but had not the power of utterance. She took a little circuit round the chamber, seeming rather to swim than walk, then stopped by the side of that Indian chest, and, looking on me with her usual sweetness, said, 'Beauclair, between the hours of twelve and one this night you will be with me.' The surprise I was in at first being a little abated, I began to ask some questions concerning that future world I was so soon to visit; but, on the opening of my lips for that purpose, she vanished from my sight.

By the time Madame de Beauclair had finished her story it was getting towards midnight. Suddenly she cried out, 'Oh! I am sick at heart!' Despite medical attention, she was dead in half an hour, just at the time the apparition had foretold.

The Tower

The Tower is supposedly haunted by the ghosts of many historical personages who have suffered there. These include the Little Princes, nephews to Richard III (r. 1483–5), who were murdered while imprisoned in the Tower, and Henry VIII's second wife, Anne Boleyn, beheaded on Tower Green in 1536. Her ghost has often been reported as haunting the Green, and also the Chapel Royal in the White Tower, according to nineteenth- and twentieth-century accounts. In 1864, a sentry who was being court-martialled for deserting his post explained that he had challenged a white shape looming through the mist, and when it failed to stop he had stabbed it with his bayonet, but the weapon passed straight through. Realizing this must be Anne Boleyn's ghost, he had fled in panic. His excuse was accepted. Lady Jane Grey is also said to appear as a white shape on the anniversary of her execution, 13 February 1554. Other famous ghosts include Sir Walter Raleigh, imprisoned for thirteen years in the Bloody Tower and finally beheaded in 1618, and Henry Percy, imprisoned for sixteen years for his share in the Gunpowder Plot, but never executed. In addition, there are anonymous monks, and unidentified figures clad in historical costumes of various eras; there are phantoms that are not seen, but heard sighing, groaning, or screaming in various parts of the building; there are footsteps, cold draughts, and strange, lingering scents.

The more historical tales are sometimes remodelled quite drastically, to suit the expectations of different generations as to what is a 'good story'. As an example, it is instructive to consider the accounts of the death of Margaret Pole, Countess of Salisbury, executed on 27 May 1541 on the orders of Henry VIII. The first description is a contemporary one, written by Eustace Chapuys, a diplomat, in a letter to the Queen of Hungary. He stresses the dignity, self-control, and edifying words of the elderly countess, giving this priority over the distressing details of the actual beheading:

> When informed of her sentence she found it very strange, not knowing her crime, but she walked to the space in front of the Tower, where there was no scaffold but only a small block. She commended her soul to God, and desired those present to pray for the King, Queen, Prince and Princesses. The ordinary executioner being absent, a blundering *garçonneau* [young lad] was chosen, who hacked her head and shoulders to pieces.

About a hundred years later comes a different version, written by the historian Lord Herbert of Cherbury in his life of Henry VIII (1649). The account he had been given was that the countess, steadfastly maintaining her innocence, refused to co-operate in her own execution, and thus created difficulties for the headsman:

> The old lady being brought to the scaffold set up in the Tower, was commanded to lay her head on the block: but she (as a person of great quality assured me) refused, saying 'So should traitors do, and I am none'; neither did it serve that the executioner told her it was the fashion; so, turning her grey head every way, she bid him, if he would have her head, to get it off as he could; so that he was constrained to fetch it off slovenly.

It is a powerful, if gruesome, scene. It has, alas, been cheapened in modern ghost lore into a grotesque melodrama, in which all sense of dignity and tragedy is lost. We are now told that the countess, 'screaming in abject terror', had to be dragged to the block by force, broke away from the guards, and ran about the courtyard, demented, while the masked executioner pursued her. Eventually 'the guards dragged her writhing body to the bloodstained block', where it took five blows to finish her off. All this is supposed to be spectrally re-enacted on the anniversary of the execution:

> Then, according to reports, her ghost is seen, screaming with terror, running panic-stricken round and round the spot where the scaffold once stood, pursued by a ghostly masked executioner, heavy axe in hand, who finally overtakes the terrified woman and 'chuckling diabolically' slowly hacks her head off with repeated dreadful blows.

Such a travesty must surely set the proud and courageous countess turning in her grave. It is some compensation to consider that in 1886 the Vatican, regarding her as a martyr, granted her the title 'Blessed'; no doubt she will eventually be canonized as St Margaret Pole.

Tyburn Tree

London's most famous gallows was the large triangular structure in the district of Tyburn, at what is now the junction of Bayswater Road and Edgware Road, colloquially known as 'Tyburn Tree' or 'the Three-Legged Mare'. In 1678, it collapsed abruptly one night, an event which caused considerable astonishment and some wild rumours. An anonymous writer immediately produced a semi-humorous pamphlet: *The Tyburn-Ghost: Or, The Strange Downfall of the GALLOWS. A most true Relation how the famous TRIPLE-TREE near PADDINTON was on Tuesday-night last (the third of this instant September) wonderfully pluckt up by the Roots, and demolisht by certain EVIL-SPIRITS*. Some people, says the writer, believed that it had grown old and sunk under its own weight; others, that 'a Company of Quack-Doctors' had planned to steal it and grind it to powder, to be sold as a 'Universal Medicine' (splinters of gallows wood were indeed used in folk medicine, for instance as a cure for toothache).

But the most probable Opinion is, That it was ruined by certain Evil Spirits, perhaps the Ghosts of some who had formerly suffered there; for if Persons Killed retain so great an Antipathy against their Murderers, that scarce a Physitian dares come near his expired Patient, lest the Corpse should fall a-Bleeding, and discover [reveal] that which the more Courteous Grave uses to hide, we may imagine amongst so many *Rank Riders* as have broke their necks by *Falls* from this skittish Three-leg'd Jade, some or other might resolve to be revenged on her.

Nay, it is reported, or may be for ought I know, That there was seen last Tuesday-evening a Spirit sitting on one of the Cross-beams with its *Neck awry*, making a strange noise like a Scrietch-Owl; which 'tis supposed did afterwards demolish all the *venerable Fabrick:* But of this there is yet no *Affidavit* made.

The gallows was of course promptly replaced, and continued in use till 1783.

Norfolk

Alderfen Broad

In the first half of the nineteenth century, the Revd John Gunn, rector of the parish of Irstead, set out to record 'The traditions of a single Parish, retained in the memory of a single individual'. This was Mrs Lubbock, widowed in 1813; when Gunn published her stories in 1849, she was eighty. Her stock of folklore she had learned from her father, so she reported things that were said and believed in the eighteenth century.

One of the things she said was:

> Before the Irstead Enclosure in 1810, Jack o' Lantern was frequently seen here on a roky [misty] night, and almost always at a place called Heard's Holde, in Alder Carr Fen [modern Alderfen] Broad on the Neatishead side ... I have often seen it there, rising up and falling, and twistering about, and then up again. It looked exactly like a candle in a lantern.

Heard's Holde was supposedly where a man called Heard, 'guilty of some unmentionable crimes', was drowned, and local people thought the light seen hovering about there was Heard's ghost.

Neatishead people finally became so annoyed with him that three 'learned' gentlemen attempted to lay the ghost by an exorcism known in some counties as 'reading a ghost down' (reciting Scripture at it while the ghost dwindled more and more, until it was small enough to be shut in a bottle – at Lowestoft, Suffolk, Parson Cunningham was famous for conjuring a devil into his hat). At first they failed, as the ghost was too canny:

> ... he always kept a verse ahead of them. And they could do nothing, till a boy brought a couple of pigeons, and laid them down before him. He looked at them and lost his verse; and then they bound his spirit.

In most counties, Jack o' Lantern seems to have been envisaged as some kind of diminutive sprite. The notion that he was a ghost fits better with the general Norfolk concept of him as the aggressive Lantern Man (*see* THURLTON).

Aylmerton

Not far from Aylmerton, below the area known as the Roman Camp, are a number of shallow, circular depressions as much as 27 feet (8 m) wide. Formerly thought to mark the site of prehistoric pit dwellings, they are now known to be iron-working pits dating from c.850–1100.

Murray's Handbook for ... *Norfolk* (1870) says that they were known as 'the shrieking pits', local folklore asserting 'that loud shrieking is sometimes heard proceeding from them; and that a white figure may be seen at certain seasons gazing into the pits and wringing its hands'. This may be the same haunt that Henry Harrod in 1852 connected with pits at Weybourne, having been told by a labourer living in the neighbouring village that cries coming from them were often heard:

> ... and that a woman, dressed in white, rose ever and anon screaming from among them, and ran from one to another, looking down into them, wringing her hands, and shrieking. He himself had seen and heard her; for she had followed him one night nearly to his own gate!

She is not always dressed in white: in 1877, the Norfolk antiquary Walter Rye, who called her the 'Shrieking Woman', described her as 'a pale woman with long hair', while in Bryant's *Norfolk Churches* (1900) she is 'an elderly woman, with long white hair'.

Neither Harrod nor *Murray's Handbook* explains why the Shrieking Woman behaves in this way, and Ernest Suffling, c.1890, says the object of her search is something 'which nobody can define'. Later writers say she is seeking the body of her child, buried in one of the pits by her husband, who killed both her and the baby in a fit of insane jealousy. This was perhaps a late attempt to explain in terms of ghosts one of the noisy supernatural storm-warnings heard around the coast – this may be the same Shrieking Woman that makes a racket at SHERINGHAM.

Blickling Hall

The present Jacobean mansion of Blickling Hall succeeded an earlier house belonging to the Boleyn or Bullen family. At one time it was owned by Sir Thomas Boleyn, father of Anne, Henry VIII's second wife.

Of Sir Thomas himself, a contributor to *Notes and Queries* in 1850 wrote:

> The spectre of this gentleman is believed by the vulgar to be doomed, annually, on a certain night in the year, to drive, for a period of 1000 years, a coach drawn by four headless horses, over a circuit of twelve bridges in that vicinity. These are Aylsham, Burgh, Oxnead, Buxton, Coltishall, the two Meyton bridges, Wroxham, and four others whose names I do not recollect. Sir Thomas carries his head under his arm, and flames issue from his mouth. Few rustics are hardy enough to be found loitering on or near those bridges on that night; and my informant averred, that he was himself on one occasion hailed by this fiendish appari-tion, and asked to open a gate, but 'he warn't sich a fool as to turn his head; and well a didn't, for Sir Thomas passed him full gallop like:' and he heard a voice which told him that he (Sir Thomas) had no power to hurt such as turned a deaf ear to his requests, but that had he stopped he would have carried him off.

The note, initialled 'E.S.T.', came from the Revd E. S. Taylor of Ormesby, who adds, 'This tradition I have repeatedly heard in this neighbourhood from aged persons when I was a child, but I never found but one person who had ever actually *seen* the phantom.' The story was also said to be 'well vouched' for in Charles Palmer's edition of Manship's *History of Yarmouth* (1854), suggesting it had been current in the eighteenth century. The bridges in question are those of the Bure Valley.

The story recounted by the Revd Mr Taylor leaves many things unexplained, which the original narrator no doubt assumed to be common knowledge, notably the flames shooting from Sir Thomas's mouth; the fact that he will carry people off if they give him half a chance; and that the surest way of preventing this is to take no notice of him. These features relate Sir Thomas's story to other tales of the phantom coach, underpinned by the medieval tradition of the 'hell-wain', which carried off the souls of the damned. The warning against taking notice of the supernatural embodied in the story – including by implication speaking – is a common theme: tradition prescribes silence for dealing with everything from the Devil to fairies.

In Taylor's version, Sir Thomas was 'doomed ... for a period of 1000 years', a supernatural penance commonly imposed on wicked ghosts. Subsequent accounts say that he is 'rumoured' to have to atone for his share in Anne's decapitation, some stating that his haunt took place on the anniversary of her execution (19 May 1536), though one from 1903 claims it occurs 'every night'. Storytellers appear to have become more interested in explaining *why* Sir Thomas haunts Blickling than in what is the dominant theme of the 1850 version: *what happens if you see him*. The focus there is on the encounter with the spectre, and the story follows a traditional pattern, telling what the consequences of such a meeting could be, and relating how someone who did encounter the apparition escaped, thus passing on to the audience the 'traditional' time-tested strategy for dealing with the supernatural.

Later-recorded versions make things bigger, and more technicolour – not twelve Bure bridges (1850, 1862), which makes sense in the context of Blickling, but forty, over the Bure and the Yare, Bass Bridge at Brundall being one of them. The lengthening of Sir Thomas's route appears to have taken place as the result of Palmer's speculation in his edition of Manship's *History of Yarmouth* that Sir Thomas's haunt was identical with the 'vision of the "Headless Horses"' seen at WEST CAISTER.

Another shift in emphasis has been from Sir Thomas to Anne, by some said to have spent her early years at Blickling. In the *Norfolk Antiquarian Miscellany*, Walter Rye in 1877 wrote:

> ... nothing is more firmly believed than that Lady Ann Boleyn rides down the avenue of Blickling Park once a year with her bloody head in her lap, sitting in a hearse-like coach drawn by four black headless horses, and attended by coachmen and attendants, who have ... also left their heads behind them.

However, the hallmark of phantom coach stories is that, if not anonymous, they are usually attached to landed proprietors against whom some kind of grudge is held. In folkloric terms, one would *expect* the passenger in the phantom coach to be Sir Thomas, whose rise to fame and fortune was somewhat rapid and must have excited envy. Anne's haunt, though more often selected for mention today, is essentially a story told by warm and well-fed people in the safety of a highly populated mansion; her father's expresses the anxieties of country people out alone in the Bure Valley after dark. This is why Rye, after saying that people had become used to Anne's visits, adds, 'But the appearance of Sir Thomas Boleyn is not to be treated with such calm indifference.'

Castle Rising

The spectacular ruins of twelfth-century Castle Rising, dominated by massive earthworks, are said to be haunted by Queen Isabella, the 'She-Wolf of France'. An old tradition that appears to have started with the French chronicler Froissart (c.1333–c.1405) says that she was imprisoned there by her son, Edward III, after the execution of her lover Mortimer, for consenting to the murder of her husband, Edward II, at BERKELEY Castle, Gloucestershire. Some claim that she lived there in obscurity for twenty-seven years, and according to the eighteenth-century Norfolk historian Francis Blomefield she finally died there. Local tradition asserted that she was buried in Norfolk, and in the mid nineteenth century a stone in Rising church bearing the words '*Isabella regina*' was pointed out as marking the site of her grave. In the twentieth century, if not earlier, it was said that she went mad from loneliness and that her shrieks could still be heard ringing out from the Norman keep.

The tradition is a fine example of folk justice at work, rewriting history the way it *should* have been. While Isabella certainly lived at Castle Rising at intervals from the death of Edward II in 1327 to her own death in 1358, this was probably because it was one of her own properties. Her son, Edward III, visited her there (tradition said by underground passage from the Red Mount chapel at Lynn), and in 1344 she celebrated his birthday with him at Norwich. She was allowed to travel and cannot have been lonely: as Dowager Queen, she lived in state at the castle, Edward allowing her £3,000, later £4,000, for expenses, which implies a large household. Her death actually took place in Hertford Castle, where she had been in continuous residence since October 1357. She is said to have chosen to be buried at Greyfriars, London, where Mortimer had been buried twenty-eight years earlier, but – duplicitous to the end – with the heart of her murdered husband on her breast.

Croxton

A tradition of a phantom funeral was reported by Charles Kent in 1910 at Croxton. He writes that, on Croxton Heath many years ago, some poachers killed a gamekeeper and, not knowing what to do with his body, put it in a cart in among the dead hares and rabbits. As they got nearer to Thetford, a chalk-pit by the road seemed a convenient place to dump him. However, as they were lifting the gamekeeper out of the cart, he partly revived and swore to haunt them all their lives. Then they finished him off and buried him.

> Ever after a strange sight might be seen, so it is said, of a hearse, coffin and bearers, coming out of the pit at dead of night and after going some little distance down the road, turning in at a field gate and returning to the place of burial.

He adds, 'Several decades ago young people of the neighbourhood used to go in parties to see this wonder.'

Great Melton

In the 1870s, a lane called Blow Hill (or Coldblow Hill) in Great Melton was known for the Great Melton Beech, an old landmark. Beneath its boughs at midnight, a ghostly woman would sit, 'rocking herself to and fro, and nursing a child, seeming in great distress'. A nearby field was visited each midnight and noonday by a phantom coach, and the lane was also the special haunt of hyter sprites, described by Walter Rye in 1872–3 as 'a kind of fairy rather beneficent than otherwise'.

Gunton Park

Gunton Park was in the nineteenth century said to be haunted by a White Lady. The eighteenth-century house was the home of Lord Suffield, of whom Mackenzie Walcott writes in 1861:

> Lord Suffield told Dr Woodward the physician that his servants had informed him that they had heard the cry of the *White* Lady, the family warning of death; and that he himself was startled by a long unearthly shriek, upon which, running to the window, he saw a pale figure, in the deep twilight, glide across the lawn; and that night Lady Suffield died.

Like *the* White Lady of the Hohenzollerns in Germany and a few other English White Ladies, this one was evidently attached to a dynasty rather than a house, and served as a death-warning in the same way as an Irish banshee.

Happisburgh

One of the most macabre hauntings in Norfolk is that of the 'Pump Hill Ghost' at Happisburgh, reported by Ernest Suffling c.1890. In the eighteenth century, farmers coming home late at night were sometimes terribly frightened at a figure they saw coming up the main street of the village from the direction of Cart Gap – he was legless and headless, his head hanging down his back between his shoulders. In his arms was a long bundle. By his dress he appeared to be a sailor, for he wore a dark blue coat and a leather belt with a big brass buckle through which a pistol was thrust. His hair was dressed in a pigtail, so long it nearly trailed on the ground, the head being where it was. Two men who lay in wait for him followed him till he came to a well, dropped the bundle down it, then disappeared down it himself. They told their story next day, and the village agreed to search the well. A volunteer was lowered down it on a rope and at first could see nothing, but just as he was being drawn up again caught sight of a piece of dark blue cloth caught on a brick. Going down again with a clothes prop, he poked about at the bottom and encountered something soft. Using an iron hake tied to a clothes line, he fished up a sodden sack tied at the mouth. When they opened it, a pair of boots stuck out, attached to legs hacked off at the thigh. Further search found a corpse whose head was only held on by a flap of skin at the back. He was wearing a dark blue coat.

After that, they searched the area near Cart Gap and discovered a large patch of blood, the partner to his pistol, three or four gold pieces, and some empty Schiedam bottles. From these they surmised that smugglers had quarrelled and murdered one of their number, but why they carried his body to the well when they could have buried it on the beach remains a mystery.

Such was the explanation of the 'Hazebru' Pump Hill Ghost, which haunted a spot – known as Well Corner before the pump was added – along Whimpwell Street (with Whimpwell Green, south of Happisburgh, all that survives of Whimpwell village). Previous to a storm, horrible groans would be heard, but they stopped when the pump was set up. This pump, which still stood there in Suffling's time, fell into disuse in the twentieth century, but for long was not removed because people said that if this was done, the groaning would return. Villagers today must be less superstitious: there is no sign of the pump on Pump Hill, now marked by a triangle of green with a signpost on it in the middle of the road. The ghost's route lay from Cart Gap, past the red and white lighthouse built in 1791 by the Trinity House Brethren, into the village street.

Hickling Broad

Ernest Suffling, in his *History and Legends of the Broad District* (*c.*1890), tells the story of the Hickling Skater, or, as he is sometimes called, the Potter Heigham Drummer. About the time of Waterloo, a young soldier was home on a month's furlough who had a sweetheart at Potter Heigham on the far side of Hickling Broad. Her father did not approve of him, as he was only a drummer boy, so they had to meet secretly. They arranged to meet in a marsh on the Heigham side of the Broad at a place called Swim Coots. The Broad was frozen and he skated to meet his sweetheart for several evenings; but, though cautioned against it, he ventured once too often – when near the wherry channel he must have gone through the ice, for only his ghost kept the appointment with the waiting girl. He was not found for several days, as the ice was too thin to walk on but too thick to pull through in a boat. Now he can be seen in February early in the evening skating across the Broad at full speed. He beats a drum while skating 'and, said a native, "he du whistle along tu, master!"' Suffling says that, at the time of writing, the ghost had not been seen for a number of years.

In a dialectal version of this story printed in *Longman's Magazine* in 1903, an old wherryman explains that 'th' folks ha' a notion that th' Hickling drummer lad go skaten' round Swim Cutes, a-beaten' o' his drum ter show that th' ice ain't safe.' In the absence of other early versions, it is hard to say if the idea of the drumming as a warning is the writer's own embroidery, or a genuine local tradition.

Long Stratton

One of the best-known tales of the phantom coach in Norfolk is attached to the massive tomb of Edmund Reve (d. 1647) and his wife (d. 1657) in the north chancel of St Mary's church, Long Stratton. Their recumbent figures are shown, she lying in front, he behind and above her, propped on his elbow. He is dressed in scarlet robes, having been a judge of Common Pleas from 1639.

John Varden tells the story in the *East Anglian Handbook . . . for 1885*, saying:

> . . . there is or was a local legend that at certain times his ghost, jokingly known as 'Old Hunch,' drives . . . round the parish. Once a country labourer returning home late at night saw the ghostly carriage being driven furiously towards him, and scrambled into a tree . . . Scarcely was he up in the branches than it went dashing by, and finding himself safe . . . he shouted . . . 'Old Hunch, Old Hunch.' Instantly a hideous face was thrust out of the carriage window, and a harsh voice yelled back, 'If I was as far behind you as I am in front, you would never call me Hunch again.'

Varden gives no reason for the haunt, but, according to a later source, 'popular legend has it that he wrongfully obtained the manor and advowson'. In other words, this is the common tale that the occupant of the phantom coach is being punished for some injustice.

At Spixworth, 'Judge Peck' rides out at midnight in similar fashion, a tradition likewise connected with a pompous church monument, dated 1634, and bearing the effigies of William Peck and his wife.

Mannington Hall

Mannington Hall was the setting for a ghost story well known in the nineteenth century. The antiquary Dr Augustus Jessopp, staying at the Hall on 10 October 1879, was working in a room off the library after everyone else had left or gone to bed when he saw a large white hand within a foot of his elbow. Turning his head he saw the figure of a large man sitting with his back to the fire and bending slightly over the table, examining the books which he, Dr Jessopp, had been reading:

> The man's face was turned away from me, but I saw his closely cut reddish-brown hair, his ear and shaved cheek, the eyebrow, the corner of the right eye, the side of the forehead, and the large high cheek-bone. He was dressed in what I can only describe as a kind of ecclesiastical habit of thick corded silk or some such material, close up to the throat, and a narrow rim or edging, of about an inch broad, of satin or velvet serving as a stand-up collar and fitting close to the chin . . .

When the doctor moved a book on the table, the man vanished, but reappeared five minutes later. Dr Jessopp continued working, and when he had finished closed his book and threw it down on the table. It made a slight noise as it fell, and the figure once more disappeared.

According to Enid Porter in *The Folklore of East Anglia* (1974), the steward of Mannington Hall had once revealed the 'ghost' to be none other than an Italian servant come in to remove the brandy. The episode was remembered in the family of Mr T. Purdy of Aylsham, who writes:

> My grandfather R.J.W. Purdy was a friend of Lord Orford and used to shoot at Mannington, and his story, as handed down to me by my father T.W. Purdy . . . was that the 'ghost' . . . was in fact

the Italian butler whose name . . . I believe was Carlo. Carlo always fancied a night cap of a glass of brandy before he retired, and the brandy decanter stood on the table in front of the Dr.: so when the latter was deep in thought and appeared to be asleep, Carlo slid quietly into the library but every time he reached for the decanter, the Dr. opened his eyes . . .

However, in Dr. Jessopp's own account of the apparition, published in the *Athenaeum* for 10 January 1880, what he had been drinking was seltzer water.

Mundesley

According to nineteenth-century report, an apparition known as 'the Long Coastguardsman' walks the Norfolk coast from Bacton to Mundesley every night just as the clock is striking midnight, but strange to say cannot be seen on moonlit nights. He loves wind, and, when a storm rages, shouts and sings at the top of his voice. During a lull, he may be heard laughing loudly, but at other times his cries for help can be heard a long way off. Who he is nobody knows, but his behaviour resembles that of other spirits haunting the English coast, such as Jan Tregeagle of TREGAGLE'S HOLE, Cornwall.

Raynham Hall

The Brown Lady of Raynham has reputedly haunted Raynham Hall, at East Rainham, for nearly three centuries. In *The Night-Side of Nature* (1848), Mrs Crowe reports:

> The Hon. H.W. — told me that a friend of his . . . had often seen her, and had one day inquired of his host, 'Who was the lady in brown that he had met frequently on the stairs?' . . . Many persons have seen her.

Charles Loftus, the brother-in-law and cousin of Lord Charles Townshend, owner of Raynham, in his autobiography *My Youth by Sea and Land* (1876), gives his account of the ghost, 'who, in 1842 and 1844, caused such excitement among the inmates, visitors and servants'. After saying that he did not himself see her, he relates the experience of three young men of the family, cousins, staying in the house in October and November 1855. Encountering her one night on the stairs, they pursued her, but when they had her cornered she waved her hand and disappeared. Next morning, after hearing their adventure, one of the family exclaimed:

> 'This is exactly what occurred to me – the same appearance on the stairs, with precisely the same dress, and high-heeled shoes. I made notes of it all at the time. And, oh! the awful expression of those glazed, hollow eyes, and the parchment-colour of her pinched cheeks! Who can she be? I said nothing about this when it occurred to me in 1844, but it is perfectly true.'

Loftus, who was a Townshend on his mother's side, knew the apparition as the 'family ghost' (his words), Lady Dorothy Walpole, sister of Sir Robert Walpole. Loftus calls her 'Lady Dorothy', and refers to her 'well-known face and figure', recognizable from a portrait at Raynham showing her in the dress in which she often appeared, 'of a brown silk brocade spangled with gold'.

Lady Dorothy married the second Viscount Townshend in 1713, but the marriage seems to have been unhappy. Norfolk tradition said she was a young and beautiful lady, forced to marry an old man against her will, but the antiquary Walter Rye remarks that never was there a tradition with less foundation. Dorothy's husband sent their children to be brought up by his mother at Raynham, and some suggest that it was to find them that, after her death from smallpox in 1726, she returned to the Hall. However, Charles Loftus writes:

> Two reasons were given by her family why she could not rest; one was that she was offended because her family had not been ennobled, and the other that some of her husband's family possessed wealth to which she conceived herself entitled. So that on one side she hated the Walpole, and on the other the Loftus, family on their appearance at Raynham.

According to his daughter Florence, Captain Marryat (1792–1848), who lived at Langham, spoke of seeing the Brown Lady. Holding up the lighted lamp she carried, she 'grinned in a malicious and diabolical manner', so enraging him that he fired his revolver at her. She immediately vanished and the bullet lodged in a door.

Though Loftus speaks of the haunting having ceased, Florence notes, 'I have heard that she haunts the premises to this day,' and indeed she reputedly appeared on 19 September 1936, when a photographer, Indra Shira, and his assistant Captain Provand, were photographing the oak staircase. Shira suddenly called out to Provand to press the trigger, and Provand had no time to see what Shira saw: a ghostly figure coming down the stairs towards them. However, a misty shape resembling a woman in a long dress appeared on their photograph published on 16 December 1936, in *Country Life*.

Lady Dorothy also haunted Houghton Hall, built on the site of her old family home. According to Walter Rye, George IV, as Prince Regent, saw a little lady dressed in brown, with dishevelled hair and ashen face, by his bed in the State Bedroom and 'with many oaths' declared, 'I will not pass another hour in this accursed house, for I have seen that what I hope to God I may never see again.'

William Dutt, in *Highways and Byways in East Anglia* (1901), says the 'Browne Lady' was introduced from Houghton into Raynham 'when one of Sir Robert Walpole's sisters married a Marquis of Townshend'. This suggests that some people believed her to be a spectre who moved to Raynham with Dorothy on her marriage, like a handful of other family apparitions that were passed down in the female line.

The change of haunt is characteristic of spirits attached to families such as banshees and dynastic White Ladies, both of which normally serve as death omens. This may be why not everyone calls her a *Brown* Lady: Walter Rye refers to her as the *Grey* Lady, and in *The Perlustrations of Yarmouth* (1875) she is called the *White* Lady, and said to have appeared a few days before the death of the Marquis of Townshend in 1863. Possibly one sort of apparition has evolved into another, a hereditary death-warning into a historical ghost.

Sheringham

Of old, the town consisted of Upper and Lower Sheringham, one a prosperous agricultural village, the other a poor fishing community. On the boundary of the parish, at a gap in the cliffs, was a place where, around the middle of the eighteenth century, twelve drowned sailors, washed up after a gale, were thrown one on the top of another into a ditch without Christian burial, and covered with a heap of stones. If anyone were bold enough to venture there at night in bad weather, he would distinctly hear a sound like shingle dropping slowly, pebble by pebble, onto a big stone.

A little way out to sea was a spot, said the fisherfolk, where the captain of some old ship was drowned. There, more than once, fishermen had heard sounds like a human voice coming up from the water; whichever way they pulled, the voice would seem to come from the other direction, till at last it would come from just beneath the boat like the last despairing cry of a sinking man. Then, if they were wise, they would row for life to shore, and consider themselves lucky if they reached home before the squall which was sure to follow.

The 'Shrieking Woman' was a noisy phantom whom the people of Sheringham also believed to be a portent of disaster. A contributor to *Notes and Queries* in 1864 wrote, 'When she is heard, bad times are coming indeed. She had been silent for a long time till last Christmas, when she threw several good people in Upper S— into great alarm with unusually hideous yellings.' The author explains away the event, saying that what was mistaken for the 'shrieks' might have been the singing, 'more hearty than melodious', of a large group of young people returning that night from a ball. At any rate, 'the storm which ... should have followed the old hag's shrieks, did not come.'

Another premonitor of storm was 'Shock', the local name for the famous East Anglian 'Shuck'. The Revd E. S. Taylor of Ormesby wrote in 1850 that he had heard of Shuck from many people in East Norfolk and Cambridgeshire, who described him as a 'black shaggy dog, with fiery eyes ... who visits churchyards at midnight', and Amelia Opie wrote in her journal in 1829 after walking by Over-strand church, 'Tradition says, that every evening, at twilight, the *ghost of a dog* is seen to pass under the wall of this churchyard, having begun its walk from the church at [Beeston] ... It is known by the name of Old Shuck.'

Shuck is not usually thought of as a ghost: he is a shape-shifting bogey beast (*see* BRIGG, Lincolnshire) whose local manifestations include 'Old Scarf' in Great Yarmouth, 'Skeff' of Garvestone, 'Old Shocks' around Tasburgh and Flordon, the 'Shucky Dog' around Magdalen, and 'Chuff' in Walberswick, Suffolk. His appearance did not always presage death or disaster, and indeed he could act as a guardian. At Sheringham the apparition was thought to come out of the sea and run along 'Shock's Lane'. He was deemed to be headless and to have a 'white handkercher' tied over the place where his head should have been, yet to possess great saucer eyes: collectors have made jokes about the seeming contradiction, but headlessness and saucer eyes are traditional signs of the supernatural.

Thetford

According to W. G. Clarke, in his *In Breckland Wilds* (1926), many years ago, a spectre known as 'the White Rabbit' haunted parts of Thetford near the Warren. 'It had large flaming eyes, could run very fast, was never caught, and was seen by a great many people.' Not only do rabbits appear as bogey beasts (*see* BRIGG, Lincolnshire) in other counties, but Thetford Warren was infested with the real thing. On 6 May 1837, John Drew Salmon wrote in his diary: 'The white rabbits very conspicuous on the Warren as they kept moving about.'

Thetford also possessed what must be a unique ghost. It haunted a mansion variously called 'The Place' or 'The Nunnery', which occupied the site of a Benedictine nunnery sold by Henry VIII to Sir Richard Fulmerston, who turned it into a house, converting the church into 'lodgings and convenient rooms'. According to *Murray's Handbook for ... Norfolk* (1870):

A long gallery was formerly shown here, in which (1569), the young heir of the Dacres, Lords of Gilsland and Greystock [Cumberland], was killed by a fall from a wooden horse. He had been placed under the care of Sir Richard Fulmerston by the Duke of Norfolk, his guardian. Spots of blood were shown on the floor.

Sir Richard's ghost troubled the gallery, and 'made night hideous' in various parts of Thetford – since ... it was asserted that he had played the part of the wicked uncle, and for the sake of lands (to which he was never in any degree entitled) had 'taken a pin' out of the 'vaulting horse,' and so caused young Dacre's death.

George, Lord Dacre, died on 17 May 1569, at the age of seven. The 'wicked uncle' story flourished, despite the fact that Sir Richard had been dead three years when little Lord Dacre met with his accident. Walter Rye, telling the story in 1877, does not mention Sir Richard's haunting of the gallery, but instead reports a tradition of Young Lord Dacre prancing up and down 'on the ghost of a headless rocking-horse'.

Clarke says that Lord Dacre's ghost got so troublesome around the Nun's Bridges (formerly the 'Blue Bridges') that it was decided to lay him. A pound of new candles was thrown into the Little Ouse and the spirit ordered not to return until they were burned completely up – for a similar piece of trickery, *see* DEBENHAM, Suffolk.

Meantime, Sir Richard was not idle. In 1850, a contributor to *Notes and Queries* wrote of a phantom coach 'in the West of Norfolk':

... where the ancestor of a family is reported to drive his spectral team through the old walled-up gateway of his now demolished mansion, on the anniversary of his death: and it is said that the bricks next morning have ever been found loosened and fallen, though as constantly repaired.

Clarke says this was the blocked red-brick gateway marking the entrance to the Nunnery, 'built up seven times, and knocked down seven times by a carriage with four horses'. Though neither he nor Rye say so, the implication is that the phantom coach belongs to Sir Richard. He may be paying for the alleged murder; more likely, he is suffering from the traditional curse falling on those who acquire or damage former Church property. Not only had he taken over the Nunnery, but in 1548 he bought Thetford priory from the Crown, and disposed of its materials.

Thurlton

In the churchyard at Thurlton, on the north side of the church, is the Wherryman's Gravestone. Carved with the picture of a Norfolk wherry, it marks the grave of Joseph Bexfield, a wherryman drowned on 11 August 1809 at the age of thirty-eight, leaving a widow and two children.

Local tradition says that Bexfield was one of the wherrymen who plied the River Yare between Norwich and Yarmouth. They used to tie up at night at Thurlton Staithe, halfway between the two places. Near where the track across the marsh from the Staithe met the old turnpike road stood the White Horse Inn. One night, after having a drink there, he was making tracks for home when he remembered he had left some things he had brought his wife from Norwich on the wherry. Though one of his drinking cronies warned him not to return to the Staithe, because the Lantern Men were about in the marsh 'popping off in hundreds', Bexfield said he knew the marsh too well to be led astray by a 'Jack o' Lantern', and off he went. That was the last they saw of him, until days later his body was washed up between Reedham and Breydon.

The Fenland storyteller W. H. Barrett says in *East Anglian Folklore* (1976) that the old Thurlton man who told him this tale ended by saying that a 'shadow figure' could still be seen on a misty night wandering over the marshes and vanishing into the river. It was the ghost of the wherryman being led to his doom.

However, in a much sparer version of the story current in oral tradition in the 1940s and 1950s there was no ghost. It is possible that Mr Barrett, who was a relative of the occupant for many years of March Farm (formerly the White Horse), and used to entertain nephews and nieces with his stories, added the ghost for extra measure. The emphasis in earlier accounts was not on what became of Bexfield (whose descendants still lived locally) after his demise, but on the dangers of the marshes, in particular the ferocious Lantern Man, long thought of in East Norfolk as a malevolent being whose attacks were provoked by not treating him with respect.

Waxham Hall

It was no doubt thanks to its combination of hoary antiquity and later neglect that Waxham Hall acquired the reputation of being haunted. By the end of the nineteenth century, there were traditions of a coach and headless horses, the tragic withering of an ancient line, a ghost, and a bloodstained floor. Similarly, W. H. Cooke, an avid collector of East Norfolk folklore, says in about 1911:

> In the spacious Attic is *The Haunted Chamber!* In it a member of the Brograve family committed suicide by cutting his throat. At certain seasons of the year, the blood stains are visible. Of the last generation of this family, not one of the males died a natural death.

The direct line of the Brograves had indeed ended with the death of Sir George Berney Brograve, who died childless in 1828, having been predeceased by his younger brother, Captain Roger Brograve, who shot himself in 1813.

Probably because of the similarity of their names, there appears to have been some confusion between Sir George and his father Sir Berney Brograve, to whom many local legends are attached. Although the romantic notion of a 'tragic ending to an ancient line' was prompted by Sir George's history, it came to be Sir Berney who was said to be the last of his race, for he lived and died a bachelor, although he dotted the countryside with his 'portrait' (bastards). Similarly a macabre story at Hempstead of a huntsman devoured by his own hounds came to be associated with both.

'Owd Sir Barney', as he was known, had several supernatural encounters. He may have been the hero of what Rye calls 'The curious tale of how one Berney's hair "turned white in a single night" by the apparition of his brother'. An informant of W. B. Gerish's heard that the 'somewhat numerous ghostly train' which haunted Waxham Hall were the unshriven spirits of the Brograves who died violent deaths.

One story ran that, on New Year's Eve, Sir Berney gave a banquet for the shades of his ancestors. Covers were laid for the six ghosts, and glasses filled for every guest. One by one, their toasts were solemnly drunk, but on the stroke of midnight they vanished, and later Sir Berney awoke, cold and disagreeable (and presumably hung over).

The exploits of this adventurer did not end with his death. Some identified the driver of the phantom coach as Sir Berney in person. In 1906, Walter Rye wrote:

> Everybody out Stalham way knew that 'Owd Sir Barney' rode on certain nights in the year along the 'Carnser' [causeway] from Waxham Hall to Worstead, and if no one could be produced who had really seen the apparition, why, there was any number who had 'heard tell' of it.

West Caister

Caister Castle was built by Sir John Fastolf in about 1420. The Revd John Gunn of Irstead wrote in 1849: 'The marvellous account of a carriage drawn by headless horses at ... Caistor [sic] Castle, is not yet utterly discarded.' He gives no details of the haunt, but Mackenzie Walcott in *The East Coast of England* (1861) writes, 'The peasants believe that at midnight yearly a dark coach, drawn up by headless horses, rolls into the dark courtyard, and carries away some unearthly passengers.'

This is in line with old beliefs in the 'hell-wain' which trundled round collecting the souls of the dead, and with many later phantom coaches with unnamed occupants. However, Charles Palmer, in a brief mention of the 'Headless Horses' in Manship's *History of Yarmouth* (1854), tried to rationalize the tradition, suggesting that, as Geoffrey Boleyn, first of the Boleyns at BLICKLING HALL, bought that manor from Sir John Fastolf, 'and complained of his bargain', it might be that the restless spirit of his descendant, Sir Thomas, 'occasionally extends his drive to Caister'.

Wolterton Hall

Wolterton was built by Horatio Walpole, the brother of the statesman Sir Robert Walpole, in 1727–41. Lady Dorothy Nevill, in *Mannington and the Walpoles* (1894), writes:

There is a family ghost at Wolterton, which at intervals is seen by old servants about the place. A white lady is said to be in the habit of appearing whenever some calamity is about to threaten our family. Some little time before my brother, the late Lord Orford, died, in 1894, I well recollect his saying to me, 'I hear from Norfolk that the white lady has been seen again. It is you or I this time, Dolly, for we are the only ones left[.]' The white lady in question is supposed to be one of the Scamler family, who were the possessors of Wolterton before my ancestor built the present mansion. There used to be some story that one of the Lords Orford unearthed the old tombstones of the Scamlers in the ruined church in Wolterton Park, and that this act of sacrilege was the cause of the poor lady's spirit being so disturbed ... In old days the Walpoles used to be driven in their hearse three times around this ruined church before being laid to rest in the family vault [at Wickmere]. Certainly Lady Walpole of Wolterton (Pierre Lombard's daughter) was buried with this ceremonial.

This custom was said by later writers to have been devised in order to placate her. Lady Dorothy Nevill, however, reports discovering that no such act of sacrilege was ever perpetrated, 'so it must be for some other reason that the ghostly dame lingers about Wolterton'.

The last burial in the churchyard at Wolterton took place in 1747, and Fadens' map of Norfolk in 1797 records it as a ruin. The ceremony connected with it perhaps inspired the tradition of a phantom hearse, 'with steeds, plumes, and attendants, according to some all headless', said to appear to Walpoles as a death-warning at both Wolterton and Raynthorpe Hall.

Lady Dorothy Nevill says also that the Lady Walpole née Lombard mentioned was herself believed to haunt the house:

In the drawing-room is a full-length portrait of Ambassador Horace Walpole. This gentleman formed part of a large picture comprising himself and wife and seven or eight children, some of which are represented as angels, apparently having died as babies. My father cut this picture up and gave the portraits to different members of the family, whose descendants they are. The unhappy wife, Miss Lombard, is said to haunt Wolterton seeking for her divided relatives.

Northamptonshire

Althorpe Park

Althorpe Park was in the nineteenth century the subject of a fairly
singular ghost story. As John Ingram, in *Haunted Homes* (1888),
remarks:

> That a residence of the antiquity and importance of Althorp
> should have a ghost is nothing unusual ... The apparition which
> is connected with Earl Spencer's palatial dwelling, however, is
> not of the character one generally finds connected with places of
> that rank ...

The story Ingram tells is that Mr (later Archdeacon) Drury was
invited by Lord and Lady Lyttleton to go with them to Althorpe
on a visit to Earl Spencer, Lady Lyttleton's father. After dinner, Mr
Drury and Lord Lyttleton played billiards, going on with their game
so late that finally one of the servants came and asked them, when
they went to bed, to put out the lights themselves as Earl Spencer
was always worried about fire. Looking at their watches, they were
amazed to see that it was past two, and both of them went to bed.

Some time later, Mr Drury was woken by a light falling on his
face. Opening his eyes, he saw at the foot of the bed a stable-man, in
a striped shirt and flat cap, who was carrying a lantern with the
bullseye turned full on him. 'What do you want, my man? Is the
house on fire?' exclaimed Mr Drury, but received no reply. Further
questions met with the same silence, and finally he told the man to
take himself off 'as an impudent scoundrel, whose conduct should
be reported to his master'. The figure then slowly lowered the
lantern and passed into the dressing room, from which there was
no exit other than the door by which he had entered. 'You won't be
able to get out that way,' called Mr Drury, then dropped off to sleep
again without waiting to see what followed.

Next morning, he remarked to Lady Lyttleton that it was a very
odd thing but he had been disturbed by a stable-man walking into
his room in the middle of the night. He said he supposed he was

drunk, though he did not seem so. When he described the man's dress and general appearance, Lady Lyttleton turned pale and said, 'You have described my father's favourite groom, who died a fortnight ago, and whose duty it was to go round the house after everyone had gone to bed, to see that the lights were extinguished, and with strict orders to enter any room where one was seen burning.'

Ingram did not know whether or not the groom was ever seen by Mr Drury or anyone else at Althorpe again. The folklorist Christina Hole connected this story of a 'faithful servitor' with others concerning the return of monks and priests to the abbeys or priories or churches they once served, saying, 'So much of a man's energy and devotion are expended in this life upon his work that it is not surprising to hear of those who returned after death to the scene of their labours.'

Apethorpe

In 1621, the Mildmay chapel was added to the parish church of St Leonard at Apethorpe, north of Oundle, to house the huge marble monument to Sir Anthony Mildmay (d. 1617) and his wife. Their effigies lie on a big sarcophagus at the corners of which stand four life-sized figures: Piety, Charity, Wisdom, and Justice. Above is a drum-shaped lantern with the seated figures of Faith, Hope, and Charity, again. The insistence on charity is not accidental, and is connected with a most benevolent ghost.

The couple who occasioned all this pomp lived at nearby Apethorpe Hall, the house as it was *c.*1500 still being the core of the present mansion. The house and manor passed through several owners before in 1550 coming to Sir Walter Mildmay, from whom it descended to Anthony, his son.

Murray's Handbook for ... Northamptonshire (1901) notes the Hall's many historical associations and points out its attractions for nineteenth-century visitors, including portraits in the long gallery. 'Here also is the "lively portraiture" of the Lady Grace, wife of Sir Anthony Mildmay, who, according to a tradition of the house, "walks" on certain nights, scattering silver pennies behind her.'

As *Murray's Handbook* suggests, this unusually gracious tradition was probably a recollection of her charity in life. It is recorded on her monument that she was 'helpful with phisick, cloathes, nourishment, or counsels to any in misery'. Moreover, she instituted four quarterly sermons in the church, as well as leaving money for the poor and for placing apprentices.

Bulwick

In the parish church at Bulwick is a bronze plaque to the memory of Admiral Sir George Tryon (1832–93), born at Bulwick Park, his family home. He entered the navy young and held a series of important appointments, including Secretary of the Admiralty. In August 1891, he was appointed to the command of the Mediterranean fleet, which by constant drill and exercise he transformed into a fighting unit. His reputation as a tactician was prodigious: it is all the sadder, then, that he is mainly remembered now for a naval blunder.

He was leading the fleet on manoeuvres aboard HMS *Victoria*, commissioned as flagship of the fleet, to replace the older HMS *Camperdown*. On 22 June 1893, en route from Beirut to Tripoli, the fleet was steaming north-north-east in parallel columns six cables (1,200 yds/1.1 km) apart when Tryon ordered the two lines of ships to turn inwards towards each other. His intention appears to have been to bring the fleet into the anchorage with the two columns (as well as the ships in column) at two cables interval. However, to finish up at this distance, they needed to start *ten* cables apart. When staff questioned the signal, Tryon would not listen. They assumed he knew what he was about.

But he seems to have made a mathematical error, with the result that the *Camperdown*'s ram struck the *Victoria* below the waterline, making a long breach. The sea's inrush was so great that she quickly went down by the bows, taking with her Tryon, 22 officers, and 336 men. As the ship was sinking, the admiral was reported as saying, 'It is entirely my fault.'

Hard on the heels of the disaster came more sensational reportage. Staff-Commander Hawkins-Smith, the navigation officer, who stood by Tryon in his last moments, said at the ensuing court martial, 'Nearly all the various yarns which have got into the papers, such as the coxswain offering the lifebuoy, and the Admiral refusing to save himself, are pure inventions.' Later, Christina Hole, for example, reports that the *Victoria* sank, 'carrying the Admiral and one midshipman who defied orders and refused to leave him with it' – a distortion of the fact that, when Tryon turned round to order the signalman to give the signal 'Send boats', he saw one of the midshipmen and said to him, 'Don't stop there, youngster – go to a boat.' A few moments later the ship turned over. One of the saddest aspects of the tragedy was that *many* midshipmen were lost.

Then there were the alleged omens, many and various: among other things, people now remembered that HMS *Victoria* was recommissioned on a Friday the thirteenth. The culmination of all this was a remarkable ghost story based on the widespread belief that a sailor's fetch would come to warn his family of his death. After the tragedy, reports began to circulate that, on 22 June, Lady Tryon had been giving an 'At Home' in her London house in Eaton Square, when one or two of her guests were surprised to see what they thought was her husband walk across the drawing room without saying a word. They knew that he was then supposed to be in the Mediterranean, and there had been no rumour of his return, nor did Lady Tryon appear to expect him. At the moment when they thought they saw him, he had already been drowned.

Clopton

On the eastern border of the county, south-west of Oundle, stood the old church of what was then Clapton, the spire of which was blown up 'to save the expense of keeping it in repair'. Not far from its site is Skulking Dudley Coppice, shown by name on large-scale maps. It gets its name from a member of the Dudley family, who held a manor here in the fourteenth century and remained in possession until 1764. Local tradition says the family was hunch-backed.

In the early years of the twentieth century, one of them returned to disturb the villagers' peace. This was 'Skulking Dudley', so-called because he was seen on moonlit nights dodging in and out of hedgerows. It was said that he could not rest because of a murder he had committed in 1349. Whether from guilt or as a penance, he would nightly 'walk' from Clopton manor past the old graveyard and demolished church, and then along the Lilford road to the small coppice later named after him. His visits caused such alarm after 1900 that in 1905 the Bishop of Peterborough came with twenty-one clergy to exorcize him, after which his wanderings ceased.

According to the version of Skulking Dudley's story given in the Reader's Digest's *Folklore, Myths and Legends of Britain* (1977), it took the combined skills of twelve clergymen to lay him. He is represented as a bullying landowner who continued to torment the villagers of Clopton long after his death. Soon after inheriting Clopton manor in the fifteenth century, Dudley so insulted a neighbouring landowner that the young man challenged him to a duel. However, Dudley was a coward, and on the appointed day took to his bed feigning illness. To save his honour, his daughter disguised herself in his armour and fought in his place. She lost but her opponent discovered who she was just as he was about to kill her, spared her life, and married her. Skulking Dudley met his end when one of his own harvesters, annoyed at being whipped, struck off his head with a scythe.

This version, which sets the story a century later than the first, combines with the Skulking Dudley legend that of the heiress Agnes Hotot, who married into the Dudley family. Before her marriage, her father, Sir John Hotot, was challenged to a duel by a certain Ringsdale. As Sir John was suffering from gout, Agnes took his place and laid low her opponent. 'When he lay prostrate on the ground she loosened her throat-latch, lifted up the visor of her helmet, and let down her hair about her shoulders, thus discovering [revealing] her sex.'

Daventry

The former Wheatsheaf Inn at the end of Sheaf Street, Daventry, was during the Civil War the scene of a historic apparition.

On 31 May 1645, Charles I, having taken Leicester by storm, marched towards Oxford, then under siege. On 7 June, the Royalist army reached Daventry, where Charles set up his headquarters. For six nights, he slept at the Wheatsheaf. His army of around 10,000 men were stationed at 'Daventry Field' (then unenclosed land), with the cavalry at Staverton and nearby villages. On 12 June, a skirmishing party of Fairfax's horse seized some prisoners and the king had the whole army encamp on Borough Hill and stood under arms all night. The battle of NASEBY followed on 14 June.

The king had gone to Daventry 'with a thorough resolution of fighting', but overnight changed his mind and decided to march north, as Prince Rupert originally advised. According to Rastall's *History of Southwell* (1787), 'The occasion off this alteration was said to be some presages off ill fortune which the King received, and which were related to me by a person off Newark att that time in his Majestie's horse.'

> About two hours after the King had retired to rest, some off his attendants hearing an uncommon noise in his chamber, went into it, where they found his Majestie setting up in bed ... The King, in a trembling voice, ... told them how much he had been agitated in a dream, by thinking he saw the apparition of Lord Strafford, who, after upbraiding him with unkindness, told him, he was come to return him good for evil, and that he advised him by no means to fight the Parliament armie that was att that time quartered at Northampton, for in it was one whom the King should never conquer by arms. Prince Rupert, in whom courage was the predominant qualitie, rated the King out off his apprehensions the next day, and a resolution was agen taken to meet the enemie. The next night, however, the apparition appeared to him a second time, but with looks of anger. Assured him, that would be the last advice he should be permitted to give him, but that if he kept his resolution off fighting he was undone.

After this, Charles remained another day at Daventry swithering between staying and going, and finally decided to take the advice of Strafford, his former counsellor, whose death warrant he had been obliged by Parliament to sign four years before. But it was too late – overnight, word reached him that Fairfax's army was now within eight miles (13 km) of his own. He decided to fight. As Rastall comments, 'If his majestie had taken the advice of the frendly ghost ... his affairs might, perhaps, still have had a prosperous issue ... After this he never could get together an armie fit to look the enemie in the face.'

Charles's defeat at Naseby was the beginning of the end:

He was often heard to say, that he wished he had taken *the warn-ing*, and not fought at Naseby; the meaning of which nobody knew but those to whom he told this appearance at Daintree, and they were afterwards all off them charged to conceal it.

Hannington

This small village midway between Northampton and Kettering was the scene of a Nine Days' Wonder. In 1675, Justinian Isham wrote from Christ Church, Oxford, to his father that 'The report of the Hannington ghost was spread all over Oxford.'

A contemporary pamphlet appeared, entitled *The Rest-less Ghost: or, Wonderful News from* Northamptonshire, *and* Southwark. This account had been taken down before witnesses from the mouth of William Clarke, a maltster of Hennington (as it is spelt in the pamphlet), and could be vouched for by William Stubbins, John Charlton, and John Stevens, 'to be spoken with any day at the Castle Inn without Smithfield-Barrs', and many others.

Clarke lived at a farmhouse known as 'Old Pells house' after earlier occupants. Twelve months previously, a series of incidents began: doors were unlocked or unbolted during the night, flung off their hinges, and windowpanes were broken. Nothing had been seen until about three weeks before when, as Clarke was walking a little way off from the house, 'the Spirit on a sudden became visible to him, at first in a very horrid, but immediately after in a more familiar and humane shape.' Although frightened, Clarke demanded in the name of God what it was, and what it wanted. To which the apparition answered 'with a pleasant friendly countenance and distinct voice' (and the pamphlet emphasizes this by going into larger print):

> I am the disturbed Spirit of a person long since Dead, I was Murthered neer this place Two hundred sixty and seven years, nine weeks, and two days ago, to this very time, and come along with me and I will shew you where it was done.

It led him to the side of a hedge and said, 'Here was I kill'd, my head being separated from my body.' When Clarke asked why he had been killed, he said it was for his estate. He was unable to rest because he had lived in London, at Southwark, and before his death had buried some money and documents there. Clarke asked why, in that case, he had not started his haunting before, and the apparition answered that it *had* haunted 'that place' (i.e. where the money was buried) for several years after his death but that a certain friar had bound him for 250 years by magic, stopping him appearing on earth. Now that time was up, and Clarke must help him by going to Southwark next day or he would give him no peace. Clarke said he could not leave so soon but agreed to meet him within the fortnight on London Bridge.

When Clarke told his neighbours and the minister of this encounter, they said he must keep his promise to the ghost 'but not to eat or drink in any place whether it should lead him' (the same taboo as existed against eating and drinking with fairies). So, on 9 January 1675, Clarke went to London and started crossing London Bridge. The spirit appeared before him, in ordinary clothes (instead of the traditional shroud) and 'with an inviting smile' led him to a house in Southwark. There, he became visible not only to Clarke, but to those living there, telling them 'very mildly' they were his descendants and showing them where to dig.

Early next morning, Clarke returned to the house and they dug on that spot, and about eight feet down found a pot of gold, with documents at the bottom, some of which crumbled away, while others, of parchment, corroborated the spirit's account by their dates. When Clarke lifted the pot, the spirit reappeared and instructed him as to the distribution of what had been found. When this had been done, the spirit appeared again 'in a very joyful contented manner', thanking him, saying that now he could rest and would trouble him no more.

Naseby

The battle of Naseby, the turning point of the English Civil War, was fought on 14 June 1645. Prince Rupert, commanding the forces of his uncle, Charles I, chose an advantageous position on Dust Hill, two miles (3 km) to the north, along the Sibbertoft road. This strategic position meant that Cromwell's men were fighting into the wind and the smoke from the cannon was blowing back on them.

Nevertheless, they won and slaughtered 200 Royalist camp followers as a moral principle.

According to legend, for years after 1645 there were times when
people witnessed the struggle re-enacted in the sky, accompanied
by the sounds of mortal combat. The Northamptonshire historian
John Morton, writing in 1712, comments:

> As to the Reports we have had of strange Appearances of Military
> Skirmishes in the Air, or of Armies of Aerial Warriours disputing
> in Battel-Array for Victory, and particularly that in the Fenn [sic]
> Countrey nigh *Peterborough* the Year before the Revolution; I
> should scarce have taken notice of them, had they not been so
> seriously mention'd by some of our Old Historians; and had they
> not of late impos'd upon some of better Rank than the Vulgar.
> Those in the Fen [sic] Countrey, who say they were Spectators of
> this strange Prodigy, peradventure saw a great many small Clouds
> of uncouth Shapes, from which there flash'd out Lightning, and
> now and then they heard a Thunder-Crack. This 'tis likely was the
> whole of the Matter, and all the rest the product of their own
> Superstitious Imaginations.

They may also have been influenced by the Wild Hunt reported in
the early twelfth century as having been witnessed in and around
PETERBOROUGH, Huntingdonshire and Peterborough. However,
similar spectral armies have been reported since classical times: in
England, one was seen in Cumberland in the eighteenth century on
SOUTHER FELL.

The battle of Naseby evidently remained the talk of the village
for many years. The Revd John Mastin, vicar of Naseby, wrote in
1792:

> The following ænigmatical anecdote was told me when I first came
> to Naseby, by Charles Wilford, master of the Bell public house.
> 'Some years ago, on a Shrove-Tuesday, two women of the village
> had a violent dispute in the church-yard; from words, they pro-
> ceeded to blows, and fought most furiously; when a man, who was
> shot at the battle of Naseby, came out of a grave and parted them.'

On investigation, it transpired that Humphrey Thompson, a parish-
ioner of Naseby and quartermaster fighting for Charles I in this
battle, was wounded, but not killed. After quitting the army, he

was made parish clerk and sexton, and was digging a grave when the women's quarrel took place.

Passenham

Passenham is, or was, much haunted. Frightful shrieks were said to be heard coming from the millpond: these are the screams of a woman called Nancy Webb, who, finding herself pregnant, threw herself into the race and was crushed to death by the mill wheel.

At the bottom of the mill dam may be 'laid' another ghost. Jack Gould writes that his early youth was spent in Passenham, where in the 1920s he heard talk of 'Bobby Bannister', who, though Gould never heard of anyone who had actually seen him, was used as a bogey to frighten naughty children.

'Bobby Bannister' was a historical person, Sir Robert Banastre, Head of Household to Kings James I and Charles I. His bust presides over his burial place in the chancel of the parish church. A fervent Anglo-Catholic, he rebuilt his 'faire chauncel' in 1626 in sumptuous style, with fine woodwork, wall paintings, and a roof painted deep blue and studded with golden stars.

But despite Sir Robert's munificence to the church, he left behind an evil reputation. In a manuscript believed written by a William Druce at the end of the nineteenth century, Banastre is said to have been owner of the manors of Passenham and Furtho, who pulled down both villages except for the churches and a farmhouse or two, to render his estate exempt from paying Poor Rates. In a versified account of his legend, we hear that he died in mid death-bed confession, with his sins upon him, and soon after his death:

> . . . rumours strange, about were noised,
> Of howlings heard, a figure seen,
> In armour clad, who walked the green
> And verdant meadow late at night,
> Causing the villagers much fright.

As Sir Robert's funeral procession approached the church, the bearers of his bier were aghast to hear a familiar voice saying 'Steady! Steady! I am not ready!' Hastily they opened the coffin, but as the corpse bore the signs of death, closed it again and proceeded to the church. But at the church porch the voice came again: 'Steady! Steady! I am not ready!' During the service, a series of bizarre accidents occurred and above the ensuing hubbub they heard again: 'Steady! Steady! I am not ready!'

Hurrying through the service, they placed Sir Robert's coffin in his tomb. But after that, the villagers became afraid to go out at night:

> For scarce would even shadows fall,
> And darkness close round the Churchyard wall
> Than dashing along at a desperate pace,
> (None e'er saw the driver's face)
> Was a coach and four with a headless team . . .
> Oh! Who is it . . . utters that piercing scream
> 'Steady, steady! I am not ready!'

Finally, things got so bad that the parson's wife said he should apply for a faculty to hold a service to lay the ghost beneath the mill wheel till Doomsday. Soon bishop, canons, and rural dean all arrived and, when the time came for Sir Robert's nightly appearance, began to read the service. At that, the ghost rose up and promised, if they stopped exorcizing him and let him work out his penance, he would never plague the village again. So the bishop bade the spirit depart in peace. 'Sir Robert's ghost then took its flight; / No one has seen it since that night.' A penny pamphlet of 1856, however, gives a different ending, saying 'six men, eminent for piety, were required to lay his spirit, once and forever afterwards, in the bottom of the mill dam.'

In T. H. White's version, 'Bobby Bannister' has *not* been laid and still haunts the area:

Then there was Robert Bannister, the huntsman . . . He rides with his whole pack of hounds in full cry . . . and marks to ground by his grave. He broke his neck out hunting, and was dragged home dead by a frightened horse with his foot in the stirrup. So now he rides like that, a rattling skeleton behind a fiery horse, and the neck is out of joint. It is a fine sight, with the pealing of the hounds and the jolting of the bones, on a roaring north-westerly night of windy December.

Whittlebury

'The hell-hounds, and their ghostly huntsmen, are still heard careering along the gloomy avenues of Whittlebury,' wrote Thomas Sternberg in 1851, using the name of the village of Whittlebury for Whittlewood, on the outskirts of which it lies. This ancient wood, called in Anglo-Saxon *Witelwuda*, is a former royal forest – an appropriate setting for the spectral chase first recorded in England at PETERBOROUGH, Huntingdonshire and Peterborough, in the early twelfth century, and commonly identified with continental tales of the Wild Hunt.

In Northamptonshire, the hunters were known as the 'wild-men' and the 'wild-hounds'. Of the Huntsman himself, Sternberg writes, 'Both Whittlebury and Rockingham contend for the honour of his presence.' The Whittlebury tradition, as narrated in the *Sporting Magazine* in 1849, ascribes to him a romantic origin. A daughter of one of the noble rangers of the forest, famed equally for beauty and coquetry, was passionately loved by a knight, but, after encouraging him, she subsequently turned cold. Driven mad, he plunged a sword through his own heart. Soon she also died and was doomed to be hunted eternally by the demon knight.

Sternberg offers the rationalizing explanation that the story was put about by poachers in Whittlewood, to keep observers away. If so, they did not invent it. This is a version of an international folk-tale which tells how the Wild Huntsman pursues a supernatural woman through the forest: usually either a man intervenes, or the Huntsman catches her, kills her, and cuts her up like game.

John Dryden is sometimes said to have got the idea of the spectral hunt in 'Theodore and Honoria' from the Whittlewood legend heard during his residence in the county. But while it is true that Dryden came of Northamptonshire landed gentry (he was born at Aldwincle), his poem, published in *Fables, Ancient and Modern* (1700), is a translation of a story told in Boccaccio's *Decameron* in the fourteenth century.

'Relentless as a rock', the fair Honoria persistently rejects Theodore's advances, and to put distance between them he goes to live in a nearby grove. One morning, walking in the woods, he hears screaming. Presently, a naked woman, young and beautiful, comes running towards him:

> Her face, her hands, her naked limbs were torn,
> With pressing thro the brakes, and prickly thorn;
> Two mastiffs gaunt and grim her flight pursu'd,
> And oft their fasten'd fangs in blood embru'd: ...
> Not far behind, a knight of swarthy face,
> High on a coal-black steed pursu'd the chace;
> With flashing flames his ardent eyes were fill'd,
> And in his hand a naked sword he held:
> He chear'd the dogs to follow her who fled,
> And vow'd revenge on her devoted head.

The knight tells Theodore that he loved the woman, but she rejected him and he killed himself. Both were damned and daily she flees before him, daily he kills her, feeding her heart and bowels to his dogs, daily she revives. Even as he speaks, she springs up from the ground and sets off again, the 'hell-hounds' in pursuit, the knight not far behind.

Theodore now invites Honoria to a feast in the grove. The hunt is enacted as before; the knight again tells his tale. Honoria takes the horrific sight as a warning and, through mingled fear and remorse, rewards Theodore's constancy by marrying him.

In both the medieval tale and the Northamptonshire story, the prevailing idea is that violent deeds may be re-enacted over and over again by the spectres of the players in the original drama. Rather than Dryden being inspired by the Northamptonshire tale, it is likely that, by the nineteenth century, someone had grafted his story onto a vaguer local tradition.

Northumberland

Bellister

In the grey of the evening 'about half a century ago', says M. A. Richardson in his *Table Book* (1842–5), a stripling was making his way to Bellister Castle to seek service there. After he had crossed the Tyne at Haltwhistle, his route lay along a broken road, and he had not gone far when he saw a traveller ahead of him. This seemed a little strange, as he knew that no one had come over the ferry much before him. He quickened his pace and shouted, wanting company on the road, but the person ahead took no notice and, try as he might, the youth could not catch up. The stranger had long white hair, and was wrapped in a grey cloak reaching to his heels. He appeared to be carrying a small bundle.

They reached the broken gateway of the old castle of Bellister. At that moment, the stranger turned round and revealed a pallid face across which was a bloody gash. His beard and garments were red with blood and, fixing his lustreless eyes on the youth and pointing with a scowl at the ruin, he melted silently away.

The boy went to the house and told the old mistress what he had seen. She was much concerned, for she had heard of a spirit haunting the place from an older generation. It had never appeared, she said, without calamity ensuing. 'It came to pass as the old lady feared and predicted. That very evening the unfortunate lad was seized with the severe illness, and before next morning was a corpse.'

Richardson gives an explanation of the haunt, pseudo-medieval in tone, perhaps someone's literary embellishment of the tradition. According to this, many years before, when the manor was occupied by the Blenkinsopps, a wandering minstrel had sought shelter one night and was admitted. Later, the Lord of Bellister began to harbour suspicions that he was a spy for a neighbouring baron and told his attendants to bring the harper before him. When he could not be found, the baron's suspicions seemed confirmed. He ordered out the bloodhounds, which overtook the poor old man by the willow trees

near the banks of the Tyne and tore him to pieces. After that, whenever the baron returned to the castle after sunset, the ghost of the
harper followed him home. Its occasional more terrifying appearances were found to be the prelude of misfortune in the house of
Bellister.

Richardson concludes, 'The Gray Man no longer appears at
Bellister, or traverses the broken pathway ... But Bellister and
its vicinity continues to be a haunted and forbidden place after
nightfall.'

Black Heddon

M. A. Richardson's *Table Book* (1842–5) includes an account, sent
him by Robert Robertson of Sunderland, of the haunting sixty or
seventy years previously of Black Heddon, near Stamfordham, by
a supernatural being known as 'Silky' from her predilection for
appearing dressed in silk:

> Many a time, when any of the more timorous of the community
> had a night journey to perform, have they unawares and invisibly
> been dogged and watched, by this spectral tormentor, who at the
> dreariest part of the road ... would suddenly break forth in
> dazzling splendour. If the person happened to be on horseback ...
> she would unexpectedly seat herself behind, 'rattling in her silks.'
> There, after enjoying a comfortable ride; with instantaneous
> abruptness, she would ... dissolve away ... leaving the bewil-
> dered horseman in blank amazement.

At Belsay, a few miles from Black Heddon, there was a crag under
the shadows of whose trees Silky loved to wander at night. At the
bottom of the crag was a waterfall, over which an ancient tree
spread its arms, amid which Silky had a rough chair, where she
used to sit, rocked by the wind. Sir Charles M. L. Monck, of Belsay
Castle, had carefully preserved this tree, still called 'Silky's seat'.

Horses were sensitive to Silky's presence and she seemed to
take pleasure in stopping them in their tracks, so that no manner of
brute force could get them moving. The only remedy was 'magic-
dispelling witchwood' (rowan, mountain ash). Once, when a farm
servant had to fetch coals from a distant colliery and was returning

after dark, Silky waylaid him at a bridge, thereafter called 'Silky's Brig', south of Black Heddon, on the road to Stamfordham. On reaching the top of the bridge, the horses and cart became fixed, and there they would have stood all night had not someone come to the rescue who had 'witchwood' upon him.

Silky is described as 'wayward and capricious'. Like many bogeys, she revelled in surprise. Women who cleaned their houses on Saturday night, ready for the Sabbath, would find them next morning turned upside-down, but, if the house had been left untidy, Silky would put it straight.

Eventually, she abruptly disappeared. People had long surmised that she must be the restless ghost of someone who had died before disclosing the whereabouts of her treasure. Supposedly, about this time, a servant, alone in one of the rooms of a house at Black Heddon, was terrified by the ceiling giving way, 'and from it there dropt, with a prodigious clash, something quite black, shapeless and uncouth'. The servant fled to her mistress screaming at the top of her voice, 'The deevil's in the house! The deevil's in the house! He's come through the ceiling!' It was some time before anyone dared to look, but finally, the mistress, stouter-hearted than the rest, ventured into the room and found there a great dog or calf's skin – 'filled with *gold*'. After this Silky was never more heard or seen.

The *Denham Tracts* (1892–5) quotes an article published in 1861 which likewise says that Silky had not been heard of for some years. However, the writer, the Revd J. F. Bigge, says, 'I was once attending a very old woman, named Pearson, at Welton Mill . . . [who] told me, a few days before her death, that she had seen Silky the night before, sitting at the bottom of her bed.' Here she seems to have taken on the role of White Ladies as death omens.

There was another apparition named 'Silky' who 'rendered untenantable' the mansion of Chinton, and a third at DENTON HALL.

Blenkinsopp Castle

Until about 1820, the old fortress of Blenkinsopp, on the western border of Northumberland, was partly occupied by some poor families.

'More than thirty years ago,' says the narrator telling its story in 1845, in two of the rooms lived the 'hind' (married farm servant) of the estate with his family. One night, shortly after they had gone to bed, the parents hearing screams rushed into the adjoining room, where they found one of their children, a boy of about eight, sitting up in bed trembling, bathed in sweat and in a state of extreme terror.

'The White Lady, the White lady!' – screamed the child, holding his hands before his eyes, as if to shut out an apparition of some frightful object; 'What lady,' cried the astonished parents . . . 'She is gone,' replied the boy 'and she looked so angry at me because I would not go with her. She was a fine lady – and she sat down on my bedside – and wrung her hands and cried sore – then she kissed me and asked me to go with her – and she would make me a rich man, as she had buried a large box of gold, many hundred years since, down in the vault – and she would give it me, as she could not rest so long as it was there. When I told her I durst not go – she said she would carry me – and was lifting me up when I cried out and frightened her away.'

That the castle was haunted by a White Lady the parents had heard from others. However, they persuaded themselves that the boy had been dreaming. But as this happened again on the next three nights, the boy telling the same tale, they moved him and were no longer troubled, though afterwards he dared not enter any part of the castle alone, even in daylight. In 1845, he was still alive and had settled in Canada. He insisted his story was true and at forty would shudder at the recollection 'as if he still felt her cold lips press his cheek and her wan arms in death-like embrace'.

The belief that there was treasure in Blenkinsopp Castle had been reinforced some years before by the arrival of a strange woman at the neighbouring inn who had dreamed of a chest of gold buried in the vault. She left without finding it, perhaps because she told her hostess the secret, 'but she . . . told it to every person in the village, accompanying it with . . . "dinna ye be speaking o'nt."'

Although traditionally White Ladies acting as treasure guardians are comparatively seldom accounted for by being given a back-history, a slightly contrived mock-medieval 'legend' existed in M. A. Richardson's day to explain the presence of the ghost. This says that she was the spirit of the mysterious foreign wife of 'Bryan Blenship' (Bryan de Blenkinsopp) atoning for hiding her treasure chest from her avaricious husband and ruining their marriage:

> Tradition tells us that his lady ... must need wander back to the old castle and mourn over the chest of wealth, the cause of all their woe ... until some one possessed of sufficient courage shall follow her to the vault, and by removing the treasure, lay her spirit to rest.

Shortly before 1895, news that the 'Lady's Vault' had been found ran like wildfire round the district and large numbers of people flocked to see it. A small doorway had been discovered at the deepest level of the castle, beyond which was a low, narrow passage. The whole place was damp and smelly, and swarmed with meat flies (suggesting the exit of an old garderobe). The only man who dared enter said he came to two flights of steps, the second long and precipitous. As he peered down into the darkness, 'thick noxious vapours' extinguished his candle so he had to grope his way back in the dark. Though he made another attempt, he never went down the second staircase and the vault was closed up.

Cuddie's Cave

A mile-long (1.6 km) walk on the Kyloe Hills leads to a natural cave in open woodland. Marked on the map as 'St Cuthbert's Cave', it was more popularly known as Cuddie's Cave, 'Cuddie' being Cuthbert's familiar Northumbrian name. Some said it was where St Cuthbert's coffin rested on the monks' flight from Lindisfarne before the marauding Danes; others that it was an occasional resting place of the saint himself when, as Bishop of Lindisfarne, he used to make journeys through his diocese.

It was said to have been much later the lurking place of a Border reiver (robber), who hoarded his gear in the crags on Belford Moor, which included Cockenheugh, Collierheugh, and Bounder's or Bowden Doors Crags, near Lyham. On one occasion, however, he was surprised by the people of the farm at Old Hazelrigg in the granary stealing corn, and they killed him. His ghost had haunted the place thereafter.

According to report, his dim form was sometimes seen about the Crags, bewailing the loss of his buried treasure, and crying:

> In Collier heugh there's gear eneugh,
> In Cocken heugh there's mair,
> But I've lost the keys of Bowden doors,
> I'm ruined for evermair.

He also sometimes appeared as a dun-coloured horse or pony, known as the 'Hazelrigg Dunnie'. His pranks seemed to consist chiefly of frightening children and villagers, and were not unlike those of other bogey beasts (*see* BRIGG, Lincolnshire). Often in the morning, when the ploughman had caught his horse (as he thought) in the field and brought him home and harnessed him, he would be horrified to see the harness hit the ground and what he had thought was his own docile animal already far away, kicking up his heels and 'scouring across the country like the wind'.

There was a quarry on the way to Hazelrigg, of which the steepest part was pointed out as the place over which the Dunnie used to dangle his legs 'when he took an airing'. During high winds, a peculiar singing coming from one of the windows of the farmhouse of North Hazelrigg was attributed to the Dunnie, although later it turned out to be made by a strip of paper.

According to other accounts, the Dunnie was a kind of brownie, who created uproar by turning the furniture topsy-turvy overnight. He was thought to be instrumental in changing human babies for fairy changelings, and, when the midwife came to a confinement, sometimes substituted himself for the horse, landing both her and the man behind whom she was riding pillion in a morass.

These traditions come from around the middle of the nineteenth century. Mrs Balfour added in 1904:

'I have made enquiries about this sprite ... Three persons to whom I have spoken claim to have seen 'Dunnie' in the shape of a donkey; others have heard complaints of his behaviour at births. But he has not been seen, so far as I can hear, of later years. However, an accident took place about two miles from Hazelrig [*sic*] last summer (1893), when an old horse (in harness) got frightened and bolted; and I heard the explanation offered: 'That's no' a cannie part over there; are ye sure it was th' au'd horse, an' no' suthin' playin' [pretending] to be him?'

Denton Hall

Denton Hall, near Newcastle, was said to be haunted by an apparition clad in rustling silks. A literary story of an encounter with this spectre contributed to M. A. Richardson's *Table Book* (1842–5) contains brief snippets of what appears to be genuine local tradition. The narrator to whom the ghost appeared, as an old lady in an old-fashioned flowered satin gown, adds:

> In the neighbourhood I found that the house was regularly set down as 'haunted,' all the country round, and that the spirit, or goblin, or whatever it was that was embodied in these appearances was familiarly known by the name of 'Silky.'

This apparition would disturb people asleep at night, seemingly coming to look at them in their beds:

> I have heard ... that midnight curtains have been drawn by an arm clad in rustling silks; and the same form clad in dark brocade been seen gliding along the dark corridors of that ancient, grey, and time worn mansion ...

Similar silk-clad apparitions are found in other mansions and old houses, notably, over the Border in Berwickshire, 'Chappie' of Houndwood and 'Pearlin' Jean of Allanbank; while in Northumberland there is another 'Silky' at BLACK HEDDON.

Silk characterizes the ghost as aristocratic, as silk was expensive and not for the lower orders. The *Denham Tracts* (1892–5) records the tradition that the profligate Duke of Argyll, while living at Chirton, near North Shields, in the reign of William III, had a mistress who died very suddenly. Neighbouring gossips concluded that she had been murdered, hence her spirit 'walked' at night, dressed in brown silk, in a shady avenue.

With the Denton Silky, there was an attempt to account for the haunt by giving the apparition a 'history':

There is some obscure and dark rumour of secrets strangely obtained and enviously betrayed by a rival sister, ending in deprivation of reason and death; and that the betrayer still walks by times in the deserted hall which she rendered tenantless, always prophetic of disaster to those she encounters.

Her role as a herald of disaster she has in common with some White Ladies, also often clad in silk.

Dilston

Dilston Hall, built in 1616, was demolished in 1768, except for its chapel, which, like the surviving tower of the earlier Dilston Castle, is now a listed ancient monument. The Hall itself had been allowed to decay, a victim of events, having been the family home of James Radcliffe, third and last Earl of Derwentwater, beheaded for rebellion on 24 February 1716.

Various collectors of folklore in the mid nineteenth century report that the inhabitants of the neighbourhood of Dilston received an omen of his execution. The aurora borealis appeared uncommonly brilliant on the night before and was consequently long after known as 'Lord Derwentwater's Lights'. The knoll on which Dilston Hall stood is surrounded on two sides by a stream called the Devil's Water ('Dilston' being a corruption of 'Devylstone', from a family of that name). When the earl was beheaded, the Devil's Water supposedly ran with blood and the corn ground that day came crimson from the mill.

Tradition claimed that Lord Derwentwater was undecided whether to join the Jacobite Rebellion (though this appears historically untrue) but that, when he was sitting in the Maiden's Walk, overlooking the Devil's Water, the figure of a woman, clad in robes of grey, appeared before him and, placing a crucifix in his hand, assured him it would keep him safe from bullet or sword. He supposedly took the figure for a hereditary apparition attached to his family and so acted on its advice.

Cynics claimed, however, that it was Lady Derwentwater herself who, when he first rode out on his grey horse to join the Jacobites but turned back at the sight of his ancestral woods, flung her fan onto his head as he passed under the window, saying 'Take that, and give your sword to me!' True or not, people blamed her for his death.

Lord Derwentwater was young, handsome, kindly, and well loved. His death came as a shock – it is said that a cry went up from the crowd at his execution on Tower Hill, and people steeped their handkerchiefs in his blood. (Such 'corporeal relics' of those considered to be saintly were cherished as charms: at the execution of Charles I in 1649, cloths were dipped in his blood and used to cure scrofula.) He was variously said to have been buried first at St Giles-in-the-Fields, London, or to have been taken to the Catholic chapel at DAGENHAM PARK, Essex. Finally, he was taken back to Dilston and laid in the chapel vault. When this was opened in 1805, the head was found beside the body. Among a number of country people gaining access to the vault was a local blacksmith, who extracted several teeth and sold them for half-a-crown apiece (such was the demand, some scores were sold as supposedly genuine). Unlike the blood-soaked handkerchiefs, these were perhaps merely grisly souvenirs.

Lady Derwentwater was thought to have returned to Dilston with her husband's body and, says *Murray's Handbook for* ... *Northumberland* (1864), 'the neighbouring peasants believe that her spirit still sits lamenting at the top of its ruined tower, and the glimmering of her lamp may often be seen ... through the darkness of the night.'

According to M. E. C. Walcott, in *The East Coast of England* (1861), she waits 'for the return of her murdered lord'; and a tradition was recorded in 1888 that Lord Derwentwater indeed returned, leading a phantom army:

> It is but a generation since the trampling of hoofs and the clatter of harness was heard on the brink of the steep here, revealing to the trembling listener that 'the Earl' yet galloped with spectral troops across the haugh. Undisturbed ... the Earl himself had rested ... for a whole century; yet the troops have been seen by the country people over and over again as they swept and swerved through the dim mist of the hollow dene.

Haltwhistle

In the second volume of M. A. Richardson's *Table Book* (1844) appears what is said to be a popular story 'of which the occurrences happened about forty years ago', and which, or so said the people telling it, had 'the credible testimony of living and faithful witnesses'.

> A farm steading situated near the borders of Northumberland, a few miles from Haltwhistle, was occupied at the period to which we refer, by a family of the name of W—k—n. In front of the dwelling house, and at about sixty yards' distance, lay a stone of vast size, as ancient, for so tradition amplifies the date, as the flood. On this stone, at the dead hour of the night, might be palpably discerned, a female figure, wrapped in a grey cloak, with one of those low crowned black bonnets, so familiar to our grand-mothers, upon her head, incessantly knock! knock! knocking, in a fruitless endeavour to split the impenetrable rock ... From this ... she gained the name of 'Nelly the Knocker.'

The inhabitants of the house grew accustomed to the noise at night and Nelly was no trouble to them otherwise. Richardson records that 'the relater of these circumstances states, that on several occasions, she has passed Nelly at her laborious toil, without evincing the slightest perturbation.'

However, two of the farmer's sons were then approaching manhood, and one of them suggested that, as Nelly was evidently signalling the presence of hidden treasure, they should blast the stone to get to it. This they did, and their labours were rewarded with a cluster of urns containing gold. They had sent the maid-servant off on a needless errand so no one should know about their find, which they managed to keep secret for many years, people attributing their steadily increasing prosperity to good management of their lucky farm.

Meldon

In 1832, the county historian John Hodgson gave a vivid account of a seventeenth-century witch, Meg of Meldon. He writes:

MEG, or, as some call her, THE MAID OF MELDON, was, according to tradition, a person of considerable celebrity in her day as a witch and a miser; and since her death has continued the subject of many a winter evening's ghost tale. That she was *Margaret Selby*, the mother of Sir Wm. Fenwick, of Meldon, is, I think, plain from the following circumstances. After her death, she used to go and come from Meldon by a subterraneous coach road to Hartington Hall, which was her residence after her husband's death. The entry into this underground way at Hartington was by a very large whinstone in the Hart.

Despite her reputation for witchcraft, all the stories he tells are about her treasure and her haunts. He goes on to say:

The traditional superstitions of the neighbourhood say that, as a retribution for her covetous disposition and practice in unearthly arts, her spirit was condemned to wander seven years and rest seven years. During the season she had to walk her nightly rounds, she was the terror of the country from Morpeth to Hartington Hall. The places of her most usual resort were those in which she had bestowed her hoarded treasure – places she always abandoned after her pelf was found ... Many nights of watching and penance are said to have been spent over a well a little to the south east of Meldon Tower, where she had deposited a bull's hide full of gold, which has never yet been discovered ... Several large fortunes, within the last century, are attributed to the discovery of bags of her gold.

One of the hoards attributed to Meg seems to have been real enough, even if it was not hers. According to Hodgson, the ceiling of Meldon schoolhouse once gave way with the weight of a bag of her money while the master was out at his dinner, and the boys lucky enough to be in, eating theirs out of their satchels, 'had a rich scramble for it'. Robert White, M. A. Richardson's source for stories of Meg in his *Table Book* (1842–5), knew a man who was a schoolboy then and managed to get two or three coins.

Like traditional bogeys, Meg appeared in all sorts of shapes. One of her favourites, says Hodgson, was that of a beautiful woman, but she was also often seen running along the parapet of Meldon Bridge in the form of a little dog. Sometimes she appeared as lights and colours, flickering over the Wansbeck, or under a row of beech trees by the river, in the lane between the bridge and Meldon Park. The people of Meldon, however, became so used to her that they would say when she passed them, 'There goes Meg of Meldon.'

Another of Meg's haunts, says Hodgson, was in an 'antient stone coffin' on the site of Newminster abbey, where people had seen her sitting 'in a doleful posture' for many nights together. The country people called this coffin 'the trough of the Maid of Meldon' and used the water that collected in it for removing warts and curing other persistent complaints. Later authors say this stone coffin was used as a cattle trough.

According to the *Denham Tracts* (1892–5), Meg's husband, William Fenwick, died in May 1652, giving us a rough date for the haunt in the second half of the seventeenth century. Pictures of Meg show her in a high-crowned, broad-brimmed hat like a conventional witch, with piercing eyes, both of which may have contributed to the popular view of her. Perhaps more important was local resentment: given fierce Border loyalties, the chief thing held against her was possibly that, as her fortune was tied up in the mortgage of Meldon, in order to get her hands on it, the young heir of the Herons, whose ancestral estate it was, had to be dispossessed.

The *Denham Tracts* records an exploit of Meg's on Meldon Bridge similar to one related of a ghost at TUDHOE, Co. Durham. A man well-known for not believing in ghosts had often heard tales of Meg's frightening people, and for a lark one night he decided to dress in white and sit on the parapet of Meldon Bridge, waiting for passers-by. He had not been there long when he found Meg herself seated beside him. 'You've come to fley [frighten],' said Meg, 'and I've come to fley, let's baith fley together.'

Shilbottle

The dangers of mining – from pit-falls to fire damp – are reflected in the beliefs of miners, especially those concerning various spirits formerly said to haunt mines. One usually appearing as a blue flame was immensely strong, and helped miners in their work if rewarded. However, if not properly treated, he brought disaster on the mine. In Northumberland, where he was known as Blue Cap or Blue Bonnet, he long haunted Shilbottle Colliery near Alnwick. He worked as a *putter* (someone who 'put' or pushed the laden *trams* or coal-tubs, or hauled them by a short rope). A writer in the *Colliery Guardian* of 23 May 1863 explains:

> Sometimes the miners would perceive a light-blue flame flicker through the air and settle on a full coal-tub, which immediately moved towards the rolly-way as though impelled by the sturdiest sinews in the working. Industrious Blue-cap required, and rightly, to be paid for his services, which he modestly rated as those of an ordinary average putter, therefore once a fortnight Blue-cap's wages were left for him in a solitary corner of the mine. If they were a farthing below his due, the indignant Blue-cap would not pocket a stiver; if they were a farthing above his due, indignant Blue-cap left the surplus revenue where he found it.

Very different in character from this helpful bogle was the dangerous Northumbrian spirit known as 'Cutty Soams' from the delight he took in cutting the rope traces or 'soams' by which the little assistant putters (boys and girls) were yoked to the coal-tub. An account of him in the *Colliery Guardian* in 1863 says that it was not uncommon for the men to go down to work and find that he had been busy overnight cutting every pair of traces to pieces. The only good he ever did was in a roundabout way. At Callington Pit, when an overseer called Nelson, suspected of causing the deaths of two miners, was killed by fire-damp, local rumour said it was a punishment. This was seemingly put down to Cutty Soams, and Cutty Soams Colliery, as the pit came to be known, never worked another day.

By many miners, Cutty Soams was said to be the ghost of a miner who had been killed in the pit and returned to warn his 'marrows' (workmates) of impending misfortune.

Some spirits were believed to reinforce traditional mining customs, notably the ban on work on certain holy days. A correspondent of *Notes and Queries* in 1855 comments on the 'almost universal aversion' miners had to entering a mine on Good Friday, Holy Innocents' Day (28 December), or Christmas Day, and says that, when he visited one of the lead mines in Allendale,

Northumberland, he found that, rather than work on those days, miners would sacrifice their employment. When asked why, they explained that some catastrophe would befall them if they defied custom.

See also MARAZION, Cornwall for the Seven Whistlers.

Troughend

A popular Border ballad was 'The Death of Parcy Reed', taken down from the 'chanting' of an old woman named Kitty Hall, by James Telfer of Saughtree, Liddesdale. Telfer presented a transcript to Sir Walter Scott and also gave one to M. A. Richardson for use in his *Table Book* (1842–5). It was Richardson's opinion that the events it describes took place not later than the sixteenth century, though there was no historical evidence to show when – or if – it occurred.

It is a story of betrayal such as might have come from a saga. 'Parcy' (Percival) Reed was owner of Troughend, a high tract of land on the west side of Redesdale. Being a keen hunter and brave soldier, he was made warden of the district, charged with ordering the apprehension of thieves. This incurred the hostility of a family of brothers named Hall, owners of Girsonfield, a farm just east of Troughend; and also of a band of mosstroopers, Crosier by name, several of whom he had brought to justice.

The Halls concealed their enmity, however, and invited Parcy Reed to go hunting with them. Ignoring bad omens, he went. Towards nightfall, they retired to a solitary hut in Batinghope, a lonely glen stretching westward from the Whitelee, a little tributary of the Reedwater. Late that evening, according to plan, the Crosiers came down and found Parcy defenceless, deserted by the Halls, who had also sabotaged his weapons. The Crosiers instantly cut him to collops – according to tradition, the pieces were later gathered up by his people 'and conveyed in *pillow slips*' back to Troughend.

According to the ballad, when he realizes the Crosiers are coming, Parcy appeals to the Halls in turn, offering them first his black horse, then his yoke of oxen, if they will help him. Each refuses, so as his final throw he increases the stakes:

O turn thee, turn thee, Tommy Ha' –
O turn now, man, and fight wi' me;
If ever we come to Troughend again,
My daughter Jean I'll gie to thee.

But Tommy gives the same answer as his brothers:

I mayna turn, I canna turn,
I daurna turn and fight wi' thee;
The Crosiers haud thee at a feud,
And they wad kill baith thee and me.

As a result of these events, the very name Crosier became abhorred throughout Redesdale and the Halls reviled as 'the fause hearted Ha's'. Local tradition embellished the affair with tales of Parcy Reed's ghost. It was said that shortly after daybreak the likeness of Parcy Reed was seen near Batinghope, hurrying over the heath, arrayed in his green hunting dress, his horn by his side, and his long gun over his shoulder. On stormy nights, the phantom was often seen near his mansion, wielding a large whip so furiously that the very trees were threatened with destruction.

John Hodgson, in his *History of Northumberland* (1827–40), says that the spirit of Parcy Reed could find no rest 'till one gifted with words to lay it to rest . . . offered it the place or form it might wish to have'. It chose the banks of the Rede between Tod Lawhaugh and Pringlehaugh. Evidently the spirit was confined for a specified time to a particular area.

One of its favourite haunts was about the Todlaw Mill, where the people on their way to the meeting house at Birdhope Cragg often saw it. They would take off their hats and bow, and the courteous phantom would bow back. Hodgson says the haunt continued till the spirit's 'certain time' was expired, when the conjurer who laid him felt something like the wing of a bird brush by. Later, he was seized with cold trembling and died. Light is shed on the unexplained wing brushing by in a letter sent to Sir Walter Scott:

There is a place in Reed water called Deadwood Haughs, where the country-people still point out a stone where the unshriven soul of Parcy used to frequent in the shape of a black hawk, and it is only a few years since he disappeared.

In the *Table Book* version of this story, the spirit appeared as a dove, perched on a large stone in the middle of the Reed at Pringlehaugh. Possibly hawk and dove were thought to be soul-birds like the Seven Whistlers (*see* MARAZION, Cornwall).

Nottinghamshire

The Bessie Stone

On the A60 between Nottingham and Mansfield, a little north of its junction with the B6020 to Kirkby, is the once conspicuous landmark of the Bessie Stone. Now standing in a dip thanks to road improvements, it is marked 'Sheppard's Stone' on the Landranger map and was erected in memory of Elizabeth Sheppard of Papplewick, murdered on this spot on 7 July 1817 by Charles Rotherham of Sheffield.

She was about seventeen, and had left Papplewick that morning to go to Mansfield to find work in service. She was later seen leaving Mansfield but did not reach her home. According to a contemporary broadsheet, some quarry men going to work next morning saw a few halfpence lying on the ground and, when they looked around for more, saw the girl's mangled body through a hedge. Her head was so battered that her features could scarcely be recognized, the brains protruding from the skull, and one eye knocked completely out of its socket and lying on her cheek.

On 25 July, Charles Rotherham, aged thirty-three, stayed overnight at the Three Crowns in Redhill. While there, he tried to sell a pair of women's shoes and an umbrella. Unsuccessful, he left the shoes behind in his room but managed to sell the umbrella at Bunny. It was not long before the connection was made between these items and the known possessions of the dead girl. As the broadsheet tells the story, he was traced along the road from Redhill to Loughborough, and was taken on the bridge leading over the canal near there. When the constable approached him, he was looking over the bridge into the water, and did not resist arrest. According to other versions of events, he was caught at Mansfield after selling the girl's shoes in Nottingham market, or at Nottingham having sold them at Mansfield.

At the coroner's inquest, Rotherham confessed to the murder but said he did not know why he had killed her. He did not know Elizabeth and did not speak to her during his brutal attack. He had beaten her over the head and other parts of the body with a hedge stake and then thrown her into a ditch. Having found no money on her (evidently the immediate object of the attack), he had taken her shoes and umbrella, and would have taken her gown but could not get it off. The verdict could be nothing other than guilty, and on 28 July he was hanged at Nottingham on Gallows Hill.

Pat Mayfield, in *Legends of Nottinghamshire* (1976), reports that not long after these events Bessie's ghost appeared at the spot where she died and coachmen often reported seeing her. It was eventually concluded that she appeared whenever her memorial was disturbed – supernatural occurrences are frequently said to follow the disturbance or removal of particular stones held for one reason or another to be numinous.

Clifton Grove

The fine avenue of trees running alongside the river from Clifton Hall towards Wilton known as Clifton Grove was a popular place of resort in the eighteenth century. In his additions to Robert Thoroton's *History of Nottinghamshire* (1797), John Throsby notes, 'Here tradition says, the Clifton Beauty, who was debauched and murdered by her sweetheart, was hurled down the precipice into her watery grave: the place is shewn you, and it has been long held in veneration by lovers.'

The tale of the 'Fair Maid of Clifton' had been told earlier in a ballad existing in several versions, one of which is known as 'Bateman's Tragedy', entered in the Stationers' Register in 1624. This later became the basis for 'Clifton Grove' (1803), a poem by the Nottingham-born poet Henry Kirke White (1785–1806). According to this, Margaret, the 'Fair Maid', is not murdered by her lover, as in Throsby's account, but destroyed by demons as a punishment for perjury.

Margaret had many suitors but disdained them all until she fell in love with a youth called Bateman. They used to meet in secret in Clifton Grove, but one autumn evening when he arrived he looked deathly pale. In broken accents, he told her:

> For three long years, by cruel fate's command,
> I go to languish in a foreign land.

When he asked if she would remain faithful, Margaret declared:

> Hear me, just God! If, from my traitorous heart,
> My Bateman's fond remembrance e'er shall part,
> If, when he hail again his native shore,
> He finds his Margaret true to him no more,
> May fiends of hell, and every power of dread,
> Conjoin'd, then drag me from my perjur'd bed,
> And hurl me headlong down these awful steeps
> To find deserved death in yonder deeps!

Drawing from her finger a gold ring, she quickly broke it in two, hid one half in her bosom, and gave the other to him.

Bateman left, and for Margaret two years passed 'in silent grief'. But in the third, another man tempted her with his wealth and she married him. Six months later, Bateman returned and came to claim her. When he heard the news that she had betrayed him, he rushed down to the scene of their former love at Clifton Grove, where, tormented by visions of her in the arms of Germain, her husband, he cast himself in the river and drowned.

Remorse now overcame Margaret, although too late. She waited until the child she carried was born, and that same night, while those who attended her in childbed were sleeping, stole away and was never seen again.

> The neighbouring rustics told that in the night
> They heard such screams, as froze them with affright; ...
> And even now, upon the heath forlorn,
> They shew the path, down which the fair was borne.
> By the fell demons, to the yawning wave,
> Her own, and murder'd lover's, mutual grave.

In the nineteenth century, Sir Robert Clifton appears to have known another version which likewise attributed Margaret's death to divine retribution. He writes, 'A perjured maid, sheltering from a storm was struck by lightning, and carried from the Grove into the Clifton Deeps below; and as many people say, curiously enough from that day to this the land down which she fell has remained arid ... !' This variant combines the punishment for oath-breaking with the old 'barren land' theme, whereby nothing grows on the ground where people have met violent deaths.

In 'A Warning for Young Maidens; or, Young Bateman', a ballad in the Roxburghe Collection, it is Bateman's ghost that overtakes the Fair Maid. Though she and Bateman have plighted their troth, after a mere two months she transfers her affections:

> Old Jerman, who a widower was,
>   he[r] husband needs must be,
> Because he was of greater wealth,
>   and better of degree.

When she denies making Bateman any vows, he hangs himself on her door and from then on she constantly fancies she sees his ghost. After giving birth to her child, she begs friends to watch by her bed, for:

> Here comes the spirit of my love,
>   with pale and gashlie face,
> Who, till he take me hence with him,
>   will not depart this place.
> Alive or dead I am his right,
>   and he will surelie have,
> In spight of me and all the world,
>   what I by promise gave.

But the friends fall asleep, and when they awake she has vanished.

The Roxburghe ballad tells the story in terms of the ghost who returns for his sweetheart, a theme found in other traditional ballads. English legend also offers many instances of the suicide by drowning of girls seduced and then abandoned by their lovers, some possibly historical. Conceivably all versions of the 'Clifton Maid' are more or less dramatic interpretations of an otherwise unrecorded local tragedy.

Newstead Abbey

Newstead Abbey was originally an Augustinian priory founded between 1165 and 1173. In 1539, during the Dissolution of the

Monasteries, the abbey was closed down, and its land and buildings were sold the following year to Sir John Byron of Colwick. It became the seat of the Byron family, and eventually came down to the poet George Gordon, Lord Byron (1788–1824).

The inheritance was a mixed blessing: Byron loved Newstead and its medieval atmosphere (and asked to be buried there beside the monument to his Newfoundland dog, Boatswain, though this request was ignored). However, by his time, the house was almost in ruins, its gardens overgrown, and the estate run down, its woods having been felled for the price of their timber. Without the means to save it himself, Byron sold it to his old schoolfellow, Colonel Thomas Wildman, in 1818 for £95,000.

Like other ancient houses, Newstead had its legends. A carved chimney piece in a bedroom was traditionally explained as showing a Saracen lady who had been rescued by a crusading Byron from her kinsfolk. There was a similar carving in the dining room, thought to depict the same scene.

Byron's immediate predecessor was known as 'Devil Byron', and among wild tales about him was the rumour that he was haunted by the ghost of a sister to whom he had refused to speak for many years on account of a family scandal. Despite her heart-rending appeals of 'Speak to me, my lord! Do speak to me, my lord!' they were still unreconciled when she died.

The 'Corn Law Rhymer' Ebenezer Elliott (1781–1849), in a ballad on this legend, has the spectres of both 'Devil Byron' and his sister sallying forth together in wild weather, he in his coach and she on horseback:

> On mighty winds, in spectre coach,
>   Fast speeds the Heart of iron;
> On spectre-steed, the spectre-dame –
>   Side by side with Byron....

> On winds, on clouds, they ride, they drive –
>   Oh, hark, thou Heart of iron!
> The thunder whispers mournfully,
>   'Speak to her, Lord Byron!'

Another ghost said to haunt the abbey was that of its first owner, remembered as 'Sir John Byron the Little, with the Great Beard'. An old portrait of him that was still hanging over the door of the great saloon 'some few years since', according to John Ingram writing in the 1880s, allegedly sometimes at midnight stepped out of its frame and walked around the state apartments. Indeed, one young lady visiting Newstead some years before Ingram's time insisted that she had seen Sir John the Little in broad daylight, sitting by the fireplace reading an old book.

Newstead Abbey was also credited with possessing a White Lady. The American writer Washington Irving (1783–1859) mentions that a young woman, Lord Byron's cousin, staying at the abbey, one night when she was in bed saw a White Lady come out of the wall on one side of the room and pass into the one opposite. In 1877, John Potter Briscoe recorded something of her history, saying that old inhabitants of the neighbourhood of Hucknall used to relate that the Honourable William Byron of Bulwell Wood Hall had a daughter who clandestinely married one of her father's dog-keepers. She had several children by him, and 'it was further added that the mysterious "White Lady," who some years ago haunted the grounds of Newstead Abbey, sprang from this ill-assorted match.'

Byron himself had a taste for Gothic fantasy: while he lived at Newstead, a skull was found of large size and unusual whiteness. Byron supposed it had belonged to one of the friars buried there, and sent it to London to be converted to a goblet. When it came back, he instituted a new order at the abbey, with himself as grand master or abbot. The members, twelve in number, were provided with black robes and, when at certain times they assembled, the skull was filled with claret and passed round. The skull is said to be buried at Newstead under the chapel floor.

It is consequently uncertain how seriously one should take the assertion of his biographer, Thomas Moore, that Byron believed his fortunes to be bound up with the life of an oak he had planted on first coming to Newstead, having an idea 'that as *it* flourished so should *he*'. Debatable, too, is Moore's note on a letter written to him by Byron on 13 August 1814:

> It was, if I mistake not, during his recent visit to Newstead, that he himself actually fancied he saw the ghost of the Black Friar, which was supposed to have haunted the Abbey from the time of the dissolution of the monasteries ... It is said, that the Newstead

ghost appeared, also, to Lord Byron's cousin, Miss Fanny Parkins, and that she made a sketch of him from memory.

This Black Friar is described by Byron in *Don Juan*, canto 16:

> [. . . a monk arrayed]
> In cowl, and beads and dusky garb, appeared,
> Now in the moonlight, and now lapsed in shade,
> With steps that trod as heavy, yet unheard.

The ghost served as a hereditary omen, its appearance portending misfortune to the Byrons:

> By the marriage-bed of their lords, 'tis said,
> He flits on the bridal eve;
> And 'tis held as faith, to their bed of death
> He comes – but not to grieve.

> When an heir is born, he is heard to mourn,
> And when aught is to befall
> That ancient line, in the pale moonshine,
> He walks from hall to hall.

Byron says nothing directly about whether or not he believed in, much less saw, this spectre, or if this was just his fantasy. According to later authors, however, the ghost appeared in 'the Haunted Chamber' adjoining Byron's bedroom, though at night he walked the cloisters and other parts of the old abbey, and Byron claimed to have seen him shortly before his ill-fated marriage to the heiress Anne Millbanke in 1815. All this may have been deduced from *Don Juan* combined with Thomas Moore's note.

If authentic, however, the 'Goblin Friar' tradition was probably connected with a belief that grew up in the course of the seventeenth century that the descendants of those who had been granted possession of monastic buildings and estates at the Reformation would be punished for this sacrilege, and would never prosper. The idea was strongly argued by Sir Henry Spelman in his *History and Fate of Sacrilege* (written in the 1640s and posthumously published in 1698), and remained influential even in Victorian times, recurrent misfortunes in landowning families whose seat had once been monastic property being readily interpreted as the result of a curse.

Nottingham

Nottingham Castle stands on the summit of a precipitous rock. Although a castle was built here by William the Conqueror, the present building was erected in 1679.

The castle rock is honeycombed with tunnels, used for various purposes. The best-known of these is Mortimer's Hole, excavated through the sandstone from the level on which the castle stands almost to the level of the River Lene flowing at its foot. It was probably created to make traffic easier between the castle and the corn-mill and brewhouse on the river below.

It is said to have been so-called in remembrance of an event in the time of Edward III (r. 1327–77). According to early historians, one night in 1330, on his orders, a party of men entered the castle through a secret tunnel. They surprised Mortimer, Earl of March, the co-regent and lover of Queen Isabella, the young king's mother, and seized him despite her impassioned pleas. He was taken to the Tower of London and there executed for betraying his country to the Scots 'and for other mischiefs'.

The oldest description of Mortimer's Hole is by William Camden (1551–1623), who says that on his visit to Nottingham Castle they descended 'by many steps into a subterraneous cavern called Mortimer's hole, from Roger Mortimer's concealing himself in it'. Later historians argued that Camden had made a mistake, for if the tunnel was known to Mortimer it was not a secret entry. In fact, what was known to Camden as Mortimer's Hole, and what is so-called today, is not the tunnel in the story, which was subsequently discovered by investigation, having been partly filled in.

There are modern claims that Mortimer can sometimes be heard pacing the cell in which he is supposed to have been held in the castle, and that Queen Isabella haunts Mortimer's Hole, as she does CASTLE RISING, Norfolk, to which she was banished.

Rufford Abbey

At the Dissolution of the Monasteries, Rufford abbey, founded in 1148, was given by King Henry VIII to the Earl of Shrewsbury in exchange for lands he owned in Ireland. The refectory of the former

Cistercian abbey was incorporated into a wing (now ruined) of a house built here in the 1600s.

The abbey ruins are said to be haunted by the ghost of a monk: Antony Hippisley Coxe, writing in 1973, reports that one witness, who saw the phantom in a mirror, described how it was dressed and was told that this was not the habit of the Cistercian order, which is white. However, it was later discovered that a monk answering exactly to the description had once visited Rufford abbey and indeed died there.

The Reader's Digest's *Folklore, Myths and Legends of Britain* (1977) gives a more sensational account of the apparition, saying that only a skull showed beneath the cowl of this monk (much like images of the Grim Reaper). To this piece of Gothicism it adds that an entry in the parish register of Edwinstowe records the death of a man 'from fright from seeing the Rufford ghost'. As neither Hippisley Coxe nor the Reader's Digest cite chapter and verse for any of their information, it is hard to say which is the more authentic report.

Oxfordshire

Burford

In this town, and in several villages of the area, there is a strong tradition that the malevolent ghosts of two seventeenth-century grandees, Sir Laurence Tanfield and his wife, might be encountered riding in a spectral coach, either separately or together. People of whom such stories are told would have had a reputation for 'wickedness' when alive, and in this case it is easy to see why. Sir Laurence, a successful lawyer and judge, became rich enough to buy Burford priory in 1617 and, as lord of the manor, deprived the burgesses of Burford of various rights and privileges which they had long enjoyed on the assumption that their town was a royal borough. He died in 1625; his effigy and that of his widow can be seen on their fine tomb in Burford parish church. Lady Tanfield is equally reviled in popular tradition; she is said to have behaved with great arrogance. According to the folklorist Katharine Briggs, who herself lived in Burford, Lady Tanfield allegedly declared that she 'would like to grind the people of Burford to powder beneath her chariot wheels'. The ghostly tales are described by several writers of the 1920s and '30s in terms which show that they go back well into the nineteenth century; Muriel Groves, for example, writing in 1934, passes on an account from her father, who in turn got it from his own mother's nurse:

> Old Dame Taylor, my grandmother's nurse, told father that Lord and Lady Tanfield used to drive over the roofs of the Burford houses – up one side of the street and down the other. This became such a nuisance that the townspeople got seven clergymen to come and 'lay' them under Burford Bridge – the first arch – seven priests with bell, book and candle. If ever the arch gets dry they will come again. One dry season, it began to 'hiss and bubble', so the people watered it till the river rose.

Katharine Briggs, collecting in the 1960s, was told some further details: that the airborne coach was fiery, that its appearance was an omen of misfortune, and that the parsons had corked up Lady Tanfield's ghost in a bottle before throwing it into the river. One of her informants, whose grandparents had lived at Whittington in Gloucestershire, reported that because Sir Laurence had owned an estate there he was remembered there too as 'the Wicked Lord', who drove his coach up and down a particular lane. Whoever saw it would die. She remembered an incident in her childhood when a groom assured her that he himself had found a man lying dead in the lane, killed by the sight of the Wicked Lord; the truth of the matter, it turned out, was that a man had indeed been taken seriously ill while being driven along that lane, and the driver had thought best to leave him at the roadside while he went to find help.

Sir Laurence's ghost was also reported to appear at Great Tew, where the manor house had at one time been his home. In the 1930s, Ethel Williams was talking to a young gravedigger and his friends in the churchyard there, to see how much they knew about local historical figures:

> When I asked about Lord Falkland, they could tell me nothing, but when Judge Tanfield was mentioned, their faces brightened, and they told me of the great elm in the park, a mile or so away, round which, when the clock strikes at midnight, Chief Baron Tanfield can be seen driving in a coach and six.
>
> 'So it is said,' concluded the gravedigger, as a concession to modern scepticism.
>
> 'Not that I would like to be there to see,' added one of his friends quickly.

Some writers identify the aristocratic ghosts of NORTH LEIGH and WILCOTE as Lord and Lady Tanfield; certainly their reported behaviour follows similar patterns, and the two traditions may well have become confused. The belief that wicked landowners are doomed to ride for ever in a gruesome spectral coach is fairly common; it is found, for example, at OKEHAMPTON, Devon, and BLICKLING HALL, Norfolk. It may well reflect popular resentment at their power and wealth.

North Leigh

The parish church at North Leigh includes a medieval chantry chapel for the Wilcote family, with fifteenth-century effigies of Sir William Wilcote or Wilicotes (d. 1413) and his widow Lady Elizabeth Blacket, who remarried after Sir William's death but is buried beside him. They are the focus for several legends recorded in the 1920s, linked both to this village and to nearby WILCOTE. One collector, Angelina Parker, was told in 1923:

> In the village [of North Leigh] these figures were always called the 'Lord and Lady'. The Lady is lying with her hands near together as if in prayer. There is a story that the hands were once closer together, but are gradually falling apart, and that, when they are quite apart, the Lady will 'come again' and haunt the village.

A few years later, in 1929, Violet Mason was told a slightly different version: that local children would, 'quite recently', anxiously examine the hands of both effigies to see if they had moved, believing that when they parted their hands they would go up Perrott's Hill 'to look for their treasure'. This refers to an alleged treasure hidden in a partly demolished mansion after the death in 1765 of the last of the Perrott family to have owned it, and supposedly found in the mid nineteenth century by a later owner, who suddenly became very rich. There is no logical reason why the ghosts of the medieval Wilcotes should concern themselves about it; possibly some confusion has arisen from the fact that North Leigh church also contains in its vaults many coffins of the Perrott family, though not of the same branch as lived on Perrott's Hill.

Violet Mason knew another tale about something that supposedly happened in this church, or rather its churchyard, almost a hundred years before her time. Three girls had gone there at midnight on Christmas Eve to carry out a well-known form of love divination by flinging hempseed over the left shoulder, saying:

> Hemp-seed I scatter, hemp-seed I sow;
> He that is my true love, come after me and mow.

This was believed to summon up a brief vision of the wraith of one's future husband, but on this occasion everything went wrong:

Three girls crept out of their beds and went down to the church-yard on Christmas Eve. The eldest went first and performed the rite duly, but saw nothing. She died a spinster at the age of 83. The next oldest then started, but after a few minutes began shriek-ing terribly, saying that a coffin was following her, and got into a dreadful state. A few months later she died. Of course the third did not take her turn, and the rite was absolutely forbidden and no one has since been known to go through it.

Wilcote

Traditionally, there are several ways to lay ghosts. Some require their bones to be found and buried; some are laid by prayer and Masses; others, who cannot rest because of some injustice done or suffered, vanish once this has been put right. Medieval Christians regarded them as souls undergoing punishment for sin, who could find peace through the prayers of the living.

Folk legends recorded in the nineteenth and twentieth centuries frequently describe a form of ghost-laying which is both religious and aggressive. These stories are set in the eighteenth or early nine-teenth century; the ghosts are the stubborn, malevolent spectres of local evildoers (often gentry) which disturb a whole community until a parson, or more often a group of parsons, confronts them and eventually subdues them by fierce and unceasing Bible-reading and prayer. The parsons usually hold lighted candles, which the ghost will try to extinguish; only men of the strongest faith can keep their candles burning and never falter in their prayers, a process which is often called 'reading down' the ghost.

The purpose of this ritual is not to obtain entry into Heaven for the ghost, but to keep it bound to a specific spot on this earth. Generally this is somewhere local, but sometimes it is the Red Sea. The ghost may be set an endless task, for example making ropes of sand, emptying a lake with a small perforated shell, or stripping a hill of grass at the rate of one blade a night. Alternatively it may be physically confined, often by being 'read down' into smaller and smaller forms and imprisoned in a bottle, snuff-box or boot, which is then thrown into a pool or river or buried under a boulder.

Theo Brown, the only folklorist who has examined stories of this type in detail, believed that the idea of ghosts bound in confinement on this earth, or condemned to repetitive or impossible tasks, replaced belief in Purgatory, forbidden at the Reformation; close comparison with traditions from Catholic countries would be required to test this interpretation.

A tale of haunting and exorcism in Wilcote is recorded in several versions in the 1920s, the restless spirits being those of the fifteenth-century Sir William and Lady Wilcote, buried in NORTH LEIGH church. Violet Mason was told by some members of North Leigh Women's Institute, who had been compiling a book on their village history, that the 'Lord and Lady' (as they were locally called) used to drive up and down Wilcote Avenue in a spectral coach and four, while others told her:

> They used to drive round the sky above Wilcote, and I was told by Mrs — how her father used to tell her they went round and round over North Leigh too, and they got so strong they could be seen in full daylight, and all the people were terrified of them. But twelve clergymen laid their spirits in North Leigh church.
>
> Another story is that a 'very wicked Lord of Wilcote' used to toll the bell of Wilcote church in the night. The rector, who used to come over for Sunday and slept in a little room with an outside staircase, very courageously got up and went into the church to question the ghost. The answer was that he could not sleep in his grave so long as the clapper remained in the bell; the clapper must be thrown into the pond and the bell buried in the wood. Another version says that the bell was recast and the clapper thrown in the pond. For a long time there was a belief that something terrible would happen if the ponds were cleaned. Some years ago it was decided to clean them. Most untoward things kept on hindering the work, but it was done at last. However, the clapper was not found, nor did anything terrible happen.

Katharine Briggs, collecting folklore here in the 1960s and '70s, found one informant who had heard from her grandmother that the Wilcote ghost had been laid by seven or twelve clergymen, one standing in the middle and the rest in a ring around him. They asked, 'Why troublest thou us?' and the ghost replied, 'I shall haunt as long as the clapper and the bell hang together,' so the bell was melted down and the clapper thrown into the pond. Another informant spoke of 'ghosts which are supposed to have happened in Wilcote woods': in her version the spirit to be laid was in dog form, and she took the clapper to be not part of a church bell, but the wooden instrument used for scaring birds:

> At one time of day they got a newly-born baby and clappers and a priest and there were two small ponds, and they said a prayer over the baby, they threw one clapper into one pond and one into another to lay a big black dog, and if all these should return together, they say the ghost will reappear.

Rutland

Barrowden

In 1977, a lady from Morcott reported to the Rutland Local History Society that when she walked her dog down Green Lane, at Barrowden, the dog would never pass a certain spot without making a detour.

What upset the dog may have been a haunt, arising from events nearly a hundred years before. The didicoys (gypsies) used to camp on Redhill, on the lane leading to Turtle Bridge. One night in 1880, a terrible fight broke out among them, resulting in one being killed and buried under the hedge on the right side of the lane. No one knew anything about this until a didicoy told a villager sometime later, but the matter was never pursued.

Braunston

In the seventeenth century, Braunston was the scene of poltergeist activity. As the first of four 'Stories' accompanying a letter by Mr Thomas Woodcocke dated 17 July 1691, Richard Baxter records:

> Mr *Mun*, Rector of *Stockerson* in *Leicestershire*, had a Daughter married to one Mr *Beecham*, Rector of *Branston* in *Rutland*; in whose House it was frequently observed, that a Tobacco-pipe would move it self from off a Shelf at one end of the Room, to another Shelf at the other end of the Room, without any Hand. Mr *Mun* visiting his Son-in Law, took a Pipe of Tobacco in that Room, and looked for some such Motion; but a great Bible, instead of a Pipe, moved it self off from a Desk at the lower end of the Room, and cast itself into his Lap. Whereupon he opened the Bible at *Gen*.3.15. saying, *Come, Satan; I'll shew thee thy Doom: The Seed of the Woman shall break the Serpent's Head. Avoid* [Begone] *Satan.*
>
> This Mr *Mun* himself told me, when in the Sickness Year, 1665,

I lived in *Stockerson-Hall*. I have no reason to suspect the Veracity
of a sober Man, a constant Preacher, and a good Scholar.

The 'Sickness Year' is that of the Great Plague of London, when
anyone who could avoided the metropolis.

Mr Mun's brisk dismissal of the spirit is paralleled only by the
sangfroid of another gentleman whose encounter with the Devil at
Lambeth is narrated by Baxter:

> Mr *Samuel Clark* hath published the Apparition to Mr *White* of
> *Dorchester*, Assessor to the *Westminster*-Assembly, at *Lambeth*.
> The Devil, in a light Night, stood by his Bed-side: He looked
> a while whether he would say or do any thing, and then said, *If*
> *thou hast nothing else to do, I have*; and so turned himself to sleep.

Brooke Priory

Brooke priory, an Augustinian foundation from before 1153, was
the only monastic house in Rutland. The mansion today called
Brooke Priory is commonly believed to have been built over the
earlier building, of which the original cellar is still in existence, the
rest having been destroyed by Oliver Cromwell.

According to *The Villages of Rutland* (1979), tradition has it that a
ring fixed to a heavy studded door in the courtyard is where
Cromwell tied his horse when he visited the house. When the old
building was being knocked down by Cromwell's men, it is said that
a man ran in his shirt from the priory through the park, climbing
into an oak tree there. When the way was clear he ran to warn the
people of Martinsthorpe, but collapsed and died of exposure after
arrival; his ghost is said to haunt the area.

Cottesmore

Recorded by the Rutland Local History Society is the tradition of
an animal ghost – and unusually an animal actually known in the
village rather than a shape-shifting bogey.

Cottesmore Hall was the home until 1913 of the Countess of
Lonsdale, remembered for her generosity in giving blankets to the

widows and poor people, and presents to the children at Christmas, not to mention a fine supper for the bell-ringers.

> The Countess brought back from Egypt a donkey she named 'Pharoah', and she would ride this round and round the covered exercising ring, or at the 'treadmill', a path around the adjoining field. After the death of the animal, it was said to haunt the Hall yard.

Perhaps he was treated more kindly at Cottesmore than he had been in Egypt, and after death was loath to leave the place he loved.

Edith Weston

Towards the end of the nineteenth century, Edith Weston endured a remarkably noisy outbreak of activity by a poltergeist or 'rapping ghost'. In an old farmhouse at the bottom of the village street, a loud banging on doors, floors, and cupboards used to be heard. In 1896, in order to 'lay' this ghost, the estate bailiff stood on one side of the door on which the loudest knocks were heard, and the keeper stood on the other, but loud knockings took place even while they stood there. On another occasion, there were thunderous knockings on the inside of the cellar door, but when it was opened there was no one below. The knockings had been so loud they had been heard fifty yards (46 m) up the street.

Snelston

North of Caldecott, the Uppingham road (A6003) leads past the site of the deserted medieval village of Snelston. The sole remaining trace of the village, now a listed ancient monument, is the line of the village street, appearing as a hollowway among the roots of trees. But there was once a church on the hill here, and local legend says its bells still lie buried where the church used to be.

The Uppingham road continues after Snelston to the ominously named Galley Hill. Once a gallows was a grim landmark against the skyline here. Galley Hill was said to be haunted by the sound of trotting hooves always preceding traffic whether going up or down, making the horses sweat and shy, though nothing could be seen. This is 'an almost forgotten legend', say the Stokeses in *Just Rutland* (1953) and give no local explanation of the haunt. Maybe it was thought to be a last echo of the cart bearing some unfortunate on his final journey, or of some coaching accident on the hill, or simply of some lone phantom rider unable to rest.

Stocken Hall

Stocken Hall, just north of Clipsham, is an early Georgian house with neo-Elizabethan additions, which later became an open prison farm. Hidden in its own woods, it is said to be haunted by several ghosts.

One was the spectre of a woman in black, with touches of white, who passed by with bowed head or vanished down a corridor as soon as she was seen. In the early 1900s, occupants of the house and their visitors sometimes encountered her, one visitor reporting that, taking her for a servant, she spoke to her, whereupon the figure disappeared. The ghost was thought to be that of a girl who was strangled in the attic.

At a quarter to three in the afternoon of one December day, three of the house's occupants who were walking across the park towards Clipsham noticed their terrier pricking up his ears and showing signs of fright. When they looked to see what was wrong, they saw the figure of a man hanging from the bough of an old oak tree. He was clad in a brown smock, with something white over his face, and they could see the rails of the fence behind him quite clearly through his body. When they got to within about forty yards (37 m), he suddenly disappeared. He is rumoured to have been a sheep-stealer who was hanged in the park.

But the phantom most often in evidence was a little white pup, who was seen by many people over a period of about eighteenth months. They would frequently open doors for it, only to find that it had disappeared. Once, as the woman then living in the house and her daughter were ascending a narrow staircase, the little dog passed them: they felt it touching them as it squeezed between them but they saw nothing. They said that they experienced a sensation of 'burning chill' for hours afterwards where it had touched them. Otherwise, the little dog seems perfectly harmless: perhaps this was once his house.

Shropshire

Bagbury

One of the finest tales of ghost-laying in the region is shared between Bagbury on the English side of the Border, and Hyssington, just across the border in old Montgomeryshire (Wales). There are two excellent renderings of it dating from the Victorian period. One was told to Charlotte Burne, the great collector of Shropshire folklore, in 1881 by an old farmer named Hayward; Hayward had heard it some sixty years previously from the parish clerk of Hyssington, who claimed to remember the blind parson who was responsible for laying the ghost. The other version was printed earlier, in 1860, by the antiquarian Thomas Wright.

Both versions agree that the story starts in Bagbury, with the death of a particularly wicked farmer or squire (neither his name nor his dates are given) who made his men work over hours, swore at them, and gave them nothing to drink. Charlotte Burne was told that 'he had never done but two good things in his life, and the one was to give a waistcoat to a poor old man, and the other was to give a piece of bread and cheese to a poor boy, and when this man died he made a kind of confession of this.' His spirit reappeared in the form of a huge, savage bull which haunted the farm, terrifying people with its flaming eyes and sharp horns, and roaring 'till the boards and the shutters and the tiles would fly off the building, and it was impossible for anyone to live near him'. Some called him the Roaring Bull of Bagbury, and others the Flayed Bull, for the phantom creature was said to be skinless. He also occasionally appeared in human shape, as a 'black man' (demonic, presumably, rather than of African descent). Late one night a servant was alarmed to see the locked back door burst open and the black man walk through the kitchen and out by the front door, which also opened of its own accord, though locked; the servant relocked both doors, but the same thing happened again and again, all through that night. To put an end to this reign of terror, an exorcism was required.

According to Wright's version, people came to Bagbury from

miles around and, led by a single parson, surrounded the Bull and drove him towards Hyssington, and finally into the church there, while the parson read texts to him all the way, and the Bull continually grew smaller and tamer. But it was a slow process, and night came on, and there was only one candle stump available. When it burned out, and the parson could read no longer, the Bull (which by then was no larger than a dog) started to grow again till it filled the church and burst the wall. But next day the parson and people returned with plenty of candles, and this time they made the bull so small that they could bind him up in a boot.

They then buried him deep under the door-stone, where he lies to this day. There are believers in this story who affirm that were the stone to be loosed the bull would come forth again, by many degrees worse than he was at the first, and that he could never again be laid.

In the other version of the tale, that given to Charlotte Burne in the 1880s by Farmer Hayward, a whole group of parsons, nine or twelve of them, assembled in Hyssington church for the exorcism, carrying lighted candles. But the Bull 'made a great rush' and every candle but one was blown out, the exception being that of one old blind parson who, knowing what was likely to happen, had put his candle inside his top-boot. The others relit their candles from his, and then, despite the Bull's attacks (which made the wall crack), they resumed the praying.

Well, they got the bull down at last, into a snuff-box, and he asked them to lay him under Bagbury Bridge, and that every mare that passed over it should lose her foal, and every woman her child; but they would not do this, and they laid him in the Red Sea for a thousand years. I remember the old clerk at Hyssington. He was an old man then, sixty years ago [1820s], and he told me he could remember the old blind parson well.

Bridgnorth

In the 1880s, a strange supernatural manifestation was reported to the folklore collector Charlotte Burne as having occurred on a road near Bridgnorth some thirty years previously. A young woman was out driving with some friends when the horse drawing their carriage came to an abrupt halt and would not move, however much the driver whipped it. The young woman got down and took the horse by the bridle, thinking she would be able to coax it forward, but felt herself struck and flung back against the fence by some powerful yet invisible force. A few moments later, 'a gigantic arm and hand slowly became visible, holding the poor horse by the neck in its cruel grasp, but no more of the monster form appeared.' Just then, the church clock at Bridgnorth struck midday, and at the sound 'the hand slowly unclasped its hold and faded away.' The horse was able to move, though it was never fit for work again.

The young woman had an aunt with whom she was on very bad terms, the aunt having so often been unkind and unjust to her that the two had ceased to see each other. This aunt was living in Paris, and it turned out that she had died there just before noon on the very day her niece had this uncanny experience. Charlotte Burne thought the tale carried implications not only of haunting but of witchcraft, since witches were so commonly said to have the power of halting horses.

In modern times, according to the local writer Christine McCarthy, many buildings in the town are reputed to be haunted. One is the Magpie House Restaurant in Cartway, which has marble busts of a little boy and girl in the garden, and a notice in the hallway claiming that the building has been haunted by a woman in black for over 300 years:

> The legend says that she was the mother of two children who, in the 1600s, whilst playing at Hide and Seek, were inadvertently locked in the cellar. The river, which was in flood, burst its banks, quickly flooding the cellar, and the two unfortunate children drowned. The grief-stricken parents erected marble images in memory of the two children which can be seen today in the Terrace Garden.

A previous owner of the restaurant told a local paper around 1980 that she had often heard the children's ghosts calling out and banging on the cellar door on stormy nights when the river was high; she had also seen the apparition of an old woman, weeping and dressed in black, which entered her bedroom and lay down beside her in bed.

Cayhowell Farm (Myddle)

Richard Gough, writing his *History of Myddle* in 1701–2, gives an account of an omen which had regularly foreboded death for members of whichever family owned the farm at Cayhowell; he had personally observed it on three occasions, and was well placed to do so, for his sister had married into the Bradocke family, the then owners. The omen was that a pair of pigeons would come to the farm and remain there for about a week or fortnight before the person's death, but would leave immediately afterwards. Those that Gough saw were 'pretty large pigeons', whose markings he describes; he was sure it was the same pair each time. When the farm was later let out to a tenant, they came for this man's death also. On the other hand, if someone at the farm was sick and the birds did not appear, this meant he or she would recover.

Chetwynd

A well-known legend of the nineteenth century concerned the ghost of Madam Pigott of Chetwynd. Some said she was killed by a fall from her horse while out hunting; more usually it was said that she died in childbirth, her cruel husband having remarked that he did not care, provided the baby lived, for 'one must lop the root to save the branch.' In the event, the baby died too, and Madam Pigott became a very troublesome ghost, not only in her former house but in the lanes round about. She would sit on a certain steep bank, or in a tree, or on a high wall, sometimes combing her baby's hair, or accompanied by a cat; from these vantage points she would leap down onto the horse of any rider passing by late at night, and cling on till he crossed running water. She was especially vindictive (for obvious reasons) towards anyone who was riding to fetch a midwife. On the other hand, one woman described her simply as a 'pale white figure sadly and silently wandering in the garden' of her old home, and recalled being warned as a child to 'put your apron over your head when she goes by, and she'll do you no harm'.

In the end Madam Pigott, like many other Shropshire ghosts, was exorcized by a group of parsons who drove her into a bottle, which they threw into Chetwynd Pool. But one winter when there was skating on the pond this bottle got broken, and so she came again, worse than ever. Twelve more parsons repeated the exorcism, with a fresh bottle, and this time they threw it into the Red Sea, and she was never seen again.

Clun

Edric Salvage ('Wild Edric'), a Shropshire landowner whose name is recorded in the Domesday Book, was involved in a revolt against William the Conqueror in 1069, though by 1072 he had made peace with him. Later he rebelled again, thus forfeiting his estates; his death is not recorded.

A romantic legend about Edric was recorded in the following century by Walter Map (c.1180). It happened once that Edric, returning late from hunting, lost his way in the Forest of Clun and wandered there till nightfall. At length he saw a large building at the edge of the forest, and a light shining inside it; coming closer, he saw many tall, lovely ladies dancing in a circle, and all sweetly singing, though he could not understand the words. He rushed in, caught hold of the fairest of them, and in spite of the fierce resistance of the others he managed to carry her away.

After three days and nights of total silence, she at last spoke to him, saying she would be his wife and would give him luck, health, peace, and plenty, but on one condition: if he should ever reproach her about her sisters, or about her life in the woods, not only would she leave him but he would lose all his good fortune, and his life too. He willingly agreed, and they were married; he took her to William the Conqueror's court, where her beauty convinced everyone she was of fairy race, but he was careful to say nothing about how he had found her. All went well for many years, until one day that Edric came home from hunting and did not find his wife there to greet him. When she returned, he shouted angrily, 'I suppose it was those sisters of yours that kept you so long?' Instantly she vanished and, though he searched desperately, he never found her again, and pined away with grief.

This tale of Map's fits a common medieval pattern, where a human hero wins a fairy bride, only to lose her because he breaks some taboo she has laid on him. Map adds that Edric's son was named Elfnoth, and was the only man born from the marriage of a human and an elf who ever lived and prospered.

Later stories about Edric are quite different. According to a servant girl from Rorrington in the 1860s, he and his wife Lady Godda, and all his followers, are still alive in the depths of the lead mines of western Shropshire, imprisoned there for his foolishness in ever trusting the Conqueror; they cannot die till all wrongs have been righted and England is as it was before the troubles of his time. Meanwhile, they help the lead miners by knocking underground to show where the best lodes can be found, or to warn of danger.

If they are seen above ground, it is a sure sign that a serious war is about to break out, and the direction in which they are going indicates where this war will be. The girl who talked of this said she had seen them herself, in 1853 or 1854, just before the Crimean War. She had been walking near Minsterley with her father, a miner, when they heard a horn blowing. Her father told her Edric and Lady Godda were about to ride past, and she must on no account speak till they were gone, or she would go mad; she should cover her face too, but not her eyes. She was therefore able to describe the riders, who were in colourful medieval attire. Her father said he had seen them before, heading south, in the times of Napoleon.

Charlotte Burne got this story at second hand from the girl's former mistress, since the girl herself could not be traced and Burne never found another informant who knew it; however, she felt confident that its similarities to sleeping hero traditions showed it was authentic folklore. From her book it passed into the general corpus of Shropshire tales, being repeated by one author after another, often with updatings of the alleged apparitions of Edric to take account of the two World Wars.

Fitz

Collecting folklore in the late nineteenth century, Charlotte Burne encountered a curious tradition at Fitz, which combines horror with grotesque humour. There was once a lady at Fitz who was buried with all her jewels, and a wicked parish clerk who opened the grave to steal them. The lady (unlike the heroines of other versions of this tale such as that told at STANTON ST BERNARD, Wiltshire) was well and truly dead, and did not revive. But from then on her ghost haunted the clerk, whose name was Holbeach (locally pronounced 'Obitch'), in the form of a spectral colt. The first time he saw it he fell to his knees in terror, crying, 'Abide, Satan, abide! I am a righteous man and a psalm-singer!' Then the colt grew bolder, getting in front of him when he wanted to cross a stile, as if to force him to get on its back, so that he had no peace, and gradually lost his wits. Even after Holbeach was dead, 'Obitch's colt' continued to walk in Cutberry Hollow.

Hampton's Wood

Here, not far from Ellesmere, another tale of traditional exorcism was current in the late nineteenth century. By praying incessantly for three days and three nights, a parson forced a ghost which used to appear in the form of a headless man to change into that of a cat, and then shrank it till it was small enough to be imprisoned in a glass bottle. This bottle he put into three iron chests, one inside the other, and buried the whole lot under a barn, where the ghost would have to remain for ninety-nine years. 'But the poor minister was so exhausted by the task that he died.'

Kinlet

In Kinlet church is a monument to Sir George Blount, who died in 1581; it was a focus for many tales about him in the nineteenth century. His two sons had died in childhood, but he had a daughter, Dorothy, who made a runaway match with a gentleman of the neighbourhood whom her father disliked. Tradition embroidered upon this, claiming that it was her own pageboy whom she fell in love with and married, to the fury of her father. He did not, how-ever, disinherit her; instead, his ghost 'came again' to plague her and her husband, and their descendants, so that they had no peace. He lurked in a pool where women used to do their washing, and terrified them by rising up out of the water on horseback; he would even drive into Kinlet Hall in a phantom coach with four white horses, which he drove through the rooms and even over the dining table. Things got so bad that the family pulled down the original Kinlet Hall and built a new one, abandoning cellars full of wine and beer which nobody dared touch, for fear of angering Squire Blount's ghost.

But trouble still went on, till at last a group of parsons with lighted candles contrived to lay him by their prayers, banishing him to the sea. However, several local people told Charlotte Burne that Blount's fate was in some way linked to a small, flat bottle lying under his monument in the church, 'with a little glass stopper in it which nobody can get out'. If the women cleaning the church saw children touching the bottle they would warn them, 'Take care you dunna let that fall, for if it breaks old Blount will come again.' By the time Charlotte Burne printed the tale, this bottle had been removed, but two of her informants remembered seeing it quite often in the 1870s, when they were schoolgirls; they told her how 'on one occasion one of their school-fellows had offered to try and pull the stopper out, at which they were so frightened that they ran out of the church.' Other informants also recalled seeing the bottle, but gave a rational explanation for its presence; they said it had contained 'some chemical liquid used for photography' and had been left in the church by accident. This was also the explanation given to a later folklorist, Christina Hole, in the 1930s; as she sen-sibly says, no exorcist would risk leaving a bottled ghost where it could so easily be found and released.

Longnor

On the outskirts of this village there is, or was, a pool which was believed to be bottomless, and was known as the Black Pool. At night a ghostly White Lady rises from its depths and wanders about the roads. In 1881 the vicar's servant, a man named Hughes, told Charlotte Burne how he had met this phantom once, in his younger days, without at first realizing what she was. He was crossing a narrow footbridge by the ford at Longnor Brook:

> I sid [saw] 'er a-cumin', an' I thinks, 'ere's a nice young wench. Well, thinks I, who she be, I'll gi'e 'er a fright. I was a young fellow then, yo' know – an' I waited till 'er come up close to me, right i' the middle o' the bridge, an' I stretched out my arms, so – an' I clasped 'er in 'em, tight – so. An' theer was nothin'!

On one occasion, Hughes said, the White Lady had appeared at a nearby public house, the Villa, but again she had not at first been recognized:

> Joe Wrigley, he told me. There was a great party held in the garden, and he was playing the fiddle. And they were all daincin', an' she come an' dainced, all in white. An' everyone was saying, 'What a nice young 'ooman – Here's the one for me – I'll have a daince wi' 'er' – and so on, like that. And she dainced and dainced wi' 'em, round i' the ring, but they could'n' niver ketch 'old on 'er hand. And at last she disappeart all of a sudden, and then they found out who it 'ad bin, as 'ad bin daincin' along wi' 'em. And they all went off in a despert hurry, and there was niver no daincing there no more.

Charlotte Burne was inclined to classify this White Lady as a fairy, in view of her association with water and her skill at dancing in a ring, although another of her local informants declared the apparition was the ghost of a lady who drowned herself in the pool, having been disappointed in love. (There is even something demonic in her sinister manifestation in the dance hall.)

Millichope

One of Charlotte Burne's elderly informants told how a certain squire in days long past fell to his death from an upper window of Millichope Hall, causing an indelible bloodstain on the ground below. Moreover, for some reason his estate 'didna go to the right heir'. And so the old squire 'came again' – and, said the informant in low and solemn tones, 'The form as he come in was that of a flayed bull!'

Spectral cattle are mentioned fairly frequently in other counties too, either as the ghosts of humans or, more commonly, as supernatural creatures in their own right, but the gruesome idea that the creature is *flayed* seems to be a Shropshire speciality, found also in some versions of the BAGBURY legend. To find parallels one must go to Scotland or Scandinavia.

Ratlinghope

An anecdote from the mid nineteenth century given by Charlotte Burne illustrates the differing ways in which a paranormal occurrence could be explained. A man from Longnor set out one evening to visit some relations at Ratlinghope. As he was crossing the Longmynd, he saw, in a hollow of the road, a funeral procession walking rapidly towards him – the hearse with its bearers and pallbearers, followed by a long line of mourners. There were so many that they quite filled the lane, and he had to stand aside to let them pass. He was surprised to meet a funeral at that hour, and that it should travel so fast, so when he reached Ratlinghope he asked his relatives who it was who had died. 'There's no one dead,' they said, and asked him where he had seen the procession. He described the place. 'Oh,' they said, 'that's no funeral. Theer's allays summat to be seed about theer!'

There was a deep and widespread folk belief in the second sight, particularly premonitory visions connected with death; these could be a sign that someone had just died, or an omen that this would happen soon, or a warning of the percipient's own approaching death. On the other hand, such a vision could be a ghostly repetition of some past event rather than relating to the present or future, and in that case would be linked to a particular site. This ambiguity is the point of this legend.

Somerset

Chilton Cantelo

A farmhouse in this village, Higher Chilton Farm, displays a skull in a cabinet on a high shelf in its hall, facing the main door of the house. It has been in the building since at least 1791, when it was mentioned by John Collinson in his *History and Antiquities of Somerset* in connection with the epitaph of a certain Theophilus Brome who died in 1670, aged sixty-nine, and was buried in Chilton church. Collinson writes:

> There is a tradition in this parish that the person here interred requested that his head might be taken off before his burial and preserved at the farmhouse near the church, where a head, chop-fallen enough, is still shown, which the tenants of the house have often endeavoured to commit to the bowels of the earth, but have as often been deterred by horrid noises portentive of sad displeasure; and about twenty years since (which was perhaps the last attempt), the sexton, in digging a place for the skull's repository, broke the spade into two pieces, and uttered a solemn asseveration never more to attempt an act so evidently repugnant to the quiet of Brome's head.

The reason for this curious request, according to local tradition, was that Brome had fought in the Civil War on the Republican side, and had been shocked to see how after the Restoration some of those responsible for the death of Charles I had been exhumed and posthumously beheaded, with their heads displayed at the Tower. Rather than be disgraced in this way, he preferred to arrange for his head to be kept safe in what had been his home in the latter part of his life. According to some authors who repeat the story (but not all), Brome's grave was opened and restored in the mid nineteenth century, and it was noted that the skeleton was indeed headless.

Nowadays, popular ghost books and folklore collections regularly refer to all house skulls as 'screaming skulls', on the model of the one at BETTISCOMBE MANOR, Dorset, but this is not fair to Theophilus

Brome, whose 'horrid noises' might well have been groans rather than screams. Recent owners of the farm, Mr and Mrs Kenton, regarded the skull as friendly and protective, provided it is not handled too much, and in 1990 Mr Kenton wrote to a researcher:

> I would be interested to know where the 'screaming skull' information came from; my family have lived here for 75 years, and he has always been a quiet and respected gentleman.

Ilminster

At a crossroads outside the town, on the Dowlish road, is a spot marked on the map as Mary Hunt's Grave, where people occasionally lay flowers. Stories about Mary (or Molly) have been collected in the latter part of the twentieth century by the folklorists Kingsley Palmer and Roy Patten, but there is no indication how much earlier they may be; they are so contradictory that it is doubtful whether Mary ever existed. She is variously called a witch, a gypsy, a prostitute, a woman who murdered her husband, a victim of murder, or a girl who killed herself because she was pregnant; but all informants agree that her ghost walks at midnight, or at least can be heard rattling its chains and turning in the grave. Apparently not everyone takes this very seriously, since some informants say the ghost is riding on a go-kart, or 'a kind of trolley', or even on roller skates; sometimes it is seen knitting, because, they say, she was knitting when she was murdered.

Nether Stowey

A little way outside the village, on the Crowcombe road, is a wooded bank called Walford's Gibbet, in reference to a murderer's fate in 1789. Historical records show that Walford, a young charcoal burner, killed a wife to whom he had not been long married; local tradition, as recorded in the twentieth century, supplies a background story. It is said that he was engaged to one girl, but entered into sexual relations with another – the half-witted daughter of an older charcoal burner – who used to hang around his hut in the woods and make herself available to him. In due course she became pregnant, and her father and the parish overseer forced him to marry her, much against his will. This led to quarrels, violence, and eventual tragedy; on the night of 5 July 1789, as both were returning home drunk from the inn at Nether Stowey, Walford strangled his idiot wife and hid her body in a ditch (now called Dead Woman's Ditch). The crime was soon discovered, and he was condemned to be hanged at the scene of his crime, and his body then gibbeted there. The gibbet remained there till the early nineteenth century, when it is said to have been sawn in half and used as a pair of gateposts; the name was then transferred to one of the nearby trees. Some people still say they hear the gibbet's iron chains rattling on windy nights, or smell rotting flesh – for the remains of Walford's body were buried on the spot. His ghost, and that of his murdered wife, are said to haunt the area.

Nunney

In August 1977, the road linking this village to Frome, three miles (5 km) away, became famous in the press as the setting for an encounter with a phantom hitchhiker. Some time previously (probably in 1975), a driver had given a lift to a middle-aged man in a check jacket who was standing by this road; this man sat in the back of the car, complained of being cold, and then vanished from inside the car while it was still in motion. The horrified driver reported this to the police at Frome. On another occasion, the same driver saw the same man standing in the centre of the road; in trying to avoid hitting him, he crashed his car into a lamppost (or into the hedge).

It was alleged that this had caused such panic in Nunney that people were afraid that attendance at their Silver Jubilee celebrations would be affected, and a posse of vigilantes began patrolling the lane in search of the ghost. This was only a publicity stunt by the Jubilee Committee (as their chairman admitted to a researcher a few years later), based on their awareness of the driver's account of his experiences. However, it drew a response from a retired lorry-driver who recalled that some of his mates in the 1940s used to report seeing a ghost at this spot; they thought it was due to the dying curse of a cyclist knocked down by a car. If this was indeed a local tradition, it would account for the sex of the Nunney apparition and its unusual garb (phantom hitchhikers are more commonly women).

While he was inquiring into these rumours, Michael Goss found that some of his informants recalled a belief that Judge Jeffreys had ordered some men who had supported Monmouth's rebellion in 1685 to be hanged from the trees bordering this road, and that the creaking of these gibbets can sometimes be heard at night. It is unlikely that hangings actually occurred here; the ruthless sentences Jeffreys passed on the rebels are so well remembered in Somerset that horror stories about him are found in many places where he did not in fact go.

Porlock

Porlock is the setting for a tale of ghost-laying reported by the Somerset folklore collector Ruth Tongue in the 1960s, the ghost being that of a local pirate named Lucott or Luckett – an evil man, but a rich one, who was given Christian burial because of his wealth after his ship was sunk in battle. But the ghost would not rest, and even appeared in Porlock church during a service. Twelve priests tried to lay him, but fled from him in terror. So the priest from Watchet was sent for; he engaged Lucott in a riddle contest and defeated him with a question he could not answer. He then forced Lucott to mount a donkey and ride to Watchet. The ghost still had some power left, for on the way he knocked out the eye of a man who laughed at his plight. But at Watchet the priest ordered him to enter a small iron box, and hurled it out to sea.

Shepton Mallet

South of this village, at an intersection of five roads, stands Cannard's Grave Inn. This is named after Giles Cannard, a former landlord in the eighteenth century who grew rich by helping highwaymen and smugglers; he is also alleged to have deliberately made customers drunk in order to rob them, or even to murder them. He also committed forgery, and when this was discovered he hanged himself rather than stand trial. He was buried at the crossroads, which he now haunts.

Wellington

An elaborate tomb in Wellington church contains Sir John Popham, who died of sickness, aged seventy-two, in 1607. According to John Aubrey's comments on him in his *Brief Lives* (1669–96), he had neglected his studies in youth, preferring the 'profligate company' of criminals, with whom he 'was wont to take a purse', i.e. go out robbing. However, when he was about thirty his wife persuaded him to work seriously at the law, after which he had a fine career, rising to be Speaker of the House of Commons and Chief Justice. He presided at the trials of the Earl of Essex, Sir Walter Raleigh, and the Gunpowder Plotters. However, he was widely considered to have been both cruel and corrupt in his judgements. There were scandalous rumours that he had unjustly enabled his cousin 'Wild Will' Darrell to escape a charge of murder, in exchange for being made heir to the latter's estate at LITTLECOTE HOUSE in Wiltshire.

In popular tradition, as collected by Ruth Tongue, Theo Brown, Kingsley Palmer, and other twentieth-century folklorists, Popham is said to have been killed while out hunting, when his horse stumbled on a steep hillside near the present Wellington Monument and flung him into a pit in the gulley below, where he either broke his neck or drowned. It is supposed to be bottomless, leading straight down to Hell; it is now called Popham's Pit. His ghost was held captive there for a while, but thanks to the prayers of his pious wife he was allowed to emerge and begin a slow return to the tomb in Wellington church, three miles (5 km) away, crawling through an underground tunnel at the rate of one cockstride a year. If he can complete the journey his soul will be safe, but he has had setbacks, and is still on the way. Some say his underground route passed under a certain farm, where people were so disturbed by the noises under their floor that they called in a white witch who conjured him right back into his pit.

Popham's ghost was also associated with an oak tree in the woods of Wilscombe Bottom. A letter to the *Wellington Weekly News* on 23 June 1909 related how woodmen who were felling trees in the

1850s decided to spare this oak because, when they laid axes to it, it uttered pitiful groans; they concluded that the ghost must be sheltering there and decided to spare it for a few years to give him time to move on. In another version, a ploughman succeeded in uprooting the tree when others had failed, because of the piety of his own life and the fact that he used a team of ten oxen, which are sacred beasts.

Wincanton

A road junction at Bratton Seymour, on the A371 about two miles (3.2 km) west of Wincanton, is still called Jack White's Gibbet in memory of an eighteenth-century murderer, though the gibbet itself is of course long gone. In 1730, a traveller named Robert Sutton, while drinking at an inn at Castle Cary, foolishly bragged that he was carrying a good deal of money, so when he went on his way he was trailed by Jack White, a local ruffian. Jack caught up with his victim at the Bratton Seymour junction, and robbed and killed him. When the corpse was found it was laid out in the inn at Wincanton, where many people gathered to view it. Jack was among them, and as he drew near he noticed a trickle of blood beginning to ooze from the dead man's wound; others saw it too, and though Jack tried to run away he was caught and forced to actually touch the corpse, which at once gushed with blood. This was taken as proof of guilt, so he was hanged at the site of the crime, after which his body was gibbeted there and left to rot.

According to some informants speaking to twentieth-century folklorists, Jack was more cruelly punished by being locked alive into the iron cage of the gibbet and left to starve to death – a hideous form of punishment known in Elizabethan times and said to have been employed in the late seventeenth century on Bagshot Heath, Surrey. A further elaboration of the Wincanton tradition, recorded by Kingsley Palmer in 1968–9, is that the victim was Jack's own long-lost brother, returning home anonymously to surprise his family after making his fortune abroad. In any case, Jack's ghost still haunts the spot, and the story still circulates vigorously.

It is hard to tell just where history merges into legend in a tale like this. The murder is certainly factual, as are the names of murderer and victim. That the corpse should be displayed in an inn would be quite normal procedure at that time. That it would bleed when the murderer approached was a common popular belief, and witnesses might have persuaded themselves that they saw it happen, though it is (one hopes) unlikely that such an observation would be admitted as 'proof' in a court of law. Live gibbeting, at this date, is surely impossible, while the theme of a robber unwittingly killing his own brother is known to be an international legend.

Withycombe

In 1612, a wealthy widow named Madam Joan Carne, of Sandhill Manor, was buried at Withycombe. Indeed, she was triply widowed, and popular tradition remains convinced that she had murdered all three husbands – and, furthermore, was a witch. The tale of what happened after her death is well known locally; one version, as told to Ruth Tongue in 1959, goes:

> When at last she died they made sure of her. They nailed her coffin with iron nails, they hurried her body off to the church for Christian burial, and when the service was over they came dancing with joy back to Sandhill Manor. One of them flung open the kitchen door and there stood Madam Joan Carne frying eggs and bacon quite placidly. Then she turned her head and smiled at them. Well, they sent post haste to Watchet for a priest who was hiding there [i.e. a Roman Catholic?] – their own Parson had failed badly, and the Watchet priest had succeeded with another ghost. Now, the Priest must have known a lot about Madam Carne, for he sent her spirit into a pond not a mile away and she can only return by one cock-stride each year, despite her smile.
>
> Our people are now saying that she turned into a hare and someone shot her with a silver bullet and lamed her, and that she is now a ghost. Some of our older men say she's about if things go wrong.

In 1969, Ruth Tongue repeated the story personally to Kingsley Palmer, adding a few variant details: that the whole coffin, not just its nails, was of iron; that the priest turned the revenant into a greyhound before sending it into the pool (which she said was still called the Witch's Pool); and that 'everyone is waiting for Sandhill Manor to burn' once Madam Carne does get back home.

Staffordshire

Adbaston

A fine house called 'The Lea', near the village of Adbaston, was believed in the nineteenth century to be haunted by the ghost of a certain Madam Vernon, widow of its owner. She had only the use of the house after his death, as both house and estates would eventually pass to their three daughters. Madam Vernon, however, married again, and had a son and daughter by this marriage.

She put aside whatever money she could to provide for these children, for her second husband was very extravagant and fast-living. She hid her savings in a pot in the cellar, but was struck down by an illness which robbed her of the power of speech, and could only gasp 'mun, mun' as she died, pointing downwards. The children guessed what she was trying to say, but too late – there was nothing left of the money, for their spendthrift father had also understood and taken it all.

So the three Vernon sisters took the house and land, the second husband spent all the money, and the children of the second marriage had to earn their living in humble callings. This angered Madam Vernon's ghost so much that she haunted the Lea and made it almost impossible to live there, 'till they got the parsons to come to her, and they laid her in a pond below the house'.

The folklorist Charlotte Burne was told this story by the grand-daughter of Madam Vernon's son who was cheated out of the money she had wished him to have:

In her youth [she] was a servant in the house which was once her great-grandmother's. Her fellow-servants knew of her descent, and one day the coachman offered to show her the place where her ancestor's spirit was laid. 'So he took me and showed me, and a nasty little pit it was too, all covered with green slime, and shaped just for all the world like a coffin.'

327

Broughton Hall

The black-and-white manor house of Broughton Hall was once the seat of the Broughton family. The older parts of the present house (enlarged in the twentieth century) were built by the Royalist Thomas Broughton in 1637.

It was Thomas's house that the Victorian novelist Rhoda Broughton (1840–1920) knew, at first from visits to her grandfather Sir Henry Delves-Broughton. Later, while Rhoda was still a child, her father, a clergyman, was presented with the living at Broughton, and moved with his family into the Hall.

According to Rhoda Broughton's biographer, Marilyn Wood, writing in 1993, Broughton had a ghost, which Rhoda learned about as part of her family history. The story was set in Civil War times, when Thomas Broughton had been captured by Parliamentarians, imprisoned at Stafford, and heavily fined, while his wife was compelled to provide board and lodging at Broughton for 'divers souldiers'. According to the family legend, the young heir of the day had leaned out of the window of the second-floor long gallery and taunted some Roundheads with the cry 'I am for the King.' Upon hearing this, one of the soldiers fired and the boy fell back into the room mortally wounded. He was wearing scarlet stockings at the time and these were one of the distinctive features mentioned in various sightings of his ghost, earning him the familiar name of 'Redsocks'.

Burslem

Burslem, in the Staffordshire Potteries, was haunted by 'Old Molly Lee', who sold milk in the town and was reputed to be a witch. After her death, she was seen going about the streets with her milk pail on her head, uttering the 'cry':

> Weight and measure sold I never,
> Milk and water sold I ever.

According to Charlotte Burne and Georgina Jackson's *Shropshire Folk-Lore* (1883):

At other times she would 'get' in the cottages, and sit knitting in the corner. She came both day and night, and annoyed the people so much that they got the neighbouring clergy to meet together in Burslem Church to lay her. So six parsons came, and brought a stone pig-trough into the middle of the church, and 'prayed and prayed that her spirit might rest.' And at last they saw her hovering in the air up in the roof of the church, and they went on praying, and they saw the form of her come face downwards, gradually 'drawing' down towards the trough. And so they got her into it at last, and took the pig-trough, and put it on her grave in the churchyard, and so she was laid. 'But three of the parsons died of it, and the other three had a big job to get over it. That's true, that is; for I've been over to Burslem Churchyard myself, on purpose to see the pig-trough, and I stood and put my foot in it.' So ended the tale-teller, but a few weeks ago, (1882).

The 'pig-trough' can still be seen in the churchyard much as John Ward described it in his history of Stoke-on-Trent in 1843: 'A very remarkable stone coffin, hewn to the shape of the body . . . brought hither (it is said) from Hulton Abbey, when its foundations were dug up several years ago.' The long, narrow coffin was thought to have belonged to Lady Elizabeth (d. post 1400), widow of Nicholas, fifth Baron Audley. Ward says nothing of the story told of it.

However, he also describes a table-tomb near the south door of the church. Its axis is north–south instead of the usual east–west, an arrangement explained by local tradition. Though without inscription, the tomb was 'well-known to be the tomb of Miss Margaret Leigh, of Jackfield, who (as appears by the Register,) was buried the 1st of April, 1748'. He continues:

It has been attested as an undoubted fact, by old persons, who well-remembered the occurrence, that after the body had been interred some days, it was taken up, and placed in its present transverse position, for the purpose of pacifying the ghost of the deceased, which found no rest until this fortunate expedient was adopted.

From 'Margaret Leigh' to 'Molly Lee' is an obvious transition, and one version of the story now current is that the day after Old Molly Lee was laid to rest, parishioners saw her sitting on her gravestone crying that she could not rest until she was laid 'side-erts on'. The grave was opened and Molly's coffin examined, but as nothing seemed to be wrong she was buried as before. Next day she was sitting on her gravestone again, crying that she wanted to be laid 'side-erts on'. Again, they opened the grave, found nothing wrong, closed it, and Molly reappeared, crying 'side-erts on'. So finally they re-opened the grave, widened it, and turned Molly sideways, laying her finally to rest in the position the table-tomb occupies today.

The question is whether both the 'pig-trough' and the table-tomb stories existed in Ward's time, or whether someone, seeing the objects in question mentioned consecutively in his text, assumed a connection and associated both with Molly Lee. Whatever the explanation, the exorcism of Molly Lee into a 'pig-trough' was well known around Burslem in the 1880s. Whereas the table-tomb story arose to explain a physical anomaly, the 'pig-trough' version belongs to a handful of tales of ghosts atoning for watering milk, including the Shouter of Gatley Carrs near STOCKPORT, Cheshire. In the Shouter's case, being prayed down made him smaller and smaller, but it looks as if at Burslem the expression 'praying down' was taken literally, hence Old Molly floating down from the roof.

Children ignored the fact that Molly was supposedly 'laid': they used to dare one another to run three times round her grave, calling out:

> Molly Leigh, Molly Leigh,
> Follow me into all the holes I see.

They believed that her ghost would leap out and chase them.

Etruria

The name of Etruria is synonymous with Wedgwood porcelain. Its founder, Josiah Wedgwood (1730–95), finding his original premises at Burslem too small, migrated to a new site on the banks of the canal he largely funded, and established a works and village called Etruria after the Etruscans' homeland of that name.

Subsequently, the village became locally notorious for the 'White Rabbit of Etruria', a phantom rabbit that would appear in a secluded grove. Henry Wedgwood writes in *The Romance of Staffordshire* (1877–9):

> Deep was the terror which the 'Grove' – as it was called – inspired after the sun had gone down. The voice of a boy was sometimes heard piercing the stillness with piteous cries for help, that made the lonely pedestrian shiver with horror, for no sooner was the cry heard than a beautiful milk-white rabbit was seen to cross the pathway. It seemed to be in no hurry, but went quietly along: sometimes the horrid cry for help breaking out before it appeared, and at others after it had escaped from sight. But the villagers were in awful dread; and should any of the wild rakes stay later at Hanley than they bargained for, if drunk and alone, they would generally become sober before they reached the 'haunted spot'.

Once, an effort was made to catch the rabbit and prove whether it was really a phantom or solid flesh and blood. In Wedgwood's time, the man who tried the experiment was still living in the village. He waited for it one night at the usual place, for it always appeared virtually on the same spot and ran in the same direction. When finally it came, he fell on it, as he thought, but the rabbit escaped, and his shoulder was dislocated. 'After this experiment the terror deepened, and people were more afraid than ever to pass the lonely grove.'

The White Rabbit's appearance was connected with the spot where a murder had taken place. Fourteen-year-old John Holdcroft of Burslem had been strangled by his friend Charles Shaw after a gambling argument. In March 1834, Shaw was sentenced to death, but because he was only sixteen years old the sentence was commuted to transportation for life.

This idea that revenants (ghosts of dead persons) might appear in the form of animals, including rabbits, was once a widespread belief in Staffordshire as elsewhere (for example in Lincolnshire: *see* BOLINGBROKE CASTLE).

Hammerwich

At Hammerwich (or, as Charles Poole in the 1880s calls it, Hammerwick), just north of Blackhills, in 1668, a man called Francis

Aldridge heard a whistling in the air, 'the tune more melodious to him than any he had ever listened to in his life'. Poole associates this with the Gabriel Hounds or Gabble Ratchets, a phenomenon in which bird calls are ascribed a supernatural origin. In many places, people, especially miners, took the sound of the Gabriel Hounds to be a portent of disaster.

Poole, however, notes, 'Some say that it is the music of angels, transporting some blessed soul to its eternal home.' This connects with another tradition concerning the Gabriel Hounds, that they were souls of infants who died before being baptized and so were condemned to wander. The blessed souls version was perhaps a reshaping of this tradition in the light of milder religious beliefs.

Lower Gornal

Charles Poole, whose undated *Customs, Superstitions and Legends of ... Stafford* must have been published soon afterwards, quotes a report as 'recently' appearing in the *Daily Telegraph* in 1881 that the village of Lower Gornal, about two miles (3.2 km) north-west of Dudley, had for several weeks been in a ferment because of rumours that ghosts were to be seen walking about St James's churchyard.

Two years previously, the vicar, the Revd J. Y. Rooker, had been fired at and badly injured, and several people said they had seen the would-be assassin lurking about, while others claimed that figures had been seen walking up and down the field leading from the vicarage into the churchyard and performing all kinds of antics. Although the police were called, they were unable to solve the mystery.

Meantime, as a consequence of these reports, a number of villagers grew so frightened that they declared openly that on no account would they go near the churchyard after dark, and the women in the choir refused to go to evening choir practice unless men went with them for protection.

Knowing that the vicar had been permanently injured by the attack on him, a band of young men pledged themselves to keep watch and mete out summary justice to anyone who attempted to harm him or his family. This appears to have proved more of a hindrance than a help. On the very first night of their vigil, one of the volunteers, arriving later than the others, was not recognized in the dark and taken for the vicar's assailant. A cry was raised and he only escaped by scaling a wall and getting into the back of a house.

On the Saturday night, voices were heard in the vicarage garden and the police sent for, but though they searched everywhere no one was found. In a yard at the back of the house, more voices were heard, and Mr Rooker, going out to investigate, was grabbed by a man who said, 'You have come to kill the vicar, have you? I've sworn to take your life, you villain, and I'll do it quick.' Lights were brought and the man turned out to be a neighbour, who had been drinking in a public house.

Whether this 'scare' was a malicious hoax that got out of hand or deliberate victimization of the vicar and his family, the village people became convinced that it was the work of ghosts. The *Daily Telegraph* notes that:

> . . . a woman a few nights ago called at the vicarage, and requested the Rev. Mr Rooker to permit her to cut a turf four inches square from a particular grave in the churchyard, in which she alleged was a young man, who could not lie at ease in his grave in consequence of a guilty conscience. She stated that if the turf were put under the communion table, and allowed to remain four days, all ghosts would disappear, and be laid at rest for ever.

This seems an easier exorcism to perform than the traditional 'reading down' of a ghost such as was performed for Old Molly Lee of BURSLEM, but whether or not the vicar tried it the newspaper does not say. Unlike clergymen in the eighteenth century, if one is to believe local legends, a Victorian Protestant vicar would almost certainly have had strong reservations about performing such blatant folk magic in his church.

Lud's Church

Lud's Church, in the Dane Valley near Gradbach, is a narrow cleft in Forest Wood on the slopes of Black Forest. The result of a geological fault in the rock, it runs for about two hundred feet (61 m) into the hillside and is about fifty feet (15 m) deep but only nine or so (3 m) wide. Stone steps lead down into this gloomy place, where it is said the sun never shines.

Regularly mentioned in guidebooks since the mid nineteenth century, Lud's Church is said to have been a meeting place in the fifteenth century of the Lollards, one of the first breakaway religious movements in the lead up to the Reformation. Followers of the reformer John Wycliffe or Wycliff, they were obliged to meet in secret because they were considered heretical. The name 'Lud's Church' purportedly derives from an adherent of Wycliffe, Walter de Ludauk, who met with other Lollards here but was captured by passing soldiers. According to legend, his granddaughter was killed during the skirmish and buried close to the entrance to the cleft or cave. Here for many years, until destroyed by vandals, stood a white, wooden effigy known as 'Lady Lud', said to be a memorial to her, but in fact the figurehead from the ship *Swythamley*, Swythamley Hall lying just south-west of Lud's Church.

David Clarke, in *Ghosts and Legends of the Peak District* (1991), prefers to derive the name 'Lud's Church' from Lugh, the pagan Irish sun-god, whose festival of Lughnasa was held on 1 August. A stone on the path leading out of Lud's Church and down toward the River Dane is sometimes said to be an altar where sacrifices were made to the gods. Another recent identification is with the Green Chapel in the fourteenth-century medieval romance *Sir Gawain and the Green Knight*, whence perhaps the report of headless green men being seen here, and the claim that this was one of the hiding places of the outlaw Robin Hood.

Popular oral tradition speaks rather of this being a haunted place. According to a contributor to *The Reliquary* in the 1860s, various tales of terror were told 'by the lowest and most ignorant of the inhabitants', among them the story of the 'Ghost of the Black Forest', who haunted the neighbourhood of Lud's Church and frightened travellers making their way towards Castle Cliff; and of the 'Bosley Boggart', a fearsome spectre and the terror of the countryside for miles. Now it is said that Ludauk's granddaughter, whose name was Alice, haunts Lud's Church, and there are reports of weird floating lights being seen.

Micklow

Staffordshire has a number of revenants taking the form of spectral animals, including the White Rabbit of ETRURIA and possibly the headless White Dog of Leek Brook, although there appears to be no story explaining his appearance.

Haunting the Eccleshall Road near Micklow is a greyhound, said to have been seen by a number of people in the late nineteenth century. He comes out of the hedge, walks down the road for fifty or so yards (46 m) on the right-hand side of any late-night traveller, then disappears into a culvert. The haunt is said to have begun after a Mrs Bratt had drowned herself in a nearby pit.

Onecote

A story recorded in about 1900 tells of a Onecote farmer who was returning from Leek market late one night when he was suddenly whirled up from the ground and found himself seated on horseback behind a headless horseman. The horse leaped forward over the fields, effortlessly clearing the trees and hedgerows. Close to his home, the farmer was flung to the ground, dazed and injured, and a few days later died. Another man who encountered the spectre survived the experience, but his horse and his dog both died.

Seven clergymen were gathered to exorcize the demon apparition, and managed to compel it to speak. Whether or not the clergymen tried to dismiss the spirit or bind it in traditional fashion is not recorded: perhaps because it was a divine ban that had been placed on the spirit, it could not be lifted.

It was said that the headless horseman was one of four evil spirits cast out of Heaven and forced to roam the earth until the 'Crack of Doom' released it from its haunt. W. P. Witcutt, writing in *Folk-Lore* in 1942, adds two further explanations: that he is the ghost of a pedlar murdered by robbers who for a joke struck off his head and set the headless body on a horse; or that he is the spirit of a knight killed in a great battle with the Scots in Yorkshire, whose horse brought his master's headless body home. (These explanations accounting for the headlessness of the spectre are unlikely to be old:

traditionally, headlessness in a ghost is not a reflection of how a person died, but simply a sign of the supernatural.)

Witcutt describes the spectre as riding a white horse and says that belief in him still flourished among 'the country folk', one of whom had met him at a crossroads not long before and thought him 'an awful gory sight!' Another headless horseman on a white horse and clad in armour haunted Barberry Gutter, on the road from Alton to Farley.

Ranton

In *Shropshire Folk-Lore* (1883), Charlotte Burne gives the story of an encounter with one of the more unusual bogey beasts or ghosts in English folklore.

In January 1879, a labourer from Ranton reported being sent with a cart-load of luggage to Woodcote, in Shropshire, and driving home after dark somewhat slowly, his horse being very tired. As he came to the bridge where the road crossed the Birmingham and Liverpool Canal, 'a strange black creature with great white eyes sprang out of the plantation by the road side and alighted on his horse's back'. When he tried to knock it off with his whip, the whip passed right through, and in his terror the labourer dropped it. Exhausted as it was, the horse broke into a canter with the black thing still clinging to its back.

After a while the creature disappeared, though how and where the carter could not say. He stopped at the nearest village and told his story, causing great alarm, and when he reached home he lay sick in bed for some days. The whip was found in the road near the bridge, just where he said he had dropped it.

Meanwhile, the tale he had told was much talked of in the neighbourhood, with many variations. As a result, a policeman came to ask the carter's employer whether it was true that he, the employer, had been attacked and robbed on the bridge over the canal. The employer, much amused, told the policeman that nothing of the sort had happened to him, and told him about the carter's experience. 'Oh, was that all, sir?' said the policeman. 'Oh, I know what *that* was. That was the Man-Monkey as *does* come again at that bridge ever since the man was drowned in Cut!'

Although explained by the policeman as a revenant (the ghost of a person) habitually 'coming again' on the bridge, this apparition sounds somewhat like a relative of Shuck (*see* SHERINGHAM, Norfolk).

Rowley Regis

William Green (1834–1924), whose father had been a gardener on the Haden Hall estate at Rowley Regis, told the story of a young priest at nearby Hales (Halesowen) abbey who broke his vows by falling in love with a local girl, Elaine or Eleanor of Hayseech Mill. They would meet secretly, often on the wooded banks of the Stour, but either the abbot was told of their meetings or he had seen them. They decided one night to flee together using an underground passage to the hall. Unhappily, they were caught and walled up alive there. From that time forward, the ghost of Elaine, dressed in white, would appear in the neighbourhood of the hall, wringing her hands and searching for her lover. J. Wilson Jones, in his *History of the Black Country* (1950), says that William Green told him this as the 'true' story of the 'friendly ghost' that he had heard mentioned in connection with the old Haden Hall.

Although Britain has a number of macabre 'walled up alive' traditions, mostly relating to nuns, they seem to have arisen from a combination of antiquarian surmise over the reasons for intramural burials in churches, and post-Reformation confusion over the nature of 'enclosed' monastic orders. These are contemplative orders dedicated to prayer, and nuns in such orders may not leave their cloister, except under special circumstances, nor may others enter. Monks in contemplative orders are not so strictly confined. Medieval 'solitaries' were also commonly envisaged as being shut up in their cells, but, if they were anything like Mother Julian of Norwich (1342–c.1416), they received visitors and had servants to cook food and do the chores.

Uttoxeter

Frederick Hackwood, in *Staffordshire Customs, Superstitions and Folklore* (1924), tells the legend accounting for the custom once prevailing in Uttoxeter of ringing a curfew bell. He writes:

> It is told of Lady Tansley, the Abbess, who, journeying from Tutbury to Uttoxeter, was lost in the forest; but, hearing the curfew rung ... was enabled to direct her steps by the sound, and where she safely arrived, though much wearied by her wandering. In remembrance of the adventure, she gave a bell full of money to ensure the perpetual ringing of the curfew bell ... The story does not end here. For centuries the curfew was regularly rung, preceded always by three tangs of the bell in honour of the pious benefactress, both night and morning, till a newly appointed sexton, either wilfully or forgetfully, omitted the usual preliminary tangs; whereupon, says tradition, the ghost of the Lady Abbess appeared in the belfrey, ascended the bell-rope, and vanished as suddenly as she had appeared.

Lady Tansley was evidently taken to be abbess of the priory of Tutbury, probably founded in the 1080s.

Suffolk

Acton

In a contribution to *Notes and Queries* in 1852, W. Sparrow Simpson wrote:

> In the little village of Acton, Suffolk, a legend was current not many years ago, that on certain occasions ... the park gates were wont to fly open at midnight 'withouten hands,' and a carriage drawn by four spectral horses, and accompanied by headless grooms and outriders, proceeded with great rapidity from the park to a spot called 'the nursery corner.'

The park in question was that of Acton House, built in the early eighteenth century and since demolished. Sparrow Simpson had never been able to find out what happened to the coach on reaching the 'nursery corner', and none of the inhabitants of Acton then living had ever seen it, but some had heard the noise it made. People in other counties, too, sometimes claimed to have heard phantom coaches but not seen them.

The 'nursery corner' seems to have been one of those places disliked by local people, as tradition also said that it was the spot where a very bloody battle had taken place, 'in olden time, when the Romans were governors of England'. Perhaps they had found physical evidence of some conflict and this gave it an eerie reputation. For Sparrow Simpson adds:

> ... near this haunted corner is a pool called Wimbell Pond, in which tradition says an iron chest of money is concealed: if any daring person ventures to approach the pond, and throw a stone into the water, it will ring against the chest; and a small white figure has been heard to cry in accents of distress, 'That's mine!'

Other places in England have treasures in ponds guarded by a ghost, but this could be one of England's many White Ladies.

These legends seem to have been current around Acton in the eighteenth century.

Barsham

According to James Hooper and William Dutt in *The Norfolk Broads*
(1903), the Blennerhassett family acquired property at Barsham,
near Beccles, by marriage. One of their number thereafter haunted
the area in a phantom coach:

> It is an old tradition at Barsham that 'Old Blunderhazard' drives
> out every *Christmas Eve*, just before midnight, to visit Hassett's
> Tower, at Norwich, and to return to Barsham *before he may snuff
> the morning air*. The horses were headless, but always with fire
> flashing from their nostrils.

A similar anomaly can be found in traditions of Shuck (*see* SHERING-
HAM, Norfolk), sometimes described as headless and yet with saucer
eyes. Headlessness is in neither case to be taken literally, but only as
a traditional way of expressing the weird.

What happened when Old Blunderhazard *got* to Norwich is
suggested by nineteenth-century traditions from the city itself.
These say that a coach with four headless horses and a headless
coachman used to cross Bishop's Bridge over the Wensum late at
night going towards Pockthorpe or up to Mousehold Heath. First
the crack of the whip would be heard, then the coach and horses
seen. Sometimes it appeared flying through the air over trees and
houses 'while ever and anon the whole city would be illuminated
by the flashes of fire from the (headless) coachman's whip'. The
passenger in this coach was named as 'Old Hassett', said after the
dissolution of the priory of Norwich to have become a tenant of
the Grange.

The Grange or Monk's Grange was a Leet House built in the
thirteenth or fourteenth century by the prior of Norwich at the foot
of St James's Hill, Thorpe. At the Reformation it passed to the dean
and chapter, who in 1540 leased it to one Harrison, whose widow
married a William Blennerhassett. From his time to 1792 it was
known as Hassett's Manor House, but in that year it was pulled
down to make way for a cavalry barracks. John Varden, writing
in the *East Anglian Handbook for 1885*, says the house had prior to
its destruction already become derelict and was rumoured to be
haunted:

... strange sights and sounds were seen and heard in the old Grange itself. A dead body had been seen to roll across a room, there were doors that could never be opened, and two men attempting to open two doors that had been plastered up were struck blind.

As often with ghost stories, the rationalizing suggestion had been made that the dilapidated house was deliberately given its evil reputation by smugglers to keep the curious away.

But, if so, they were working with authentic materials. The flashes of fire from his coachman's whip and from his horses' nostrils place Old Blunderhazard in the company of the damned, and almost certainly this is a penitential legend concerned with the Blennerhassetts' occupation of the Grange. The acquisition of Church property after the Reformation is often punished in tales, one reason why Sir Francis Drake also rides out from BUCKLAND ABBEY, Devon, in a phantom coach.

Blythburgh

On the north door of Blythburgh church are long black marks said to be the claw marks left by the Black Dog of BUNGAY. According to the seventeenth-century pamphleteer Abraham Fleming, the Black Dog appeared at Blythburgh on the same day as at Bungay, and 'placing himself uppon a maine balk or beam ... sodainly he gaue a swinge down through ye Church', killing two men and a boy, and burning someone's hand in his progress. He went out through the north door (traditionally the Devil's Door) and, when this was cleaned in the 1930s, long black marks were found which people connected with the Black Dog's visitation. Today, they are sometimes pointed out to children as the claw marks of Shuck (*see* SHERINGHAM, Norfolk).

Toby's Walks, now a picnic site off the A12 south of the village, just before the B1387 turn-off for Walberswick and Minsmere, are paths on gorse-covered common land said to be haunted by 'Black Toby'. He is supposed to have been Tobias Gill, a black drummer in Sir Robert Riches's regiment of dragoons, who were quartered at Blythburgh for a week in 1750. One night, walking very drunk on the common, Toby met a servant girl, Ann Blakemore, whose dead body was found next morning with Toby, in a drunken stupor, close beside it. He was convicted of her murder at Ipswich Assizes and hanged in chains at the crossroads.

It was a local belief in the nineteenth century that those out late at night near the scene of his execution would see a funeral hearse drawn by four headless horses driven by Toby himself. Denied a grave in consecrated ground because of his crime, he was doomed to drive himself every night to Hell.

The Suffolk County Council information board at the picnic site gives a version of this story which omits the fact that Toby was black. This gives a different slant to it. If there were a real Toby, he would have been a conspicuous outsider and therefore a convenient scapegoat. His ghost would then belong, not with those unable to rest because they had not been given Christian burial in a church-yard, but among those who died unjust deaths.

Boulge

Boulge is perhaps best known as the last resting place of Edward Fitzgerald (1809–83), translator of *The Rubáiyát of Omar Khayyám*. The FitzGerald family lived at Boulge Hall (since demolished) from 1835 onwards, and were remembered at Boulge in connection with a haunt. Camilla, Lady Gurdon, writing in 1893, gives 'Mr Redstone' (the English master at Woodbridge Grammar School) as her source for the following:

> At Boulge Hall, upon the stroke of twelve at midnight, a coach drawn by a pair of headless horses, and driven by a headless coachman, who dismounts to open the lodge gates, takes back the ghost of the late owner, Mr Fitzgerald. A man from Debach stayed up one night to see if it were true, and 'he was wholly frightened by the sight.'

The 'Mr Fitzgerald' mentioned here is probably not the poet himself but his brother John, who inherited the Hall. Why he should be supposed to haunt it is uncertain.

Perhaps this is a later version of another tradition given to Mr Redstone:

Boulge is said to be haunted by a Mrs Short, who is called the 'Queen of Hell.' She murdered a gentleman at Boulge Hall. The stain is on the floor where she murdered him. Now ... she come [sic] out of the gate in a carriage with a pair of horses that have got no heads. She wears a silk dress. There is a light on the carriage, and a man drives the horses. About three years ago a servant girl lived there. Mrs Short went into her room and pulled all her things off her. The girl said she felt its (the ghost's) breath like a wolf upon her.

This story is a notable combination of the widespread theme of phantom coaches with the equally widespread one of 'indelible bloodstains', and it has a historical foundation.

The 'Queen of Hell', so-called from her furious temper, was the previous owner of Boulge Hall who came into it in 1792 on the death of her second husband, William Whitby. Subsequently she married Henry Hassard, later Short, a former lieutenant-colonel in the Royal Dragoons. Their marriage was turbulent: Thomas Wright in his *Life of Edward Fitzgerald* (1904) says she was an imperious and bad-tempered old lady, adding:

She and her husband, Colonel Short, often fell out and at such times the colonel would speak only to his dog, she to her cat. After a particularly bitter quarrel Mrs Short declared that she would not live with her husband again.

Instead, she built herself Boulge Cottage (now also gone) in the grounds and periodically withdrew there when life at the Hall became intolerable.

A letter survives written by the Suffolk antiquary Henry Jermyn (1767–1820), dated 14 March 1802, and partly based on information derived from Mrs Short's nephew by marriage, Charles Thomas Rissowe. It describes her activities on New Year's Day 1800, when she threatened to burn down the farm house or buildings, destroyed the windows in the dining room and evidently broke down a door, though, so she said, 'only to regain her Liberty'. This was after the colonel had had four men restrain her and remove from her a knife (she subsequently had them indicted for assault, complaining of 'unnecessary Violence'). 'The Hole burnt in the middle of the room far away from the Door was not, I believe, discovered till after the Retreat.'

It was evidently from the knife and the 'Hole' in the floor that rumour constructed the local tale of a murder and an ineradicable bloodstain. As for the phantom coach, it was habitually associated in popular tradition with overbearing or (in the general opinion) unjustly wealthy landowners.

Bungay

Bungay became famous in the annals of the supernatural following the publication of a tract by Abraham Fleming entitled 'A straunge *and terrible Wunder wrought* very late in the parish Church *of Bongay* . . .' Fleming relates that, on Sunday, 4 August 1577, between nine and ten in the morning, when people were in church, 'a great tempest' broke over Bungay, hard upon which there appeared 'an horrible shaped thing' resembling a great black dog. 'This black dog . . . running all along down the body of the Church . . . passed between two persons, as they were kneeling . . . and . . . wrung the necks of them bothe at one instant clene backward.' Another man received 'such a gripe on the back, that therwithall he was presently drawn togither and shrunk up, as it were a peece of lether scorched in a hot fire: or as the mouth of a purse or bag, drawen togither with a string'. Fleming adds, 'there are remaining in the stones of the Church, and likewise in the Church dore which are meruelously renten & torn, ye marks as it were of his clawes or talans.'

The Black Dog's activities have been ascribed to ball lightning. However, in the sixteenth and seventeenth centuries, people still interpreted tempests, whirlwinds, and related phenomena as the work of the Devil. Diabolical Black Dogs were reported as appearing during tempests in 857 at Trèves, and in 1341 at Messina.

Though this may be how the people of Bungay thought of the event, the Churchwarden's Books for 1577 simply note in the margin: 'M^d. A great terryble & ferfull tempest at the tyme of procession vpon the Sondaye, such darknes, Rayne, hayle, Thunder & lightnyng as was never seen the lyke.' An account of the same storm, likewise with no mention of a Black Dog, appears under the year 1577 in the second edition of Holinshed's *Chronicles*. There are slight differences between the pamphlet account and the one in Holinshed, and Fleming speaks of the man shrunk up like 'a peece of lether' as thought to be 'yet alive', which might suggest a local informant. However, Fleming was one of the editors of the Holinshed second edition, and also a Puritan preacher. It is likely that he seized his chance to make a moral point – he represents the appearance of the dog as divine punishment for the congregation's sins.

The connection between thunderstorms and the supernatural was preserved in East Anglian speech into the nineteenth century. Edward Moor, in *Suffolk Words and Phrases* (1823), defines 'SPERIT' as 'A ghost, the soul, lightning. A spirit', and the Revd Forby in 1830 gives as an example: 'In the great tempest, a spirit lit upon the church steeple.'

That an oral tradition of the Black Dog has persisted in Suffolk since the sixteenth century is doubtful. The local historian Christopher Reede in the 1980s suggested that the memory of the Black Dog died out as a result of the Great Fire of Bungay in 1688, when many inhabitants are thought to have left the area, and was only revived much later. The story was known to at least some in the Bungay area in the nineteenth century, possibly as a result of a poem on the Black Dog's advent included in a new edition of Fleming's pamphlet published in 1826 (with a lurid illustration). He appears on a carved wooden Dole Cupboard in St Mary's church, bearing the date 1675 but thought to be a nineteenth-century fake, and a proverb adapted to fit him in the sixteenth century survived, so that in East Anglia in the nineteenth century it was said of a hardened sinner that he 'could no more blush than the Black Dog of Bungay'. The novelist Sir Henry Rider Haggard, of nearby Ditchingham House, also says in *A Farmer's Year* (1898) that a vague belief persisted 'that the devil is ... to be met with in these parts, and especially on Hollow Hill, in the concrete shape of the black dog of Bungay'. However, the Black Dog probably only became well known in the 1930s when accounts of him were published locally, notably in Ethel Mann's *Old Bungay* (1934).

From then on, visible reminders of the Black Dog played a part in keeping the story alive. In the teeth of his original connotations, he has become a symbol of civic identity: he can be seen near the Butter Cross as a weathervane on a lamp-standard originally erected in 1933, and in Bungay's coat of arms, granted in 1953, which has the Dog standing on forked lightning as its crest. He likewise appears on the town sign, and the town football team is known as Bungay Black Dogs.

The story is still growing. Some twentieth-century authors claim that the marks of the Black Dog's claws are still to be seen on the door of Bungay church, but little remains of the original north door, largely destroyed in the Great Fire. There may have been confusion with BLYTHBURGH. The Black Dog is now also spoken of as a ghost, sometimes identified as Hugh Bigod, haunting BUNGAY CASTLE. Sometimes he is identified with Shuck (*see* SHERINGHAM, Norfolk), but perhaps the most curious tradition collected by Reede was that the Black Dog was a black *cat*, the Devil in disguise.

Bungay Castle

According to Morley Adams, writing in 1914, the later Bigods of Bungay Castle were notorious for profanity and wickedness, and part of their penance was to haunt the scenes of their crimes. On certain nights every year, they drove out in a huge coach drawn by four steeds, their mouths and nostrils pouring flames and smoke, and driven by a headless coachman with his head under his arm.

The coach would go from Bungay along the top road to Geldeston, Norfolk, past the church, down a lane called Lover's Lane, then down a narrow, sandy lane called Bigods' Hill, onto the 'low road' and so home to Bungay.

> It is never both *seen* and *heard* . . . It comes rumbling down Bigods' Hill, the horses snorting and panting; nearer and nearer it comes, and louder and louder grow the sounds of it, until it passes you and the sounds diminish and gradually die away in the distance. To those who have been privileged to see it . . . like a silent wraith the phantom coach glides by, and though the prancing hoofs of the horses strike fire from the ground, no sound is heard.

This alternation between an auditory and a visual phenomenon is unusual: most phantom coaches are either one or the other. At Bradenham Hall, Norfolk, for example, the family home of the novelist Sir Henry Rider Haggard in his youth, Haggard's father used to tell the story of how, one Christmas, a coach was heard driving up to the door but when they ran to look there was nothing.

Burgh

In 1892, Camilla, Lady Gurdon, wrote in the pages of *Folk-Lore* of a lane in Burgh known as 'White-foot Lane' because a ghost with white feet walked up it. It was accordingly shunned at night. She also writes:

> The Rev. Arthur Maude, Rector of Burgh, tells me that a particular place underneath the Burgh Road, where a stream has made a deep hole, is supposed to be haunted. In or after wet weather, when there is much noise caused by the gurgling of the water in this spot, children are afraid to pass the place; an old woman below is washing her skellets, and it is called the Skellet Hole. Our gardener says his mother has a skellet – a brass tripod pot – the 'bale' or handle of which had a crook or twist in it, by which it could be hung upon the iron bar that always, in those days, went across the cottage chimneys. Skellets are never seen now, and the name has died out; but the place is still said to be haunted, and a young man told me it was called '*Skeleton* Hole' – a curious corruption.

Perhaps, like tales of freshwater mermaids, this story was told to children to keep them away from the water.

Clopton

In 1928, Clopton Hall was bought by Justin and Edith Brooke. In their *Suffolk Prospect* (1963), Justin Brooke says that he bought a farm which adjoined the Hall and which was supposed to be haunted. A successful farmer had lived there 'in the old days' and when he died no one could find where he had hidden his money. They knew he must have been rich, however, because not only was he a good farmer but he was a bachelor. Three days after his funeral, a man entering the farmyard saw the farmer standing there. But when he went up to speak to him, he had vanished. From this people supposed that his money was hidden somewhere in the yard, but still no one found the money, either there or anywhere else.

An old man told Brooke that, when he was a 'little old boy', his father was a farmworker and they lived in the farmhouse. The boy himself had a bedroom at the back, and one night woke up to see a tall figure standing by his bedside. This figure drew the blankets down a little and motioned him to get up. He was so frightened, however, that he said 'Go away' and the figure vanished. Next night the same thing happened, only this time the blanket was pulled halfway down. Again he said 'Go away' and the figure vanished. On the third night, the ghost stripped the bed altogether and, even more terrified than before the boy said, 'Go away, damn you.' Then the ghost vanished and never after that came back. For the rest of his life, the old man lamented the fact that he had been too scared to get out of bed and follow the ghost, who had clearly meant to show him where the money was hidden. Had he found the money, he said, he could have lived as a 'gentleman' and never had to work.

A number of places have similar tales of the dead unable to rest until they have led someone to their hidden riches. Not everyone was as reluctant to follow a ghost as this old fellow, who clearly told this story out of regret, as Justin Brooke adds that he was a charming old man but just a bit workshy.

Dallinghoo

Towards the end of the nineteenth century, Camilla, Lady Gurdon, heard from Mr Redstone, the same teacher who had told her the story of Mrs Short of BOULGE, the tradition that under the high post of a gate at Dallinghoo lay a hidden treasure. The ghost of its former owner haunted the spot, the combined efforts of twelve clergymen having failed to 'lay' his spirit.

Dallinghoo also had a 'footless' ghost. Lady Gurdon writes:

> In years gone by there lived at Dallinghoo a Widow Shawe who committed suicide by cutting her throat. She now haunts the lanes and flits by without feet. She has been seen by many, and amongst those whom she has startled is Mrs H., a thatcher's wife (my informant for this and other Dallinghoo tales.) This person is a firm believer in ghosts, for she has seen spirits track the footsteps of her children.

'Mrs H.' evidently did not explain why the ghost of Widow Shawe
was thought to be footless: perhaps like some other apparitions she
was walking on a former ground level.

Debenham

In the later nineteenth century, 'Mrs H.', probably the thatcher's
wife who also told Lady Gurdon stories of DALLINGHOO, said to her:

> 'I once lived in a curious old house – the Barley House, out
> Debenham way – and that were haunted. There were a great
> horse-shoe nailed into the ceiling on one of the beams, and they
> say that were to nail in a spirit so as he couldn't get out – a lot of
> clergymen done it. There were a pond close by, round which a
> man (*i.e.*, a ghost) always walked at night. So a clergyman he come
> with a rushlight, and put that into the pond, and he say the spirit
> were not to come out until the rushlight were burnt out. So he
> could never come out, for a rushlight could never burn out in
> a pond.'

The exorcism containing a ruse of this sort is often mentioned in
English folk traditions. This is an ancient theme, exemplified in the
classical story of 'Althaea's Brand'. The Fates foretold at Meleager's
birth that he would die when a certain brand then burning in his
mother Althaea's hearth had been entirely consumed by fire. But
Althaea seized the brand, stopped it burning, and hid it away.
Later, on hearing the news that Meleager had killed her brothers,
she took the brand from its hiding place and threw it on the fire,
causing his death.

Hintlesham Hall

Hintlesham Hall is a Tudor red-brick house much altered in the
eighteenth century by elaborate rebuilding and facings of stone.
Gambled away in the days of Queen Anne by Henry Timperley, in
1747 it came into the possession of Sir Richard Lloyd and passed
from him to his son and grandson, both named Richard Savage
Lloyd.

The great staircase and library were said to be haunted by the second wife of one of the Richard Savage Lloyds, who reputedly starved her stepson to death. Charles Beard, author of *Lucks and Talismans* (1934), who had stayed in the house, wrote how one night he saw the library door swing open 'as though propelled by an invisible but purposeful hand' and then shut again. Once his nerves were steady enough, he made a dash to his bedroom.

For years a dummy figure supposedly modelled from the features of the murdered boy was kept locked in the attic. It was known as the 'Luck of Hintlesham', and at one time was preserved behind a curtain on the staircase. It was said that, if the figure were broken or harmed or removed, the house would pass out of the inhabitant's family and disaster follow. Beard writes, 'I believe it was so removed at one time and the house was sold by Colonel Lloyd Anstruther.' (This was to Sir Gerald Ryan.) According to Mary Lewes, in *Stranger than Fiction* (1911), the figure (she says that of a girl) was removed from the staircase for a dance: 'But mark what happened! That very night occurred a shock of earthquake enough to cause part of the house to fall down!'

Beard says that the 'Luck' was made of wax and was perhaps a funerary effigy. The fact that it was kept on the staircase would account for the tradition of its being haunted.

Lowestoft

Jack Rose, in *Tales and Tall Stories* (1992), tells the story of the Lowestoft North Quay ghost, said to roam the dock area. This is supposedly the ghost of Edward Rollahide, who fell to his death during an argument with a fellow labourer, George Turner, in 1921, when they were working on the construction of the North Quay West. Rollahide appears to have started arguing while playing cards, and the story goes that he picked up an axe and, swinging it wildly, began to chase Turner. During one such wild swing, Rollahide lost his footing, fell into a pit of cement and was not seen alive again. Later, when Turner was coming home from an evening's drinking, Rollahide's misshapen ghost appeared before him swinging his axe and dripping wet cement. Cursing and wailing, it disappeared through a wall. Turner was so shocked that he took to his bed and died. Rose adds that the ghost has been seen on at least three other occasions.

Oulton Broad

In 1861, Mackenzie Walcott recorded the melodramatic story of Oulton High House (now the Manor House), built in the middle of the sixteenth century:

> It was long known as the 'haunted house,' where some deed of darkness had been committed, and at midnight a wild huntsman and his hounds, and a white lady carrying a poisoned cup, were believed to issue and go their fiendish rounds. According to the legend, the spectre, in the time of George II., was the wife of a roystering squire, who, returning unexpectedly from the chase, surprised her toying with an officer, his guest, whose pity for her had ripened into guilty love. High words followed, and when the husband struck the vile suitor of his wife, the paramour drove his sword through his heart. The murderer and lady fled with her jewels and the gold of the murdered man. Years after, her daughter, who had been forgotten in the haste of departure, having grown up into a beautiful woman, was affianced to a young farmer of the neighbourhood. Being on the eve of marriage, she was sitting with him in the old hall one bleak November night, when a carriage, black as a hearse, its curtains closely drawn, and with servants dressed in sable liveries, stopped at the door. The masked men rushed in, and carried off the young girl to her unnatural mother, having stabbed the lover, who had endeavoured in vain to rescue her. In a convent cemetery at Namur was a grave, said to cover the unhappy daughter, who had been poisoned by her mother.

Pakenham

Towards the end of the nineteenth century, a house near Pakenham was said to be persistently disturbed by strange noises and the sound of footsteps, supposedly made by the ghost of the man who

built the house with suspect money. The Revd Harry Jones, reporting the story in 1900, writes:

> They *du* sah one time there allus used to be a knife and fork laid
> for he ivery night, but at last they couldn't stand it no longer, and
> they got the passon in, and he read he down into a closet agin the
> fireplace in the best bedroom, and they papered the closet door
> up, and he worn't heard no more iver so long. Then there come
> some new people, and took the house, and they undone the closet,
> and aout he come rasher nor iver, knockin' here and knockin'
> there, tell you couldn't hardly sleep for he ... Then they read he
> daown agin. That time they read him daown of a clock case, and
> they took the pendle (pendulum) aout, and put it down a well.
> So he was squat (quiet) of a long time; but arterwards they git the
> pendle agin, and set the clock agoin' and aout he come rasher nor
> iver ... So that time they got a heap of passons to read he down
> for good. I don't know zackly haow many there was, but there
> was over thutty passons ... and they read he daown of an owd
> well, and they built a summer haous over it ... and that haven't
> been interfered with sence.

The knife and fork laid for the ghost is paralleled in the Norfolk
story of 'The Dauntless Girl' recorded by Walter Rye in 1920, in
which the Dauntless Girl pleases the old ghost of the squire's
mother, who haunts the house 'specially at meals', by always laying
a place for her at table and handing her the vegetables 'just as if
she were real'. For the rest, there are enough verbal similarities
(for example 'aout he come rasher nor iver') to folktales from
other counties to suggest that this may not be an authentic Suffolk
narrative, but a composite of printed ghost stories.

Easier to accept as genuine is an extract from a letter sent to Lady
Gurdon's regular informant, Mr Redstone, and published by her in
1893. It reads:

> I do know one tale which is true – at least the man who saw firmly
> believes it, and was perfectly sober at the time. He was a carter,
> and driving one night by moonlight saw a funeral procession
> coming – mourning coaches, etc. As the road was narrow, he
> stopped and drew aside to let it pass, noticing how quietly it went
> by. Afterwards he made enquiries, and found that there was no

funeral; but that on the anniversary of the death of some old chap who died long ago, the said procession was seen, and had been seen by others. The man who tells this was living at Pakenham at the time.

Phantom funerals have been reported from time to time in most counties.

Seckford Hall

In St Mary's church, Woodbridge, there is a monument on the north side of the chancel to Thomas Seckford (d. 1587), who built the north chapel. It takes the form of a tomb-chest with open arcades, and originally had brasses but these together with inscriptions were stripped from the tomb by the Puritan iconoclast William Dowsing (c.1596–1679). Thomas Seckford was a wealthy man, Master of the Court of Requests in the reign of Queen Elizabeth I, and a great benefactor of Woodbridge. The Seckford Charity, endowed with lands at Clerkenwell, supported almshouses, the grammar school, and other institutions.

A secret passage is supposed to exist between his town house, Woodbridge Abbey, and nearby Seckford Hall, a most beautiful red-brick mansion built between 1553 and 1585. By the mid nineteenth century, it had declined into a farmhouse, and was partly in ruins by the Second World War, but has since been restored and is now a hotel and restaurant. Current tradition says that Thomas Seckford's ghost may be seen there, wearing a steeple-crowned hat and magnificent period costume (or, according to some, dressed all in white), carrying his wand of office. He is said to perpetually bemoan the fact that the money he left in the Seckford Trust for the poor has been appropriated by the rich.

Surrey

Albury

Here, a deep, clear, pool surrounded by trees, which was formerly called Shirebourne Pond, has been known since the mid nineteenth century as the Silent Pool; it is said to be bottomless and haunted, and its name implies that it is one of the many places where, supposedly, no bird ever sings. It is in fact a flooded chalk-pit. Such sites very often attract supernatural beliefs, and it is common for water-haunting ghosts to be female. A Victorian novelist named Martin Tupper, who lived at Albury Park, provided a melodramatic explanation in his novel *Stephan Langton* (1858); it is now impossible to tell what form the legend took before his time, if indeed it existed at all.

According to Tupper, Emma, a virtuous village maiden, used often to bathe naked in this pool. One day, she realized that a horseman was spying on her from between the trees – it was none other than King John (that stereotypical bad king in popular history and folklore). Rightly guessing that he meant to rape her, she tried to escape by moving to deeper water, but he followed, riding his horse into the pool. Before long she reached a spot where the pool deepens sharply, and with a despairing shriek she sank down. A further tragedy followed, since her brother was not far off and heard the scream; he plunged in to save her, but since he too could not swim the brother and sister drowned together, while the callous king made no move to save them. Later, the girl's father denounced King John before his assembled retinue at Guildford Castle, producing as proof a feather from his hat, which had caught in the branches of a tree near the pond. The indignation caused by this crime contributed to the barons' revolt, which led to the signing of Magna Carta at nearby Runnymede.

Tupper's tale no doubt appealed to Victorian taste, since it managed to be at the same time morally uplifting, tragic, patriotic, and discreetly sexy. He also claimed, quite falsely, that it was true history, and 'may be depended upon for historical accuracy in every detail'. It has since been repeated in virtually every guide-book to the district, and has fed back into local tradition. It is said that Emma's ghost still haunts the spot.

Epsom

In November 1779, the 35-year-old Thomas Lord Lyttelton, well known for his wild life and the many women he had seduced, died suddenly at his Epsom home, Pitt Place (demolished in the 1960s). The event created a great stir, because it was said that he had seen a vision a few days previously which correctly predicted the time of his death, but had ignored it. On 12 June 1784, Boswell recorded Dr Johnson as saying, 'It is the most extraordinary thing that has happened in my day. I heard it with my own ears from his uncle, Lord Westcote. I am so glad to have every evidence of the spiritual world, that I am willing to believe it.'

An account of the affair was preserved at Pitt Place and published in the *Gentleman's Magazine* in 1816; it is said to be a contemporary record by Admiral Wolseley, who was in the house at the time. He explains that Lord Lyttelton had suffered several 'suffocating fits' [asthma attacks?] in the preceding weeks, and was in London:

> While at his house in Hill-street, Berkeley-square, he dreamt, three days before his death, he saw a Bird fluttering, and after-wards a Woman appeared in white apparel, and said, 'Prepare to die, you will not exist three days.' He was alarmed, and called his servant, who found him much agitated and in a profuse per-spiration. This had a visible effect the next day on his spirits. On the third day, while at breakfast ... he said, 'I have jockeyed [cheated] the ghost, for this is the third day.'
>
> The whole party set off for Pitt Place. They had not long arrived when he was seized with a usual fit. Soon recovered. Dined at five. To bed at eleven. His servant, about to give him rhubarb and mint water, stirred it with a toothpick; which Lord Lyttelton perceiving, called him a slovenly dog, and bid him bring a spoon. On the servant's return, he was in a fit. The pillow being high, his chin bore hard on his neck. Instead of relieving him, he ran for help; on his return found him dead.

A more detailed account, printed in the *Gentleman's Magazine* the previous year (1815) but not claimed to be contemporary, shows some embellishments. The bird is not mentioned, and the visionary woman ('one of the most angelic female figures that imagination could possibly paint') specifies that he will die 'at the hour of twelve'. To help keep his spirits up his friends, unknown to him, had put his watch, and all the clocks in the house, forward by half an hour; so when it was, as he thought, 12.15, he went off to bed, saying, 'This mysterious lady is not a true prophetess, I find' – only to die a few moments before the real midnight. The same account says that at this very moment Miles Andrews, a friend of Lyttelton's who had invited him down to Dartford, woke to see him looking at him from between his bed-curtains, wearing dressing-gown and nightcap. Thinking his friend had arrived at an unexpectedly late hour and needed a bed, Andrews rang for a servant, who denied that Lord Lyttelton was in the house. Puzzled, and suspecting a practical joke, Andrews went back to sleep. Only late next day did he learn the truth, and fainted.

An account said to be that of the Lord Westcote whom Dr Johnson mentions, and supposedly written in February 1780, was published long afterwards in *Notes and Queries* (1862). It tells much the same story, adding some further details, for instance that Lyttelton explained his dream of the bird by recalling that a few days previously he had actually seen a robin fly into somebody's room. This is interesting, for it was already a superstition in his time that birds entering a house were a death omen, and there is ample evidence in the following century that robins were especially feared. A further point, reported by Charles Harper in 1907, was a suggestion that the ghostly woman was the recently deceased mother of a girl (or two girls) whom Lyttelton had seduced.

Guildford

Guildford Gaol was the scene for the manifestation of a ghost, come to seek justice for its own murder. The story is given by Joseph Glanvill, who in 1681 wrote a treatise to disprove 'Saduceism' (the idea that there is no afterlife) by assembling what he considered trustworthy accounts of ghostly apparitions. Glanvill says that a few years previously, in about 1670, a certain Mr Bower, an elderly man from Guildford, was found on the highway 'murdered very barbarously, having one great cut across his throat, and another down his breast'. Two men were arrested on suspicion and put in gaol to await trial. They shared a cell there with a highwayman imprisoned for some other matter. That night, the highwayman was woken around 1 a.m. by an old man who came in silently, pointing to a great gash on his throat and a wound on his breast; he tried to rouse the other two, but 'they grumbled at him, but made no answer', and next morning told him it was only his fancy.

However, the highwayman was so convinced of the reality of what he had seen that he talked about it to others, and the story came to the ears of Mr Reading, the Justice of the Peace who would try the case, and who was a cousin of the victim. He sent for the highwayman and asked him to describe the apparition; the description of the spectre's colouring, beard, hair, and so on tallied exactly with those of the late Mr Bower. Realizing such evidence was not admissible in law, Mr Reading noted it, but kept it secret from the jury until after the two accused men had been convicted on quite different circumstantial evidence, though they denied their guilt to the last. Glanvill heard the story 'from Mr Reading himself, who is a very honest person and not credulous'.

Tadworth

In Tadworth Court, there hangs a portrait of an unknown lady in seventeenth-century costume; she stands among flowering shrubs and trees, while an area of partly erased paint gives the impression of a second face looming between the branches behind her. Writing about the Court in the 1920s, Frances Leaning found that a story centred upon this picture was known verbally and with many variations to nearly everyone in Tadworth (a hamlet in the Banstead area), and had been so known since the 1850s.

It was said that the portrait showed one of a pair of sisters who had lived in that house long before; both were in love with the same man, one happily, and one in vain. One day, he came to visit the one he loved, and she, hearing his voice in the main entrance hall, leaned over the balusters of the upstairs gallery to greet him. In a frenzy of jealousy her sister seized her from behind and tipped her over the balusters, so that she fell to her death on the stone-flagged hall; then, maddened by horror at her own crime, she rushed through a certain room, up a certain narrow staircase, and out onto the roof, from which she threw herself down. Shortly afterwards, it was observed that the shadowy face of the murderous sister had appeared in the background of her victim's portrait, and could not be erased. Nor could the painting itself be removed from its place; whenever it was disturbed in any way, the ghostly sounds of the tragedy would be heard again in the house. There had at one time also been indelible bloodstains on the hall floor, but later the stone paving was replaced.

Being a historian, Frances Leaning had hoped to pin down names and dates for this tragedy, but could find no evidence; despite the strong conviction of local people that 'there must be something in it', she was forced to conclude that someone simply invented it, to fit the unknown lady's portrait, and perhaps to impress 'Christmas guests assembled round the blazing logs in the great hall fireplace, where the gallery showed dimly at dusk and the ceiling was lost in shadows'.

West Horsley

Headless ghosts are a cliché of folklore, but according to a Surrey writer, William Hurst Chouler, in 1978, the church in this village is haunted by the reverse phenomenon, a head without a body – that of Sir Walter Raleigh, executed by decapitation in 1618. Normally, heads of criminals were kept on display at Tower Bridge or else-where till they rotted, but Raleigh's wife persuaded the judges to spare him this final disgrace and allow her to embalm the head and keep it herself. It is said that she carried it with her everywhere until she herself died, some twenty years later; it was eventually buried at West Horsley, where Raleigh's son Carew lived for a few years, from 1656 to 1664.

Sussex

Burpham

In 1771, a certain Jack Upperton of Burpham, together with another man, attempted to rob a post-boy who was carrying mail across the Downs from Steyning to Arundel, in Blakehurst Lane on the outskirts of the village of Burpham. Upperton was the only one caught, though local tradition has always maintained that he was the less guilty of the two; he was hanged in Horsham, and the judge added, 'and afterwards let him be hung in chains on the most convenient spot on Burpham New Down in the parish of Burpham, nearest to the gate at the end of Blakehurst Lane'. The corpse was duly brought home and hoisted in chains on a gibbet. On the following Sunday, the whole village came out, children and all, to view the spectacle.

By the 1850s, not only the skeleton but the gibbet itself had crumbled away, though its stump could still be seen; trees were beginning to invade that area of downland – a process which has continued to the point where nowadays the site of the gibbet is hidden in impenetrable woods. A post and plaque bearing the inscription 'J. U. 1771' was erected by Lawrence Graburn, a local historian who wrote under the pen name Newall Duke, in 1951; it has since been vandalized, lost, and replaced on several occasions.

Even in the twentieth century the site was reputed eerie, and Jack's spirit was thought to walk there; people were said to get hopelessly lost if they tried to go that way at night. However, the only fully developed narrative is a humorous one, showing how the locals played tricks on strangers. In 1959, 'Newall Duke' wrote:

A Burpham man told a story which took place about eighty years ago [i.e. about 1880]. After his day's work, he was cutting wood for himself near the gibbet, of a March evening between the lights. He had just finished when he heard several people approaching, and stood still in the underwood. A little party of men and women stopped close to him, and an elderly man said, 'Somewhere just near here is where the last highwayman was hung in chains, and it is said his ghost walks these paths at night.' Whereupon the man shouted, 'And here he is, too!' Never before had he seen a party bolt so quickly.

Such a tale is too good to be dropped. A later historian, Chris Hare, was told it again in 1999, this time set in the 1920s. Two smart young Londoners were challenged by the locals to visit the gibbet site on a dismal October night; arriving there, rather drunk, one of them inquired, 'Well, how are you tonight, Jack?' 'Wet and cold! Wet and cold!' replied a hollow voice, at which the Londoners fled, and were last seen 'heading for Chichester at a hundred miles an hour'. At least they did not go mad, as the victim of a similar trick is supposed to have done at Winterborne St Martin, Dorset.

Chalvington

There was an honest miller in Chalvington in the 1750s, 'the only honest miller ever known', according to M. A. Lower, writing in 1854. This man, finding success in business impossible, in a fit of despair hanged himself in his own mill. He could not be buried in the churchyard, for until 1823 it was forbidden for suicides to lie in consecrated ground; instead, coroners frequently ordered that they be buried in the roadway, usually (but not necessarily) at a cross-roads. This seems to be an extension of the legal and ecclesiastical rule that persons condemned to death should not receive church burial, for suicide was a crime equivalent to murder, and the death of the 'culprit' was deemed equivalent to execution. As a further mark of ignominy, the bodies of suicides often had a stake driven through them, as was done in this case. Lower explains:

An oaken stake driven through his body grew into a tree, and threw a singular shrivelled branch, the only one it ever produced, across the road. It was the most singular abortion of a tree we ever saw, and had something extremely hag-like and ghostly in its aspect. The spot was of course haunted, and many a rustic received a severe shock to his nerves on passing it after nightfall. The tradition ... [was] looked upon as fabulous, until about twenty-seven years ago [c.1827], when a labourer employed in digging sand near the roots of the scraggy oak discovered a human skeleton. For this part of the history we can vouch, having in our boyish days seen some of the bones.

Chanctonbury Ring

Chanctonbury is a high spot (883 ft; 269 m) along the ridge of the South Downs, just east of the village of Washington, and its Ring was originally the name given to a small Iron Age hill-fort whose barely noticeable earthwork overlooks its steep northern face. But in 1760, at a period when landscape improvement was in fashion among the gentry, Charles Goring, the sixteen-year-old son of the family whose estate included the hill, began planting a thick clump of beeches on the site. In time, this became perhaps the best-loved Sussex landmark, and it was these trees, not the earthwork, which everyone called Chanctonbury Ring. It was a favourite goal for walkers, and a site for family picnics. The great gale of 1987 virtually destroyed it, but hopefully the young trees now planted there will one day be worthy successors.

The spot has become the focus for several brief but memorable tales – or rather, groups of tales, for each shows considerable fluidity and variation – all of which were current in the 1960s, and probably still are. They were collected by one of the present authors in the late '60s and '70s.

Concerning the actual planting, it is often said that whenever he climbed the hill, Charles Goring carried a bottle of water with him to water his young trees; some, more cynical, say he sent footmen up with buckets every day. Another story is that when he was a little boy his father gave him a handful of seeds to do as he liked with, so he ran round the earthworks on the hill, scattering them as he went, and so the clump of trees was made. For other storytellers, the figure of the rich young landowner has dropped out, to be replaced by that folktale favourite the Lowly Hero or Heroine; for them, it was 'a poor village boy', or 'three little girls from the vicarage below the hill', who laboured to create the Ring.

The major factor in legend-building here was the nature of the clump itself, as it was in its prime: its density, its circularity, its coolness and silence contrasting with the sunny open Downs full of lark-song and the hum of insects. To some, this made it an eerie spot, and they would tell how they, or their dogs or horses, were unwilling to go close to the trees; alongside this general feeling of unease, there were more specific claims that it was haunted by phantom horses (heard but not seen), or 'a lady on a white horse', or a Druid, or a white-bearded Saxon killed at Hastings who had buried treasure there before going into battle and now wanders about looking for it. Run three times round the Ring, and one or other of these ghosts will appear to you.

Running or walking round the Ring is the stable core in a whole group of assertions well known in the area. The tradition goes back at least as far as Arthur Beckett's *Spirit of the Downs* (1909), where we read: 'If on a moonless night you walk seven times round the Ring without stopping, the Devil will come out of the wood and hand you a basin of soup.' Nowadays, there are many variations on this theme, usually making the conditions more demanding; for instance, that the circuits should be done at midnight, or on a specified date, or by walking backwards. It is also asserted that it is impossible to count the number of trees in the Ring correctly, because there is some magic in them; moreover, in the 1930s it was also said that if anyone happened to reach the correct total, the ghosts of Julius Caesar and his legions would be seen marching across the Downs – a piece of pseudo-history, for the Roman invasion did not affect this part of Sussex.

Chichester

Daniel Defoe recorded a curious tale current here in the 1720s:

They have a story in this city, that whenever a bishop of that diocese is to die, a heron comes and sits upon a pinnacle of the spire of the cathedral. This accordingly happened about 1709 when Dr John Williams was bishop. A Butcher standing at his shop door, in the South Street, saw it, and ran in for his gun, and being a good marksman shot the heron and killed it, at which his mother was very angry with him, and said he had killed the bishop, and the next day news came to the town that Dr Williams, the last bishop, was dead; this is affirmed by many people inhabitants of that place.

Somewhat similar is the belief that a cormorant perching on the church tower at BOSTON, Lincolnshire, is a death omen.

Cuckfield

In 1848, a rich old lady named Mrs Ann Pritchard Sergison died at the age of eighty-five at her home, Cuckfield Park. She had been notorious for a bitter lawsuit in which she wrested ownership of the estate from the woman commonly thought to be her niece by proving the latter was not really her brother's daughter but had been bought by him as a baby in a Dublin pub in order to provide himself with an heir. Mrs Sergison was also notable for her harsh treatment of her tenants, and for a vindictive temper, which led her into feuds with her neighbours and relatives, even with her own son. She was locally nicknamed 'Wicked Dame Sergison', and she had not been long dead when country people claimed her ghost was walking, for she was too wicked to rest in her grave. In particular, she haunted the road that passed her home; she could be seen swinging on the oak gates at the entrance to its park, causing horses to shy in terror. No one dared go that way at night. Finally, it is said, the vicar and curate of Cuckfield, together with the vicar of Balcombe, held a service of exorcism in the village church at midnight and drowned the ghost in the font. At about the same time, her son replaced the old oak gates by spiked iron ones, and the haunting stopped.

Iron is a good safeguard against malevolent spirits, and if it is in the form of a sharp object its power is all the greater, as is seen in the frequent use of knives, shears, scythes, or scissors as protection against witchcraft.

Highdown Hill

On the slopes of this hill, just west of Worthing, stands the isolated table-tomb of a certain John Oliver (or Olliver), a miller who died in

1793. Many years before his actual death he had persuaded the owner of this land to allow him to erect it there and to build a summerhouse alongside; there he would go every day, allegedly to meditate on death and to compose pious verses. He is said also to have kept his coffin under his bed, storing bread and cheese in it. Local opinion, both then and now, is sharply divided about him. Some take his piety at face value, but many regard him as a rogue who was in league with smugglers; they say he used the hill as a lookout post, the mill as a means of signalling, and the tomb itself as a place to hide contraband and/or the money he made from it. Some believe his wealth still lies somewhere near, and that the copious verses he composed and had carved on the tomb contain clues to its hiding-place.

Two stories are told locally about the tomb, and have been known to one of the present authors since the 1930s. One is that John Oliver arranged to be buried upside down because he believed that on Judgement Day the earth would turn topsy-turvy, and he wanted to be the only person facing the right way. By this, most people mean that he is head down, not merely lying on his face. Curiously, there would have been an opportunity to check whether this is authentic oral history or fictional legend in July 1982, when drunken vandals smashed the tomb with a digger, and it was suggested that before repairing the superstructure the contents could be examined; however, Oliver's remaining descendants refused permission. But the silence of contemporary documents makes it almost certain that the story is not true. There is, for instance, a long, mocking press report of his eccentric funeral, involving a white coffin, white-clad bearers, and a little girl reading the service and giving a sermon; the reporter would hardly have failed to mention such a ludicrous detail as upside-down burial if it in fact occurred. Even more telling is the silence of John Oliver's will, drawn up only two years before his death, which makes provision for the upkeep of the tomb but leaves no instructions about any special positioning of the coffin. So we can assume this is a rumour which grew up later; it may have been stimulated by what actually happened at Box Hill, Surrey, where Major Peter Labellière was indeed buried head downwards, at his own request.

The second story is that if you run round the grave seven times, the miller's ghost will jump out and chase you; again the verses on the tombstone are said to threaten this, though of course they do not. There is, however, a carving on the west side, now much weathered, which might well have set the story going; this shows a skeleton holding a spear, pursued by another figure which clutches its shoulder and is possibly meant to be Time, though it has no hourglass. Below are lines of versified dialogue, in which the first speaker must be the living visitor to the tomb and the second could be either the dead miller or a personified Death:

> Death, why so fast? Pray stop your hand
> And let my glass run out its sand;
> As neither Time nor Death will stay,
> Let us employ the present day.
> Why start you at that skeleton?
> 'Tis your picture that you shun;
> Alive it did resemble thee,
> And thou when dead like that shalt be.

Clearly, John Oliver was aware of the long tradition of *memento mori* funerary art and verse, even if his rendering of it was somewhat eccentric. He certainly succeeded in being remembered and discussed long after his death; generations of Victorian sightseers from Brighton and Worthing would visit the tomb, take tea at the miller's former home, and admire the fine view. And to this day people argue about whether John Oliver was a pious believer who expected a literal Doomsday, a rebel against Church orthodoxy, a smuggling rogue, or a joker.

Warwickshire

Alveston

One of the brief items of folk tradition recorded by J. Harvey Bloom in the 1920s is as follows:

> At Alveston a plough lad named Charles Walton met a dog on his way home nine times on successive evenings. He told both the shepherd and the carter with whom he worked, and was laughed at for his pains. On the ninth encounter a headless lady rustled past him in a silk dress, and on the next day he heard of his sister's death.

In itself, this simply reflects the common belief that a phantom dog is an omen of death. However, it is made more memorable by what happened sixteen years later, when the same Charles Walton was murdered in 1945, in circumstances which suggested to the police that local people suspected him of black magic. At the time of his death he was aged seventy-four, so he must have been in his fifties when he told Bloom about his supernatural encounter when young. This anecdote might well have played a part in building up his occult reputation.

Aston Hall

In 1872, the folklorist J. S. Udal inquired through the pages of *Notes and Queries* whether there was any basis for the 'rather startling and fearsome legend' popularly linked with this fine Jacobean mansion in Birmingham. The story was that at some unspecified time in the past one of the Holte (or Holt) family who owned the estate suspected his wife of conducting a love affair (or rather, in Udal's Victorian phrase, having 'too great a familiarity') with one of the servants. He punished her by keeping her imprisoned in a small room at the top of the house, just below the roof; food was passed to her through a narrow hole in the wall, and she survived there for some years until eventually she died. The place was reputed to be haunted, with rattling chains and other sinister sounds. A more recent tale is that one of the top-storey rooms (the same one?) has been called Dick's Garret ever since a man of that name hanged himself in it because of an unhappy love affair, and that he now haunts it.

Burton Dassett

In 1923–4, there were repeated rumours of strange lights moving around this village and the nearby ones of Fenny Compton and Northend; nowadays they would be classified as UFO apparitions, but at that time the local explanation was 'ghosts'. The then president of the Folklore Society, A. R. Wright, quoted some of the current reports in his address to the Society, to illustrate the curious fact that a haunting may shift from one place to another within a neighbourhood:

> A 'ghost light', a yellow and blue ray, has been said to flit over the lonely range of hills between [Fenny Compton] and Burton Basset. It appeared in 1924 on the exact anniversary of its appearance in 1923, and in 1924 was said to have left its haunt in the hills to dance and caper in the churchyard. Many people have been scared by it, and say that the ghost has the traditional large eyes of fire. The explanation that it is due to marsh gas is, of course, scouted.

Wright's references are a mere summary of the narratives which those who believed they had actually seen the lights gave at the time, as can be seen from many contemporary press reports quoted by the local writer Meg Atkins when she investigated the matter for a book published in 1981. One man described watching the light, which was strong and dazzling, 'of a very beautiful mingled blue and red', later changing to orange, as it moved quickly among trees and bushes, occasionally hovering and sweeping the ground 'as if searching for something'. Some people saw it on the hills, others in the churchyard. A motorcyclist told how he saw a brilliant light hurtling along a road towards him, then vanishing; a railwayman spoke of an oval light hovering about two feet above the ground; a woman gave a lengthy account of seeing a yellow-blue flame bobbing about among derelict farm buildings and then suddenly turning into a dazzling glare, which returned on later nights as a milder but still uncanny glow which would light up her bedroom.

Edgehill

The battle of Edgehill, the first major encounter in the Civil War, was fought on 23 October 1642. Three months later, in January 1643, a pamphlet entitled *A Great Wonder in Heaven* described how, on several nights around Christmas, phantom armies had been seen and heard in the sky, re-enacting the battle in every detail:

> Between twelve and one of the clock in the morning was heard by some sheepherds, and other countrey-men, and travellers, first the sound of drummes afar off, and the noyse of souldiers, as it were, giving out their last groanes; at which they were much amazed ... But then, on the sudden ... appeared in the ayre those same in-corporeall souldiers that made those clamours, and immediately, with Ensignes display'd, Drummes beating, Musquets going off, Cannons discharged, horses neyghing (which also to these men were visible), the alarum or entrance to this game of death was struck up ... Till two or three in the morning, in equal scale continued this dreadful fight ... so amazing and terrifying the poore men, that they could not give credit to their ears and eyes; run away they durst not, for feare of being made a prey to these infernall souldiers, and so they, with much feare and affright, stayed to behold the outcome of the business.

The vision having ended with the defeat of the Royalists, those who had seen it reported it to a magistrate and a clergyman, and swore it was true. Next night, and on several subsequent occasions, many people of all classes gathered to watch the skies, and saw the same sights. Reports of the affair having reached King Charles at Oxford, he sent six reliable officers to investigate; not only did they take sworn statements from witnesses, but they themselves saw the phantom armies, and recognized several people they knew who had died at Edgehill. All this they reported to the king on oath. The pamphleteer concludes:

What this doth portend, God only knoweth, and Time will perhaps discover; but doubtlessly it is a sign of His wrath against this Land for these civil wars, which may He in His good time finish, and send a sudden peace between his Majestie and Parliament.

Some recent writers on the supernatural, such as Antony Hippisley Coxe (1975), say that people occasionally hear or see the spectral battle again on 23 October, the anniversary. The local author Meg Atkins was told in the 1970s that some Victorian journalists had visited the site on that date and 'returned upset and frightened, and made a very hurried departure'. Individual ghosts, notably those of Prince Rupert and Sir Edmund Verney, have been seen on the battlefield; a phantom white horse has been reported from the area where some of the slain are said to be buried.

Ilmington

Many traditions about ghosts have been collected from this village by various writers between c.1930 and 1980, including J. Harvey Bloom, Alan Burgess, Roy Palmer, and Meg Atkins. One report concerns the relatively peaceful spirit of Edmund Golding, who was the parish clerk and died in 1793; he walks up and down the church aisle, muttering the service responses, as he did when alive. Another tells of a phantom coach, with the traditional headless horses and coachman, which drives along Pig Lane and is said to carry the ghost of a local landowner who had murdered one of his neighbours. Alternatively, it is sometimes described as a coach that has only one wheel, carrying the ghost of a murdered man; it drives straight across fields and up hills, leaving the track of its single wheel.

The third tradition is of a dangerous ghostly huntsman, sometimes identified as a seventeenth-century owner of Ilmington Manor, sometimes as a plain yeoman. In life he had owned a pack of hounds and had been so keen on the chase that he neglected everything else, including church-going, for he would go hunting even on a Sunday. There are two accounts of his end. One is that the ground swallowed him up, together with his hounds, during a Sunday hunt. The other is that one night, hearing the hounds howling in their kennels, he went out in his nightshirt to see what was disturbing them; not recognizing him in this unfamiliar garb, they tore him to pieces. Ever since, he and the ghostly pack can be seen on Christmas Eve and New Year's Eve, as they set out in pursuit of some phantom fox in the fields below Meon Hill. The cry of the hounds can be heard for miles, and they are locally referred to as 'Hell Hounds' or 'Night Hounds'. Those who meet this huntsman should take good care not to do anything he asks – not, for instance, to open a gate for him – for this would give him the power to carry them away to their eternal destruction. This tale is one of the clearest examples in Britain of the widespread European folk tradition of the demonic Wild Hunt (see PETERBOROUGH, Huntingdonshire and Peterborough).

Finally, there are tales of witchcraft attached to the village. One old woman is said to have been hanged at a crossroads and then buried there with a stake through her body. She is alleged to have repeatedly caused a man's horse to stumble there when he was carrying medicine home to his sick wife (whom the witch hated); as a result the medicine was spilt, the woman died, and the witch was blamed for her death.

Nowadays, it is a matter of pride for a village to claim multiple hauntings; others that do so include PAINSWICK and PRESTBURY, both in Gloucestershire, and PLUCKLEY, Kent.

Little Lawford

A complex and persistent tale of haunting is set in and around the now-demolished Little Lawford Hall, for a long time the seat of the Boughtons – a family with the sinister Red Hand of Ulster in their armorial bearings. This heraldic emblem is in fact the badge of baronetcy, but is accounted for in popular imagination, here and elsewhere, by various tales of bloodshed. In the case of the Boughtons the most generally accepted version, given for instance by George Morley in *Shakespeare's Greenwood* (1900), is that one of them, in Elizabethan times, heroically lost an arm in battle and was thereafter nicknamed One-Handed Boughton. Alternatively, the local writer Meg Atkins states (1981) that his hand was amputated as a penalty for moving his neighbour's landmark – a heinous sin, according to the Bible, but not one which English law has ever punished in this way. In either case, it was he who returned as a ghost; Morley tells how he would terrify anyone who attempted to sleep in the chamber which had been his, and drove round the district in a phantom coach. By the eighteenth century, the situation had become so intolerable that one of his descendants, Sir Edward Boughton, summoned a team of twelve parsons to conduct an exorcism, each armed with a candle. Once the ghost appeared, eleven of them were unable to keep their candles burning, but the twelfth, Parson Hall of Great Harborough, was a man of great faith; his candle remained alight, and his unfaltering prayers eventually forced the ghost down into a bottle, which was tightly corked and thrown into a nearby marl-pit. But even he could not obtain an unconditional surrender; before entering the bottle, One-Handed Boughton stipulated that he must be allowed two hours of freedom every night in which to ride round the lanes in his coach. Like the anonymous spectral huntsman at ILMINGTON, Boughton sometimes orders those who meet him to open a gate for him, but (according to traditions current late in the nineteenth century) it is inadvisable to obey.

Lawford Hall was demolished in 1784. Early in the nineteenth century, there was some excitement over a bottle found in a pond in what had been its grounds. Could this be the one in which Boughton was confined? Meg Atkins reports that it was given to the nearest relatives, the Boughton-Leighs of Brownsover Hall – whereupon the spectral coach was seen heading in that direction. The bottle was locked away in a massive cupboard, and the family maintained that if it were removed, one of them would die. Eerie sounds of footsteps, hoofbeats, and carriage wheels continued to be heard in and around the house until the family left it after the Second World War, having buried the bottle in concrete at a secret place. The house is now a hotel, and is no longer haunted.

Princethorpe

W. P. Witcutt noted in the journal *Folk-Lore* in 1944 that from 1922 to 1929 the attic of the manor house here was reputedly haunted by a phantom known as Plantie's Ghost. The trouble began when workmen re-slating the roof disturbed a box made of lath and plaster, with a highly polished wooden door, and various bits of metal and wire fixed to the sides of it. The villagers called this contraption a 'husher', and said it had been put there 'to amuse the ghost and keep it from harming people'. 'Plantie' was not, apparently, the name of the ghost itself, but that of a previous owner of the house who had tried to catch it and imprison it in a bottle; presumably the attempt failed and the 'husher' was installed as a second line of defence.

Though no exact parallel to this find has been reported, the underlying principles are sound, in folkloric terms. The roof-space is vulnerable to attacks from external evil forces, so protective charms of various kinds are sometimes placed there; various distracting devices, such as tangles of coloured threads in a bottle, can also be used to divert a supernatural creature from its harmful purposes.

Ragley Hall

Two separate tales of haunting are told of Ragley Hall, in the parish of Arrow, and its park. First, as reported by J. Harvey Bloom c.1930, there is the claim that a White Lady may appear occasionally at midnight and sit upon a certain stile, after which she goes down to a brook to drink. This rather vague tradition incorporates two commonplaces of ghost lore: the association of White Ladies with water, and of apparitions with stiles or gates. It is now impossible to tell whether the story did or did not pre-date the discovery in 1833 of a woman's skeleton unearthed nearby, which was assigned to the Anglo-Saxon period by its brooches and dagger. However, the link is now firmly established in local tradition.

Then there is the tale of a duel and its outcome, as told by a local man to Alan Burgess in the 1940s:

> A black man and a white man had a duel up at the Hall. The white man was waiting in a room for the darkie, and when the darkie came in through the door, he said, 'I thought we were supposed to fight this duel alone?' And as the darkie turned to see who had come in with him, the white man shot him dead. They do

say the blood's still on the wall, but I ain't been up there lately to see.

It is possible that this is a confused memory of an actual duel fought here in 1699 between the then owner, Popham Seymore-Conway, and a Colonel Kirk, in which the former was killed, but if so, why one of the combatants has been turned into a black man in the telling remains unexplained.

Southam

T. F. Thiselton-Dyer, a late Victorian writer on the supernatural, drew attention to the fact that the journal *Ackerman's Repository* in November 1820 carried an account of an unusual legal case which had recently arisen. A farmer returning from market at Southam was murdered, and next morning a man called on the farmer's wife and told her a curious story. He said that, the night before, her husband's ghost had appeared to him, showed him several stab wounds on his body, and told him he had been murdered by so-and-so and his body thrown into a marl-pit. A search was made, the body found, and the person whose name was alleged to have been mentioned by the ghost was committed for trial on the charge of murder.

The trial came on at Warwick before Lord Chief Justice Raymond. The magistrate committed the prisoner on the strength of this story, and the jury would have convicted him had not Justice Raymond intervened. He said he placed no credence on the 'ghost-story', as the accused had a hitherto unblemished reputation and there was no evidence that any ill-feeling existed between him and the murdered man. He added that he knew of no law that admitted that a ghost could give evidence, and, even if any did, the ghost had not appeared to give it.

The crier was then ordered to summon the ghost as a witness, which he did three times. No ghost appeared. Then Justice Raymond acquitted the prisoner, but ordered that his accuser be detained on suspicion of being himself the murderer. A search of this man's house having revealed strong proofs of his guilt, he confessed to the crime and was executed at the next assizes.

Stratford-on-Avon

About a mile (1.6 km) outside the town stands Clopton House, originally an Elizabethan mansion but remodelled in the eighteenth century, which is reputedly haunted by the ghosts of several family members who came to tragic ends. Unfortunately, though their names and the dates of their deaths can be checked, the details have been passed on only by Victorian writers, who tend to dramatize the events. One of the family, Margaret Clopton, was found drowned in 1563 in a well in the grounds (still called Margaret's Well). It is alleged that she killed herself because her father would not let her marry the man she loved; she can be seen by the well, and in her old bedroom. Another, Charlotte, met an even worse fate, according to William Howitt's account in 1844:

> In one of the bed-rooms (said to be haunted ...) hung a portrait ... singularly beautiful ... and that was the likeness of Charlotte Clopton, about whom there was so fearful a legend told at Stratford church. In the time of some epidemic, the sweating-sickness or the plague, this young girl had sickened, and to all appearance died. She was buried with fearful haste in the vaults of Clopton chapel, attached to Stratford church; but the sickness had not stayed. In a few days another of the Cloptons died, and him they bore to the ancestral vault; but as they descended the gloomy stairs, they saw, by the torchlight, Charlotte Clopton in her grave-clothes leaning against the wall; and when they looked nearer, she was indeed dead, but not before, in the agonies of despair and hunger, she had bitten a piece from her round white shoulder! Of course, she had *walked* ever since. This was 'Charlotte's chamber'.

A generation later, an Alice Clopton was kidnapped on her wedding day by a rejected lover who, realizing he would not be able to outrun his pursuers because the double weight was slowing his horse, flung her into a river to drown, and made good his escape. Recounting these tales at the beginning of the twentieth century, George Morley rather implausibly claimed that the first two had inspired two famous writers: Shakespeare, in his description of Ophelia's drowning, and Poe, in 'The Fall of the House of Usher'.

Finally, the folklorist Roy Palmer in 1976 mentioned a tradition that the ghost of a Catholic priest, caught and murdered while hiding in the house, haunts certain stairs and corridors; an indelible bloodstain marks the spot where his body was dragged along a landing to a bedroom. There is probably some connection here with the historical fact that Ambrose Rookwood, one of Guy Fawkes's co-conspirators, was living in Clopton House as a tenant at the time of the plot, and that when the place was searched after the arrest of the plotters, various Catholic objects were discovered.

Westmorland

Appleby

About the end of the seventeenth century, says Jeremiah Sullivan, in *Cumberland and Westmorland, Ancient and Modern* (1857), a man well known in the neighbourhood of Appleby as 'Old Shepherd', who had been bad enough when alive, became so troublesome as a 'boggle' (shape-shifting apparition) after death that he had to be forcibly ejected from the house he had lived in. A Catholic priest came to exorcize him and 'laid' him under a large stone not far from the door.

Sullivan's informant had lived in that part of the country about forty years before and had helped at a bonfire during election celebrations not far from Old Shepherd's house:

> Whilst they were enjoying themselves round the fire, and 'cracking' [telling stories] of Old Shepherd, lo! the old fellow made his appearance from under the stone in the shape of a large white something; but he turned off sideways, and *sailed* down the 'beck,' in which they could hear him splashing like a horse.

They let the fire burn out and moved further down the beck to where they knew some wood was lying. Here they made another fire, and again Old Shepherd hove in sight. Sullivan's informant did not see him this time, but someone gave the alarm and the party broke up for the night.

Calgarth

To Calgarth Hall, once the home of the Philipson family, was attached one of the oldest and best-known traditions of screaming skulls. What may have been the earliest form of the story was known to James Clarke, who in his *Survey of the Lakes* (1789) writes:

At Crowgarth were two human sculls [sic] of which many strange stories are told: they were said to belong to persons whom Robin [Philipson] had murdered, and that they could not be removed from the place where they then were; that when they were removed they always returned, even though they had been thrown into the Lake, with many other ridiculous falsehoods of the same stamp: some person, however, has lately carried one of them off to London, and as it has not yet found its way back again, I shall say nothing more on so very trivial a subject.

From 1819 comes a statement supporting Clarke's assertion that only one skull remained.

In Clarke's day, the tale of the skulls was evidently one of the stories told of Robert Philipson, 'Robin the Devil', a supporter of Charles I during the Civil War, by some reviled as a sacrilegious murderer and by others celebrated as a daredevil hero. Nineteenth-century accounts, however, attach the legend to Myles Philipson. In 1858, Alexander Craig Gibson retold the story in verse as he had heard it from John Long, the ferryman of the former Ferry Inn on Lake Windermere. It was also told by the American Moncure D. Conway in *Harper's Magazine*.

According to Conway's version, as repeated by John Ingram in the 1880s, Myles Phillipson (with two *l*'s), a wealthy local magistrate, coveted a little bit of ground known as Calgarth and wanted to add it to his estate, but the owners, a humble farmer named Kraster Cook and his wife Dorothy, refused to sell it. Myles thereupon 'swore he'd have that ground, be they "live or deead"'. However, as time went on, he appeared better disposed and invited them to a Christmas banquet. Afterwards, he pretended that they had stolen a silver cup, and it was of course found in their house, an obvious 'plant'. Theft being a capital offence, and Phillipson the magistrate, they were both sentenced to death. In the courtroom, Dorothy rose and, glaring at Phillipson, said:

'Guard thyself, Myles Phillipson! Thou thinkest thou has managed grandly; but that tiny lump of land is the dearest a Phillipson has ever bought or stolen; for you will never prosper, neither your breed; whatever scheme you undertake will wither in your hand; the side you take will always lose; the time shall come when no Phillipson will own an inch of land; and while Calgarth walls shall stand, we'll haunt it night and day – never will ye be rid of us!'

Dorothy's curse came true, for after that the Phillipsons never prospered. Having built a new house at Calgarth, they acquired two troublesome skulls as guests. They were found at Christmas at the head of some stairs, and were buried a long way off, but then turned up in the house again. 'The two skulls were burned again and again; they were brayed [crushed] to dust and cast to the wind; they were several years sunk in the lake; but the Phillipsons never could get rid of them.'

In some accounts, the skulls are represented not as mysteriously self-returning but as being manipulated by ghosts. Writing in 1860, Mackenzie Walcott notes, 'Calgarth was said to be haunted by two spirits, the guardians of two sculls [sic] which ... if removed from a particular window, were immediately replaced by these unearthly guests.'

It is said that Bishop Watson of Llandaff (d. 1816), who bought the Calgarth estate, while living there went through a solemn form of 'laying' the two ghostly skulls in order to allay the fears of the locals. He is alleged to have had them walled up in the niche on the staircase where they were kept. Whether these measures had the desired effect is uncertain: whereas John Ingram says that 'Dorothy and Kraster have remained quiet of late years', Wilson Armistead in 1891 says that the spectres 'still are seen'.

Various attempts to explain the skulls' origin have been made: that they came from a burial ground attached to Old Calgarth where human bones frequently turned up; or that a lady doctor who had lived in the house kept two skeletons for professional purposes, of which the skulls survived. Others suggest that the story was inspired by an early form of the name Calgarth, referred to as *le Calvegartrige* in 1390–4, which resembles Calvary, otherwise Golgotha, 'the place of the skulls'; or that it was started as Round-head propaganda, the Philipsons' decline in fortune being attributed not to Dorothy's curse but to their being ardent Royalists during the English Civil War.

Brougham Hall, near Penrith, also had a screaming skull: after many attempts to get rid of it, the old Westmorland family of the

Broughams finally bricked it up in a wall. A number of other old houses contain, or have contained, human skulls, generally regarded as protective talismans. In every case, there is a strong tradition that the skull or skulls must never be removed. At some point, apparently in late Victorian times, the term 'Screaming Skull' was coined with reference to the specimen at BETTISCOMBE MANOR, Dorset, and is now the standard term even where screams are not specified as part of the manifestations.

Crackenthorpe

Probably the best-known ghost in and around Appleby is one from Cromwellian times known as 'Peg Sneddle', an account of whom is given in E. Bellasis' *Machells of Crackenthorpe* (1886). Here she is identified as Elizabeth Sleddall, the wife of Lancelot Machell of Crackenthorpe Hall, and mayor of Appleby (1660–71). She was said to haunt Crackenthorpe Hall and appear to the heads of the family shortly before their deaths.

> The country folk say that she has been seen driving along the Appleby road at a great pace with 'amber leets [lights]' in the carriage, and disappears suddenly in Machell wood near a spot marked in the ordnance survey Peg Sneddle's trough. When storms come from the Fell, Peg is said to be angry, and *vice versa* in fine weather . . .

The 'Fell' in question is Cross Fell, in Cumberland, from which a sudden icy wind called the Helm Wind is traditionally said to blow.

The country people said that Peg was 'laid' under a big stone called 'Peg's stone' in the River Eden just below Crackenthorpe Hall for 999 years. Bellasis had been told that this stone had disappeared, 'albeit a stone there still . . . was pointed out to me as Peg's, just off the right bank below the hall.'

Bellasis quotes from a Machell family manuscript book the tradition that an old oak tree in the neighbourhood of Cracken-thorpe was known as Sleddall's Oak, 'where a female figure is seen to sit and weep when any misfortune is about to befall any member of the Machell family'. Some later writers say that Peg Sneddle and Elizabeth Sleddall were two separate ghosts. In the 1960s,

Gerald Findler reported that, when he was a soldier convalescing at Appleby during the First World War, wounded 'Tommies' often came in at night with tales of having seen Peg.

Lake Windermere

Today a modern ferry takes passengers across the narrow part of Lake Windermere from Rawlinson's Nab on the east bank to the Ferry House on the west, passing between the lake's islands, the largest of which is Belle Isle. Coming from the Bowness side, one sees the Claife Heights of Cumberland towering above the opposite shore.

In the days when ferrymen crossed in a rowing boat, Rawlinson's Nab was the home of a mysterious spirit who came to be known as the Crier of Claife. Only his voice was heard, calling to the boatmen, and it was a presage of doom.

Harriet Martineau, writing in 1855, tells the story:

> It was about the time of the Reformation, one stormy night, when a party of travellers were making merry at the Ferry-house, – then a humble tavern, – that a call for the boat was heard from the Nab. A quiet, sober boatman obeyed the call, though the night was wild and fearful. When he ought to be returning, the tavern guests stepped out upon the shore, to see whom he would bring. He returned alone, ghastly and dumb with horror. Next morning, he was in a high fever; and in a few days he died, without having been prevailed upon to say what he had seen ... For weeks, after, there were shouts, yells, and howlings at the Nab, on every stormy night: and no boatman would attend to any call after dark. The ... monk from Furness who dwelt on one of the islands of the lake, was applied to to exorcise the Nab. On Christmas day, he assembled all the inhabitants on Chapel Island, and performed in their presence services which should for ever confine the ghost to the quarry in the wood behind the Ferry, now called the Crier of Claife. Some say that the priest conducted the people to the quarry and laid the ghost, – then and there. – Laid though it be, nobody goes there at night.

Mackenzie Walcott, in 1860, immediately before giving the legend of the Crier of Claife, tells how, in 1635, a marriage party of fifty people, along with the bride, a young girl from Sawrey, and the bridegroom, a yeoman of the same place, was drowned here on return from Hawkshead church. Though Walcott himself does not explicitly lay the blame on the Crier, other writers on the Lake District connect this accident with the ghost.

Levens Hall

Levens Hall is a mainly Elizabethan house built round a fortified pele tower of the late 1200s. The Elizabethan parts of the house are largely the work of James Bellingham, who inherited Levens in about 1580. A century later, it had to be sold, allegedly in order to settle the gambling debts of his grandson, Alan. Levens was bought by his kinsman, Colonel James Grahme, Privy Purse to King James II until his abdication in 1688, and tradition says that he won the house on the turn of the ace of hearts. True or not, the lead down-spouts on the front of the house are decorated with gilded hearts and the initials of James Grahme and his wife Dorothy.

During his long occupancy, Colonel Grahme (d. 1730) restored the house and it has remained largely unchanged since then, possibly because it has remained in the same related group of families down to its present owners, the Bagots. Among its treasures are the Levens Constables, long-stemmed ale glasses twenty inches (51 cm) high, out of which the toast 'Luck to Levens whilst the Kent flows' was traditionally drunk.

The 'Luck of Levens Hall' is also tied up with a herd of fallow deer in the park. It is said that the birth of a white fawn in the herd heralds some event of importance in the family. Consequent on this idea is the belief that it is unlucky to kill any of the white deer. It is said that Lord Templeton, at one time the owner, gave orders to shoot a white buck he had seen, and told the gamekeeper, when he demurred, that such a belief was superstitious nonsense. The gamekeeper nevertheless refused to carry out the order, and the task was given to someone else. Following the death of the buck, all sorts of trouble followed: Levens Hall twice changed hands, the staff lost their jobs, and local people attributed this to the shooting of the buck.

Connected with the 'Luck' is the tale of the 'Curse of Levens'.

J. G. Lockhart, telling the story in 1938, says that an unidentified person, 'for some reason which is not disclosed', put a curse on the owners of Levens, saying that strangers would always separate them from their lands, and that no son would succeed his father until a white doe was born in the park and the waters of the Kent stood still. Lockhart writes, 'The Curse appears to have been literally fulfilled. The estate went continuously from father to nephew, brother or cousin, or else through the female line.' Then, in 1896, Mrs Bagot bore a son, a doe in the herd gave birth to a white fawn, and the River Kent froze solid.

Such a romantic house as Levens was bound to have its ghosts, one of whom has supplanted the unidentified person (and filled in the gaps) in Lockhart's story. This is the 'Grey Lady', said to be the ghost of a gypsy who in the early part of the eighteenth century called at Levens Hall seeking food and shelter. On being turned away, she died of starvation, but not before cursing the house and its occupants, as before. Peter Walker, relating this tradition in 1993, says that the Grey Lady has been seen several times since then, sometimes by motorists on the A6, when she is accompanied by a small black dog.

Perhaps this is the same black dog who others say manifests himself on the stairs at Levens Hall but is not malevolent.

Lowther Castle

Plans were announced in 2003 for the restoration of Lowther Castle, in 1957 reduced to a shell. The castle was built between 1806 and 1814 on the site of Lowther Hall, home in the eighteenth century of Sir James Lowther, first Earl of Lonsdale.

Following his death, it became celebrated for its haunt by this classic member of the 'wicked gentry'. Jeremiah Sullivan in 1857 wrote:

> Westmorland never produced a more famous boggle – infamous as a man, famous as a boggle – than Jemmy Lowther, well known ... as the 'bad Lord Lonsdale.' This notorious character ... became a still greater terror to the country after death, than he had been even during his life. He was with difficulty buried; and whilst the

clergyman was praying over him, he very nearly knocked the reverend gentleman from his desk. When placed in the grave, the power of creating alarm was not interred with his bones. There were disturbances in the Hall, noises in the stables; neither men nor animals were suffered to rest. Jemmy's 'coach and six' is still remembered and spoken of, from which we are probably to understand that he produced a noise, as boggles frequently do, like the equipage of this description. There is nothing said of his shape, or whether he appeared at all; but it is certain he made himself audible. The Hall became almost uninhabitable, and out of doors there was constant danger of meeting the miscreant ghost.

It seems to have been thought, says Sullivan, that the only help to be had in such cases was that of a Catholic priest, one reason being that the exorcism had to be in Latin. One was brought in, but Jemmy held out against him for a long time and when he finally capitulated would only agree to go for a year and a day to the Red Sea (to which ghosts were traditionally banished). These terms were not accepted, and the priest read on and on until he finally mastered the stubborn ghost 'and *laid* him under a large rock called Wallow Crag, and laid him for ever'. (Wallow Crag is WALLA CRAG, Cumberland.)

Shap Fell

Following their survey of local folklore, L. F. Newman and E. M. Wilson in 1952 wrote:

> It is still a current belief in Westmorland and North Lancashire that black dogs haunt certain places. Where the belief is associated with a given locality, the ghost may perhaps assume other manifestations . . . The belief in the appearance of a phantom black dog as a death omen also exists in the area.

An apparition that may have changed categories from shape-shifting animal bogey to death omen in dog-form (if indeed in local belief they were ever separate) is one haunting Shap Fell. The Revd Joseph Whiteside in *Shappe in Bygone Days* (1904) reports the existence near Shap of a 'dobby' or bogey that *generally* appeared as a large black dog. Later, in 1988, J. A. Brooks writes that the A6 over Shap Fell used to be extremely hazardous in winter and local people believed that fatal accidents on it would be presaged by the sight of a black dog. He always appeared at the same spot, running in front of cars for a little way, before jumping over a stone parapet between the road and a drop of three hundred feet (91 m). He apparently made newspaper headlines in the autumn of 1937 when he was seen on several nights.

See also BRIGG, Lincolnshire; SHERINGHAM, Norfolk.

Wiltshire

Heytesbury

In 1901, J. U. Powell reported to *Folk-Lore* that people of this village were telling vivid tales about how the ghost of a prominent member of the local gentry had been laid by a posse of parsons in 1854. This was done at the request of the dead man's wife, who was troubled by the revenant and used to speak with it once a year, wearing a sheepskin turned inside out as a protection against its attacks. It was believed that though a ghost might easily tear a living man to pieces, it had no power to harm a lamb's skin (this, presumably, is because it symbolizes Jesus Christ, the Lamb of God). Parsons from several parishes gathered at Heytesbury for this exorcism, but almost all of them were mastered by the ghost's power and could not keep up their prayers. One, however, a certain Parson Smith, stood firm, and correctly replied, 'A lamb', when the ghost asked, 'What is the simplest thing in the world?' He then began the formula to banish the ghost to the Red Sea, but the spirit pleaded so earnestly not to be sent there that some other place of confinement was chosen, though what this was is not said.

Highworth

In 1922, the writer Alfred Williams, describing the countryside of this area, mentioned a story of ghost-laying which provides a humorous variation on this popular theme. At one time, it is said, the people of Highworth were troubled by the ghost of their late landowner, Squire Crowdy, who would roam the streets at midnight with a rope round his neck, or noisily drag a coach round the yard of the manor house. The vicar, together with a bailiff and some jurymen, went to the empty house to conduct an exorcism, but the ghost proved obstinate; it would only submit if it were laid in a barrel of cider and allowed to remain there. So that was done;

Squire Crowdy's ghost was sealed up in a barrel in his own cellar, and the cellar securely bricked up.

Littlecote House

This mansion is the setting for an Elizabethan tale of crime and detection which, if true, is exceptionally horrible. John Aubrey certainly believed it, and records it in his *Brief Lives* (1669–96) to explain why Littlecote House passed to Sir John Popham in 1589, having previously belonged to the Darrells.

> Sir John Dayrell, of Littlecote in com. Wilts [the county of Wiltshire], having gott his Ladie's waiting woman with child, when her travel [labour pains] came, sent a servant with a horse for a midwife, whom he was to bring hood-winked [blindfolded]. She was brought, and layd the woman, but as soon as the child was borne, she saw the Knight take the Child and murther it, and burn it on the fire in the chamber. She having donne her businesse was extraordinarily rewarded for her paines, and sent blindfold away. This horrid Action did much run in her mind, and she had a desire to discover [reveal] it, but knew not where 'twas. She considered with her selfe the time she was riding, and how many miles might be rode at that rate in that time, and that it must be some great person's house, for the roome was twelve foot high; and she could know the chamber if she sawe it. She went to a Justice of the Peace, and a search was made. The very chamber found. The Knight was brought to his Tryall; and, to be short, this Judge [i.e. Popham] had this noble howse, parke, and manor, and (I thinke) more, for a Bribe to save his life; Sir John Popham gave Sentence according to Lawe; but being a Great person, and a Favourite, he procured a *Noli prosequi* [a ruling that no further steps be taken].

Aubrey is wrong on some points. Darrell's Christian name was William; he died in 1588, and since Popham did not become a judge until 1602 he cannot possibly have presided at Darrell's trial, if there ever was one. But rumours certainly were current at the time. A letter of 2 January 1578, preserved in the archives of Longleat and addressed to the owner, Sir John Thynne, contains a message for a certain Mr Bonham, living at Longleat, whose sister was known to be Darrell's mistress; the writer 'desires that Mr Bonham will enquire of his sister concerning her usage at Will Darrell's, the birth of her children, how many there were, and what became of them; for that the report of the murder of one of them was increasing foully, and will touch Will Darrell to the quick'.

Sir Walter Scott retold the story in the notes to his novel *Rokeby* (1811), and his is now the best-known version. He sets the event in 1575, and says the villainous Darrell (whom he nicknames 'Wild Will') threw the baby alive into the flames. The midwife, whom Scott calls 'Mother Barnes of Shefford', was determined to bring him to justice, so she secretly cut a strip of cloth from the hem of the bed-curtains, and though blindfolded still managed to count the steps of the staircase as she left. These clues led to the house being identified. Darrell was tried, but acquitted after bribing Popham; however, he died soon after, being thrown from his horse while hunting.

Ralph Whitlock and Kathleen Wiltshire recorded some twentieth-century elaborations of the tale. These include the idea that the baby was conceived in incest, its mother being Darrell's sister, whose ghost haunts the house; also, that Darrell's horse threw him because it was terrified by the apparition of a ghostly burning baby at a place since called 'Darrell's Stile'. Darrell's ghost is said to haunt this stile, with a pack of phantom hounds, and to drive up to the entrance of Littlecote House in a phantom coach as a sign that the owner's heir will shortly die. For instance, in 1861 the heir was a six-month-old baby, Francis Popham, who was seriously ill; his nurse had sent urgently for his parents, who were away. In the middle of the night she heard a coach galloping up to the door, to her great relief – but when she looked out of the window, there was nothing there. The baby was dead by morning.

Longleat

A story reported by V. S. Manley in his book *The Folk-Lore of the Warminster District* (1924) claimed that there had once been a Marquis of Bath who returned to haunt Longleat House after his death and made himself so troublesome to his widow that she called upon twelve parsons to come to the house to lay him in the Red

Sea. This much is common in folklore, but the remainder of the procedure is unusual. In Manley's words:

> A sheepskin was procured, into which the Marquise was wrapped, and in a cradle they laid her, and carried her to her room. The twelve parsons sat around a table and waited. At midnight the ghost appeared and stood among them. Each parson in turn asked the ghost what troubled him. It begged to be allowed to touch the hem of his wife's garment. They told him this was impossible, because she was wrapped in lamb's wool. Then they walked through the house reciting the Lord's Prayer backwards, which proved effective in ridding the place of the ghost.

It is an enigmatic tale. The protective power of the sheep's or lamb's fleece is clearly related to the religious symbolism in which these animals stand for innocence, as at HEYTESBURY; the Marquise is also laid in a cradle, like an innocent newborn babe. But what was the ghost's intention towards his living wife? Would he have murderously attacked her? There are Danish legends in which a revenant begs to touch his wife's hand but she, forewarned, holds out her kerchief, which he rips to pieces. Or is he amorous? Katy Jordan, retelling the story in the year 2000, says the lamb's wool 'protect[s] her from the ghost's advances'. Sexuality in ghosts rarely features in British sources, most of which have been filtered through the respectability of nineteenth-century informants and collectors, but can be deduced from some accounts of the undead, as for instance the twelfth-century writings of William of Newburgh, who mentions a dead man entering the bed where his wife was sleeping. Or is his gesture meant as a humble plea for her prayers, rather as the ghost of Sir John Popham at WELLINGTON, Somerset, had his fate alleviated by the prayers of his pious wife? It is, alas, impossible to get past the collector to question the informant, so the questions must remain unanswered.

Semley

A sinister story was collected by the folklorist Kingsley Palmer in 1969 about a skeleton nicknamed 'Molly' kept in Pythouse, a mansion near Semley:

Molly is the remains of a female who was hanged at Oxford for the murder of her baby girl by scalding, the father of which is rumoured to have been a member of the Benet Stanford family [owners of the house]. The crime is supposed to have been committed in what is known as the 'Pink Room' at Pythouse, which Molly is supposed to haunt, as well as walking in the nearby corridors. There is also a curse which states that should Molly be taken away from Pythouse misfortune will fall upon the family.

Three times Molly has been removed. The first time a wing of the house caught on fire. The second time the son and heir died. The third time the daughter died.

The explanation of Molly's back-history is a mixture of plausible and implausible. In 1752, a law 'for better Preventing the horrid Crime of Murder' allowed judges, at their discretion, to replace gibbeting, which was the normal sequel to hanging, by handing over the corpse to medical students for dissection, and this remained the case until the Anatomy Act of 1832. A skeleton originating in this way could well have ended up as a memento in a private house, if a member of the family had trained as a surgeon. But that Molly should have been guilty of infanticide in the same house, and that the father of her child was one of the family there, is more dramatic than convincing. The rest of the tale echoes the widespread traditions about skulls kept in houses from which they should never be removed, on pain of supernatural disturbances and/or misfortunes to the household (*see* CALGARTH, Westmorland).

Stanton St Bernard

Ralph Whitlock's book on the folklore of Wiltshire includes a macabre tale which his informants said had happened about a hundred years earlier, i.e. in the 1870s. The wife of a wealthy farmer of this parish died and was buried in the family vault, wearing some of her fine rings. The sexton, who had observed the jewels when the body was being laid out, went back into the vault after dark in order to steal them, and broke the coffin open. One of the rings was so tight-fitting that he could not pull it off, so he took out his pocket-knife and cut the whole finger off. At the shock of this pain, the woman revived and sat up, for she had only been in a deep coma. The sexton ran off, terrified, leaving the door of the vault open. The woman made her way home, her hand bleeding as she went, and rejoined her astonished husband, with whom she lived for many more years.

The story so far is one that occurs in several other places in England and abroad, but there is a further development. The woman's ghost is said to appear every year on the anniversary of the false funeral, walking from the church to the farm and then into the dining room; her finger drips blood all the way. Kathleen Wiltshire was told in 1940 that several maids in the household had seen this ghost; 'one dropped a trayful of china, another gave notice on the spot, and a third ran screaming home.'

Stourton

In 1930, the local writer Edith Olivier described various apparitions to be seen in and around Stourton. On New Year's Eve, on a road near there, one might encounter a headless horseman accompanied by a black dog. He was said to be a man who foolishly betted that by going across country he could ride home from Wincanton Market to Stourton in seven minutes – and broke his neck galloping down the Sloane track.

Also in this village was Brook House, one window of which was at that time kept bricked up, supposedly because the room it belonged to was haunted by a black dog and by an old woman. An old man told Edith Olivier that he had once slept in that room, and saw the woman at the foot of his bed; in the morning he found that all his bedclothes had been pulled off, and even the bolster removed from its case.

Tidworth

In 1681, Joseph Glanvill published his treatise *Saducismus Triumphatus*, 'Saduceism Defeated' – meaning by 'Saduceism' the doctrine of the Sadducees mentioned in the New Testament, who denied that there is an afterlife. In this he defended the reality of the supernatural with well-attested accounts of apparitions, demons, and witchcraft. Among them was the story of the 'Drummer of Tedworth' (as Tidworth was spelled at that time).

Just twenty years earlier, in March 1661, John Mompesson of Tedworth, a magistrate, confiscated the drum of a vagrant called William Drury who had been wandering about for some days, beating his drum and demanding money from the town constable. The drum was later taken to Mr Mompesson's home while he was away in London. Strange noises were heard that night, making Mrs Mompesson think there were burglars in the house. On his return, John Mompesson too heard 'thumping and drumming on top of the house, which continued a good space, and then by degrees went off into the air', and knockings on the external walls of the house. A few weeks later, the trouble shifted indoors, to the children's room:

> It ... vexed the youngest Children, beating their Bedsteads with that violence, that all present expected when they would fall in pieces. In laying Hands on them, one should feel no blows, but might perceive them to shake exceedingly ... After this, they should hear a scratching under the Childrens Bed, as if by something that had Iron Talons. It would lift the Children up in their Beds, and follow them from one Room to another ...
>
> During the time of the knocking, when many were present, a Gentleman of the Company said, Satan, if the Drummer set thee to work, give three knocks and no more, which it did very distinctly and stopt ...
>
> Another night, strangers being present, it purr'd in the Childrens Bed like a Cat, at which time also the cloaths and Children were lift up from the Bed, and six men could not keep them down ... After this it would empty the Chamber-pots into their Beds, and strew them with Ashes, though they were never so carefully watcht. It put a long piked iron into Mr *Mompesson's* Bed, and into his Mothers a naked Knife upright.

Poltergeist phenomena continued for two years. Meanwhile William Drury had been caught thieving, and sent to prison in Gloucester. One day in 1663 he asked a visitor if he had heard about the drumming at a gentleman's house at Tedworth. Yes indeed, said the visitor. 'Aye,' said the drummer, 'I have plagued him, and he shall never be quiet, till he hath made me satisfaction for taking away my drum.' This was reported, and as a result the drummer was tried as a witch at Salisbury:

> The fellow was condemned to Transportation, and accordingly sent away; but I know not how ('tis said by raising Storms and affrighting the Seamen) he made shift to come back again. And 'tis observable, that during the time of his restraint and absence the House was quiet, but as soon as ever he came back at liberty, the disturbance returned. He had been a Souldier under *Cromwell*, and used to talk much of Gallant Books he had from an odd Fellow, who was counted a Wizzard.

The case roused great interest. Glanvill was himself one of those who went down to Tedworth while the trouble was at its height and heard scratching noises in the children's room; since he could see their hands, and since there was no animal in the room, he 'was then verily perswaded, and am still, that the Noise was made by some Daemon or Spirit'. Others were sceptical; it was noticed that when a Commission of Inquiry was sent from London by Charles II to investigate, nothing happened while they were there. John Aubrey recalled that Sir Christopher Wren observed that the knockings only occurred if a certain maidservant was in the next room, and that the partitions were only of thin board.

Despite its first publication in a context of theological debate, the tale has proved widely popular and appears in many books on supernatural lore in Britain.

Wilcot

The manor house here is built on the site of a former monastery, and like others of similar history is said to be haunted by a monk. The story of this monk, however, is unusually tragic; when the monastery was dissolved on the orders of Henry VIII, he hanged himself rather than leave. He now appears in the bedrooms of the manor house, where he is seen by anyone who is visiting the manor for the first time, as he bends over the bed to examine the newcomer.

A curious tale, given by Kathleen Wiltshire in her collection of local folklore from the 1970s, but allegedly going back to 1761, tells of the magical ringing of an invisible bell. 'A debauched person who lived in the parish' came to the vicar very late one night, demanding the keys of the church because he wanted to ring a peal. It is not said whether the man was simply drunk, or whether he had reasonable excuse – he might, for example, wish to ring a passing bell for someone dying or to toll for someone just dead, as was sometimes done even at night. The vicar refused, saying it was far too late, and the noise would disturb Sir George Wroughton and his family, whose house adjoined the churchyard.

Furious, the 'debauched person' went off to Devizes to ask a famous wizard or cunning man called Cantle to help him take revenge on the vicar. 'Does he not like ringing?' said Cantle. 'He shall have enough of it!' From then on, a bell tolled incessantly inside the vicarage, although, oddly, anyone who stuck his head out of a window would no longer hear it. People came from far and near to listen to it; even the king sent a gentleman from London to check the truth of the report. Eventually Cantle, who had been arrested on some other charge, confessed in prison that it was he who was causing the trouble, but did not withdraw the spell; the ringing continued as long as he was alive.

There are strong similarities here to the circumstances surrounding the story of the Drummer of TIDWORTH, leading to a suspicion that the Wilcot legend is less old than is claimed, and is modelled on the more famous Tidworth one.

Worcestershire

Besford

Roy Palmer, who wrote *The Folklore of Hereford and Worcester* (1992), commented on various macabre traditions involving ghosts and hunting hounds. The owners of Church Farm at Besford used to have the task of kennelling foxhounds for the local hunt, on a part of their land known as Dog Kennel Place. A tale current in the nineteenth and twentieth centuries alleged that on one occasion, in the eighteenth century, the kennelman was woken by hearing some disturbance among the hounds, and went out to investigate. He did not return. Next day, people found his boots, with the feet and legs still in them, but nothing more, for the dogs had eaten the rest of him. From then on, ghostly boots, with their spurs jingling, could sometimes be heard tramping across Dog Kennel Place. Palmer notes that the story received fresh impetus from its apparent confirmation in 1930, when a skeleton lacking its lower legs was discovered at Church Farm; however, this skeleton, and others subsequently found there, were probably men killed in the battle of Worcester in the Civil War.

A similar story was told at Broadway, about the ghost of a kennelman, who walks in his nightshirt. He was killed by his own hounds when he went out during the night to quieten them; they did not recognize him, as he was wearing a nightshirt. Killer hounds are also mentioned in the more romantic legend told at CHADDESLEY CORBETT, and in connection with WAXHAM HALL, Norfolk.

Chaddesley Corbett

Harvington Hall, about a mile (1.6 km) north-west of the village, is a late Elizabethan mansion, much remodelled in the seventeenth century; it is notable for its many priest holes and secret passages, one of which had a pulley whereby one could descend from an upper floor to ground level, and then exit from the house by a hidden door near the moat.

According to local tradition, as reported by the folklorist Roy Palmer in 1992, the surrounding district is haunted by a ghostly huntsman and a pack of demonic hounds. The hunter is said to be a medieval nobleman, Sir Peter Corbet, who died in about 1300, and whose home was on the site where the present Hall stands; he had been granted the unusual privilege of a permission to hunt in the royal forests, in order to keep down the number of wolves in the district. The place where he is said to have kept his pack of wolfhounds can still be seen as a stone-lined pit called the Kennels, which was said to be linked to the Hall itself by an underground tunnel passing under the moat – an imaginary extension, presumably, of the real passage described above.

Sir Peter had a daughter, and she was in love with a young man from Wolverley whom she used to meet secretly, for fear of her father's anger, in the tunnel. One night the hounds were baying so persistently that the kennelman sent for Sir Peter, and together they discovered the cause: the girl and her lover were keeping a rendezvous in the tunnel, where Sir Peter overheard them arranging to meet there again next night. He did nothing for the moment, but when the next night came he locked his daughter in her room and let the hounds loose in the tunnel. In due course, fierce baying and agonized screams were heard, and in the morning all that was left of the lover was his hands and his feet; his feet were encased in stout boots, and as for the hands, it was believed that dogs would never eat human hands – an idea based on the Bible story of Jezebel's death (2 Kings 9:10, 35). Sir Peter's daughter, mad with grief, drowned herself in the moat. Sir Peter, suddenly smitten with remorse, hanged every one of his precious hounds and flung their bodies into a nearby pond, now called Gallows Pool. However, this was not enough to expiate his cruelty, and when he died his ghost was doomed to hunt night after night, accompanied by a pack of spectral hounds.

The theme of a spectral Wild Hunt is found in many places (see PETERBOROUGH, Huntingdonshire and Peterborough), but the usual explanation given is that someone had been so sinfully fond of hunting that he is doomed to hunt for ever after death.

Hanley Castle

Though spectral dogs are commonplace in British lore, it is not often that one is interpreted as the actual ghost of a named dog, with a story to explain the haunting. But such is the case at Hanley Castle, according to local contributors to *The Worcestershire Village Book* compiled by members of the Women's Institute in 1988.

During the Civil War, the castle belonged to Thomas Holroyd, a zealous Royalist, and after the battle of Worcester in 1651 it was sacked by the victorious Parliamentary army. The local tradition explains that Holroyd owned a fine but one-eyed bulldog, which he had named Charlie in honour of the king, and that when the Roundheads rampaged through the castle they hanged the bulldog from an oak, simply because of its name. Holroyd was charged with treason against Parliament and forfeited much of his estates, though these were returned to him after the Restoration. But nothing could restore the bulldog, whose ghost has haunted the village ever since.

Leigh

Jabez Allies, writing in 1852, recalled a tradition of his boyhood, which on his evidence seems to have been current in the eighteenth century:

> I well remember, in my juvenile days, hearing old people speak of a spectre that formerly appeared in the parish of Leigh, in this county, which they called 'Old Coles'. They said that he frequently used, at dead of night, to ride as swift as the wind down that part of the public road between Bransford and Brocamin, called Leigh Walk, in a coach drawn by four horses, with fire flying out of their nostrils; and that they invariably dashed right over the great barn at Leigh Court, and then on into the river Teme. It was likewise said that this perturbed spirit was at length *laid* in a neighbouring pool by twelve parsons, by the light of an inch of candle; and, as he was not to rise again until the candle was quite burned out, it was, therefore, thrown in to the pool, and to make all sure the pool was filled up . . .

The ghost that haunts a particular stretch of road and the ghost laid in a pool have many parallels, but this particular haunting has a slight basis in history. The manor of Leigh, which belonged to the abbots of Pershore, at the Dissolution of the Monasteries came into the hands of the king. In the reign of Elizabeth I it was sold to Edmund Colles, a county justice, whose family had been tenants of the estate since the time of the abbots. But they were soon to lose it at the hands of another Edmund Colles, the first Edmund's grandson, who sold it to meet his debts, and who is generally identified as the 'Old Coles' of the story. Remorse for severing a centuries-old family connection may have been deemed the cause of Edmund's restless spirit – but in his day any unpopular landowner might be remembered as a ghost of the worst description.

A crime is sometimes laid at Edmund's door as a cause of the haunting, but Allies says nothing of this, so it may be a later addition. In this version, it is said that the sale of his house and land was not enough to clear his debts, so he turned to robbery. One dark night, knowing that a friend of his would be riding home from Worcester to Cradley with a large sum of money, he ambushed him on the road, clutching at the horse's bridle to drag it to a halt. But the man slashed with his sword at the masked robber's arm, and broke free. Reaching home, he was horrified to find a severed hand still entangled in the bridle, and even more horrified to recognize on its little finger the signet ring of his friend Colles.

Next day he went to Leigh Court, where Colles, whose hand was indeed severed at the wrist, confessed his crime and begged to be forgiven. The friend willingly forgave him, and Colles died soon after from loss of blood.

Quite apart from its place in local tradition, this story is of interest to folklorists because the severed hand caught in the bridle foreshadows the plot of two modern urban legends well known in Britain and America. In one, some louts try to hijack a car while it is waiting at traffic lights, and one has his fingers torn off when it accelerates away; the driver later finds them caught in the radiator grille or some other part of the car. In the second tale, a one-handed maniac with a hook is about to open the door of a car where two courting teenagers are sitting when they unexpectedly drive off; when they get home, they find his hook dangling from the door handle.

The unfortunate Edmund may be seen in Leigh parish church – one of the twelve children surrounding his father William's tomb. The tithe barn over which Old Coles used to drive his coach and horses is still standing at Leigh Court Farm. At about 141 feet (43 m) long and 35 feet (10.7 m) wide, it is the world's largest timber cruck-barn, built around 1300 as a storage barn for Pershore abbey. As both a Grade I listed building and a scheduled ancient monument, it is maintained and managed by English Heritage.

Upton-on-Severn

Here there is a ghost legend about a Captain Thomas Bound, a supporter of Cromwell, who died in 1667 and was remembered as a wicked man, very cruel and covetous, and hard on the poor. Traditions about him were collected by the local historian Emily Lawson in the 1860s. He lived first at Soley's Orchard and was married three times, his first two wives dying within a year of marriage – not in childbirth, but, according to local rumour, because he had murdered them. He was also alleged to have shifted the boundary stones defining a riverside meadow called the Ham, so as to enlarge it to his own advantage, thus incurring the biblical condemnation 'Cursed be he that removeth his neighbour's land-mark' (Deuteronomy 27:17). The final crime attributed to him was to have obtained a second house, Southend Farm, by guiding the hand of a dying woman who was trying to write her will, in such a way that his name appeared instead of the one she thought she was writing. In revenge for this trick, her ghost is said to have driven him to despair, so that he drowned himself in a pool near the house he had inherited from her.

Suicide was considered the ultimate, unforgivable sin in traditional Christian theology, and is frequently regarded in folk-lore as a reason why a dead person's spirit cannot rest. On the day Bound died, a phantom funeral procession was seen – a fairly common phenomenon in folk belief, but in this case regarded as sinister. Then his ghost was seen roaming round both his houses and also several lanes nearby, so a parson was asked to lay him. This he attempted to do by throwing a lighted candle into the pool where Bound had drowned himself, and ordering him not to return until it had burnt out – which, in the circumstances, was hardly likely to happen. But the ghost coolly disregarded the exorcism and behaved more boldly than ever, appearing on horseback in broad daylight. Three more parsons were sent for, and they gathered in the cellar at Soley's Orchard, held hands inside a circle drawn on the floor, and tried to banish the ghost to the Red Sea. However, one of them accidentally stepped with one foot outside the circle, which broke the power of their invocations; as he did so, something whizzed through the air and struck him on the cheek, and his whiskers could never grow on that spot again. The three parsons retreated, leaving orders that the cellar be bricked up.

There were no more attempts to exorcize Bound, who would often be seen on the banks of the Severn, or sitting on a stone near the fatal pool, or riding up the lane leading to Southend Farm dragging a long chain, of the sort used by surveyors to measure land – the fitting penalty, no doubt, for his dishonest shifting of boundary stones. Some said the ghosts of his three wives were also sometimes seen.

A final macabre twist to the saga, which appears to be historically true, is that during alterations to Upton church in the middle of the nineteenth century Bound's grave in the chancel was opened, and his skull taken as a souvenir. It was set in metal as a drinking cup; the folklorist Roy Palmer reports that its present whereabouts is unknown. The houses and lanes associated with Bound are now demolished or much altered.

Yorkshire

Beverley

Beverley, like most ancient cities, has its ghosts. One of the best-known apparitions was 'Sir Josceline Percy's Team'. William Henderson wrote in 1879:

> The headless ghost of Sir Josceline Percy drives four headless horses nightly above its streets, pausing over a certain house ... tenanted a few years back by a Mr Gilbey. This house was said to contain a chest with 100 nails in it, one of which dropped out every year. Tradition avers that this nocturnal disturbance is connected with Sir Josceline once riding on horseback into Beverley Minster.

Why he did so is unexplained. Possibly it was to visit his ancestral tombs in Beverley Minster. Sir Josceline was evidently condemned to ride through the air in his phantom coach until all hundred nails were out of the chest, as a punishment for sacrilege.

One Beverley ghost was unusual in serving law and order. According to *A Glossary of Words used in Holderness* (1877):

> A phantom, popularly supposed to be the ghost of a prisoner who had committed suicide, and called 'Awd *simmon* beeather,' was said to haunt the gaol and appear to the prisoners, which acted usefully as a deterrent to criminals, who dreaded him much more than the confinement and punishment.

The glossary explains the *simmon* in Old Simmon Beater's name as the pounded brick or tiles used by bricklayers to colour mortar. The back-breaking work of beating simmon was given to men in Beverley Borough Gaol who had been condemned to hard labour.

Bulmer

In the third volume of his *History ... of Durham* (1823), Robert Surtees tells 'an old story' also recorded by others concerning the history of the manor of Bulmer.

This was given by Sir Antony Bec or Bek, bishop and count palatine, who held the see of Durham from 1283 to 1310, to an infamous outlaw, Hugh de Pontchardon. On account of his many wicked deeds, 'Black Hugh' had been driven out of the king's court and had come to the North to live by stealing. Bishop Bec, who had made use of him in war on Scotland, granted him the lands of Thickley, south-east of Bishop's Auckland, thereafter called Thickley Punchardon, and made him his chief huntsman.

Black Hugh died before Bishop Bec, and some time after his death, when the bishop was hunting deer in the Forest of Galtres, in Bulmere Wapentake, North Yorkshire, suddenly Pontchardon galloped past him seated on a white horse. 'Hugh, what maketh thee here?' asked the bishop. Black Hugh answered never a word but lifted up his cloak and showed his ribs *'set with bones'*. None of the hunters saw him except the bishop, and he called up his dogs and rode away. This Hugh was known to the 'silly people' of Galtres as *le gros veneur* ('the big huntsman'). He was seen twice after that by ordinary people before the trees were felled.

For other spectral huntsmen, *see* PETERBOROUGH, Huntingdonshire and Peterborough.

Burton Agnes Hall

According to tradition, the Jacobean mansion of Burton Agnes Hall in the East Riding was built by the three Griffiths sisters in the reign of Queen Elizabeth I (1558–1603). At the time, the family were living in the old Norman manor house near the church. All three were impatient to see the new house completed, but none more so than the youngest, Miss Anne. However, this was not to be. According to the Bradford periodical *Yorkshire Chat*, cited by Eliza Gutch in her *East Riding of Yorkshire* (1912):

One day, when wandering alone in the park, Miss Ann [*sic*] was murderously attacked and robbed by an outlaw, who seriously wounded her. This brought on a fever of which she died. Before her death she grieved incessantly that she would never see the grand structure complete, and made her sisters promise to remove her head to the new grand Hall, where it was to be placed on a table. This they agreed to do, but after her death they buried her without fulfilling the compact. Nothing happened until they took up their abode at Burton Agnes. Then strange moanings and weird sounds made the sisters' lives a burden to them. No servants would stay; so at last after two years they caused the body to be dug up and decapitated, and placed the now fleshless head upon the table.

For many years, the skull remained there and there were no more disturbances. Some time later, however, a maid tried to discredit the story by throwing the skull on to a wagon standing outside the Hall. The horses immediately reared up, and the whole house shook, so that the pictures fell off the walls. Things only quietened down when the skull was put back on the table. Other attempts to get rid of the skull ended the same way.

It is said that belief in the skull was 'a second religion' with the Boynton family (who succeeded to Burton Agnes by marriage in 1654). They appear to have regarded it as a kind of 'luck', believing that, as long as it was left undisturbed, nothing serious would happen to any of the Boyntons, but woe betide the family if it were moved. To prevent accidents, they had a niche in the wall constructed especially for it and bricked it up inside. There it has remained: it is said to be now hidden behind panelling in one of the bedrooms, and though family and staff know where it is they do not tell.

Despite the fact that her wishes have been complied with, the ghost of Anne Griffiths, 'Owd Nance', as she was known in the village in the nineteenth century, reputedly haunted the Hall. Indeed, it is still said at Burton Agnes today that the Queen's State Bedroom is haunted by 'the blue lady', thought to be Anne, seen by some, though others only sense her presence.

The Hall was in fact built for Sir Henry Griffith (d. 1620), said to be the father of the three sisters. One clue to the origin of the story is a group portrait of three ladies that hangs in the Inner Hall. Painted by Marc Gheeraerts in 1620, it is labelled 'Frances, Margaret and Catherine Griffith' (though only Frances and Margaret are named on Sir Henry's memorial tablet in the church). Anne, nowhere mentioned in contemporary records of his family, is traditionally identified as the one on the right, distinguished from her sisters by wearing black. As with the portrait of Lady Hoby, also clad in black, at BISHAM ABBEY, Berkshire, her striking funereal garb may have inspired the story.

See also CALGARTH, Westmorland.

Calverley

William Henderson, in his *Notes on the Folk-Lore of the Northern Counties* (1866), writes:

> The village of Calverley, near Bradford ... has been haunted since the time of Queen Elizabeth by the apparition of Master Walter Calverley, now popularly called Sir Walter. It is averred that this man murdered his wife and children, and, refusing to plead, was subjected to the *'peine forte et dure.'* In his last agony he is said to have exclaimed, 'Them that love Sir Walter, loup on, loup on!' which accordingly became the watchword of the apparition, which frequented a lane near the village of Calverley. There is no fear, however, of meeting it at present; the ghost has been laid, and cannot reappear as long as green holly grows on the manor.

But he adds that his friend, the Revd J. Barmby, had told him that his grandfather, as a child, riding behind his father on horseback, saw the apparition, and was terrified by it. His father, to allay his boy's fears, said, 'It's only Sir Walter.'

This Walter Calverley is the hero of *The Yorkshire Tragedy*, a play once attributed to Shakespeare, and the tradition was used by Harrison Ainsworth in his novel *Rookwood* (1834). The *peine forte et dure* ('strong and harsh punishment') was pressing to death.

T. F. Thiselton Dyer, in *Strange Pages from Family Papers* (1895), says that in a particular room at Calverley Hall there were indelible bloodstains, and also a particular flagstone in the cellar that was never dry. In March 1874, the writer of an article entitled

'Calverley, Forty Years Ago' in a Bradford paper related how he had once tried to raise the ghost of the old squire. About a dozen boys used to assemble after school near Calverley church, and place their hats and caps on the ground in the shape of a pyramid. Then they took each other's hands and, making a circle, recited:

> 'Old Calverley, old Calverley, I have thee by the ears,
> I'll cut thee into collops, unless thou appears.'

While this was going on, they strewed breadcrumbs saved from dinner and mixed them with pins on the ground. Some of the more adventurous had to go to the church doors, whistle through the keyholes, and repeat the rhyme. The ghost was expected to appear at this point, and once did – whereupon they scampered off, leaving their caps behind.

Flamborough

A circular pit near Flamborough was said in the nineteenth century to be where a girl named Jenny Gallows committed suicide. It was a common belief along the coast that anyone running nine times round it could hear the fairies. Another was that, when the eighth circuit was complete, the spirit of Jenny dressed in white would rise from the pit and cry out:

> Ah'll tee [tie] on me bonnet
> An' put on me shoe,
> An' if thoo's nut off
> Ah'll seean [soon] catch thoo.

John Nicholson, recording this story in 1890, says that, some years previously, a farmer had ridden round the pit and to his terror Jenny rose and chased him. Just as he entered the village, she gave up the pursuit but bit a piece out of his horse's flank, and the old mare had a white patch there to her dying day.

Sexhow

The ghost who cannot rest until his or her hidden treasure has been found is a theme of a number of international folktales. Not always, however, do things turn out so badly as, according to a story from the nineteenth century, they did at Sexhow, near Stokesley.

An old woman there appeared after her death to a farmer and told him that, under a certain tree in his apple orchard, he would find a hoard of both gold and silver, which she had buried there. He was to dig it up, keeping the silver for his pains but giving the gold to her niece, who was living in poverty. At daybreak, the farmer went to the spot she had indicated, and found the treasure, but kept it all for himself. From that day on, however, he knew no peace. Though a sober man before, he took to drink, but still his conscience troubled him, and every night, at home or away, 'old Nannie's' ghost dogged his steps, reproaching him with his faithlessness.

> At last, one Saturday evening, the neighbours heard him return-
> ing from Stokesley Market very late; his horse was galloping
> furiously, and as he left the high road to go into the lane which led
> to his own house, he never stopped to open the gate at the
> entrance of the lane, but cleared it with a bound. As he passed a
> neighbour's house, its inmates heard him screaming out, 'I will – I
> will – I will!' and looking out, they saw a little old woman in
> black, with a large straw hat on her head, whom they recognized
> as old Nannie, seated behind the terrified man on the runaway
> nag, and clinging to him closely. The farmer's hat was off, his hair
> stood on end, as he fled past them, uttering his fearful cry, 'I will –
> I will – I will!' But when the horse reached the farm all was still,
> for the rider was a corpse!

Although other nineteenth-century writers agree that the place where this happened was Sexhow, William Henderson, who recorded this story in 1866, calls it 'Lexhoe', possibly to disguise its identity.

On the surface, the tale warns against avarice, one of the seven deadly sins. The underlying message, however, is that, where treasure is concerned, do exactly what a ghost tells you: it is all that will give the troubled and troublesome spirit rest.

Thirsk

W. Hylton Dyer Longstaffe, in his *History ... of Darlington* (1854), says that his former residence at Thirsk had a White Lady attached to a nearby stream. This stream indeed took its name from the haunt and was known as the White-lass-beck.

Longstaffe says that, like the spirit haunting GLASSENSIKES, Co. Durham, the 'White-lass' was a shape-shifter:

> ... turning into a white dog, and an ugly animal which comes rattling into the town with a tremendous clitter-my-clatter, and is there styled a barguest. Occasionally, too, she turns into a genuine lady of flesh and blood, tumbling over a stile.

Longstaffe also gives the local explanation of the haunt, saying, 'The Thirsk maid was murdered; and, some years ago, when a skeleton was dug up in a gravel pit near the beck, it was at once said to be that of the poor girl.'

Although in later folklore very often accounted for by traditions of murders and suicides as ordinary revenants or ghosts, neither shape-shifting bogey beasts (*see* BRIGG, Lincolnshire) nor White Ladies needed explanation: they appear earlier to have been independent spirits.

The 'White-lass' was not the only apparition haunting the neighbourhood of Thirsk. The Revd Sabine Baring-Gould, in his *Yorkshire Oddities* (1874), retails an eyewitness account of an apparition seen by an old farmer nicknamed 'John Mealyface', who died at the age of eighty-four in 1868. John told him that he was riding to Thirsk one night, when he suddenly saw a 'radiant boy' passing him on a white horse. As he drew near, his horse's hooves made no sound, and John first became aware of his approach by seeing the shadow of boy and horse cast on the road ahead of him.

Thinking that a carriage with lamps might be approaching, he only became alarmed when, the shadow growing shorter, he realized the light must be close and yet he could hear no sound. At that, he turned in his saddle, just as the boy went by. 'He was a child of about eleven, with a fresh, bright face.' The boy continued on his way until he came to a gate leading into a field, when he stooped as if to open it, rode through, and instantly all was dark.

Baring-Gould asked if the boy was wearing clothes and, if so, what they were like, but John Mealyface had not noticed the particulars. This in itself makes his story sound like an account of a genuine experience (on seeing apparitions, people are normally too taken aback to notice details). As for the name 'radiant boy', it is not clear if this was what John Mealyface himself called the apparition, or if Baring-Gould applied a term borrowed from other places.

The most celebrated Radiant Boy was one seen by Lord Castlereagh before his suicide (*see* KNEBWORTH HOUSE, Hertfordshire). After Castlereagh's death and the subsequent circulation of his story by Sir Walter Scott, Radiant Boys are recorded elsewhere under that name – Chillington Castle, Northumberland, had one 'till lately' according to *Murray's Handbook* (1873), and so did CORBY CASTLE, Cumberland. However, they seem to have been a traditional form of apparition: Baring-Gould also mentions a boy with a shining face being seen in houses in Lincolnshire and elsewhere.

Whirlow

In his *Household Tales* (1895), S. O. Addy writes:

> The ghost of one of the Brights of Whirlow Hall, near Sheffield, was said to appear in a lane near the house in the shape of a black bird with a white tail or wing. Sometimes it was felt, but not seen, as in the case of a man from Dore, who, returning home late one evening on the back of his ass, was lifted from his seat in the deepest part of the lane, and fixed upright in the middle of the lane, the ass going on as if nothing had happened. He was paralysed with fear and unable to move until the spirit allowed him to proceed.

The old belief in metempsychosis, or the transmigration of human souls, was still current in parts of England in the nineteenth century, and perhaps later. Other soul-birds included the raven or red-legged chough, said at MARAZION, Cornwall, to embody the soul of King Arthur, and another soul-bird in the North was the dove that held the soul of 'Parcy Reed', at TROUGHEND, Northumberland.

Bibliography

Abbreviations

HALS   Hertfordshire Archives and Local Studies
VCH   *The Victoria County History*

For each book, the author's name, title, etc. are given in full the first time it is mentioned in a particular chapter, but abridged for the rest of the chapter. If it is mentioned again in a different chapter, full details will be given again at the first reference in that chapter. We have not included page references, which can be found in full in the bibliography for *The Lore of the Land* (Westwood & Simpson, Penguin 2005).

Bedfordshire

Apsley Guise Peter Underwood, *The A–Z of British Ghosts* (London, 1971; new edn, 1992; repr. 1993). **Battlesden** [Reader's Digest,] *Folklore, Myths and Legends of Britain*, 2nd edn (London, 1977). **Chicksands Priory** Andrew Green, *Our Haunted Kingdom* (London, 1975); F. W. Kuhlicke, 'Medieval Spooks in Bedfordshire', *Bedfordshire Magazine* 15:119 (Winter 1976); Laurence Meynell, *Bedfordshire* (London, 1950); Betty Puttick, *Ghosts of Bedfordshire* (Newbury, Berkshire, 1996; repr. 2003); Roger W. Ward, *Legend and Lore including Extracts from History and Annals of Chicksands Priory* (pr. pub., 1983). **Kensworth** Richard Baxter, *The Certainty of the Worlds of Spirits* ... (London, 1691); [Daniel Defoe,] *Essay on the History and Reality of Apparitions. Being an account of what they are, and what they are not* ... (London, 1727); Peter Haining, *A Dictionary of Ghosts* (London, 1982; 2nd edn, Waltham Abbey, 1993); Doris Jones-Baker, *The Folklore of Hertfordshire* (London, 1977). **Knocking Knoll** James Dyer, 'Barrows of the Chilterns', *Archaeological Journal* 116 (1959, pub. 1961); W. B. Gerish, in Gerish Collection, HALS (Gerish Box – Pirton, part of D/Gr61); Ellen Pollard, 'Some Points of Interest in and around Hitchin', *Hertfordshire Illustrated Review* 2 (1894). **Millbrook** Matthew Edgeworth, 'The beautiful lady and a headless spectre', *Ampthill and Flitwick Times* (19 July 1984), cutting from Local Studies Library, Bedford Central Library; Menzies Jack, 'Man, Myth and Millbrook', *Bedfordshire Times* (5 February 1971), cutting from Local Studies Library, Bedford Central Library; Puttick, *Ghosts of Bedfordshire*. **Odell** Janet Bord, *Footprints in Stone* (Wymeswold, Loughborough, 2004); [John Leland,] *The Itinerary of John Leland in England and Wales in or about the Years 1535–1543*, ed. Lucy Toulmin Smith, 5 vols. (London, 1906–10; pa. edn, 1964), vol. 5; Puttick, *Ghosts of Bedfordshire*; [Reader's Digest,] *Folklore, Myths and Legends of Britain*. **Wilden** Christina Hole, *Haunted England* (London, 1940; new edn, Bath, 1964, re-iss. 1972), calling the village 'Willesden'. **Woburn Abbey** Janet and Colin Bord, *Atlas of Magical Britain* (London, 1990); Antony D. Hippisley Coxe, *Haunted Britain* (London, 1973; pa. edn, 1975); Puttick, *Ghosts of Bedfordshire*.

Berkshire

Bisham Abbey *Bisham Abbey, Berkshire* (National Sports Council Booklet, n.d.); Charles Harper, *Haunted Houses* (London, 1907; 3rd edn, 1927; pa. repr. 1996); Jerome K. Jerome, *Three Men in a Boat*, ch. 13 (London, 1889; repr. Bristol, 1946); Anne Mitchell, *Ghosts along the Thames* (Bourne End, 1972); *Murray's Handbook for Travellers in Berkshire*, ed. J. M. Falkner (London, 1902); *The Story of All Saints Parish Church Bisham*, comp. H. A. Jones, rev. H. Douglas Sim (1967), rev. and suppl. Patricia Burstall (1990). **Bucklebury** Cecilia Millson, *Tales of Old Berkshire* (Thatcham, 1977). **Caversham** [Hon. John Byng,] *The Torrington Diaries*, ed. C. Bruyn Andrews, 4 vols. (London, 1934–8), vol. 1. **Cumnor Place** Alfred Bartlett, *Historical and Descriptive Account of Cumnor Place* (Oxford and London, 1850); Sir Bartle Frere, *Amy Robsart of Wymondham* (Norwich, 1937); John H. Ingram, *The Haunted Homes and Family Traditions of Great Britain*, 4th edn (London, 1888); Elizabeth Jenkins, *Elizabeth the Great* (London, 1958; club edn, 1971); *VCH: Berkshire*, vol. 4, ed. William Page and P. H. Ditchfield, (London, 1924). **Hampstead Marshall** Information to J.W. from Rachael Arthur, daughter of Robert Graham, August 2003. **Inkpen** Leslie V. Grinsell, *Folklore of Prehistoric Sites in Britain* (Newton Abbot, 1976); Jeremy Harte, 'Stormy Weather', *3d Stone* 47 (2003). **South Moreton** Berkshire Local History Recording Scheme (1924), cited in David Nash Ford, *Royal Berkshire History*, website *www.berkshirehistory.com/legends*, 2003. **Windsor Castle** Hector Bolitho, *The Romance of Windsor Castle* (London, c.1943). **Windsor Great Park** Jeremy Harte, 'Herne the Hunter: A Case of Mistaken Identity?', *At The Edge* 3 (1996); Michael Petry, *Herne the Hunter* (London, 1972).

Buckinghamshire

Calverton [Reader's Digest,] *Folklore, Myths and Legends of Britain*, 2nd edn (London, 1977); *VCH: Buckinghamshire*, vol. 4, ed. William Page (London, 1927). **Creslow Manor** Robert Chambers, *The Book of Days*, 2 vols. (London and Edinburgh, n.d. [1863–4]), vol. 1, 'Creslow Pastures. A Ghost Story'; John H. Ingram, *The Haunted Homes and Family Traditions of Great Britain*, 4th edn (London, 1888); Revd W. Hastings Kelke, 'Creslow Pastures', *Records of Buckinghamshire*, vol. 1 (Aylesbury, 1858); *Murray's Handbook for Travellers in Berks, Bucks and Oxfordshire* (London, 1860). **Eton** George Sinclair, *Satan's Invisible World Discovered ...* (Edinburgh, 1789), Relation 8. **Gibraltar** H[orace] Harman, *Sketches of the Bucks Countryside* (London, 1934); Revd Frederick George Lee, *Glimpses in the Twilight ...* (Edinburgh and London, 1885); [Reader's Digest,] *Folklore, Myths and Legends of Britain*. **Middle Claydon** Maurice Ashley, *The English Civil War* (London, 1974; pa. edn, 1980); Antony D. Hippisley Coxe, *Haunted Britain* (London, 1973; pa. edn, 1975); *A Great Wonder in Heaven: shewing The late Apparitions and prodigious noyses of War and Battels, seen on Edge-Hill ...* (London, 1642); *Murray's Handbook for ... Berks, Bucks and Oxfordshire*; Lord Nugent, *Some Memorials of John Hamden*, 2 vols. (London, 1832), vol. 2; Frances Parthenope Verney, *Memoirs of the Verney Family ...*, 4 vols. (London, 1892), vol. 2; Peter Verney, *The Standard Bearer: The Story of Sir Edmund Verney ...* (London, [1963]); C. V. Wedgwood, *The King's War 1641–1647*

(London, 1958; pa. edn, 1966; 6th imp., 1973). **West Drayton** Lee, *Glimpses in the Twilight* ... **Woughton-on-the-Green** Harman, *Sketches of the Bucks Countryside*; Christina Hole, *Haunted England* (London, 1940; new edn, Bath, 1964; re-iss. 1972).

Cambridgeshire

Abington Enid Porter, *Cambridgeshire Customs and Folklore* (London, 1969). **Cambridge, Abbey House** Porter, *Cambridgeshire Customs and Folklore*. **Cambridge, Corpus Christi College** 'A College Ghost', in *Occult Review* 1:3 (March 1905), ed. Ralph Shirley. **Litlington** G. L. Gomme, *Folklore as an Historical Science* (London, 1908); *VCH: Cambridgeshire*, vol. 7, *Roman Cambridgeshire*, ed. J. J. Wilkes and C. R. Elrington (Oxford, 1978). **Little Abington** William Cole MSS, 'Diary' and 'Parochial Antiquities', MSS, BL; W. M. Palmer, *William Cole of Milton* (Cambridge, 1935); Porter, *Cambridgeshire Customs and Folklore*. **Littleport to Brandon Creek Road** Porter, *Cambridgeshire Customs and Folklore*. **Southery** W. H. Barrett, *Tales from the Fens*, ed. Enid Porter (London, 1963). **Wandlebury Camp** William Camden, *Britannia*, trans. Philemon Holland (London, 1610); Gervase of Tilbury, *Otia Imperialia*, ed. Felix Liebrecht (Hannover, 1856), ch. LIX 'De Wandlebiria'; C. C. Oman, 'The English Folklore of Gervase of Tilbury', *Folk-Lore* 55 (March, 1944). **Whittlesford** 'Urbs Camboritum' [W. R. Brown], *Cambridgeshire Cameos* (Cambridge, *c.*1895), Cameo No. 7; Porter, *Cambridgeshire Customs and Folklore*.

Cheshire

Brereton Green William Camden, *Britannia*, trans. Philemon Holland (London, 1610); Christina Hole, *Haunted England* (London, 1940; repr. 1990). **Burleydam** D. Haworth and W. M. Comber, *Cheshire Village Memories*, 2 vols. (Chester, 1952, 1961), vol. 1. **Congleton** Fred Gettings, *The Secret Lore of the Cat*, pa. edn (London, 1990). **Coombs Moss** Fletcher Moss, *Folk-Lore: Old Customs and Tales of my Neighbours* (Didsbury, 1898). **Duddon** Haworth and Comber, *Cheshire Village Memories*, vol. 2; Jacob Larwood and J. C. Hotten, *English Inn Signs* (a revised and modernized version of *The History of Signboards*, 1866; London, 1951); Frederick Woods, *Legends and Traditions of Cheshire* (Nantwich, 1982). **Gawsworth** Haworth and Comber, *Cheshire Village Memories*, vol. 1. **Lyme Park** Egerton Leigh, *Ballads and Legends of Cheshire* (London, 1867). **Marbury Hall** Haworth and Comber, *Cheshire Village Memories*, vol. 2; Woods, *Legends and Traditions of Cheshire*. **Neston** Christina Hole, *Traditions and Customs of Cheshire* (London, 1937). **Stanney** Haworth and Comber, *Cheshire Village Memories*, vol. 2. **Stockport** Charlotte Burne and Georgina Jackson, *Shropshire Folk-Lore: A Sheaf of Gleanings* (London, 1883); Robert Holland, *Glossary of Words used in the County of Cheshire* (London, 1886); Fletcher Moss, *History of the Old Parish of Cheadle, in Cheshire* (Manchester and Didsbury, pr. pub. 1894) and *Folklore: Old Customs and Tales of My Neighbours* (Didsbury and Manchester, pr. pub. 1898); Jacqueline Simpson, *The Folklore of the Welsh Border* (London, 1976).

Cornwall

Bodmin Moor Robert Hunt, *Popular Romances of the West of England* (London, 1865), ser. 2; [Matthew Paris,] *Matthæi Parisiensis Chronica Majora*, ed. Henry Richards Luard, vol. 2 (London, 1874); John Timbs and Alexander Gunn, *Abbeys, Castles and Ancient Halls of England and Wales: South* (London and New York, n.d.). **The Irish Lady** J. T. Blight, *A Week at the Land's End* (London, 1861); Hunt, *Popular Romances of the West of England*, ser. 1. **Marazion** Julian del Castillo, *Historia de los Reyes Godos ...* (Burgos, 1582), libro 4, discurso 18; J. O. Halliwell-Phillipps, *Rambles in Western Cornwall By the Footsteps of the Giants* (London, 1861); Hunt, *Popular Romances of the West of England*, ser. 2; Roger Sherman Loomis, 'The Legend of Arthur's Survival', *Arthurian Literature in the Middle Ages*, ed. Roger Sherman Loomis (Oxford, 1959); Edgar MacCulloch, 'Cornish Folk Lore: King Arthur in the Form of a Raven', *Notes and Queries* vol. 8 (24 December 1853). **Pengersick Castle** William Bottrell, *Traditions and Hearthside Stories of West Cornwall* (Penzance, 1870); ser. 2; Hunt, *Popular Romances of the West of England*, ser. 2; *Pengersick Castle* (leaflet, n.d.). **Penzance** William Bottrell, *Stories and Folk-Lore of West Cornwall*, ser. 3 (Penzance, 1880); M. A. Courtney, *Cornish Feasts and Folk-Lore* (Penzance, 1890). **Porthcurno** Bottrell, *Traditions and Hearthside Stories of West Cornwall*, ser. 2. **St Agnes** Hunt, *Popular Romances of the West of England*, ser. 2. **St Levan** Bottrell, *Traditions and Hearthside Stories of West Cornwall*, ser. 2; Stanfords Charts 13, *Start Point to Trevose Head* (Maldon, rev. edn, 1997). **Talland** Bottrell, *Stories and Folk-Lore of West Cornwall*, ser. 3; Tony Deane and Tony Shaw, *The Folklore of Cornwall* (London, 1975); Hunt, *Popular Romances of the West of England*, ser. 1. **Tregagle's Hole** Bottrell, *Traditions and Hearthside Stories of West Cornwall*, ser. 2; [Richard Carew,] *Carew's Survey of Cornwall*, ann. Thomas Tonkin, ed. Francis, Lord de Dunstanville (London, 1811); Hunt, *Popular Romances of the West of England*, ser. 1; *The National Trust: Coast of Cornwall*, leaflet no. 12, 'Loe Pool and Gunwalloe' (1987); H. M. Cresswell Payne, *The Story of the Parish of Roche* (Newquay, n.d. [1948]); M. and L. Quiller-Couch, *Ancient and Holy Wells of Cornwall* (London, 1894); B. C. Spooner, *John Tregagle: Alive or Dead* (St Peter Port, Guernsey, 1979). **Trencrom Castle** Bottrell, *Traditions and Hearthside Stories of West Cornwall*; James Dyer, *The Penguin Guide to Prehistoric England and Wales* (London, 1981); Hunt, *Popular Romances of the West of England*, ser. 1.

Cumberland

Aira Force Wilson Armistead, *Tales and Legends of the English Lakes* (London and Glasgow, 1891); Brian J. Bailey, *Lakeland Walks and Legends* (London, 1981); *Black's Picturesque Guide to the English Lakes*, 5th edn (Edinburgh, 1851); Jessica Lofthouse, *North-Country Folklore in Lancashire, Cumbria and the Pennine Dales* (London, 1976); Harriet Martineau, *A Complete Guide to the English Lakes* (Windermere and London, 1855); *Murray's Handbook for Travellers in Westmoreland and Cumberland* (London, 1866); Thomas De Quincey, *Recollections of the Lake Poets (Lake Reminiscences)*, in *The Works of Thomas de Quincey*, Riverside Edition (1876–7), vol. 3, *Literary Reminiscences* (Cambridge, Mass., and New York, 1876); Mackenzie E. C. Walcott,

A Guide to the Mountains, Lakes and North-West Coast of England (London, 1860); Peter N. Walker, *Folk Stories from the Lake District* (London, 1993); William Wordsworth, 'The Somnambulist', in *The Poetical Works of William Wordsworth*, ed. E. de Selincourt (vols. 3–5 ed. E. de Selincourt and Helen Darbishire), 5 vols. (Oxford, 1940–9), vol. 4. **Carlisle** Augustus Hare, *The Story of My Life*, 6 vols. (London, 1896–1900), vol. 4. **Corby Castle, near Carlisle** Catherine Crowe, *Ghosts and Family Legends* (London, 1859); and *The Night-Side of Nature*, 2 vols. (London, 1848; pa. edn in 1 vol., Wellingborough, 1986); T. F. Thiselton Dyer, *Strange Pages from Family Papers* (London, 1895; new issue, 1900). **Gilsland** William Henderson, *Notes on the Folk-Lore of the Northern Counties of England and the Borders* (London, 1866). **Helvellyn** *Murray's Handbook for ... Westmoreland and Cumberland*. **Lake Thirlmere** A.G. Bradley, *Highways and Byways in the Lake District* (London, 1901); A. Hall, *Lakeland Ghosts* (St Ives, Cornwall, 1977); Martineau, *A Complete Guide to the English Lakes*; Walcott, *A Guide to the Mountains, Lakes and North-West Coast of England*. **Solway Firth** Gerald Findler, *Legends of the Lake Counties* (Clapham via Lancaster, 1967, repr. 1976); Elliott O'Donnell, *Dangerous Ghosts* (London, 1954); and *The Midnight Hearse and More Ghosts* (London, 1965). **Souther Fell** *Gentleman's Magazine* 17 (London, 1747); William Hutchinson, *The History and Antiquities of the County of Cumberland*, 2 vols (Carlisle, 1785–94), vol. 1; *The Lonsdale Magazine or Provincial Repository for the year 1821*, ed. Briggs, vol. 2, no. 20 (August 1820); Martineau, *A Complete Guide to the English Lakes*. **Ulpha** *Black's Picturesque Guide to the English Lakes*; *Murray's Handbook for ... Westmoreland and Cumberland*; Walcott, *A Guide to the Mountains, Lakes and North-West Coast of England*; Frank Welsh, *The Companion Guide to the Lake District* (Woodbridge, 1989; rev. edn, 1997). **Walla Crag** *Black's Picturesque Guide to the English Lakes*; Walcott, *A Guide to the Mountains, Lakes and North-West Coast of England*. **Whitehaven** Henderson, *Notes on the Folk-Lore of the Northern Counties ...* (London, 1866); *The Unseen World; Communications with it, real or imaginary, including apparitions, warnings, haunted places, prophecies, aerial visions, astrology, &c. &c.* (London, 1847).

Derbyshire

Arbor Low James Dyer, *The Penguin Guide to Prehistoric England and Wales* (London, 1981); *The Place-Names of Derbyshire*, ed. Kenneth Cameron, 3pts (cont. pag.) (Cambridge, 1959); D. Thompson, *Arbor Low, and Three Other Prehistoric Sites in Derbyshire* (London: HMSO, 1963); W. M. Turner ['John Guyt'], *Romances of the Peak* (London, 1901). **Bolsover Castle** Louis J. Jennings, *Rambles Among the Hills in the Peaks of Derbyshire and the South Downs* (London, 1880); Nikolaus Pevsner, *The Buildings of England: Derbyshire* (London, 1953); Ebenezer Rhodes, *Peak Scenery; Or, The Derbyshire Tourist* (London, 1824). **Bradwell** Seth Evans, *Bradwell: Ancient and Modern* ([n.p.], 1912). **Derwent Woodlands** David Clarke and Andy Roberts, *Twilight of the Celtic Gods* (London, 1996); *Gentleman's Magazine* 54 (1874). **Dunscar Farm** S. O. Addy, *Household Tales With Other Traditional Remains Collected in the Counties of York, Lincoln, Derby, and Nottingham* (London and Sheffield, 1895); Clarence Daniel, *Ghosts of Derbyshire* (Clapham via Lancaster, 1973; 2nd edn, 1974, repr. 1983). **Eckington** Addy, *Household Tales ...* **Great Longstone** Daniel, *Ghosts of*

Derbyshire. **Hayfield** Addy, *Household Tales* . . .; Paul Barber, *Vampires, Burial, and Death: Folklore and Reality* (Newhaven and London, 1988). **Heage Hall** Daniel, *Ghosts of Derbyshire*. **Highlow Hall** Addy, *Household Tales* . . .; Daniel, *Ghosts of Derbyshire*; Revd M. F. H. Hulbert, *Legends of the Eyres* (Hathersage: Hathersage Parochial Council, 1981); Pevsner, *The Buildings of England: Derbyshire*; Frank Rodgers, *Curiosities of the Peak District* (Ashbourne, 1979; repr. 1985). **Magpie Mine** David Clarke, *Ghosts and Legends of the Peak District* (Norwich, 1991); Daniel, *Ghosts of Derbyshire*; R. A. H. O'Neal, 'T' Owd Mon', *Derbyshire Countryside* 2:4 (June–July 1957); Lynn Willies, *Lead and Leadmining* (Princes Risborough, 1982). **Parson's Tor** Llewellynn Jewitt, *The Ballads and Songs of Derbyshire* (London and Derby, 1867); *Murray's Handbook for Travellers in Derbyshire, Nottinghamshire, Leicestershire, and Staffordshire* (London, 1868). **Renishaw** [Charles Lindley, Viscount Halifax,] *Lord Halifax's Ghost Book* (London, 1936); Pevsner, *The Buildings of England: Derbyshire*. **Shirebrook Colliery** Daniel, *Ghosts of Derbyshire*; *The Star*, Thursday, 27 November 1958. **Tunstead Farm** Addy, *Household Tales* . . .; Clarke and Roberts, *Twilight of the Celtic Gods*; Daniel, *Ghosts of Derbyshire*; John Hutchinson, *A Tour through the High Peak of Derbyshire* (Macclesfield, 1809); G. Le Blanc Smith, *Derbyshire Reliquary* (1905); Andy Roberts and David Clarke, 'Heads and Tales: The Screaming Skull Legends of Britain', *Fortean Studies* 3 (1996). **Wormhill** William Camden, *Britannia*, trans. Philemon Holland (London, 1610); Clarke, *Ghosts and Legends of the Peak District*; Rhodes, *Peak Scenery; Or, The Derbyshire Tourist*.

Devon

Berry Pomeroy Elliott O'Donnell, *Screaming Skulls and Other Ghost Stories* (London, 1964); Deryck Seymour and Jack Hazzard, *Berry Pomeroy Castle* (Torquay, 1982). **Black Anne Pool** Elias Tozer, *Devonshire and Other Original Poems* (Exeter, 1873). **Buckfastleigh** Theo Brown, *Devon Ghosts* (Norwich, 1982); J. R. W. Coxhead, *The Devil in Devon* (Bracknell, 1967); A. W. Smith, 'A Custom Inaugurated?', *FLS News* 16 (November 1992); Ralph Whitlock, *The Folklore of Devon* (London, 1977). **Buckland Abbey** Mrs Anna Eliza Bray, *Traditions, Legends, Superstitions and Sketches of Devonshire*, 2 vols. (London, 1838), vol. 2; E. M. R. Ditmas, *The Legend of Drake's Drum* (St Peter Port, Guernsey, 1973) and 'The Way Legends Grow', *Folklore* 85 (1974); Robert Hunt, *Popular Romances of the West of England*, 2nd edn (London, 1881); Alfred Noyes, 'The Silent Hand', *The Times*, 28 August 1916. **Coffinswell** Sabine Baring-Gould, *A Book of the West*, 2 vols. (London, 1899), vol. 1. **Cranmere Pool** Theo Brown, *The Fate of the Dead* (Ipswich and Totowa, N.J., 1979); William Crossing, *Amid Devonia's Alps* (Plymouth, 1888); J. M., *Notes and Queries*, ser. 1, vol. 3, no. 82 (24 May 1851); James Spry, 'Benjamin Gayer: An Okehampton Legend', *The Western Antiquary; or Devon and Cornwall Note-Book*, ed. W. H. K. Wright, January 1884, in vol. 3, April 1883–April 1884 (Plymouth, 1884); 'Tickler', *Devonshire Sketches: Dartmoor and its Borders* (Exeter, 1869). **Dean Prior** Brown, *The Fate of the Dead*; R.J.K., *Notes and Queries* (28 December 1850). **Dewerstone Rock** Baring-Gould, *A Book of the West*, vol. 1; R.J.K., *Notes and Queries* (28 December 1850); *Murray's Handbook for Travellers in Devon and Cornwall*, 9th edn, rev. (London, 1879). **Dunsford** Brown, *The Fate of the Dead*; *Transactions of the Devon Association*

68 (1936). **Lapford** Brown, *The Fate of the Dead*; B. M. H. Carbonell, notes made
c.1923–31, in James Wentworth Day, *A Ghost Hunter's Game Book* (London, 1958);
Belinda Whitworth, *Gothick Devon* (Princes Risborough, 1993). **Martinhoe** W. R.
Halliday, 'The Story of Sir Robert Chichester', *Folk-Lore* 65 (1954); George Tugwell,
The North Devon Scenery Book (Ilfracombe and London, n.d. [c.1863]); Mrs H. P.
Whitcombe, *Bygone Days in Devon and Cornwall*, (London, 1874). **Mortehoe** Paul
Alonzo Brown, *The Development of the Legend of Thomas à Becket*, Ph.D. thesis
(Philadelphia, 1930); *The National Trust Guide*, comp. and ed. Robin Fedden and
Rosemary Joekes, 3rd edn (London, 1984); Lady Rosalind Northcote, *Devon* (London,
1919); *Notes and Queries*, ser. 4, vol. 6, no. 141 (10 September 1870); Tristram Risdon,
The Chorographical Description, or Survey, of the County of Devon (1605-30), 2 pts
(London, 1714); Arthur P. Stanley, *Historical Memorials of Canterbury* (London, 1854;
3rd edn, 1857). **Okehampton** Baring-Gould, *A Book of the West*, vol. 1; Brown,
The Fate of the Dead; *Murray's Handbook for ... Devon ...*; Kingsley Palmer, *Oral
Folk-Tales of Wessex* (Newton Abbot, 1973); Whitcombe, *Bygone Days in Devonshire
and Cornwall*. **Peter Tavy** Sally Jones, *Legends of Devon* (Bodmin, 1981); J.M., *Notes
and Queries*, vol. 3, no. 82 (24 May 1851). **Roborough Down** Sarah Hewitt, *Nummits
and Crummits: Devonshire Customs, Characteristics, and Folk-Lore* (London, 1900).
Salcombe Regis J. Y. Anderson-Morshead, 'Salcombe Regis Parish Documents', MS,
Exeter City Library; and *A History of Salcombe Regis* (Sidmouth, 1930); Brown, *The
Fate of the Dead*; Iona Opie and Moira Tatem, *A Dictionary of Superstitions* (Oxford,
1989); Steve Roud, *The Penguin Guide to the Superstitions of Britain and Ireland*
(London, 2003). **Zeal Monachorum** Richard Cotton, *Transactions of the Devonshire
Association* 14 (1882); Jennifer Westwood, *Albion* (London, 1985).

Dorset

Badbury Rings A. Hadrian Allcroft, *Earthworks of England* (London, 1908); Stanley
J. Coleman, *Hants and Dorset Folklore* (Dorchester, n.d. [?1970s]); *Dorset Magazine* 2
(1968); Edwin Guest, *Origines Celticae (A Fragment)*, ed. William Stubbs and
C. Deedes, 2 vols. (London, 1883), vol. 2; Jeremy Harte, *Cuckoo Pounds and Singing
Barrows* (Dorchester, 1986); R. Bosworth Smith, *Bird Life and Bird Lore* (London,
1909). **Bagber** Frederick Treves, *Highways and Byways in Dorset* (London, 1906;
repr. 1980). **Bettiscombe Manor** Kingsley Palmer, *Oral Folk-Tales of Wessex*
(Newton Abbot, 1973); Andy Roberts and David Clarke, 'Heads and Tales: The
Screaming Skull Legends of Britain', *Fortean Studies* 3 (1996); J. S. Udal, 'The Bettis-
combe Skull', *Notes and Queries*, ser. 4, vol. 10 (1872); and *Dorsetshire Folk-Lore*
(Hertford, 1922; repr. St Peter Port, Guernsey, 1970). **Bridport** Udal, *Dorsetshire
Folk-Lore*, citing an article on 'Dorsetshire Ghosts' by M. F. Billington in the *Dorset
County Chronicle* for August 1883. **Cranborne Chase** Edward R. Griffiths, *The
Cranborne Chase Path* (Bournemouth, 1995); W. Chafin, *Anecdotes and History of
Cranbourn Chase* (London, 1818); Palmer, *Oral Folk-Tales of Wessex*. **Lulworth**
Marianne Dacombe, *Dorset Up-Along and Down-Along* (Gillingham, 1936); Harte,
Cuckoo Pounds and Singing Barrows; John Hutchins, *The History and Antiquities of the
County of Dorset* (London, 1774; 3rd edn, ed. W. Shipp, 4 vols., London, 1861–70),
vol. 1. **Netherbury** Udal, *Dorsetshire Folk-Lore*. **Pimperne** Palmer, *Oral Folk-Tales*

of Wessex. **Stourpaine** Palmer, *Oral Folk-Tales of Wessex*. **Tarrant Gunville** Edward R. Griffiths, *Dead Interesting Dorset* (privately printed, 1996); Charles Harper, *Haunted Houses* (London, 1907; 3rd edn, 1927; pa. repr., 1996); Antony D. Hippisley Coxe, *Haunted Britain* (London, 1973); John H. Ingram, *The Haunted Homes and Family Traditions of Great Britain* (London, 1884); Palmer, *Oral Folk-Tales of Wessex*. **Winterborne Abbas** E. H. Bates, 'Extracts from a Pamphlet Entitled Emiamsoz Seqasioz, *Mirabilis Annus, or the Year of Prodigies and Wonders, &c'*, *Notes and Queries for Somerset and Dorset* 4 (1894).

Palatinate County of Durham

Bishopswearmouth William Brockie, *Legends and Superstitions of the County of Durham* (Sunderland, 1886; repr. East Ardsley, Yorkshire, 1974); *Murray's Handbook for Travellers in Durham and Northumberland* (1864); Sir Cuthbert Sharp, *A History of Hartlepool* (Durham, 1816); John Wesley, *Journal*, ed. N. Curnock, 8 vols. (1909–16), vol. 5. **Chester-le-Street** Joseph Glanvill, *Saducismus Triumphatus; Or Full and Plain Evidence concerning Witches and Apparitions* (London, 1681); John Webster, *The Displaying of Supposed Witchcraft* (London, 1677). **Darlington** Revd. J. Hudson Barker, 'Ghost Legends', in *Bygone Durham*, ed. William Andrews (London, 1898); Brockie, *Legends and Superstitions of . . . Durham*; W. Hylton Dyer Longstaffe, *The History and Antiquities of the Parish of Darlington . . .* (Darlington, London, and Newcastle, 1854); *Murray's Handbook for . . . Durham . . .* **Glassensikes, Darlington** Longstaffe, *The History and Antiquities of the Parish of Darlington . . .* **Glowrowram** Brockie, *Legends and Superstitions of . . . Durham*. **Hurworth** Brockie, *Legends and Superstitions of . . . Durham*; Longstaffe, *The History and Antiquities of the Parish of Darlington . . .* **Hylton Castle** 'The Frog with the Golden Key', no. 18 in *Folktales of Germany*, ed. Kurt Ranke, trans. Lotte Baumann (London, 1966); William Howitt, *Visits to Remarkable Places*, ser. 2 (London, 1842); M. A. Richardson, *The Local Historian's Table Book*, Legendary Division, 3 vols. (1842–5), vol. 3; Robert Surtees, *The History and Antiquities of the County Palatine of Durham . . .*, 4 vols. in 2 (London, Durham, 1816–40), vol. 2. **Langley Hall** William Henderson, *Notes on the Folk-Lore of the Northern Counties of England and the Borders* (London, 1866). **Neville's Cross, Durham** Brockie, *Legends and Superstitions of . . . Durham*; *Murray's Handbook for . . . Durham . . .* **Raby Castle** Brockie, *Legends and Superstitions of . . . Durham*. **Sedgefield** Brockie, *Legends and Superstitions of . . . Durham*. **Staindrop** Brockie, *Legends and Superstitions of . . . Durham*. **Stob-Cross** Surtees, *The History . . . of Durham*, vol. 3. **Tudhoe** Richardson, *The Local Historian's Table Book*, vol. 1.

Essex

Ambresbury Banks Revd Sabine Baring-Gould, *Mehalah: A Story of the Salt Marshes* (London, 1880; repub. London, 1920; ed. edn London, 1950); Thomas Frost, 'Historic Essex', in *Bygone Essex*, ed. William Andrews (Colchester, Hull, and London, 1892); Charles Kightly, *Folk Heroes of Britain* (London, 1982; pa. edn 1984); *The London Encyclopaedia*, ed. Ben Weinreb and Christopher Hibbert, rev. edn (London, 1993); David Smurthwaite, *The Ordnance Survey Complete Guide to the*

Battlefields of Britain, pa. edn (Exeter, 1984); Tacitus, *Annales*, xiv; *VCH: Essex*, vol. 1, ed. H. Arthur Doubleday and William Page (London, 1903; repr. Folkestone, 1977). **Barrow Hill, Mersea Island** Baring-Gould, *Mehalah: A Story of the Salt Marshes*; Leslie V. Grinsell, *The Ancient Burial Mounds of England* (London, 1936; 2nd edn, rev., 1953); Archie White, *Tideways and Byways in Essex and Suffolk* (London, 1948). **Dagenham Park** William Howitt, *Visits to Remarkable Places*, ser. 2 (London, 1842); *Murray's Handbook for Travellers in Durham and Northumberland* (London, 1864); Mackenzie E. C. Walcott, *The East Coast of England from the Thames to the Tweed ...* (London, 1861). **Earls Colne** Richard Baxter, *The Certainty of the Worlds of Spirits ...* (London, 1691); Katharine Briggs, *A Dictionary of Fairies* (London, 1976; pa. edn, Harmondsworth, 1977). **Hadleigh Castle** Philip Benton, *The History of Rochford Hundred ...*, 3 vols. in 2, cont. pag (Rochford, 1867–88), vol. 1. **Hockley** Benton, *The History of Rochford Hundred ...*, vol. 1. **Loughton** Peter Haining, *A Dictionary of Ghosts* (London, 1982; 2nd edn, Waltham Abbey, 1993); Edward Hardingham, *Lays and Legends of the Forests of Essex* (London, 1907); Christina Hole, *Haunted England* (London, 1940; new edn, Bath, 1964; reiss. 1972). **Rochford** Charlotte Craven Mason, *Essex: Its Forest, Folk, and Folklore* (Chelmsford, 1928); Fred Roe, *Essex Survivals* (London, 1929). **The Strood, Mersea Island** James Wentworth Day, *Ghosts and Witches* (London, 1954); Peter Haining, *The Supernatural Coast* (London, 1992), citing Baring-Gould, *A Book of Ghosts* (1904); Nikolaus Pevsner, *The Buildings of England: Essex*, 2nd edn rev. Enid Radcliffe (Harmondsworth, 1965; repr. 1991); White, *Tideways and Byways in Essex and Suffolk*. **Walden Abbey, Saffron Walden** Doris Jones-Baker, *The Folklore of Hertfordshire* (London, 1977); *VCH: Essex*, vol. 2, ed. William Page and J. Horace Round (London, 1907); John Weever, *Ancient Fvnerall Monvments* (London, 1631). **Wormingford** Winifred Beaumont, *The Wormingford Story* (Ipswich, 1958).

Gloucestershire

Alvington Roy Palmer, *The Folklore of Gloucestershire* (Tiverton, 1994). **Bisley** Edith Brill, *Cotswold Ways* (1985), cited in Palmer, *The Folklore of Gloucestershire*; J. B. Partridge, 'Cotswold Place-Lore and Customs', *Folk-Lore* 23 (1912). **Chipping Sodbury** Palmer, *The Folklore of Gloucestershire*. **Cold Ashton** Antony D. Hippisley Coxe, *Haunted Britain* (London, 1973). **Dover's Hill** Palmer, *The Folklore of Gloucestershire*. **Dursley** Katharine M. Briggs, *The Folklore of the Cotswolds* (London, 1974). **Painswick** Kenneth Cooke, typescript in Gloucestershire Record Office (1962). **Prestbury** Palmer, *The Folklore of Gloucestershire*. **Upton St Leonards** Palmer, *The Folklore of Gloucestershire*.

Hampshire and the Isle of Wight

Basing W. G. Beddington and E. B. Christy, *It Happened in Hampshire* (Winchester, 1937; 5th edn, 1977); [Reader's Digest,] *Folklore, Myths and Legends of Britain* (London, 1973). **Brading (Isle of Wight)** Abraham Elder, *Tales and Legends of the Isle of Wight* (London, 1839); E. C. Hargrove, *Wanderings in the Isle of Wight* (Newport, Isle of Wight, 1913); Adrian Searle, *Isle of Wight Folklore* (Wimborne

1998). **Braishfield** Beddington and Christy, *It Happened in Hampshire*. **Bramshill** Thomas Haynes Bayly, *Songs, Ballads and Other Poems*, edited by his widow, 2 vols. (London, 1844), vol. 1; Beddington and Christy, *It Happened in Hampshire*; *The Best Loved Poems of the American People*, ed. Hazel Felleman (Garden City, N.Y., 1936); Katharine M. Briggs, *A Dictionary of British Folk-Tales in the English Language*, 2 pts, 4 vols. (London, 1970–1), pt B, vol. 2; Robert Chambers, *The Book of Days*, 2 vols. (London and Edinburgh, n.d.), vol. 1; Joan Penelope Cope, *Bramshill* (Winchester, 1938); Samuel Rogers, *Italy: A Poem* (London, 1830). **Ellingham** Beddington and Christy, *It Happened in Hampshire*; J. Hallam, *The Haunted Inns of England* (London, 1972); Christina Hole, *Haunted England* (London, 1940; repr. 1990). **Michael Morey's Hump, Arreton (Isle of Wight)** Wendy Boase, *The Folklore of Hampshire and the Isle of Wight* (London, 1976); Leslie V. Grinsell and G. A. Sherwin, 'Isle of Wight Barrows', *Proceedings of the Isle of Wight Natural History Society* 3 (1941). **Vernham Dene** Beddington and Christy, *It Happened in Hampshire*; Hole, *Haunted England*; *VCH: Hampshire and the Isle of Wight*, vol. 4, ed. William Page (London, 1911).

Herefordshire

Acton Cross Andrew Haggard, *Dialect and Local Usages of Herefordshire* (London, 1972). **Avenbury** Haggard, *Dialect and Local Usages of Herefordshire*. **Bronsil Castle** William Camden, *Britannia*, ed. and enl. Richard Gough, 4 vols., 2nd edn (London, 1806), vol. 1; Ella M. Leather, *The Folk-Lore of Herefordshire* (Hereford and London, 1912). **Dorstone** Leather, *The Folk-Lore of Herefordshire*; Sir John Rhys, *Celtic Folklore: Welsh and Manx*, 2 vols. (Oxford, 1901), vol. 1; Steve Roud, *The Penguin Guide to the Superstitions of Britain and Ireland* (London, 2003). **Hereford** 'Nonagenarian', *Hereford Times*, 15 April 1876, cited in Leather, *The Folk-Lore of Herefordshire*. **Hergest Court** Leather, *The Folk-Lore of Herefordshire*; Roy Palmer, *The Folklore of Radnorshire* (Little Logaston, 2001).

Hertfordshire

Agdell Edwin Grey, *Cottage Life in a Hertfordshire Village* (St Albans, 1935). **Aldbury** John Cussans, *History of Hertfordshire*, 3 vols. (London and Hertford, 1870–81; repr. East Ardsley, Wakefield, 1972), vol 3, Hundred of Dacorum; Doris Jones-Baker, *The Folklore of Hertfordshire* (London, 1977). **Cassiobury** Cussans, *History of Hertfordshire*, vol. 3, Hundred of Cashio; W. B. Gerish, *The Folk-Lore of Hertfordshire* (Bishop's Stortford, 1911). **Cheshunt** Catherine Crowe, *The Night-Side of Nature*, 2 vols. (London, 1848; pa. edn in 1 vol., Wellingborough, 1986); William Howitt, *History of the Supernatural . . .*, 2 vols. (London, 1863), vol. 2; David Hughson, *Walks through London . . . with the Surrounding Suburbs*, 2 vols. (London, 1817), vol. 2. **Codicote** H. C. Andrews and E. E. Squires, 'Codicote past and present', *East Hertfordshire Archaeological Society Transactions* 5:1 (1912); Gerish Collection, HALS (Gerish Box – Codicote, part of D/EGr26); William Branch Johnson, *The Codicote Story* (Welwyn, 1948). **Gubblecote** *Gentleman's Magazine* 21 (London, 1751), reports for April, May and August; inquisitions on the deaths of the Osbornes, and *West Hertfordshire Notes and Queries, Watford Observer* (2 December 1911), all Gerish Collection, HALS (D/EP F272); Revd Frederick George Lee, *More Glimpses of the World Unseen* (London, 1878). **Hatfield House** Augustus Hare, *The Story of My Life*, 6 vols. (London, 1896–1900), vol. 4. **Hitchin** Reginald Hine, *Hitchin Worthies* (London, 1932) and *The Story of the Sun Hotel, Hitchin, 1575–1945*, 2nd edn (Hitchin, 1946). **Hog Hall and Hog Hall Lane** Vicars Bell, *Little Gaddesden* (London, 1949). **Knebworth House** [Edward Robert Bulwer, 1st Earl of Lytton,] *The Life, Letters and Literary Remains of Edward Bulwer, Lord Lytton, by his son*, 2 vols. (London, 1883), vol. 1; Crowe, *Night-Side of Nature*; Cussans, *History of Hertfordshire*, vol. 2, Hundred of Broadwater; Sybilla Jane Flower, *Knebworth House* [guide] (Derby, 1987); Gerish, *The Folk-Lore of Hertfordshire*; inf. rec. Nicholas Maddex, Archivist, Knebworth House, 1987; Knebworth inventory 1797, HALS K479; Coleman O. Parsons, *Witchcraft and Demonology in Scott's Fiction* (Edinburgh and London, 1964). **Markyate Cell** bfi screenonline (*www.screenonline.org.uk*); Cussans, *History of Hertfordshire*, vol. 3, Hundred of Dacorum; *Gentleman's Magazine* 26:2 (November 1846); Hare, *Story of My Life*, vol. 6; Jennifer Westwood, *Gothick Hertfordshire* (Princes Risborough, 1989). **Sawbridgeworth** Gerish Collection, HALS (Gerish Box – Sawbridgeworth, part of D/EGr67); Gerish, *The Folk-Lore of Hertfordshire*. **South Mimms Castle** Cussans, *History of Hertfordshire*, vol. 2, Hundred of Broadwater; Jones-Baker, *The Folklore of Hertfordshire*; J. H. Round, *Geoffrey de Mandeville: A Study of the Anarchy* (London, 1892); *VCH: Middlesex*, vol. 2, ed. William Page (London, 1911), and vol. 5, ed. T. F. T. Baker (Oxford, 1976). **Tewin** *Gentleman's Magazine* 53:1 (June 1783); Gerish, *The Folk-Lore of Hertfordshire*. **Tring Station** Gerish Collection, HALS (Gerish Box – Aldbury, part of D/EGr3); Arthur Jacobs, *The New Penguin Dictionary of Music*, 4th edn (Harmondsworth, 1977; repr. 1978); Sheila Richards, *A History of Tring* (Tring Urban District Council, 1974). **Ware** Robert Chambers, *The Book of Days*, 2 vols. (London and Edinburgh, n.d. [1863–4]); P. K. Thornton, *Victoria and Albert Museum Masterpieces Sheet 8: The Great Bed of Ware* (1976).

Huntingdonshire and Peterborough

Barnack *Charles Kingsley: His Letters and Memories of His Life*, edited by his Wife (London, 1895). **Castor** [Hugh Candidus,] *The Peterborough Chronicle of Hugh Candidus*, trans. Charles Mellows, ed. William Thomas Mellows (Peterborough, 1941); W. C. Lukis, *The Family Memoirs of the Rev. William Stukeley*, 3 vols. (Durham, London, and Edinburgh, 1883–7), vol. 3; John Morton, *The Natural History of Northampton-shire* ... (London, 1712); *Murray's Handbook for Travellers in Northamptonshire and Rutland*, 2nd edn (London, 1901); *The Place-Names of Northamptonshire*, ed. J. E. B. Gover, A. Mawer, and F. M. Stenton (Cambridge, 1933). **Helpston** Christina Hole, *Haunted England* (London, 1940; new edn, Bath, 1964; re-iss. 1972). **Holywell** Joan Forman, *Haunted East Anglia* (London, 1974; pa. edn, 1976); Guy Lyon Playfair, *The Haunted Pub Guide* (London, 1985); Peter Underwood, *The A–Z of British Ghosts* (London, 1971; new edn, 1992; repr. 1993). **Peterborough** Revd J. C. Atkinson, *A Glossary of the Cleveland Dialect* (London, 1868); Theo Brown, *The Fate of the Dead* (Ipswich and Totowa, N.J., 1979),

citing *Devon and Cornwall Notes and Queries* 17 (1932–3), and 'various local inform-
ants'; William Henderson, *Notes on the Folk-Lore of the Northern Counties of England
and the Borders* (London, 1866); Thomas Heywood, *The Hierarchie of the Blessed
Angells* (London, 1635); Robert Hunt, *Popular Romances of the West of England*
(London, 1865; 3rd edn, new imp., 1908); John Leyden, *Scotish Descriptive Poems;
with some Illustrations of Scotish Literary Antiquities* (Edinburgh, 1803); [Walter
Map,] *Walter Map's De Nugis Curialium*, trans. M. R. James, ed. E. Sidney Hartland
(London, 1923); *Middle English Dictionary*, vol. 4, G–H, ed. Sherman M. Kuhn and
John Reidy (Ann Arbor, 1963–7); *Sir Orfeo*, ed. A. J. Bliss, 2nd edn (Oxford, 1966)
(Auchinleck MS *c.*1330); J. M. Thiele, *Danmarks Folkesagn*, 3pts (Copenhagen,
1843–60), pt 2; Ordericus Vitalis, *The Ecclesiastical History of England and Normandy*,
trans. T. Forrester, 4 vols (London, 1854–6), vol. 2. **Upwood** *Murray's Handbook for
. . . Huntingdonshire*; Tebbutt, *Huntingdonshire Folklore* (St Ives, Cambridgeshire,
1984).

Kent

Blue Bell Hill Michael Goss, *The Evidence for Phantom Hitch-Hikers* (Wellingborough, 1984); *Kent Today*, 9 November 1992; 10 November 1992; 24 November
1992; (Maidstone) *Gazette*, 10 September 1968; 16 July 1974; *www.tudor34.
freeserve.co.uk*. **Faversham** Richard Jones, *Haunted Britain and Ireland* (London,
2001). **Goodwin Sands** Jennifer Chandler, 'The *Lady Lovibund'*, *FLS News* 27 (June
1998); *Daily Chronicle*, 13 February 1924; George Goldsmith-Carter, *The Goodwin
Sands* (London, 1953); Bill Mouland, 'Riddle of the Sands', *Daily Mail*, 13 February
1998; Paul Sieveking, 'Sunken schooners that keep on sailing', *Sunday Telegraph*,
22 November 1998. **Marden** Sir Charles Igglesden, *A Saunter through Kent with
Pen and Pencil*, 34 vols. (Ashford, 1900–46), vol. 1. **Pluckley** Alan Bignell, *Kent Lore*
(London, 1983); *Independent*, 27 October 2000, Review section; Jones, *Haunted
Britain and Ireland*. **Rainham** Bignell, *Kent Lore*.

Lancashire

Bardsea James Bowker, *Goblin Tales of Lancashire* (London, 1883). **Clitheroe** John
Harland and T. T. Wilkinson, *Lancashire Folk-Lore* (1867; 2nd edn, London and
Manchester, 1882, repr. Wakefield, 1972); William Henderson, *Notes on the Folk-Lore
of the Northern Counties of England and the Borders* (1866; 2nd edn, London, 1879);
Thomas Parkinson, *Yorkshire Legends and Traditions*, 2 vols. (London 1888–9), vol. 2.
Crank Terence W. Whitaker, *Lancashire's Ghosts and Legends* (London, 1980;
pa. edn, 1982). **Dilworth** John Harland and T. T. Wilkinson, *Lancashire Legends,
Traditions, Pageants, Sports, &c., . . .* (London, 1873); Ken Howarth, *Ghosts, Traditions
and Legends of Old Lancashire* (Wilmslow, 1994); Jessica Lofthouse, *North-Country
Folklore in Lancashire, Cumbria and the Pennine Dales* (London, 1976); Whitaker,
Lancashire's Ghosts and Legends. **Radcliffe Tower** Howarth, *Ghosts, Traditions and
Legends of Old Lancashire*; 'The Lady Isabella's Tragedy', in Thomas Percy, *Reliques
of Ancient English Poetry* (1765; Everyman edn, 2 vols., London, 1906), vol. 2;
Roby, *Traditions of Lancashire*, 2 vols. (London, 1829), vol. 1. **Samlesbury** Harland

and Wilkinson, *Lancashire Legends, Traditions, Pageants, Sports, &c.* **Timberbottom Farm** Harland and Wilkinson, *Lancashire Legends, Traditions, Pageants, Sports, &c.*; John Harris, *The Ghost Hunter's Road Book* (London, 1968); Lofthouse, *North-Country Folklore ...*; Andy Roberts and David Clarke, 'Heads and Tales: The Screaming Skull Legends of Britain', *Fortean Studies* 3 (1996). **Walton-le-Dale** Bowker, *Goblin Tales of Lancashire*; John Weever, *Ancient Fvnerall Monvments* (London, 1631).

Leicestershire

Bradgate House (Hall) Charles James Billson, *County Folk-Lore, Printed Extracts, No. 3: Leicestershire and Rutland* (London, 1895); *Black's Guide to Leicestershire and Rutland* (Edinburgh, 1884); A. B. Evans, *Leicestershire Words, Phrases and Proverbs*, ed. Sebastian Evans (London, 1881); William Kelly, *Royal Progresses and Visits to Leicester* (Leicester, 1884); Roy Palmer, *The Folklore of Leicestershire and Rutland* (Wymondham, Leicestershire, 1985); Nikolaus Pevsner, *The Buildings of England: Leicestershire and Rutland* (Harmondsworth, 1960); John Timbs and Alexander Gunn, *Abbeys, Castles and Ancient Halls of England and Wales: Midland* (London and New York, n.d.). **Hinckley** Billson, *County Folklore, Printed Extracts, No. 3: Leicestershire and Rutland*, citing the *Leicester Chronicle*, 20 June 1874; *Black's Guide to Leicestershire and Rutland*; Thomas Harrold, 'Old Hinckley', *Transactions of the Leicestershire Architectural and Archaeological Society* 6 (1888). **Husbands Bosworth** Antony D. Hippisley Coxe, *Haunted Britain* (London, 1973; pa edn, 1975); Palmer, *The Folklore of Leicestershire and Rutland*; Pevsner, *The Buildings of England: Leicestershire and Rutland*. **Kibworth Harcourt** Palmer, *The Folklore of Leicestershire and Rutland*. **Kilncote** *Gentleman's Magazine* 60:1 (1790). **Lubenham** Palmer, *The Folklore of Leicestershire and Rutland*. **Lutterworth** Richard Baxter, *The Certainty of the Worlds of Spirits ...* (London, 1691). **Sapcote** John Nichols, *The History and Antiquities of the County of Leicester*, 4 vols. (London, 1795–1811), vol. 4. **Staunton Harold** Robert Chambers, *The Book of Days*, 2 vols. (London and Edinburgh, n.d. [1863–4]), vol. 1; *Encyclopaedia Britannica*, 11th edn, vol. 10 (Cambridge, 1910); T. B. Howell, *A Complete Collection of State Trials*, vol. 19 (London, 1816); Palmer, *The Folklore of Leicestershire and Rutland*; Timbs and Gunn, *Abbeys, Castles and Ancient Halls of England and Wales: Midland*. **Stoke Golding** Palmer, *The Folklore of Leicestershire and Rutland*. **Wymondham** Palmer, *The Folklore of Leicestershire and Rutland*.

Lincolnshire

Bolingbroke Castle Gervase Holles, *Lincolnshire Churches Notes made by Gervase Holles 1634–1642 (from Harleian MS 6829)*, ed. R. E. G. Cole (Lincoln, 1911), citing Holles; Edward Peacock, 'The Spirit at Bolingbroke Castle', *Notes and Queries*, ser. 1, vol. 6, no. 146 (4 August 1852); M. G. W. Peacock, 'Folklore and Legends of Lincolnshire', Folklore Society Archives T26. **Boston** Jennifer Chandler, 'Lincolnshire Death-Birds', *FLS News* 17 (June 1993); Mrs Gutch and Mabel Peacock, *County Folk-Lore 5, Printed Extracts No. 7: Lincolnshire* (London, 1908), citing *Antiquary* 14 and 31, *Fenland Notes and Queries* 1, and *Notes and Queries*, ser. 7, 11; pers. corr. Bob Lane, Boston (9 December 1992); Mackenzie E. C. Walcott, *The East*

Coast of England from the Thames to the Tweed (London, 1861); W. H. Wheeler, *A History of the Fens of South Lincolnshire* (Boston and London, 1868). **Brigg** John Clare, *The Village Minstrel and Other Poems*, 2 vols. (London, 1821); W. Hylton Dyer Longstaffe, *The History and Antiquities of the Parish of Darlington* ... (Darlington, London, and Newcastle, 1854); Peacock, 'Folklore and Legends of Lincolnshire'; Thomas Sternberg, *The Dialect and Folk-Lore of Northamptonshire* (London and Northampton, 1851; repr. East Ardsley, Yorkshire, 1971). **Snakeholme** Peacock, 'Folklore and Legends of Lincolnshire'. **South Ferriby** Peacock, 'Folklore and Legends of Lincolnshire'. **Stainsby** Peacock, 'Folklore and Legends of Lincolnshire'. **Thorpe Hall** [Thomas Deloney,] *The Works of Thomas Deloney*, ed. F.O. Mann (Oxford, 1912); Gutch and Peacock, *County Folk-Lore 5, Printed Extracts 7: Lincolnshire*, citing Revd Cayley Illingworth, *A Topographical Account of the Parish of Scampton* (1810); Peacock, 'Folklore and Legends of Lincolnshire'; Thomas Percy, *Reliques of Ancient English Poetry*, ed. Henry B. Wheatley, 3 vols. (London, 1876–7), vol. 2; Walcott, *The East Coast of England* ...; Jennifer Westwood, *Albion* (London, 1985).

London and Middlesex

Berkeley Square J. A. Brooks, *Ghosts of London* (Norwich, 1991); Antony D. Hippisley Coxe, *Haunted Britain* (London, 1973); John o' London, *London Stories* (London, 1882; repr. 1985); R. Thurston Hopkins, *Cavalcade of Ghosts* (London, 1956). **Cock Lane** Oliver Goldsmith (attributed), *The Mystery Revealed: A Series of Transactions and Testimonials Concerning the Supposed Cock Lane Ghost* (London, 1762); Douglas Grant, *The Cock Lane Ghost* (London and New York, 1965); Andrew Lang, *Cock-Lane and Common-Sense* (London, 1894). **Drury Lane** Brooks, *Ghosts of London*; Peter Underwood, *Haunted London* (London, 1973). **Garlick Hill** Brooks, *Ghosts of London*; Underwood, *Haunted London*. **Gower Street** Brooks, *Ghosts of London*; Underwood, *Haunted London*. **Hammersmith** Brooks, *Ghosts of London*; G. T. Crook, *The Complete Newgate Calendar*, vol. 4 (London, 1926). **Hampton** Peter Haining, *A Dictionary of Ghosts* (London, 1982; 2nd edn, Waltham Abbey, 1993); J. Gilbert Jenkins, *A History of the Parish of Penn* (London, 1935); [Reader's Digest,] *Folklore, Myths and Legends of Britain*, 2nd edn (London, 1977). **Highgate** [John Aubrey,] *Aubrey's Brief Lives*, ed. Oliver Lawson Dick (Harmondsworth, 1962); Underwood, *Haunted London*. **Highgate Cemetery** Bill Ellis, 'The Highgate Cemetery Vampire Hunt', *Folklore* 104 (1993); Bill Ellis, *Raising the Devil* (Kentucky, 2000); 'Ghostly walks in Highgate', *Hampstead and Highgate Express*, 6 February 1970; 'Letters', ibid, 13 February, and 27 February. **Holland House, Kensington** John Aubrey, *Miscellanies* VI (1696), in *Three Prose Works*, ed. John Buchanan-Brown (Fontwell, Sussex, 1972). **Islington** Brooks, *Ghosts of London*. **Montpelier Square, Kensington** Charles Harper, *Haunted Houses* (London, 1907; 3rd edn, 1927; pa. repr. 1996). **Soho Square** 'The Shrouded Spectre', *Mother Shipton's Miscellany*, quoted in full in Brooks, *Ghosts of London*. **St James's Palace** T. M. Jarvis, *Accredited Ghost Stories* (London, 1823). **The Tower** For a general survey, see G. Abbott, *Ghosts of the Tower of London* (London, 1980). Eustace Chapuys' account of the countess's execution is in the *Calendar of State Papers: Spanish*; Lord (Edward) Herbert of

Cherbury, *The Life and Reign of King Henry the Eighth* (London, 1649), ed. White Kennett as *The History of England under Henry VIII* (London, 1870); modern versions, Andrew Green, *Our Haunted Kingdom* (London, 1973); Underwood, *Haunted London*. **Tyburn Tree** *The Tyburn-Ghost: Or, the Strange Downfall of the Gallows* (London, 1678).

Norfolk

Alderfen Broad Revd John Gunn, 'Proverbs, Adages and Popular Superstitions, Still Preserved in the Parish of Irstead', *Norfolk Archaeology* 2 (Norwich, 1849). **Aylmerton** T. Hugh Bryant, *Norfolk Churches: Hundred of North Erpingham* (Norwich, 1900); Henry Harrod, 'On the Weybourne Pits', *Norfolk Archaeology* 3 (Norwich, 1852); *Murray's Handbook for Travellers in Essex, Suffolk, Norfolk, and Cambridgeshire* (London, 1870; 3rd edn, 1892); Walter Rye, 'The Prophecies, Traditions, Superstitions, Folklore, Sayings, and Rhymes of Norfolk', in *The Norfolk Antiquarian Miscellany*, ed. W. Rye, 3 vols. (Norwich, 1877–87), vol. 1; E. R. Suffling, *The History and Legends of the Broad District* (London, n.d. [c.1889]); 'T.D.P.', 'Norfolk Folk Lore', *Notes and Queries*, ser. 3, vol. 5, no. 116 (19 March 1864). **Blickling Hall** James Hooper and William A. Dutt, 'Folk-Lore – Some Local Legends and Sayings', in William Dutt, *The Norfolk Broads* (London, 1903); Henry Manship, *The History of Great Yarmouth*, ed. Charles John Palmer (Great Yarmouth, 1854), sec. 1; *Murray's Handbook for ... Norfolk ...*; Walter Rye, 'Norfolk Superstitions', *Eastern Counties Collectanea: Being Notes and Queries on Subjects Relating to the Counties of Norfolk, Suffolk, Essex, and Cambridge*, ed. John L'Estrange (Norwich, 1872–3); Rye, 'The Prophecies, Traditions, Superstitions, Folklore, Sayings, and Rhymes of Norfolk'; Suffling, *The History and Legends of the Broad District*; E.S.T., 'Sir Thomas Boleyn's Spectre', in *Notes and Queries*, ser. 1, vol. 1, no. 29 (18 May 1850). **Castle Rising** Francis Blomefield, *An Essay Towards a Topographical History of the County of Norfolk*, fol. edn, 5 vols. (vol. 1, Fersfield, 1739; vol. 2, Norwich, 1745; vol. 3 cont. by Charles Parkin, Lynn, 1769; vols. 4 and 5, by Charles Parkin, Lynn, 1775), vol. 4; R. Allen Brown, *Castle Rising, Norfolk* (London, 1978; repr. 1984); Antony D. Hippisley Coxe, *Haunted Britain* (London, 1973; pa. edn, 1975); Agnes Strickland, *Lives of the Queens of England*, 12 vols. (London, 1840–8), vol. 2; John Timbs, *Abbeys, Castles, and Ancient Halls of England and Wales*, 2 vols. (London, n.d. [1st edn, 1870]), vol. 1. **Croxton** Revd Charles Kent, *The Land of the 'Babes in the Wood'* (London and Norwich, n.d. [c. 1914]). **Great Melton** Rye, 'Norfolk Superstitions'; 'The Prophecies, Traditions, Superstitions, Folklore, Sayings, and Rhymes of Norfolk'; and 'The Vocabulary of East Anglia', in *The Norfolk Antiquarian Miscellany*, vol. 3, pt 2 (1887). **Gunton Park** Mackenzie E. C. Walcott, *The East Coast of England from the Thames to the Tweed* (London, 1861). **Happisburgh** Suffling, *The History and Legends of the Broad District*. **Hickling Broad** Charles Fielding Marsh, 'The Drummer of Hickling', *Longman's Magazine*, vol. 41, no. 241 (November 1902); Suffling, *The History and Legends of the Broad District*. **Long Stratton** 'William de Castre', Norfolk folklore collections compiled by William de Castre, 7 vols., Norfolk County Library (holograph, 1916–18), vol. 3, 'Ghostly Visions' (newspaper cutting, n.d., no source); W. B. Gerish, 'Phantom Hearse at Spixworth', *Norfolk and Norwich Notes and Queries*

(26 January 1901); Frederick Hibgame, reporting a cutting from an unidentified newspaper dated October 1881, *Norfolk and Norwich Notes and Queries* (2 February 1901); Walter Rye, *Songs, Stories, and Sayings of Norfolk* (Norwich, 1897); John T. Varden, 'Traditions, Superstitions, and Folklore, Chiefly Relating to the Counties of Norfolk and Suffolk', *The East Anglian Handbook ... for 1885* (Norwich, Lowestoft, and London [1885]). **Mannington Hall** Augustus Jessopp, 'An Antiquary's Ghost Story', *The Athenaeum*, no. 2724 (10 January 1880); repr. in *Frivola* (London, 1896); pers. corr. T. Purdy, Aylsham, 11 September 1991; Enid Porter, *The Folklore of East Anglia* (London, 1974). **Mundesley** Suffling, *The History and Legends of the Broad District.* **Raynham Hall** Jennifer Chandler, 'Smuggler's fakelore', in *FLS News* 32 (November 2000); *Country Life* 16 December 1936; Catherine Crowe, *The Night-Side of Nature* (London, 1848; repr. Wellingborough, 1986); William A. Dutt, *Highways and Byways in East Anglia* (London, 1901; repr. 1923); Christina Hole, *Haunted England* (London, 1940; new edn, Bath, 1964, reiss. 1972); Charles Loftus, *My Youth by Sea and Land* (London, 1876); Florence Marryat, *There is No Death* (London, 1891); Charles John Palmer, *The Perlustration of Great Yarmouth, with Gorleston and Southtown*, 3 vols. (Great Yarmouth, 1872–5), vol. 3; Rye, 'The Prophecies, Traditions, Superstitions, Folklore, Sayings, and Rhymes of Norfolk'; and *Songs, Stories and Sayings of Norfolk*; Lucia C. Stone, 'The Brown Lady of Rainham', *Rifts in the Veil*, ed. W. H. Harrison (London, 1878). **Sheringham** 'T.D.P.', 'Norfolk Folk Lore', *Notes and Queries*, ser. 3, vol. 5 (19 March 1864); Cecilia Lucy Brightwell, *Memorials of the Life of Amelia Opie*, 2nd edn (Norwich and London, 1854); 'E.S.T.' [Revd E. S. Taylor], 'Shuck the Dog-fiend', *Notes and Queries*, vol. 1 (1850); Jennifer Westwood, 'Friend or Foe? Norfolk Traditions of Shuck', in *Supernatural Enemies*, ed. Hilda Ellis Davidson and Anna Chaudhri (Durham, North Carolina, 2001); and in *Explore Phantom Black Dogs*, ed. Bob Trubshaw (Loughborough, 2005). **Thetford** 'Cuthbert Bede' [Edward Bradley], *The Curate of Cranston ...* (London, 1862); Blomefield, *An Essay towards a Topographical History ... of Norfolk ...*, fol. edn, vol. 1; *Castle Hill*, Breckland Council leaflet (Dereham, n.d.); 'William de Castre', 'Norfolk Legends', gathering 5; W. G. Clarke, *In Breckland Wilds* (London, 1925; 2nd imp. 1926); Kent, *The Land of the 'Babes in the Wood'*; Thomas Martin, *The History of the Town of Thetford* (London, 1779); *Murray's Handbook for ... Norfolk ...*; *Norfolk and Norwich Notes and Queries* (3 September 1904); *Notes and Queries*, vol. 1, no. 29 (18 May 1850); Rye, 'The Prophecies, Traditions, Superstitions, Folklore, Sayings, and Rhymes of Norfolk'. **Thurlton** W. H. Barrett and R. P. Garrod, *East Anglian Folklore and Other Tales* (London, 1976); oral tradn to J. W. 1940s–; pers. comm. to J. W. from Mrs Bridget Hickling 1991. **Waxham Hall** W. H. Cooke, 'Places of Interest in East Norfolk' [1911], MS 4311, Norfolk Record Office, 206; James Wentworth Day, *Here Are Ghosts and Witches* (London, 1954); Oliver G. Ready, *Life and Sport on the Norfolk Broads ...* (London, n.d.; ill. edn, 1910); Walter Rye, *The Recreations of a Norfolk Antiquary* (Holt and Norwich, 1920); and *Norfolk Families* (Norwich, 1913). **West Caister** Gunn, 'Proverbs, Adages and Popular Superstitions, Still Preserved in the Parish of Irstead'; Manship, *The History of Great Yarmouth*, ed. Palmer, sec. 1; Walcott, *The East Coast of England ...* **Wolterton Hall** 'William de Castre', Norfolk folklore collections compiled by William de Castre, vol. 3, 'Ghostly Visions', (newspaper cutting, dated by hand 22.9. [19]17, no source given); Lady Dorothy Nevill,

Mannington and the Walpoles, Earls of Oxford (London, 1894); and *The Reminiscences of Lady Dorothy Nevill*, ed. Ralph Nevill (London, 1906).

Northamptonshire

Althorpe Park Christina Hole, *Haunted England* (London, 1940; new edn, Bath 1964, re-iss. 1972); John H. Ingram, *The Haunted Homes and Family Traditions of Great Britain*, 4th edn (London, 1888). **Apethorpe** *Murray's Handbook for Travellers in Northamptonshire and Rutland*, 2nd edn (London, 1901); Nikolaus Pevsner, *The Buildings of England: Northamptonshire*, 2nd edn, rev. Bridget Cherry (Harmondsworth, 1973). **Bulwick** Hole, *Haunted England*; Hilary Mead, 'The Loss of the Victoria', *Mariner's Mirror* 47 (1961); *The Oxford Companion to Ships and the Sea*, ed. Peter Kemp (Oxford, 1988); Lincoln P. Paine, *Ships of the World: An Historical Encyclopedia* (Boston, 1997). For a first-hand report of a sailor's fetch, see Florence Marryat, *There is No Death* (London, 1891). **Clopton** Jack Gould, *Gothick Northamptonshire* (Princes Risborough, 1992); *Murray's Handbook for ... Northamptonshire ...*; *The Place-Names of Northamptonshire*, ed. J. E. B. Gover, A. Mawer, and F. M. Stenton (Cambridge, 1933); [Reader's Digest,] *Folklore, Myths and Legends of Britain*, 2nd edn (London, 1977). **Daventry** W. Dickinson Rastall, *A History of the Antiquities of the Town and Church of Southwell, in the County of Nottingham* (London, 1787); *Murray's Handbook for ... Northamptonshire ...* **Hannington** *The Rest-less Ghost: or, Wonderful News from Northamptonshire, and Southwark* (London, 1675; repr. Northampton, 1878). **Naseby** Gould, *Gothick Northamptonshire*; Revd John Mastin, *The History and Antiquities of Naseby* (Cambridge, 1792); John Morton, *The Natural History of Northampton-shire ...* (London, 1712). **Passenham** [William Druce,] 'The Passenham Ghost', in O. F. Brown and F. J. Roberts, *Passenham, The History of a Forest Village* (London and Chichester, 1973), Appendix 5; Gould, *Gothick Northamptonshire*; T. H. White, 'Soft Voices at Passenham', in *The Maharajah and Other Stories*, ed. Kurth Sprague (London, 1981). **Whittlebury** Giovanni Boccaccio, *The Decameron*, trans. G. H. McWilliam (Harmondsworth, 1972; repr. 1986); [John Dryden,] *The Miscellaneous Works of John Dryden*, 4 vols. (London, 1760); *The German Legends of the Brothers Grimm*, ed. and trans. Donald Ward, 2 vols. (Philadelphia, 1981), vol. 1; Bengt af Klintberg, *Svenska Folksägner* (Stockholm, 1972); Thomas Sternberg, *The Dialect and Folk-Lore of Northamptonshire* (London and Northampton, 1851; repr. East Ardsley, Yorkshire, 1971); Benjamin Thorpe, *Northern Mythology*, 3 vols. (London, 1851–2; pa. edn in 1 vol, 2001).

Northumberland

Bellister M. A. Richardson, *The Local Historian's Table Book*, Legendary Division, 3 vols. (Newcastle, 1842–5), vol. 3. **Black Heddon** [M. A. Denham,] *The Denham Tracts*, ed. James Hardy, 2 vols. (London, 1892–5), vol. 2, citing *Transactions of the Tyneside Naturalists' Field-Club* (1861); Richardson, *The Local Historian's Table Book*, vol. 2. **Blenkinsopp Castle** Richardson, *The Local Historian's Table Book*, vol. 3. **Cuddie's Cave** M. C. Balfour, *County Folk-Lore Vol. 4, Printed Extracts No. 6:*

Northumberland (London, 1903); [Denham,] *The Denham Tracts*, ed. Hardy, vol. 2; William Henderson, *Notes on the Folk-Lore of the Northern Counties of England and the Borders* (London, 1866). **Denton Hall** [Denham,] *The Denham Tracts*, ed. Hardy, vol. 2; Richardson, *The Local Historian's Table Book*, vol. 3. **Dilston** Balfour, *County Folk-Lore Vol. 4, Printed Extracts No. 6: Northumberland*; 'The Derwentwater Insurrection', *The Monthly Chronicle of North-Country Lore and Legend*, vol. 4, no. 37, March 1890 (Newcastle-upon-Tyne, 1890); William Howitt, *Visits to Remarkable Places*, ser. 2 (London, 1842); *Murray's Handbook for Travellers in Durham and Northumberland* (London, 1864); John Stokoe, 'The North-Country Garland of Song: Derwentwater's Farewell', *The Monthly Chronicle of North-Country Lore and Legend*, vol. 2, pt 19, September 1888 (Newcastle-upon-Tyne, 1888); Mackenzie E. C. Walcott, *The East Coast of England from the Thames to the Tweed* (London, 1861). **Haltwhistle** Richardson, *The Local Historian's Table Book*, vol. 2. **Meldon** [Denham,] *The Denham Tracts*, ed. Hardy, vol. 2; John Hodgson, *A History of Northumberland, Part II*, 3 vols. (Newcastle, 1832), vol. 2; Richardson, *The Local Historian's Table Book*, vol. 1. **Shilbottle** *Colliery Guardian* (23 May 1863), quoted by Jones (below); [Denham,] *The Denham Tracts*, ed. Hardy, vol. 2; Robert Hunt, *Popular Romances of the West of England*, 3rd edn, new imp. (London, 1908); William Jones, *Credulities Past and Present* (London, 1880); *Notes and Queries* vol. 12, no. 307 (15 September 1855); Stephen Oliver the Younger [W. A. Chatto], *Rambles in Northumberland* ... (London, 1835). **Troughend** Hodgson, *History of Northumberland, Part II*, vol. 2; Richardson, *The Local Historian's Table Book*, vol. 2; Jennifer Westwood, 'Soul-Birds', *The Macmillan Encyclopedia of Death and Dying*, ed. Robert Kastenbaum, 2 vols. (Woodbridge, Conn., 2002), vol. 2; Lowry Charles Wimberly, *Folklore in the English and Scottish Ballads* (Chicago, 1928; pa. edn, 1965).

Nottinghamshire

The Bessie Stone *www.ashfield-dc.gov.uk*; Pat Mayfield, *Legends of Nottinghamshire* (Clapham, North Yorkshire, 1976); *www.paranormaldatabase.com* **Clifton Grove** Sir Robert Clifton, quoted by Mayfield, *Legends of Nottinghamshire*; John Glyde, *The Norfolk Garland* (London, [1872]); *Murray's Handbook for Travellers in Derbyshire, Nottinghamshire, Leicestershire, and Staffordshire* (London, 1868); Hyder E. Rollins, *An Analytical Index to the Ballad Entries in the Stationers' Registers 1557–1709* (1924; repr. Hatboro, Penn., 1967), no. 167, and see nos. 1007, 2864; *The Roxburghe Ballads*, ed. William Chappell, 3 vols. (London, 1871–80), vol. 3; [Robert Thoroton,] *Thoroton's History of Nottinghamshire* ... republ. with addns by John Throsby, 3 vols. (London, 1797), vol. 1; 'A Wanderer' (Captain Barker), *Walks Around Nottingham* (London, 1835); Henry Kirke White, *Clifton Grove*, in *The Remains of Henry Kirke White* ..., 2 vols. (London, 1807; repr. New York and London, 1977). **Newstead Abbey** John Potter Briscoe, *Nottinghamshire Facts and Fictions*, ser. 2 (Nottingham, 1877); Lord Byron, *The Complete Poetical Works*, ed. Jerome J. McGann, vol. 5 (Oxford, 1986); T. F. Thiselton Dyer, *Strange Pages from Family Papers* (London, 1895; new issue, 1900); Ebenezer Elliott, *More Verse and Prose by the Cornlaw Rhymer*, 2 vols. (London, 1850), vol. 1; John Ingram, *The Haunted Homes and Family Traditions of Great Britain*, 4th edn (London, 1888); Thomas Moore,

Letters and Journals of Lord Byron: with notices of his Life, 3rd edn, 3 vols. (London, 1833), vols. 1 and 2; *Murray's Handbook for ... Nottinghamshire ...*; Damien Noonan, *Daily Telegraph Guide to Britain's Historic Houses* (London, 2004). **Nottingham** Revd John Hodgson and F. C. Laird, *The Beauties of England and Wales: or, Original Delineations Topographical, Historical, and Descriptive, of each County*, vol. 12, pt 1 (of 2 parts), *Northumberland and Nottinghamshire* (London, 1813); *Murray's Handbook for ... Nottinghamshire ...* **Rufford Abbey** Antony D. Hippisley Coxe, *Haunted England* (London, 1973; pa. edn, 1975); *Murray's Handbook for ... Nottinghamshire ...*; [Reader's Digest,] *Folklore, Myths and Legends of Britain*, 2nd edn (London, 1977).

Oxfordshire

Burford Katharine M. Briggs, *The Folklore of the Cotswolds* (London, 1974); Muriel Groves, *The History of Shipton-under-Wychwood* (London, 1934); Mary Sturge Gretton, *Burford Past and Present*, 3rd edn (Gretton, 1945); E. C. Williams, *Companion into Oxfordshire*, 2nd edn (London, 1943). **North Leigh** Violet Mason, 'Scraps of English Folk-lore XIX: Oxfordshire', *Folk-Lore* 40 (1929); Angelina Parker, 'Oxfordshire Village Folk-lore', *Folk-Lore* 34 (1923); Steve Roud, *The Penguin Guide to the Superstitions of Britain and Ireland* (London, 2003). **Wilcote** Briggs, *The Folklore of the Cotswolds*; Theo Brown, *The Fate of the Dead* (Ipswich and Totowa, N.J., 1979); Mason, 'Scraps of English Folk-lore XIX: Oxfordshire'; Parker, 'Oxfordshire Village Folk-lore'.

Rutland

Barrowden [Rutland Local History Society,] *The Villages of Rutland*, vol. 1, pt 1 (Oakham, Rutland, 1979). **Braunston** Richard Baxter, *The Certainty of the Worlds of Spirits ...* (London, 1691). **Brooke Priory** [Rutland Local History Society,] *The Villages of Rutland*, vol. 1, pt 1. **Cottesmore** [Rutland Local History Society,] *The Villages of Rutland*, vol. 1, pt. 1. **Edith Weston** [Rutland Local History Society,] *The Villages of Rutland*, vol. 1, pt 1. **Snelston** J. and A. E. Stokes, *Just Rutland* (Uppingham, 1953). **Stocken Hall** Antony D. Hippisley Coxe, *Haunted Britain* (London, 1973; pa. edn 1975); Stokes, *Just Rutland*; Peter Underwood, *The A–Z of British Ghosts* (1971; new edn, London, 1992; repr. 1993).

Shropshire

Bagbury Charlotte Burne, *Shropshire Folk-Lore* (London, 1883); Thomas Wright, 'On the Local Legends of Shropshire', *Collecteanea Archaeologica* 1:1 (1860), summarized in Burne. **Bridgnorth** Burne, *Shropshire Folk-Lore*; Christine McCarthy, *Some Ghostly Tales of Shropshire* (Shrewsbury, 1988). **Cayhowell Farm (Myddle)** Richard Gough, *The History of Myddle* (1701–2), ed. David Hey (Harmondsworth, 1981). **Chetwynd** Burne, *Shropshire Folk-Lore*. **Clun** Burne, *Shropshire Folk-Lore*; Walter Map, *De Nugis Curialium*, ed. and trans. M. R. James, C. N. L. Brooke, and R. A. B. Mynors (Oxford, 1983). **Fitz** Burne, *Shropshire Folk-Lore*. **Hampton's Wood** Burne, *Shropshire Folk-*

Lore. **Kinlet** Burne, *Shropshire Folk-Lore*; Christina Hole, *Haunted England* (London, 1940; repr., 1990). **Longnor** Burne, *Shropshire Folk-Lore*. **Millichope** Burne, *Shropshire Folk-Lore*. **Ratlinghope** Burne, *Shropshire Folk-Lore*.

Somerset

Chilton Cantelo Andy Roberts and David Clarke, 'Heads and Tales: The Screaming Skull Legends of Britain', *Fortean Studies* 3 (1996); Jennifer Westwood, *Albion* (London, 1985), citing John Collinson, *History and Antiquities of Somerset*, 3 vols. (Bath, 1791). **Ilminster** Kingsley Palmer, *The Folklore of Somerset* (London, 1976), and *Oral Folk-Tales of Wessex* (Newton Abbot, 1973); R. W. Patten, *Avon and Somerset Folklore and Legends* (St Ives, 1977). **Nether Stowey** Katharine M. Briggs and Ruth L. Tongue, *Folktales of England* (London, 1965); Antony D. Hippisley Coxe, *Haunted Britain* (London, 1973; pa. edn, 1975). **Nunney** Michael Goss, *The Evidence for Phantom Hitch-Hikers* (Wellingborough, 1984). **Porlock** Ruth Tongue, *Somerset Folklore* (London, 1965). **Shepton Mallet** Antony D. Hippisley Coxe, *Haunted Britain* (London, 1973); C. H. Poole, *The Customs Superstitions and Legends of the County of Somerset* (London, 1877). **Wellington** [John Aubrey,] *Aubrey's Brief Lives* (1669–96), ed. Oliver Lawson Dick (Harmondsworth, 1962); Theo Brown, *The Fate of the Dead* (Ipswich and Totowa, N.J., 1979); Palmer, *The Folklore of Somerset*; Patten, *Avon and Somerset Folklore and Legends*; Tongue, *Somerset Folklore*. **Wincanton** Bari Hooper, 'A Cruel Punishment', *FLS News* 30 (November 1999); H. A. Irving, 'Jack White's Gibbet', *The Somerset Year-Book* (1922); Sally Jones, *Legends of Somerset* (Bodmin, 1984); Palmer, *Oral Folk-Tales of Wessex*; Patten, *Avon and Somerset Folklore and Legends*; Tongue, *Somerset Folklore*. **Withycombe** Jack Hurley, *Legends of Exmoor* (Dulverton, 1973); Palmer, *The Folklore of Somerset*; Tongue, *Somerset Folklore*.

Staffordshire

Adbaston Charlotte Burne, *Shropshire Folk-Lore* (London, 1883). **Broughton Hall** Nikolaus Pevsner, *The Buildings of England: Staffordshire* (Harmondsworth, 1974); Marilyn Wood, *Rhoda Broughton: Profile of a Novelist* (Stamford, 1993). **Burslem** Charlotte Burne and Georgina Jackson, *Shropshire Folk-Lore: A Sheaf of Gleanings*, ed. Charlotte Sophia Burne from the collections of Georgina F. Jackson (London, 1883); inf. rec. by J.W. 1983 from the Revd Philip L. C. Smith, rector of Burslem; Richard Jones, *Haunted Britain and Ireland* (London, 2001); G. T. Lawley, 'Staffordshire Customs, Superstitions, and Folk-Lore' (Bilston Library, n.d. [c.1922]); Revd A. L. Lumb, *A Short Historical Survey of Burslem Parish Church*, with addns by the Revd P. L. C. Smith (Burslem parish church, 1930; new edn, 1969); John Ward, *The Borough of Stoke-upon-Trent* (London, 1843). **Etruria** H. A. Wedgwood, *The Romance of Staffordshire*, 3 vols. (Manchester, Hanley, and London, 1877–9), vol. 1. **Hammerwich** Charles Henry Poole, *The Customs, Superstitions and Legends of the County of Stafford* (London, n.d. [c.1875]). **Lower Gornal** Poole, *The Customs, Superstitions and Legends of the County of Stafford*. **Lud's Church** David Clarke, *Ghosts and Legends of the Peak District* (Norwich, 1991); *Murray's Handbook for Travellers in Derbyshire, Nottinghamshire, Leicestershire, and Staffordshire* (London,

1868); Frank Rodgers, *Curiosities of the Peak District and Derbyshire* (Ashbourne, Derbyshire, 1979; repr. 1985), no. 99; Rob Talbot and Robin Whiteman, *The Peak District* (London, 1997). **Micklow** W. Wells Bladen, 'Notes on the Folk-Lore of North Staffordshire, Chiefly Collected at Stone', *North Staffordshire Field Club Annual Report and Transactions*, 35 (Stafford, 1900–1). **Onecote** *The Staffordshire Sentinel*, Summer Number 1909; W. P. Witcutt, 'Notes on Staffordshire Folklore', *Folk-Lore* 53:2 (June 1942). **Ranton** Burne, *Shropshire Folk-Lore*. **Rowley Regis** J. Wilson Jones, *The History of the Black Country* (Birmingham, n.d. [1950]). **Uttoxeter** Frederick W. M. Hackwood, *Staffordshire Customs, Superstitions and Folklore* (Lichfield, 1924; repr. East Ardsley, Yorkshire, 1974).

Suffolk

Acton W. Sparrow Simpson, 'Suffolk Legend', *Notes and Queries*, vol. 5, no. 122 (28 February 1852). **Barsham** Revd James Bulwer, 'Hassett's House, Pockthorpe', *Norfolk Archaeology* 7 (Norwich, 1872); James Hooper and William A. Dutt, 'Folk-Lore – Some Local Legends and Sayings', in William Dutt, *The Norfolk Broads* (London, 1903); Mark Knights, 'Norfolk Tales and Legends', *Norfolk and Norwich Annual and East Anglian Gleaner* (Norwich, 1888); John T. Varden, 'Traditions, Superstitions, and Folklore, Chiefly Relating to the Counties of Norfolk and Suffolk', in *East Anglian Handbook ... for 1885* (Norwich, Lowestoft, and London [1885]). **Blythburgh** *East Anglian Magazine* 20: 6 (April 1961); Abraham Fleming, 'A straunge and terrible Wunder ...' (London, n.d. [1577]); pers. inf. J.W. *c*.1945–; Enid Porter, *The Folklore of East Anglia* (London, 1974), citing *East Anglian Notes and Queries* 7, and informants; Suffolk County Council information board as at 30 January 2005. **Boulge** Camilla Gurdon [The Lady Eveline Camilla Gurdon], *County Folk-Lore: Suffolk* (London, 1893); Harold L. Lingwood, 'Madam Short of Boulge', *East Anglian Magazine* 11:5 (January 1952); Nikolaus Pevsner, *The Buildings of England: Suffolk*, 2nd edn, rev. Enid Radcliffe (Harmondsworth, 1974; New Haven and London, 2002); Thomas Wright, *The Life of Edward Fitzgerald*, 2 vols. (London, 1904), vol. 1. **Bungay** Patricia Dale-Green, *Dog* (London, 1966); 'Extracts from the Churchwardens' Books. No. 16. Bungay St Mary ...', in *The East Anglian; or Notes and Queries ...*, ed. Samuel Tymms, vol. 3 (Lowestoft and London, 1869); Fleming, 'A straunge and terrible Wunder ...'; Antony D. Hippisley Coxe, *Haunted Britain* (London, 1973; pa. edn, 1975); Hooper and Dutt, 'Folk-Lore – Some Local Legends and Sayings'; Alasdair Alpin MacGregor, *The Ghost Book: Strange Hauntings in Britain* (London, 1955); Edward Moor, *Suffolk Words and Phrases* (Woodbridge and London, 1823); *Notes and Queries*, vol. 6, no. 161 (27 November 1852); Christopher Reede, *A Straunge and Terrible Wunder: The Story of the Black Dog of Bungay* (Bungay, 1988); Jennifer Westwood, 'Friend or Foe? Norfolk Traditions of Shuck', in *Supernatural Enemies*, ed. Hilda Ellis Davidson and Anna Chaudhri (Durham, N.C., 2001); extended version in *Explore Phantom Black Dogs*, ed. Bob Trubshaw (Wymeswold, Loughborough, 2005). **Bungay Castle** Morley Adams, *In the Footsteps of Borrow and Fitzgerald* (London, n.d. [1914]); Augustus Jessopp, *Frivola* (London, 1896). **Burgh** Camilla Gurdon, 'Folk-Lore from South-east Suffolk', *Folk-Lore* 3:4 (December 1892). **Clopton** Justin and Edith Brooke, *Suffolk Prospect* (London, 1963). **Dallinghoo**

Gurdon, *County Folk-Lore: Suffolk*. **Debenham** M. W. Burgess, 'Mysterious Stones', *East Anglian Magazine* 35:1 (November 1975); Gurdon, 'Folk-Lore from Southeast Suffolk'; oral inf. to J.W. from Debenham residents, March 2005. **Hintlesham Hall** Charles Beard, *Lucks and Talismans* (London, 1934); Mary L. Lewes, *Stranger than Fiction; being tales from the by ways of ghosts and folk-lore* (London, 1911). **Lowestoft** Jack Rose, *Tales and Tall Stories*, ed. Dean Parkin (Carlton Colville, Lowestoft, 1992). **Oulton Broad** Mackenzie E. C. Walcott, *The East Coast of England from the Thames to the Tweed* (London, 1861). **Pakenham** Gurdon, *County Folk-Lore: Suffolk*; Revd Harry Jones, 'The Heights of East Anglia', in *The Eastern Counties Magazine and Suffolk Note-Book*, 2 vols., ed. Hon. Mary Henniker (London and Norwich, etc., n.d. [1900–2]), vol. 1; Walter Rye, *The Recreations of a Norfolk Antiquary* (Holt and Norwich, 1920). **Seckford Hall** Michael Bunn, *A Short History of Seckford Hall and the Seckford Family* (Seckford Hall, n.d.); M. R. James, *Suffolk and Norfolk* (London, 1930); *Murray's Handbook for Travellers in Essex, Suffolk, Norfolk, and Cambridgeshire* (London, 1870; 3rd edn, 1892); Pevsner, *The Buildings of England: Suffolk*; Carol and Michael Weaver, *The Seckford Foundation* (Woodbridge, 1987).

Surrey

Albury Matthew Alexander, *Tales of Old Surrey* (Newbury, 1985); W. H. Moyes, *Surrey Magazine* 2 (1901); Martin Tupper, *Stephen Langton: or the Days of King John* (London, 1858). **Epsom** James Boswell, *The Life of Samuel Johnson, LL.D.* (1791; Everyman edn, 2 vols., London 1949), vol. 2; *Gentleman's Magazine* 85:1 (1816); 86:2 (1816); Charles Harper, *Haunted Houses* (London, 1907; 3rd edn, 1927; pa. repr. 1996). **Guildford** Joseph Glanvill, *Saducismus Triumphatus* (1681; 4th edn, London, 1726). **Tadworth** Frances Edith Leaning, *Tadworth Court* (Redhill, 1928). **West Horsley** W. H. Chouler, *Tales of Old Surrey* (Yeovil, 1978).

Sussex

Burpham Newall Duke, 'Tales of Jack Upperton's Gibbet', *West Sussex Gazette*, 15 October 1959; L. N. Graburn, 'Jack Upperton's Gibbet, Burpham', *Sussex County Magazine* 25 (1951); Chris Hare, *The Good Old, Bad Old Days: The Sussex of Lawrence Graburn* (Worthing, 2001). **Chalvington** M. A. Lower, *Contributions to Literature* (London, 1854); Steve Roud, *The Penguin Guide to the Superstitions of Britain and Ireland* (London, 2003). **Chanctonbury Ring** Arthur Beckett, *The Spirit of the Downs* (London, 1909); Jacqueline Simpson, 'Legends of Chanctonbury Ring', *Folklore* 80 (1969); **Chichester** Daniel Defoe, *A Tour Through the Whole Island of Great Britain* (1724–6), ed. and abr. Pat Rogers (London, 1992). **Cuckfield** Iona Opie and Moira Tatem, *A Dictionary of Superstitions* (Oxford, 1989); M. Wright, *Cuckfield: An Old Sussex Town* (Haywards Heath, 1971). **Highdown Hill** *A Description of the Famous Miller's Tomb* (handbill, n.d.); *A Description of the Miller's Tomb on Highdown Hill*, 5th edn (Worthing, 1872); John Evans, *Picture of Worthing*, 2 vols. (Worthing, 1814), vol. 1; *Gentleman's Magazine* 70:2 (1800); Jacqueline Simpson, *The Folklore of Sussex*, 2nd edn (Stroud, 2002) and 'The Miller's Tomb: Facts, Gossip, and Legend', *Folklore*

116 (2005); *Southern Weekly Advertiser and Lewes Journal*, 6 May 1793; *Worthing Archaeological Society Newsletter*, June 1983.

Warwickshire

Alveston J. Harvey Bloom, *Folk-Lore, Old Customs and Superstitions in Shakespeare Land* (London, c.1930). **Aston Hall** J. S. Coleman, *Warwickshire Folklore* (Douglas, 1952); *Notes and Queries*, ser. 4, vol. 10 (1872). **Burton Dassett** Meg Atkins, *Haunted Warwickshire* (London, 1981); A. R. Wright, 'The Folk-lore of the Past and Present', *Folk-Lore* 38 (1927). **Edgehill** Atkins, *Haunted Warwickshire*; *A Great Wonder in Heaven* (1643), cited in Lord Nugent, *Some Memorials of John Hampden, his Party and his Times*, 2 vols. (London, 1832), vol. 2; and in Katharine M. Briggs, *The Folklore of the Cotswolds* (London, 1974); Antony D. Hippisley Coxe, *Haunted Britain* (London, 1973; pa. edn, 1975). **Ilmington** Atkins, *Haunted Warwickshire*; Bloom, *Folk-Lore . . . in Shakespeare Land*; Alan Burgess, *Warwickshire* (London, 1950); Roy Palmer, *The Folklore of Warwickshire* (London, 1976). **Little Lawford** Atkins, *Haunted Warwickshire*; G. Morley, *Shakespeare's Greenwood* (London, 1900); Palmer, *The Folklore of Warwickshire*. **Princethorpe** W. P. Witcutt, 'Notes on Warwickshire Folk-lore', *Folk-Lore* 55 (1944). **Ragley Hall** Bloom, *Folk-Lore . . . in Shakespeare Land*; Burgess, *Warwickshire*. **Southam** T. F. Thiselton Dyer, *The Ghost World* (London, 1893). **Stratford-on-Avon** William Howitt, *Visits to Remarkable Places* (London, 1844; new edn, 1888); Morley, *Shakespeare's Greenwood*; Palmer, *The Folklore of Warwickshire*.

Westmorland

Appleby Jeremiah Sullivan, *Cumberland and Westmorland, Ancient and Modern: the People, Dialect, Superstitions and Customs* (London and Kendal, 1857). **Calgarth** Wilson Armistead, *Tales and Legends of the English Lakes* (London and Glasgow, 1891); James Clarke, *A Survey of the Lakes of Cumberland, Westmorland . . .*, 2nd edn (London, 1789); Alexander Craig Gibson, *The Folk-Speech of Cumberland* (London and Carlisle, 1869); John H. Ingram, *The Haunted Homes and Family Traditions of Great Britain*, 4th edn (London, 1888); Jessica Lofthouse, *North-Country Folklore in Lancashire, Cumbria and the Pennine Dales* (London, 1976); Marjorie Rowling, *The Folklore of the Lake District* (London, 1976), citing *inter alia* W. G. Collingwood, *The Lake Counties* (1933); Mackenzie E. C. Walcott, *A Guide to the Mountains, Lakes and North-West Coast of England* (London, 1860); John Pagen White, *Lays and Legends of the English Lake Country* (London and Carlisle, 1873). **Crackenthorpe** E. Bellasis, 'The Machells of Crackenthorpe', *Transactions of the Cumberland and Westmorland Antiquarian and Archaeological Society* (Kendal, 1886); J. A. Brooks, *Ghosts and Legends of the Lake District* (Norwich, 1988); Gerald Findler, *Legends of the Lake Counties* (Clapham via Lancaster, 1967; repr. 1976); and *Lakeland Ghosts* (Clapham via Lancaster, 1969 [as *Ghosts of the Lake Counties*]; new edn, 1984). **Lake Windermere** Harriet Martineau, *A Complete Guide to the English Lakes* (Windermere and London, 1855); Walcott, *A Guide to the Mountains, Lakes and North-West Coast of England*; White, *Lays and Legends of the English Lake Country*. **Levens Hall** J. G. Lockhart,

Curses, Lucks and Talismans (London, 1938; Detroit, 1971); Damien Noonan, *The Daily Telegraph Guide to Britain's Historic Houses* (London, 2004); Peter N. Walker, *Folk Stories from the Lake District* (London, 1993); Frank Welsh, *The Companion Guide to the Lake District* (Woodbridge, 1989; rev. edn, 1997). **Lowther Castle** Findler, *Legends of the Lake Counties*; and *Lakeland Ghosts*; Sullivan, *Cumberland and Westmorland, Ancient and Modern* ... **Shap Fell** Brooks, *Ghosts and Legends of the Lake District*; L. F. Newman and E. M. Wilson, 'Folklore Survivals in the Southern "Lake Counties" and in Essex', *Folk-Lore* 63 (June 1952); Rowling, *The Folklore of the Lake District*; Revd Joseph Whiteside, *Shappe in Bygone Days* (Kendal, 1904).

Wiltshire

Heytesbury J. U. Powell, 'Folk-lore Notes from South-West Wiltshire', *Folk-Lore* 12 (1901). **Highworth** Alfred Williams, *Round About the Upper Thames* (London, 1922). **Littlecote House** [John Aubrey,] *Aubrey's Brief Lives* (1669–96), ed. Oliver Lawson Dick (Harmondsworth, 1962); H.C.B., 'Moonrake Medley', *Wiltshire Archaeological and Natural History Magazine* 50 (1943); Arthur Mee, *Wiltshire* (London, 1943); Ralph Whitlock, *The Folklore of Wiltshire* (London, 1976); Kathleen Wiltshire, *Ghosts and Legends of the Wiltshire Countryside*, 2nd edn (Melksham, 1985). **Longleat** Katy Jordan, *The Haunted Landscape* (Bradford on Avon, 2000); V. S. Manley, *Folklore of the Warminster District* (Warminster, 1924); Joseph Stevenson, *The History of William of Newburgh* (1856; repr. 1996); William of Newburgh, *Historia Rerum Anglicarum*, bk 5. **Semley** Kingsley Palmer, *Oral Folk-Tales of Wessex* (Newton Abbott, 1973). **Stanton St Bernard** Whitlock, *The Folklore of Wiltshire*; Wiltshire, *Ghosts and Legends of the Wiltshire Countryside*. **Stourton** Edith Olivier, *Moonrakings* (Warminster, 1930). **Tidworth** John Aubrey, *The Natural History of Wiltshire*, ed. John Britten (1685; London, 1847); Joseph Glanvill, *Saducismus Triumphatus* (1681; 4th edn, 1726). **Wilcot** Olivier, *Moonrakings*; Wiltshire, *Ghosts and Legends of the Wiltshire Countryside*.

Worcestershire

Besford Roy Palmer, *The Folklore of Hereford and Worcester* (Logaston, 1992). **Chaddesley Corbett** Palmer, *The Folklore of Hereford and Worcester*. **Hanley Castle** [Federation of Worcestershire Women's Institutes,] *The Worcestershire Village Book* (Newbury and Worcester, 1988). **Leigh** Jabez Allies, *On the Antiquities and Folk-Lore of Worcestershire*, 2nd edn (London and Worcestershire, 1856); Palmer, *The Folklore of Hereford and Worcester*. **Upton-on-Severn** Palmer, *The Folklore of Hereford and Worcester*, citing Emily M. Lawson, *The Nation in the Parish: or, Records of Upton-on-Severn* (1884; orig. 1869).

Yorkshire

Beverley William Henderson, *Notes on the Folk-Lore of the Northern Counties of England and the Borders* (London, 1866; 2nd edn, 1879); Frederick Ross, Richard Stead, and Thomas Holderness, *A Glossary of Words used in Holderness in the East*

Riding of Yorkshire, English Dialect Society 7 (London, 1877). **Bulmer** William Brockie, *Legends and Superstitions of the County of Durham* (Sunderland, 1866; repr. East Ardsley, Yorkshire, 1974); Robert Surtees, *The History and Antiquities of the County Palatine of Durham ...*, 4 vols. in 2 (London, Durham, 1816–40), vol. 3; Mackenzie E. C. Walcott, *The East Coast of England from the Thames to the Tweed* (London, 1861). **Burton Agnes Hall** *Burton Agnes Hall* [official guidebook] (Norwich, 1969); T. F. Thiselton Dyer, *Strange Pages from Family Papers* (London, 1895); Mrs [Eliza] Gutch, *County Folk-Lore Vol. 6, Printed Extracts No. 8: East Riding of Yorkshire* (London, 1912); Margaret Imrie, *The Manor Houses of Burton Agnes and their Owners* (Beverley, 1993); inf. rec. by J.W. from custodian at Burton Agnes, 1995; John H. Ingram, *The Haunted Homes and Family Traditions of Great Britain*, ser. 2, 4th edn (London, 1888). **Calverley** Dyer, *Strange Pages from Family Papers*; Henderson, *Notes on the Folk-Lore of the Northern Counties ...* (1866); Ingram, *The Haunted Homes and Family Traditions of Great Britain*. **Flamborough** John Nicholson, *Folk Lore of East Yorkshire* (London, Hull, and Driffield, 1890). **Sexhow** Henderson, *Notes on the Folk-Lore of the Northern Counties ...* (1866). **Thirsk** Revd Sabine Baring-Gould, *Yorkshire Oddities, Incidents, and Strange Events*, 2 vols., 3rd edn (London, 1877), vol. 2; W. Hylton Dyer Longstaffe, *The History and Antiquities of the Parish of Darlington ...* (Darlington, London, and Newcastle, 1854); *Murray's Handbook for Travellers in Durham and Northumberland* (London, 1864). **Whirlow** S. O. Addy, *Household Tales With Other Traditional Remains Collected in the Counties Of York, Lincoln, Derby, and Nottingham* (London and Sheffield, 1895).

Index

PENGUIN HISTORY

THE ENGLISH YEAR
STEVE ROUD

This enthralling book will take you, month-by-month, day-by-day, through all the festivities of English life. From national celebrations such as New Year's Eve to regional customs such as the Padstow Hobby Horse procession, cheese rolling in Gloucestershire and Easter Monday bottle kicking in Leeds, it explains how they originated, what they mean and when they occur.

A fascinating guide to the richness of our heritage and the sometimes eccentric nature of life in England, *The English Year* offers a unique chronological view of our social customs and attitudes.

'The book is a delight, a fund of information' *The Times*

PENGUIN NATURAL HISTORY

HATFIELD'S HERBAL
GABRIELLE HATFIELD

From ivy-wreathed buildings to the dandelions growing through the cracks between paving stones, we are surrounded by a wealth of native plants.

In the past they were a hugely valued resource: magical, mystical and medical. When Charles I visited Staffordshire his chamberlain wrote to the local sheriff asking him to ensure that no fern should be burnt or cut during the king's visit, so that the weather would be fine. Puppies were once fed daisy flowers in milk to keep them small while children wore daisy chains to protect against fairy kidnapping.

Packed with stories and memorable information, this book is the highly personal, very readable result of a lifetime spent researching folk cures and the science behind them. Outlining the history and uses of over 150 British plants, *Hatfield's Herbal* offers a fascinating history of what life was once like, a beautifully illustrated, evocative guide to our native plants and a passionate argument for why we should better appreciate the riches we already have.

'Hatfield, a contemporary botanist and plant historian, covers remedies from agrimony to yew and the history of their use' *Sunday Times*, Books of the Year

He just wanted a decent book to read ...

Not too much to ask, is it? It was in 1935 when Allen Lane, Managing Director of Bodley Head Publishers, stood on a platform at Exeter railway station looking for something good to read on his journey back to London. His choice was limited to popular magazines and poor-quality paperbacks – the same choice faced every day by the vast majority of readers, few of whom could afford hardbacks. Lane's disappointment and subsequent anger at the range of books generally available led him to found a company – and change the world.

'We believed in the existence in this country of a vast reading public for intelligent books at a low price, and staked everything on it'
Sir Allen Lane, 1902–1970, founder of Penguin Books

The quality paperback had arrived – and not just in bookshops. Lane was adamant that his Penguins should appear in chain stores and tobacconists, and should cost no more than a packet of cigarettes.

Reading habits (and cigarette prices) have changed since 1935, but Penguin still believes in publishing the best books for everybody to enjoy. We still believe that good design costs no more than bad design, and we still believe that quality books published passionately and responsibly make the world a better place.

So wherever you see the little bird – whether it's on a piece of prize-winning literary fiction or a celebrity autobiography, political tour de force or historical masterpiece, a serial-killer thriller, reference book, world classic or a piece of pure escapism – you can bet that it represents the very best that the genre has to offer.

Whatever you like to read – trust Penguin.

read more
www.penguin.co.uk